Moving the Needle

The publisher and the University of California Press Foundation grate-fully acknowledge the generous support of the Anne G. Lipow Endowment Fund in Social Justice and Human Rights.

Moving the Needle

WHAT TIGHT LABOR MARKETS
DO FOR THE POOR

Katherine S. Newman
and Elisabeth S. Jacobs

UNIVERSITY OF CALIFORNIA PRESS

University of California Press
Oakland, California

© 2023 by Katherine S. Newman and Elisabeth S. Jacobs

First Paperback Printing 2025

Cataloging-in-Publication Data is on file at the Library of

Congress.

ISBN 978-0-520-37910-7 (cloth : alk. paper)
ISBN 978-0-520-41266-8 (pbk: alk. paper)
ISBN 978-0-520-97653-5 (ebook)

GPSR Authorized Representative: Easy Access System Europe,
Mustamäe tee 50, 10621 Tallinn, Estonia, gpsr.requests@easproject.com

In Memoriam

Alan Krueger, James Madison Professor of Political Economy, Princeton University

Devah Pager, Peter & Isabel Malkin Professor of Public Policy and Professor of Sociology, Harvard University

Sara McLanahan, William Tod Professor of Sociology, Princeton University

These colleagues and friends published foundational research that shaped our understanding of the work and family lives of the nation's poor. Their scholarship and advocacy profoundly influenced social policy for the better.

Contents

List of Tables, Figures, and Maps

TABLES

FIGURES

MAPS

Introduction

March 2020 saw the United States conclude the longest economic expansion in its history: 121 straight months of growth. A fifty-year low in unemployment lifted the wages of the lowest paid workers faster than those of anyone else.[1] In this, the "miracle economy" of nearly ten years of growth was truly remarkable. But it was not unprecedented. The roaring expansion, low inflation and low unemployment of the Clinton years, the halcyon days of the mid-1960s and, of course, the world wars of the twentieth century were also periods of persistently tight labor markets.

In the fall of 2019, unemployment was down to 3.5 percent. By the spring of 2022, it was very nearly that low again, a remarkable rebound after the devastating and abrupt disruptions wrought by the COVID-19 pandemic.[2] In both periods, low-wage employers from Target to McDonald's began offering health insurance, vacation pay, and subsidized college tuition—benefits that were previously unheard of for this workforce. Starting salaries of $15 an hour—long the goal of the "living wage" movement—became routine. The central question for this book is what economic upswings of this kind—growth that drives unemployment way down—means for the nation's poor. The labor market is at the heart of our understanding of poverty. Poverty takes hold when employment opportunities—especially for less educated workers—are persistently meager. It is amplified when discrimination—by race, gender, immigration status, and age—place these jobseekers at the end of a long queue for available jobs.

Young Black men are the most disadvantaged group in the United States when it comes to unemployment. Their rates of joblessness are routinely much higher than any other group, and it takes them longer to land a job, especially during economic downturns.[3] They were much on the mind of William Julius Wilson when he wrote *The Truly Disadvantaged* (1987) and *When Work Disappears* (1997). In those books, which were best sellers and agenda-setters for both policymakers and social scientists, Wilson argued that poverty was largely a function of persistent joblessness, which was at the root of low rates of marriage, since "marriageable men" who bring home a paycheck are in short supply. Women respond by having children outside of wedlock, which often contributes to subsequent intergenerational poverty. Growing up poor is associated with fewer years of education, higher rates of teen pregnancy, and the marginalization of men from their families, whether as sons or partners.[4]

Wilson's books came on the heels of tumultuous debates over the role of culture in perpetuating poverty, which exploded in the 1960s. Oscar Lewis, who coined the phrase "culture of poverty" in 1959, and the Moynihan Report that followed a few years later, each located the root cause of intergenerational poverty in cultural norms that emerged out of persistent conditions of deprivation and became—in their view—self-perpetuating. This school of thought argued that poverty takes on a life of its own, as children lack role models to support the kind of conventional behavior that might enable them to break free. Widely decried as stigmatizing and victim-blaming, these arguments helped spur decades of research on poor Black communities, families, and individuals. Since then, researchers have explored the connection between poverty and discrimination, incarceration, neighborhoods, families, and culture. In each of these domains, scholars have developed and debated ideas about how life circumstances of the poor differ from those of the working and middle classes and how those differences explain persistent poverty.

In the end, it all comes back to the lack of jobs—or the lack of *good* jobs. Discrimination excludes some groups from employment opportunities, locking them into poverty. Incarceration shuts people with criminal records out of the labor market, increasing the chances that they will remain jobless and broke. Poor neighborhoods arise when a lack of local jobs leaves residents out of work and in deteriorating, often dangerous, communities. Families end up poor when parents can't find a job, or when the absence of securely employed men leads women to raise children on their own, with only a single income. And when people grow up surrounded by this concentrated poverty, scholars tell us, they are socialized in cultures that prove counterproductive.

Given that inadequate employment plays such a powerful role in theories of poverty, it is surprising how little research has been done on whether, or to what extent, tight labor markets reverse these trajectories. Only recently have scholars turned their attention to the impact of tight labor markets on inequality, offering insight into how very tight labor markets have the potential to substantially close the Black-white wage, income, and unemployment gaps.[5] If persistent unemployment or low earnings are indeed the root of most poverty problems, then truly tight labor markets that last long enough to reach those at the bottom of the economic ladder should change the equation in two ways. First, low unemployment should catalyze competition among employers to attract workers, driving them to improve job quality—including raising wages for workers on the bottom rungs. Second, low unemployment should draw jobless workers off the sidelines, transforming applicants with little formal education or employment experience into viable job candidates.

These benefits should flow into the other domains tied to poverty. As hiring managers are forced to look further afield for workers, the stigma attached to a having a criminal record, especially a nonviolent one, should be less of a barrier. In theory, when men can claim steady salaries, young women have more choices in the partnership "market."[6] Tight labor markets provide women with more options as well, including raising children on their own in more economically secure households. As unemployment declines, neighborhood peace should be easier to secure since economic security begets residential stability, which increases social capital and peaceful streets. While these assumptions are plausible, we know surprising little about what the empirical record shows. There is scant scholarship, particularly of the ethnographic variety, on the changes that come about when unemployment is persistently low. That gap is the genesis of this book: to enrich our understanding of tight labor markets and their impact on the nation's poor.

In the chapters that follow, we explore the gains that can accrue for people living in poverty when labor is scarce and jobs are going begging. But that is only part of the task. Equally critical is to understand whether those gains stick or fade over time, and for whom. The time span of our qualitative research—by accident rather than by design—put those questions in stark relief. We began the fieldwork for this book in the glory days of the most robust labor market of the past fifty years. The bulk of our interviews with employers and labor market intermediaries were undertaken before anyone had ever heard of COVID-19, the pandemic that spread relentlessly beginning in 2020, driving workers and consumers into their homes, which in turn sparked a dramatic increase in unemployment. Fortunately the labor market rebounded with astounding speed. National rates of unemployment zoomed up from 3.5 percent to 14.5 percent and back down to 3.6 percent within the space of twenty-four months.

This unprecedented turn of the business cycle compressed the phenomena that motivated this book and gave us an opportunity to witness ups and downs that ordinarily unfold over months and years. But we were fortunate in that the tight labor market at the front end of our fieldwork developed without reference to the pandemic and gave us a chance to understand how extraordinarily robust job opportunities unfold and inflect the lives of both the working poor and the bystanders who sit on the edge of the economy until their options are sufficiently compelling to warrant jumping in with both feet.

Innumerable books, academic articles, white papers, news stories, and op-eds trace the impact of slack labor markets on individuals, families, and the broader economy. But the benefits of tight labor markets have not been the subject of much sociological research. And, critically, low unemployment environments are not merely the inverse of slack labor markets—particularly for low-income workers, would-be workers, and their families. If the difference were simply quantitative—for instance, if labor market outcomes for workers were just a mechanical matter of years of education—then the effects of the labor market would be consistent, and the benefits of tight labor markets would be the exact inverse of the drawbacks of slack labor markets. This is not the case, because poor Americans are caught in *qualitatively* different circumstances compared with their working-class and middle-class counterparts.[7]

Poor workers are instead marked—by race, criminal records, or past unemployment—in ways that are often stigmatized by employers. Our research shows that these qualitative distinctions mean that these workers are categorically excluded from work opportunities until the labor market becomes *especially* tight, around 4 percent unemployment, at which point opportunities open up. And once they get a foot in the door—which might only happen under these exceptional conditions—opportunities for future jobs increase dramatically. We can't know what a tight labor market will do by looking at a slack labor market and calculating its opposite. We must examine empirically what happens under the particular conditions of extremely low unemployment.

It might be argued that these favorable moments happen so rarely that there is little point in investigating their impacts. We disagree. First, we show the United States has entered periods of significantly tight labor markets more often than we generally credit. Second, we believe that even though these conditions are not the norm, they hold important insights. If we can harvest meaningful observations about employment and its implications for economic security and mobility from the best of times, we may be able to avoid some of the losses that follow during economic downturns.

We recognize that even when employment conditions favor workers, they do not solve all problems. Far from it. Indeed, nearly a half-century of rising inequality in the United States means that these sporadic-yet-significant improvements at the bottom of the labor market have been accompanied by stratospheric wealth accumulation at the top. Accordingly, absolute improvements for poor workers do not close relative gaps. Moreover, they can be undone by three trends that we touch on only briefly in this book: automation, immigration, and inflation. They deserve, and receive, far more attention than we can provide here. Suffice to say that until these forces run the economy into recession, millions more people at the bottom of the pyramid have jobs when they didn't before. Their wages are higher. And their neighborhoods reflect the benefits of a more stable employment base. They enjoy bargaining power from scarcity that translates into greater job security. At least that's the theory. The question is whether that's also the fact.

Our mission is to understand what the historical record can tell us about what happened to poor workers and jobseekers who benefited from tight labor markets in the 1960s and the 1980s when strong economies weakened. Did the opportunities they claimed in the good years stick? Or were they a flash in the pan? We answer the same questions for the Roaring 1990s when, once again, unemployment dropped, inflation disappeared, and economic growth was high. We can find out whether people who moved up the ladder kept on climbing upward or whether they tumbled back down, and how far they fell, when the economy began to weaken. We follow that historical quantitative analysis with an exploration of how tight labor markets work on the ground. For that we need fieldwork in communities, workplaces, nonprofit organizations, and government agencies where we can learn about adaptations that unfold in a tight labor market: changes in behavior, expectations, and real experience that help to explain how the outcomes visible in business cycles come about.

That fieldwork was undertaken throughout the 2019–21 period in the city of Boston. To properly situate the fieldwork, it is important to briefly explore the special nature of the time period and the place. In 2019 the spectacular decline in unemployment motivated the core ideas of this book. At that point, COVID-19 was a virus multiplying oceans away in Wuhan, China. Interviews with the employers, jobseekers, labor market intermediaries, and residents of the two neighborhoods we discuss in detail in the qualitative chapters were largely completed by February 2020. In fall 2019 we interviewed seven major Boston employers, the leaders of six labor market intermediary organizations, and ten jobseekers who were mainly "returning citizens" participating in monthly meetings sponsored by the mayor's office that drew together another fifteen jobseekers who had been formerly incarcerated, using a common interview instrument for each category. To understand the implications of tight labor markets for neighborhoods and families, we interviewed eleven leaders of community organizations and fifteen longtime residents of two Boston neighborhoods. In these ways the project that became this book was a conventional mixed-methods sociological endeavor.

By March 2020 the virus that began in Wuhan arrived in Boston.

Within a few weeks every university in the United States shut down field-work completely. It would be nearly two years until we were able to visit with anyone face to face. Accordingly, the rest of the interviews (approximately 20 percent of the total) moved into the Zoom world of virtual video and phone calls. No one would call that an ideal research method. But it was that or nothing, and we were determined to complete the research. Because we got the bulk of the work done before the pandemic—and, critically, because unemployment fell dramatically before COVID-19 was a factor in the United States—we believe that our observations of the dynamics of tight labor markets are reasonably generalizable to other periods of very low unemployment. But we dwell at length on the history and granularity of other business cycles over a seventy-year period, to calibrate the distinctive qualities of the relevant downturns and upswings and to discern the patterns we believe are compelling evidence of the advances that accrue to the poor when labor markets tighten.

As noted in chapter 1, every recession has its own victims and every recovery unfolds differently. The Great Recession of 2008 erupted first in the housing market and quickly put real-estate agents, mortgage under-writers, banks, and other white-collar financial sector employees (who are disproportionately men) out of work. As it gathered steam, the workers who serve the upper-middle class—the dry cleaners, shopkeepers, and hotel staff—began to feel the pain. By contrast, the sharp contraction that accompanied the COVID-19 pandemic hit service workers (especially women) harder and faster than anyone else. The pandemic shuttered day-care centers, restaurants, hotels, and millions of other service professions where work depends heavily on face-to-face contact. Downtown business districts turned into ghost towns. The white-collar professionals that normally inhabit those office buildings moved their work online, into their home office suites and bedrooms and dining room tables. It was the frontline service workers who were laid off, save those in critically important industries like health care who had no choice but to show up and risk contracting the plague.

The city of Boston was chosen for the fieldwork for the simple reason that this is where one of us works and could manage the team described below. But it is fair to ask whether there is anything distinctive about Bean Town that makes it somehow suspect as a place from which to generalize about the impact of tight labor markets on employers and workers. Every city has its own special characteristics, but Boston shares many important features with other urban centers in the United States. Doubtless, future research on tight labor markets needs to focus on its impact in suburbs and rural areas, which we leave for others to consider.

Like San Francisco and New York, Boston is a high-tech industry hub. It has attracted thousands of young, high-skilled, and affluent workers, most of them white, who fill the ranks of the biotech, pharmaceutical, and computer-intensive industries. Boston is one of eight "superstar" metro areas—along with San Francisco, San Jose, Austin, Seattle, Los Angeles, New York, and Washington, DC—that together account for nearly half of the nation's technology sector job creation between 2015 and 2019.[8] At the same time, Boston has a large minority population, mainly African American, as well as Haitian and Cape Verdean immigrants, and a growing Latinx population from Puerto Rico and Central America. Asian families have arrived in large numbers over the years from China, Vietnam, and South Asia. Workers from Boston's nonwhite population are concentrated in the medical industries, construction, family-owned retail businesses, and the rank-and-file labor force of the many universities in the area. In common with most big cities—with the exception of Los Angeles—Boston has a sprawling transit system that enables workers to commute to the city center, but that only partially ties its many well-heeled suburbs via subway and rail.

Boston is in every way a profoundly unequal city. In this, is it much like other parts of urban America—from Washington, DC to New York, Chicago, San Francisco, Los Angeles, and beyond. As depicted in figure 1, income inequality across the United States increased over the past two decades, but the levels of inequality in major cities is higher than the national average. Boston is no exception and, like other major cities, the run-up in inequality has been steep. Indeed, Boston narrowly beat out San Francisco as the most unequal city in the bunch as of 2019, the most recent year for which data are available. Housing prices in Boston climbed steeply and steadily through around 2015, and then declined before stabilizing at 150 percent of their 2000 value (see figure 2). And, like other major American cities, Boston experienced substantial ups and downs in unemployment in the past twenty years (see figure 3). While peak joblessness in Boston was lower in the depths of the Great Recession and during the COVID-19

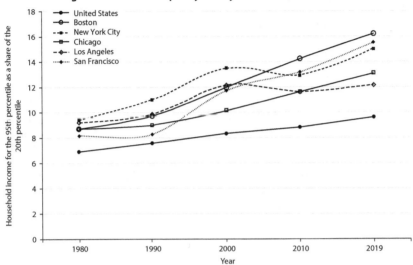

Figure 1. Income inequality in major US cities, 1980–2019

Note: Income inequality is expressed as the ratio of household incomes for those in the top 95th percentile as a share of the household income for those in the bottom 20th percentile.

Source: PolicyLink Equity Atlas, built on Integrated Public Use Microdata Series (IPUMS) data.

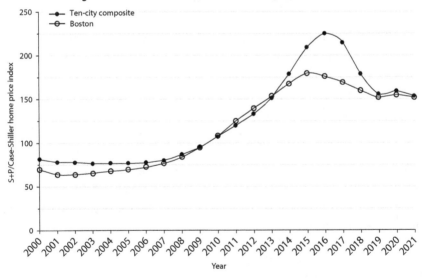

Figure 2. S+P/Case-Shiller Home Price Index, 2000–2021

Note: January 2000 = 100. The ten-city composite includes Boston, Chicago, Denver, Las Vegas, Los Angeles, Miami, New York, San Diego, San Francisco, and Washington, DC. Note that the S+P/Case-Shiller Home Price Index captures the single-family detached housing market only.

Source: Economic Research Division, Federal Reserve Bank of St. Louis.

Figure 3. Unemployment rate in major US cities, 2000–2021

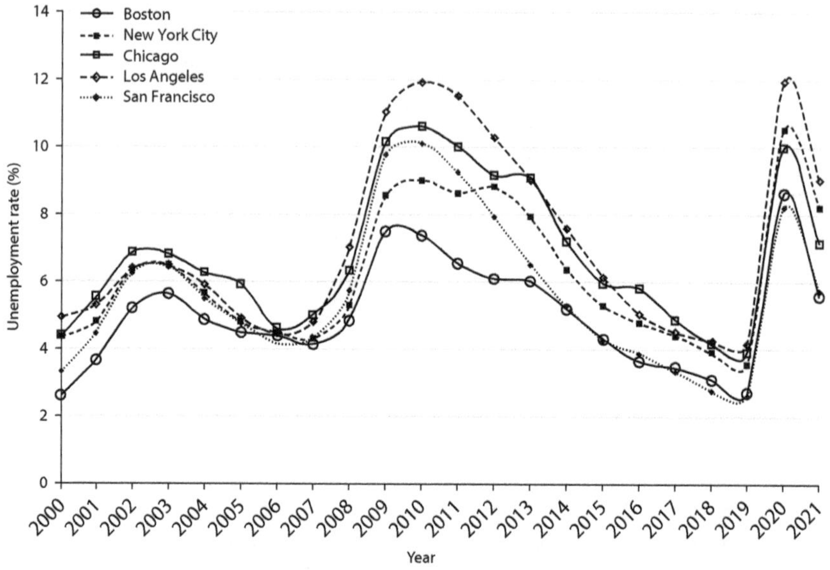

Note: Data are for Metropolitan Statistical Areas (MSAs): Boston-Cambridge-Nashua, New York-Newark-Jersey City, Chicago-Naperville-Elgin, Los Angeles-Long Beach-Anaheim, San Francisco-Oakland-Hayward.

Source: Economic Research Division, Federal Reserve Bank of St. Louis.

crisis than in other cities, Bean Town's labor market that preceded the pandemic was remarkably similar to its peers. And all appear to be on roughly the same recovery trajectory as of 2021.

Given the similarities between Boston and its counterparts elsewhere in the country, the city is a reasonable place to rely on as a location for qualitative insights into the dynamics of employers and jobseeker behavior under conditions of extremely low unemployment in the urban United States. At the same time, it is important to understand a much broader historical sweep to discern what was distinctive about this place and time relative to other tight labor markets and what we see as general patterns in the experience of the poor.

THE AGENDA

To dig into the sociological questions at the core of our project—namely the relationship between the opportunities in the labor market and the fate of the working poor and their families—we must first define that historical landscape. In chapter 1 we explore the nature of a tight labor market. This may seem a simple matter of definitions, but it is more complex than many realize. National unemployment figures—the headlines that come out the first Friday of every month, which are a widely recognized barometer of the nation's economic health—reflect an average of the data from across the country: coastal cities and boomtowns, where jobs are plentiful, along with border towns and Rust Belt communities, where huge proportions of the workforce are out of luck. But real people don't live in an aggregate national setting: they look for work near where they live. Accordingly, we direct attention to the regional characteristics of tight labor markets.

Place matters, but so does time. The duration of tight labor markets, especially how long these conditions need to last to make a significant difference for the working poor, is a rather technical question. But it is a critical one, so in chapter 1 we look over the past seventy years of economic history to answer the question of how long and just how strong tight labor markets have to be to produce positive outcomes for the poor. We decompose those results by demographic characteristics that are sociologically important. In chapter 2 we turn our attention to the consequences of tight labor markets for individuals and families. Who really gets ahead and how far are they able to go? Can poor people markedly improve their earnings, experience shorter spells of unemployment, find jobs that are more stable or offer more options for upward mobility? And if they do, how does that good fortune impact their families? If Wilson was right, we should see a meaningful impact on poor households since the absence of employment as seen as a driving force behind the pernicious consequences of poverty.

With these conceptual and empirical issues in hand, we turn to the dynamics of the labor market on the ground. How do employers react to the increasing difficulty of finding workers when unemployment dips down to historic lows? How do they change their recruitment practices? Do they think differently about who is qualified to do the work? Do they take a chance on people to whom they would not have given the time of day in a weaker labor market? And if they do begin to hire from unconventional pools of workers, how does that impact the way they onboard those new employees and try to retain them? These are the questions underlying chapter 3.

When employers venture into unknown waters, they are often uneasy about their own judgments. They can no longer rely on the familiar signals of educational credentials and traditional work experience when all those conventionally qualified people have been snapped up. Intermediaries fill that information gap and form a bulwark behind a more marginal worker that makes the employer feel more secure in their hiring decisions. But the intermediaries—the subject of chapter 4—then face the dilemma themselves. Who can *they* trust to show up to work consistently? How do *they* know whether someone they are recommending is going to pan out? Those judgments matter because the broker who recommends people that flame out will not see much repeat business. The lower reaches of the labor market have embraced these middlemen and -women as the solution to an information problem, and jobseekers must therefore find their way into these portals and impress the intermediary.

And what of the workers themselves? What is it like to struggle from the distant margins of the formal labor market and then discover a way forward, a potential path into traditional opportunity? It doesn't happen very often in "normal" job markets, but when unemployment dips to a fifty-year low, all kinds of people who had no chance at a conventional job suddenly discover they are in demand. How they learn about work opportunities and what impact this sudden good fortune has on their lives is the subject of chapter 5.

The sociological literature on poverty connects persistent unemployment to deterioration in neighborhoods. Too many unoccupied people hanging around without gainful work and too much time on everyone's hands leads to more dangerous streets. Do tight labor markets reverse these disastrous conditions? Chapter 6 looks at what happened to two predominantly Black neighborhoods in Boston that were studied extensively in the early 2000s. At that time they were plagued by catastrophically high levels of unemployment among men, high rates of single-parent households, and reliance on public benefits to (barely) make ends meet. Both neighborhoods suffered from violent crime and were among the most notoriously dangerous communities in the city. Returning to these communities in 2019–20 and tracing the changes in the census tracts that compose them, we see some of the positive outcomes of an improving economy on the quality of life and peace in the streets.

In *When Work Disappears*, Wilson hammered home the debilitating impact of persistent joblessness, especially on household stability and family cohesion. It was a bitter portrait indeed. But what happens to families when it becomes much easier to find work, and when men are not as likely to be on the sidelines? Does the flow of income from noncustodial parents to their children's households improve? Do family relationships change? Chapter 7 looks at family life in the two Boston neighborhoods to try to answer these questions.

Based on the research we have done for this book—from quantitative analyses of nationally representative data sets to qualitative fieldwork—we conclude that much is to be gained from periods when unemployment plummets. It's not an easy circumstance for employers, as it forces them to change many of their practices, often reluctantly. But for workers, tight labor markets are a shot in the arm, especially for the truly disadvantaged. Even so, tight labor markets do unravel—though not as quickly as they did in 2020, when a once-in-a-century plague descended on the country. Even in less dramatic times, normal levels of unemployment—as well as deep ones in recession—bring an end to expanded opportunity for the most disadvantaged workers. What lessons can we learn from tight labor markets that could be brought to bear during those periods of more "conventional" unemployment? Can we help families get off the hamster wheel, to consolidate some of the improvement they have experienced so that they are not so vulnerable to crashing down below the poverty line again? How might we introduce policies that favor that stability and enable workers to create "equity cushions" that can be protective against downturns? Those policy questions close the book in chapter 8.

THE RESEARCH TEAM

This research journey absorbed nearly two years and engaged a team of researchers in Boston and Washington, DC, to whom we are enormously indebted. Indeed, without them there would be no book at all. Three Harvard graduate students formed the backbone of the Boston team during the academic years 2019–21. Leah Gose in the Department of Sociology and Garry Mitchell in the Graduate School of Education formed the fieldwork team that returned to two neighborhoods in Boston originally studied by David Harding (Sociology, University of California–Berkeley), who was also a Harvard graduate student when he conducted his fieldwork in Franklin and Roxbury Crossing. Leah worked on tracking down people who have lived in the two neighborhoods for a long period of time, including the years when Harding did his fieldwork some fifteen years earlier.

In addition, Leah interviewed leaders of stable nonprofit organizations in these two communities since their perspectives on neighborhood change, public safety, and family formation were critical. Garry concentrated on interviewing employers and labor market intermediaries in the Boston region to understand how tight labor markets influenced their hiring and training practices. He focused additional attention on returning citizens, working through the Office of the Mayor of Boston to grapple with how the least-favored jobseekers—those with criminal records—were fairing in a period of very low unemployment. In ordinary times the work that Leah and Garry did would have been a challenging assignment. It is to their enduring credit that they navigated around the emerging limitations in March 2020, augmented their face-to-face interviews with virtual Zoom-type interviews, and completed the work on time and with remarkable quality. But then, Leah and Gary are remarkable scholars. We are profoundly grateful to them, not only for their time and talent but for their social scientific insights.

The quantitative team for this work was Washington, DC–based, drawing on the tremendous talent at the Urban Institute. Stipica Mudrazija worked tirelessly to clean and code the Panel Study of Income Dynamics (PSID) and the accompanying local labor market data from the Current Population Survey (CPS) and a variety of other US Census Bureau and Bureau of Labor Statistics sources. He applied his tremendous quantitative skills to a complicated set of empirical questions. In the years that we worked together on this project, Stipica managed to navigate a pandemic with a toddler (born in the early days of our research) and an infant who arrived mere months after the pandemic began. It is a testament to his dedication—and his ability to do tremendous work on very little sleep—that the book's quantitative analysis exists. Joe Peck joined the research team while an undergraduate at Yale University, as part of his internship with the Urban Institute's WorkRise initiative in summer 2020. He continued to provide invaluable data support and literature reviews while completing his degree in the months after his internship came to a close. Joe's willingness to take on the seemingly impossible with a can-do attitude combined with his ability to deliver key outputs at precisely the right time were true gifts for which we are endlessly grateful.

As the manuscript began to take shape, we needed a partner who could help us bring the sprawling document under control, train a critical eye on the arguments, bolster the scholarly framework that emerges in the text and chapter notes, and pursue some of the trickier theoretical and methodological questions that required resolution. For example, as we explain in chapter 6, we wanted to understand how the demographic composition of our two fieldwork neighborhoods had changed over the time period between Harding's research and ours. The US Census provides a window into this question, but the boundaries of census districts change over time. Correcting for that problem is no small endeavor. Solving for these dilemmas, large and small, fell to our third Harvard graduate student in the Department of Sociology, Laura Adler, who was deep into her dissertation and on the job market when she came into this project. It would be nearly impossible to credit and thank Laura for all that she did to make this book a useful contribution. Every argument, insight, and sentence in the book reflects her input. She helped us sift through a manuscript that was nearly twice the length of the resulting book, separating what was essential from what could be left by the wayside. Laura worked with our consultant, Dr. John Curiel, political scientist at Ohio Northern University, to wrestle the Census boundary problem to the ground. She worked with our research assistant, Joe Peck, to return to the PSID as well as the CPS to answer additional questions about sources of household income. Laura's maturity and intelligence are reflected on every page. That she landed a tenure-track job in the Yale School of Management while doing so much for us is a tribute to her extraordinary talent.

Finally, we owe our deepest thanks to the many people who agreed to be interviewed for this project. It would be a pleasure to acknowledge them by name. However, in keeping with the expectations of our human subjects review board, we rely on pseudonyms throughout the book and changed minor aspects of individual and organizational biographies to protect our informants as promised. Nonetheless, their lives are testimony to the payoff to sheer dedication that is rewarded more often when labor markets favor workers.

1 The Dynamics of Tight Labor Markets

Cassandra Eaton, a twenty-three-year-old single mother with a high school diploma, was working a low-paid job as a daycare teacher in Biloxi, Mississippi. In September 2017 the state's unemployment rate fell below 5 percent for the first time since the US Bureau of Labor Statistics began collecting employment data in the mid-1970s. Eaton took the opportunity to change jobs. She enrolled in an apprenticeship program that paid $19.80 per hour, learning welding for warships under construction in nearby Pascagoula. Upon completion of her two-year training program, Eaton expected to secure a full-time position paying over $27 per hour.[1]

After two years of record low unemployment, COVID-19 set in, ravaging the nation and the labor market. Millions of workers faced the existential question of whether to risk exposure at work or to elect economic hardship and remain safe at home.[2] Millions more lost their jobs altogether, as the retail and service sectors shed more than eleven million jobs, or 38.2 percent of all employment, between February 2020 and April 2020.[3] Burning Glass, a labor market analytics firm, reported that new job postings were down 43 percent nationally in March of 2020 and down as much as 75 percent in some states.[4] Yet by April 2021, employers were raising the alarm over labor shortages. Six months later, ten million jobs sat unfilled, workers were quitting at the highest rates ever recorded, and more than four million people had left the labor force—with no indication of when or whether they planned to return.[5] "Reservation wages," the offers that would-be employees deem good enough to make work worth their time, were rising all over the country.

Wages were increasing too, as businesses struggled to lure people back to work. In March 2021 wages were up 1.4 percent on average from the prior year and 4 percent higher for workers in leisure and hospitality.[6] Firms began touting prospects for promotion as part of their job descriptions. Employer postings for positions that do not require four-year degrees included the term "career advancement" 35 percent more often from March 2021 through July 2021, compared to the same span two years before.[7] "Training" was mentioned 32 percent more often. "Workers, in demand, have a new demand of their own: a career path," wrote Steve Lohr in the *New York Times*.[8] Take Ashantee Franklin, a twenty-four-year-old dog walker who lost her job early in the pandemic. She completed a four-month basic technology course with the training intermediary NPower and, with the help of their job placement service, began a contract job with Bank of America as a technology business analyst. Her starting salary is double her previous annual earnings of $20,000.[9] Even the McJob started leveling up, as franchises across the nation began advertising perks for entry-level workers in an effort to fill open positions. A McDonald's restaurant in Traveler's Rest, South Carolina, boasted: "We have a $400 hiring bonus! Come meet our team! Great starting pay and great benefits! We can offer set days off and set hours.... We have scholarships, tuition reimbursement programs, high school diploma programs—we can offer you so much!"[10] Nothing like this had been seen before under the golden arches.

This chapter answers two critical questions. First, what is a tight labor market, and when has it emerged in the past seventy years? Second, how have the poorest Americans fared during these periods of relative opportunity? Do they move into the labor market and find opportunities like the ones Cassandra and Ashantee landed more often than they do in periods of high unemployment? And do they see wage increases like theirs as a result?

THE BIG PICTURE

When employers' demand for workers outpaces the supply of workers willing or able to work, observers often refer to the market as "tight." At the opposite end of the spectrum, weak labor markets are characterized by relatively low levels of employer demand relative to the supply of workers—under these conditions the market has a great deal of slack. The labor market typically tracks the business cycle. Recessions are characterized by weak labor markets, while recoveries feature uneven labor markets with demand for some workers but not others. Expansions lead to tight labor markets.

Maximizing employment is a central goal of US economic policymaking, reflecting both the critical role that labor plays in driving economic growth and the normative value attached to the work ethic. At the conclusion of World War II, as thousands of American soldiers returned home with the specter of a return to the Great Depression looming, Congress passed the Employment Act of 1946, which emphasized maximum employment. Today this commitment to supporting job opportunities is represented by the Federal Reserve's dual mandate of "price stability" and "maximum employment." "Price stability" is defined as an annual inflation rate of 2 percent or lower. "Maximum employment" has been more difficult to quantify. Conceptually, the Fed defines maximum employment as "the highest level of employment or the lowest level of unemployment that the economy can sustain while maintaining a stable inflation rate."[11] Meeting the Fed's employment goals requires understanding what economists call the "natural rate of unemployment." Full employment rates are never zero, because even the healthiest labor market will see workers search for jobs.[12] Instead, economists define "full employment" as an economy that is operating at full capacity, using all of its available resources without driving up inflation rates.

This is the "natural" rate of unemployment, commonly known as the NAIRU (nonaccelerating inflation rate of unemployment). The indicator serves as a guide as to what "full employment" looks like at any given point in time.[13] When the unemployment rate spikes above the NAIRU, labor supply is outpacing labor demand and a slack labor market is the result. When the unemployment rate dips below the natural unemployment

Figure 4. Full employment target versus real unemployment rate, 1948–2021

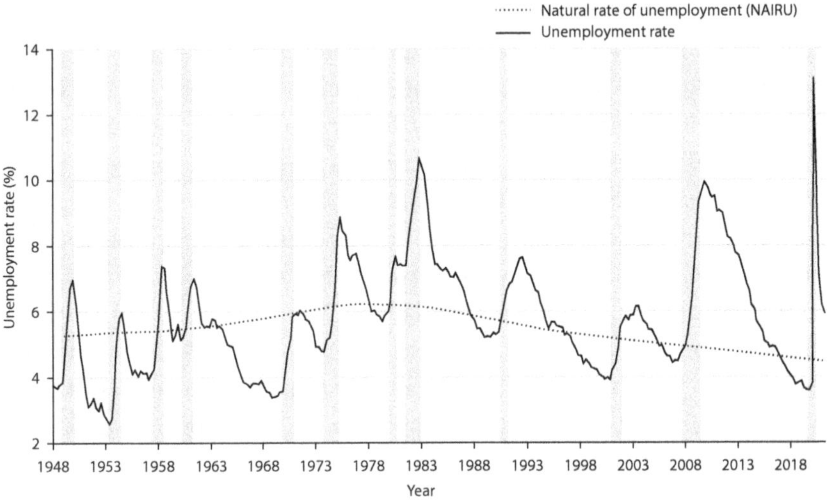

Note: Shaded areas indicate US recessions.

Source: US Congressional Budget Office, Natural Rate of Unemployment (NAIRU) and US Bureau of Labor Statistics, Unemployment Rate from FRED, Federal Reserve Bank of St. Louis.

rate, this is an indication of labor demand outpacing labor supply, or a tight labor market. The unemployment rate is one of the most important metrics of labor market health.[14] Not for nothing do journalists stand by the first Friday of every month when the national figures are released: these figures are widely accepted as a key measure of economic health by consumers, workers, employers, and policymakers. The standard unemployment rate is a simple ratio: the number of workers in the labor force who do not currently have a job (but have actively sought one in the past four weeks) as a share of the labor force. Jobseekers who become discouraged and have stopped looking are deemed out of the labor force and are not counted as officially unemployed. For this reason, unemployment rates often persist during the early stages of an economic recovery because more workers come off the sidelines to look for employment.

Figure 4 illustrates the relationship between noncyclical "full employment" rate estimates and the actual unemployment rate for the United States from 1948 through the present. The dotted line represents the natural rate of unemployment (NAIRU). The solid line represents the unemployment rate, which reflects the share of the total labor force that is out of work and actively seeking a new job.[15] The areas between the solid and dotted lines indicate the employment gap. Of those areas the portions below the dotted line indicate tight labor markets: periods where labor demand outpaced labor supply. Labor market slack, as measured by this gap between structural and cyclical unemployment, roughly aligns with the business cycle. Intuitively, the lag between labor market recoveries and the recovery in the growth of the economy makes sense. As GDP growth accelerates, businesses need time to begin to respond to the uptick in consumer demand, and responses typically include expanded hiring (or rehiring) for both existing firms as well as new business establishments. As a result, tight labor markets usually lag economic recoveries. Periods of labor market slack are typically both longer and deeper than periods of labor market tightness, and this dynamic has accelerated since the mid-1970s.

The most recent two labor market contractions are markedly different from those of the past quarter century. The labor market slack generated by the Great Recession (the first quarter of 2007 through the second quarter of 2009) was severe and sustained. The COVID-19 recession (the third quarter of 2020) was dramatic in both its severity and its brevity. Labor market slack rocketed upward and then plummeted back down at an equally breathtaking pace. That said, while the COVID-19 recession was unique in that it was driven by a once-in-a-century pandemic, nearly every recession is unique in its causes. Yet they have some common features—among them, the fact that the most vulnerable members of society shoulder a disproportionate share of the negative consequences when labor markets unravel in the wake of slowed growth.[16]

The Great Recession of 2008 was driven by a financial crisis spurred by a crash in the housing market, and the employment effects were most pronounced in financial services and housing-related industries such as construction.[17] The relatively mild 2001 recession stemmed from the collapse of the dot.com bubble and the 9/11 terrorist attack on the World Trade Center, and the effects were most pronounced in manufacturing, as businesses sharply reduced spending on machinery, computers, and other capital goods.[18] The causes of the recession of the early 1990s are myriad—a sharp rise in global oil prices resulting from Iraq's invasion of Kuwait, the savings and loan crises of the late 1980s, and the Federal Reserve's efforts to lower inflation rates.[19] Employment effects were sharpest for white-collar workers in finance, insurance, and real estate, and wholesale and retail trade employment decreased at nearly twice the rate of past contractions.[20]

In the 1980s, the combination of a global energy crisis driven by political unrest in Iran and Federal Reserve chair Paul Volcker's unprecedented aggressive increases in interest rates designed to slam the brakes on skyrocketing inflation drove a double-dip recession. The labor market effects were concentrated in goods-producing industries, like automobiles, construction, and steel. Variation in industry concentration across place as well as a legacy of occupational segregation by race and gender and industry and occupational variation in pay means that each recession has a unique impact on the labor market. However, Black workers, workers from low-income families, and especially Black workers from low-income families have been disproportionately impacted by all US recessions.

Unemployment is only one of the indicators of the health of the labor market. Indeed, economist Arthur Okun famously described it as "the tip of the iceberg."[21] The submerged portion of the iceberg too often remains unmeasured. The part under water includes (1) additional jobs for people who do not actively seek work in a slack labor market but nonetheless take jobs when they become available; (2) a longer work week reflecting less part-time and more overtime employment; and (3) additional productivity (more output per person-hour) from fuller and more efficient use of labor and capital—for instance, as workers seek out better jobs that more closely match their skills.[22] Fifty years since Okun's initial observations, assessing labor market slack remains a fundamental question in macroeconomics.[23] Researchers have generated multiple composite measures that track how tight or slack a labor market is across business cycles.[24] Labor market slack informs the decisions on interest rates and other key macroeconomic policy decisions made by the Federal Reserve Board of Governors. While the Fed relies on complex modeling, many other analysts utilize a range of more straightforward survey-driven economic indicators that offer a concise summary of labor market health. Historically, all have moved in roughly predictable ways depending on the point in the business cycle.[25]

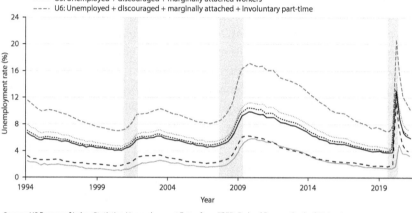

Figure 5. Alternative measures of unemployment, 1994–2021

U1: Long-term unemployed
U2: Recently unemployed
U3: Unemployment rate
U4: Unemployed + discouraged workers
U5: Unemployed + discouraged + marginally attached workers
U6: Unemployed + discouraged + marginally attached + involuntary part-time

Source: US Bureau of Labor Statistics, Unemployment Rates from FRED, Federal Reserve Bank of St. Louis.

Several measures were introduced in the mid-1990s to better capture the nuances of slack (figure 5). An especially important indicator is long-term unemployment (known as U1), defined as jobless workers who have been actively seeking work for fifteen or more weeks. The long-term unemployed are unevenly distributed across demographic groups, with disproportionately high rates for people of color, those with disabilities, and those who are not married.[26] As expected, long-term unemployment is highly sensitive to economic conditions and declines in tight labor markets. But the peaks in long-term unemployment are getting higher, and the valleys are no longer as low as they once were. Where recessions in the 1960s, 1970s, and 1980s produced long-term unemployment around 1–2 percent, the 2008 recession led to long-term unemployment over 4 percent, and it didn't fall back to 2 percent until 2014.[27] Although long-term unemployment accounts for a small portion of the population as a whole, it is a significant chunk of the total unemployed (ranging from 20 percent to more than 40 percent).[28]

How serious a problem is long-term unemployment? That depends in part on whether the long-term unemployed ultimately find work, or whether they instead drop out of the labor force entirely. Two other official Bureau of Labor Statistics measures, the U4 and U5, include not only those who are actively seeking work but also "discouraged" or "marginally attached" workers, defined as those who are no longer in the labor force but report that they want and looked for work in the past year. When the unemployment rate is decreasing, these more inclusive measures offer clues as to whether the decrease in unemployment is due to workers finding jobs (indicating a tight or tightening labor market) or leaving the labor market. As figure 5 shows, the 2011–19 recovery was characterized by elevated levels of both discouraged and marginally attached workers until the COVID-19 crisis, suggesting that the labor market rebound may have been somewhat less robust than the top-line unemployment figures indicate.

Whether workers have a job or not is one dimension of labor market slack. Whether employed workers have *enough* work is another way of looking at the submerged portion of Okun's iceberg.[29] The U6 metric from the Bureau of Labor Statistics includes not only those who are unemployed, discouraged, and marginally attached but also workers who report that they are working part-time for involuntary reasons.[30] Involuntary part-time work includes workers employed for fewer than thirty-five hours per week but who want and are available to work full-time.[31] Unsurprisingly, the U6 measure of unemployment therefore is always substantially higher than the other more restricted definitions of unemployment.

Researchers have recalculated involuntary part-time work metrics to include workers who are currently employed for fewer than thirty-five hours per week but desire additional hours, regardless of whether the worker's ideal hours are full-time. This more inclusive measure finds that underemployment in the pre-COVID-19 labor market boom was considerably higher than the official statistics suggest. Nearly 40 percent of all part-time workers preferred more hours than on offer by their current employer(s), as compared to just 11 percent of part-time workers who were working their preferred schedule.[32] Using these more inclusive measures, Black and Latinx workers were twice as likely to be underemployed as white workers.[33] Women also are more likely than men to be underemployed, as were workers in the bottom third of the family income distribution and those in low-wage occupations.[34] Over a fifth (21 per-

Figure 6. Unemployment rate by poverty status for 25- to 54-year-olds, 1976–2021

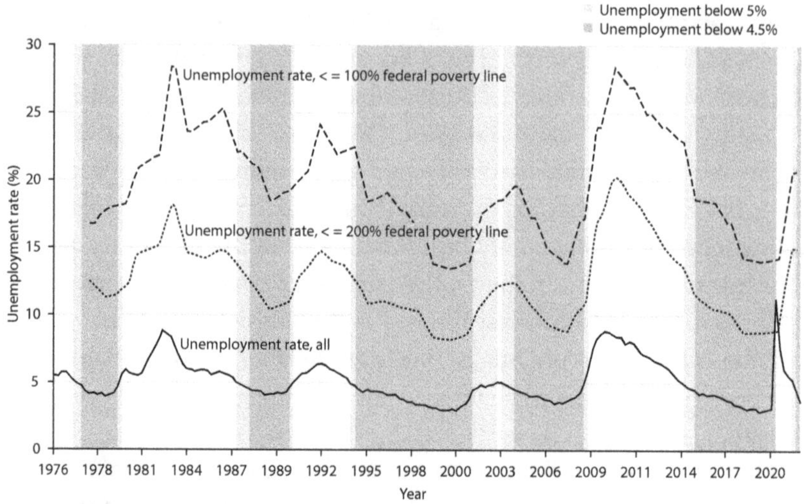

Note: Overall unemployment rate given as a quarterly average, while unemployment rate for those with incomes at 100% and 200% of the federal poverty line given as an annual average.

Source: Sarah Flood, Miriam King, Renae Rodgers, Steven Ruggles, J. Robert Warren, and Michael Westberry, Integrated Public Use Microdata Series (IPUMS), Current Population Survey: Version 9.0 (dataset), Minneapolis, MN: IPUMS, 2021. Federal poverty line measure created using CPS and authors' own calculations.

cent) of workers living in low-income households were underemployed, as compared to just 4 percent of those in the upper two-thirds of the income distribution. Workers in the service sector (21 percent), transportation and moving (12 percent), and sales (10 percent) all face disproportionate risk of underemployment.[35] Structural factors, including federal tax rules that exclude part-time workers from many types of benefits as well as the rise in just-in-time scheduling practices, help explain the increase in underemployment in these high-growth industries.[36] This industry variation in the rate of underemployment is especially notable because of the role these particular industries play as gateways to employment opportunity for workers who have been on the sideline for years.

In the seventy-three years since the United States began collecting official unemployment statistics, the unemployment rate has tracked business cycles. While significant nuance shows up when we look at the submerged portion of Okun's unemployment iceberg, the unemployment rate serves as a reliable signal of labor market health: a higher unemployment rate is an indicator of labor market slack, while a lower unemployment rate indicates a tighter labor market. As described earlier, the precise unemployment rates that characterize what the Federal Reserve refers to as "full employment" varies, but a rate of between 4 percent to 5 percent is conventionally viewed as very close to maximum employment in a healthy labor market. Our particular interest is the impact of tight labor markets on the nation's poor. We want to know whether their opportunities improve when unemployment is down. As illustrated in figure 6, unemployment rates for jobseekers with family incomes under the federal poverty threshold are substantially higher than the national average. Even more important, however, is the rapid pace at which unemployment drops among poor workers when labor markets tighten up, as depicted in the shaded lines in the figure. The darkest shaded periods represent the most conservative definition of a tight labor market—that is, an unemployment rate at or below 4.5 percent. It is during these periods that we see genuine and sustained improvement for the poor.

WHAT ABOUT WAGES?

Wages and benefits are a lagging indicator of tight labor markets. If employers are competing for a shrinking pool of available workers, one effective way to draw in talent is to raise wages and/or to sweeten the pot with benefits such as paid time off. A vast literature has documented the sluggish growth in median wage rates since the late 1970s.[37] Earners in the highest deciles have pulled away from the rest, and the middle class has been hollowed out over time. The result is an earnings ladder that stretches to outer space (literally: consider Amazon CEO Jeff Bezos's Blue Origin space adventures), but the rungs are so far apart that the climb has become nearly impossible—especially for those seeking to ascend from the bottom to the missing middle. Figure 7 charts this slow growth in real median hourly compensation, including both wages and benefits, from 1980 through 2019. While cyclical effects are indeed present in the data, they are quite muted, suggesting that employers are more reticent to raise wages in order to draw in would-be workers. But in periods like the late 1990s and the second half of the 2010s, tight labor markets did indeed lead to increased wages.

Figure 7. Real median hourly compensation, including wages and benefits, 1979–2019

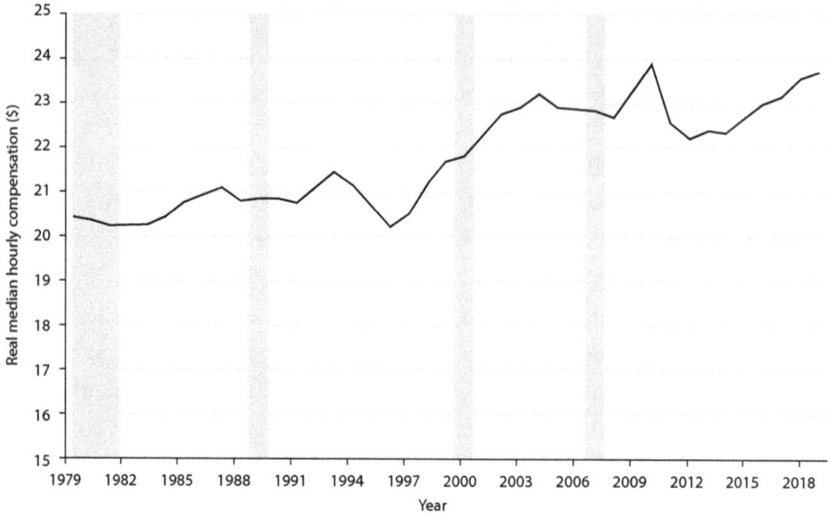

Real median hourly compensation ($)

Year

Note: Shaded areas indicate US recessions. "Compensation" refers to total compensation, including wages and benefits, of the median worker. Median hourly compensation are deflated by CPI-U-RS index.

Source: Economic Policy Institute analysis of EPI Current Population Survey extracts, v1 (2020). See Mishel and Bivens 2021.

Figure 8. Real median weekly wages by poverty status for 25- to 54-year-olds, 1976–2021

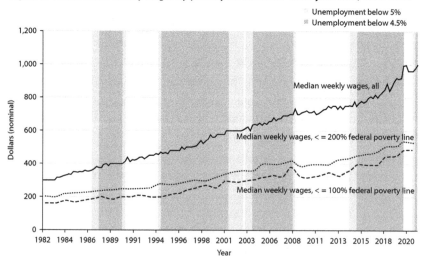

Note: Overall median wages given as a quarterly average, while median wages for those with incomes at 100% and 200% of the federal poverty line given as an annual average.

Source: Sarah Flood, Miriam King, Renae Rodgers, Steven Ruggles, J. Robert Warren, and Michael Westberry. Integrated Public Use Microdata Series (IPUMS), Current Population Survey: Version 9.0 (dataset), Minneapolis, MN: IPUMS, 2021. Federal poverty line measure created using CPS and authors' own calculations.

What about wages for those living in poverty? Figure 8 illustrates trends in weekly wages for all prime-age workers as well as the trends for workers living at or below 100 percent of the federal poverty line and the "near poor" who are at or below 200 percent of the federal poverty line. Once again, we see suggestive evidence of tight labor markets improving prospects for workers living in poverty. Wages ticked ever so slightly upward over the course of the Roaring 1990s, at the tail end of the 2000s boom, and, most recently, in the hot labor market on the eve of the COVID-19 pandemic.

VARIATION IN WORKERS' EXPERIENCE OF THE LABOR MARKET

The "headline" unemployment numbers that the country awaits every month rely on nationally representative surveys, but the fate of an individual worker isn't a matter of averages.[38] Their opportunities are determined by their local labor market, by the particulars of their educational background and skills, by their race, and by the industry in which they seek to work. Most workers look for jobs that are close to home, rather than searching throughout the country.[39] Moreover, the most vulnerable workers in areas experiencing economic shocks are the least likely to migrate to better opportunities.[40] Local labor markets vary substantially and often diverge from the national picture.

To illustrate this, we conduct a simple exercise looking at trends in state-level unemployment rates between 2010 and 2018, when national figures suggested a rapidly tightening labor market.[41] Map 1 shows the variation across state labor markets during this period. The solid gray-shaded states are "overperformers"—that is, places where unemployment rates were below the national average as the nation emerged from the Great Recession in 2010. Light gray-shaded states are "consistent overperformers," where unemployment rates were below the national average in 2010 *and* improved more rapidly than the national average between 2010 and 2018. Dark gray-shaded states are "declining overperformers" where unemployment was below the national average in 2010 but improvement was slower than average over the period. The hatch-marked states

Map 1. State variation in labor market performance during the 2010–2018 recovery

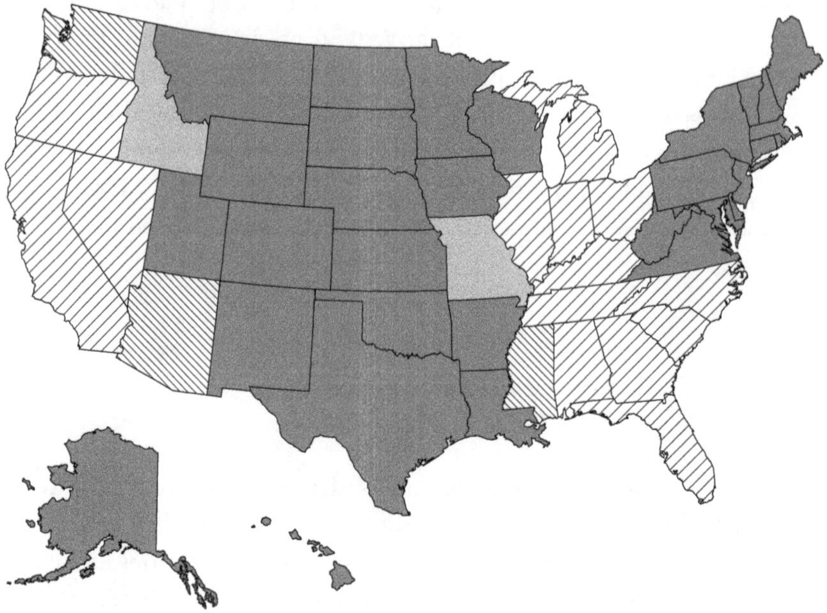

Consistent Overperformers — unemployment rate below national average in 2010, unemployment rate fell faster than national average between 2010 and 2018

Declining Overperformers — unemployment rate below national average in 2010, unemployment rate fell slower than national average between 2010 and 2018

Consistent Underperformers — unemployment rate above national average in 2010, unemployment rate fell slower than national average between 2010 and 2018

Improving Underperformers — unemployment above national average in 2010, unemployment rate fell faster than national average between 2010 and 2018

Source: Authors' calculations.

are "underperformers"—that is, places where unemployment rates were above the national average on the cusp of the recovery beginning in 2010. Lighter hatch-marked states are "improving underperformers," where unemployment rates were lower than average in 2010 but improved more quickly than the national average over the period. Darker hatch-marked states are "consistent underperformers," where unemployment was higher than average in 2010 and also improved more slowly than the national average over the period.

Much of southeastern United States, the Rust Belt, and the West Coast were improving underperformers. These regions had relatively high unemployment rates coming out of the Great Recession in 2010, but their labor markets then tightened relatively sharply over the course of the recovery period. In contrast, the Mountain West, Upper Midwest, New England, and the mid-Atlantic regions were declining overperformers. These regions entered the recovery in a relatively strong position but saw slower-than-average tightening between 2010 and 2018. Washington, Arizona, and Mississippi were troublingly consistent underperformers, coming out of the Great Recession in 2010 with relatively high unemployment rates and seeing slower improvements relative to the national average. Idaho and Missouri stand out as consistent overperformers, emerging from the recession with a lower-than-average unemployment rate and enjoying relatively more rapid declines in unemployment between 2010 and 2018.[42]

Local labor markets are not the only determinant of whether a job-seeker finds employment, of course. Workers' characteristics—including their educational credentials, race, and occupation—are also associated with variation in the labor market. Employers regularly cite a mismatch between the educational level and skills of available workers and the requirements of the jobs that they seek to fill. These claims grow louder as the labor market begins to tighten. The National Association of Manufacturers' Manufacturing Institute has tracked the "skills shortage" for nearly twenty years, highlighting what they identify as a "widening gap between the jobs that need to be filled and the skilled talent pool capable of filling them."[43] In Fall 2021, as the labor market began to pick up steam, employers once again worried about a paucity of skilled workers for available jobs. "Do we have the workforce right now to take care of this [infrastructure push]? Absolutely not," Beverly Scott, vice chair of President Biden's National Infrastructure Advisory Council told a *New York Times* reporter.[44]

To what extent are tight labor markets due to a mismatch between workers' skills and employers' demands? And how might the impacts of tight labor markets vary by education or skill? There are reasons to be skeptical of the so-called "skills mismatch." Randall Collins's 1979 classic *The Credential Society* argues the relationship between educational credentials and desirable jobs has little to do with a functional linkage between education and job requirements. Instead, he posits, educational credentials are cultural resources that impress others with importance rather than usefulness. Indeed, many of the jobs that employers report having the most difficulty filling require little to no formal education.[45] For example, in 2013, four of the ten jobs that employers across the country reported were most difficult to fill required minimal formal education: laborers, drivers, production operators, and administrative assistants. Instead of a lack of skill, the issue might be with the quality of jobs: nearly one-fifth of employers report that jobseekers were not willing to accept the positions at the rate of pay being offered.[46]

If education is culturally desirable but not functionally necessary to jobs, then demand for educational credentials will likely vary with the business cycle. This appears to be the case: media reports and surveys indicate that employer requirements increased sharply during the Great Recession, such that a college diploma was required for occupations that previously required only a high school degree.[47] Accordingly, employers raised education and experience requirements.[48] The increase in credentialism has disproportionately impacted BIPOC workers, especially Hispanic, Black, and American Indian workers, all of whom have lower rates of education attainment.[49] Tight labor markets have the potential to reverse this credentialism. Indeed, employer skill requirements fall as the labor market tightens.[50] For instance, a 1 percentage point reduction in the local unemployment rate is associated with an 0.27 percentage point reduction in the fraction of job postings requiring a bachelor's degree, and a similar decline in the fraction of job postings requiring five or more years of experience. After decades of focus on the need for "upskilling" the workforce with more formal education, we now also see moves toward *downskilling*, a reversal in the ratcheting up of education and experience requirements that takes place when unemployment is exceedingly high, as it was during the Great Recession.[51]

The persistent legacy of discrimination (both individual and structural) in the US labor market means that the impact of tight labor markets varies across racial groups, regardless of skill level or educational credentials. The disproportionate burden shouldered by Black workers in labor market contractions is well-documented. Black workers are overrepresented in consumer demand–driven low-wage occupations and industries at high risk of contraction in recession, including service and retail. The durable tracks of slavery and ensuing exclusionary policies that legally restricted

Figure 9. Unemployment rate by poverty status and race for 25- to 54-year-olds, 1976–2021

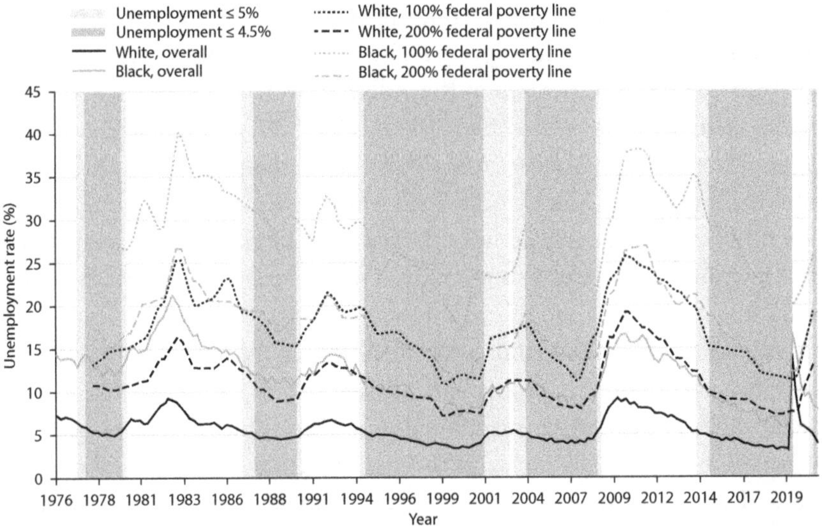

Note: Overall unemployment rate given as a quarterly average, while unemployment rate for those with incomes at 100% and 200% of the federal poverty line given as an annual average.

Source: Sarah Flood, Miriam King, Renae Rodgers, Steven Ruggles, J. Robert Warren, and Michael Westberry, Integrated Public Use Microdata Series (IPUMS), Current Population Survey: Version 9.0 (dataset), Minneapolis, MN: IPUMS, 2021. Federal poverty line measure created using CPS and authors' own calculations.

occupational choice for people of color in the United States helps to explain that concentration.[52] As a result, Black workers are disproportionately represented among low-wage workers, regardless of the health of the labor market. Indeed, in the rip-roaring tight labor market of 2019, 54 percent of Black workers earned $10.22 an hour or less and had median annual earnings of $17,950 or less—as compared to 37 percent of white workers.[53] While the share of workers across all races who are earning poverty-level wages has declined over the past three decades, Black workers are more than twice as likely to be earning poverty-level wages than white workers.[54]

This legacy is evidenced in the disaggregated data on both unemployment and wage trends, as illustrated in Figure 9. While both Black and white workers' fortunes recover sharply during tight labor markets, unemployment rates for Black workers have been substantially higher than those of white workers since the Bureau of Labor Statistics began disaggregating the unemployment rate by race in 1972. Indeed, unemployment rates for all Black workers (i.e., regardless of family income) are approximately equal to unemployment rates for white workers living in families at 200 percent of the federal poverty line. Unemployment rates for Black workers living at 100 percent of the federal poverty line are substantially higher than those of poor white workers. However, as other scholars have demonstrated—and as we'll explore further in chapter 2—unemployment rates for the poorest Black workers fall somewhat more rapidly than those of white workers during periods of very tight labor markets, suggesting that low unemployment spurs progress toward racial equity in the labor market.[55]

Although explicit discrimination has diminished (though, to be clear, discrimination remains problematically persistent), America's history of racial exclusion is woven into the fabric of the labor market in patterns of occupational segregation and through subtle mechanisms of implicit bias.[56] Even in the face of labor shortages, some employers are reticent to hire workers of color. As a result, the Black-white wage gap is substantial and has grown over the past half century.[57] Black workers today earn 20 percent less, on average, than white workers.[58] Black women earn less than white women.[59] Employed Black men earn 67 percent of employed white men's average earnings—roughly the same as in 1970s.[60] While the racial wage gap is smaller at the bottom rungs of the income distribution, Black low-income workers still earn 9 percent less than their white peers.[61] And these figures do not even account for the disproportionate share of Black men who are incarcerated.[62]

One explanation for this gap is that many less-educated Black men have withdrawn from the labor force during their prime working years—either by "choice" or as a result of incarceration.[63] Tight labor markets have the potential to draw Black workers off the sidelines by creating more meaningful opportunities (e.g., more job openings, higher wages, better benefits) and reducing employers' hesitancy to hire workers with a history of incarceration or long unexplained periods out of the labor market. Indeed, the Black-white wage gap is pro-cyclical: racial gaps in unemployment rates widen during recessions and contract during recoveries as the labor market tightens.[64] This is partly because racial discrimination declines in occupations where unemployment is low and vacancies are difficult to fill.[65] The tight labor market of 2018–19 created opportunity for Black workers. Their wage growth was exceptionally strong relative to past recoveries, and the unemployment rate for Black workers hit historic low levels.[66]

This is not the first time the United States has experienced prolonged tight labor markets. And the lessons derived from previous episodes of tight labor markets suggest that good times have positive impacts on the most disadvantaged citizens: young Black men. Harvard labor economist Richard Freeman explored just how significant tight labor markets were for young Black men, who are chronically at the bottom of the queue and subject to the greatest amount of discrimination.[67] In a paper published more than thirty years ago now, Freeman found:

> Local labor market shortages greatly improve the employment opportunities of disadvantaged young men, substantially raising the percentage employed and reducing their unemployment rate. Employment of Black youths is particularly sensitive to the state of the local labor market. Labor market shortages also significantly increased the hourly earnings of disadvantaged youths, particularly Black [youth].... Youths in areas with labor shortages [which Freeman defines as unemployment rates of 4 percent or less] had greater increases in earnings as they aged than those in other areas, implying that improved labor market conditions raise the longitudinal earnings profiles as well as the starting prospects of youths. Again, the greatest gains were achieved by young Black [people].[68]

The benefits of tight labor markets often take longer to reach Black workers, however. Despite the growth of the Black middle class, Black workers remain concentrated in the bottom rungs of the earnings and income distribution.[69] Because recessions disadvantage the disadvantaged, low-income workers are the first to feel their effects in terms of both employment and earnings.[70] Low-wage workers see few to no benefits from economic recoveries until the unemployment rate reaches between 4 percent and 5 percent.[71] And extremely tight labor markets would be needed to close the race gap entirely: closing the unemployment gap between Black and white workers would require unemployment rates of 1 percent or lower—something that is "well outside historic experience."[72] But perfection shouldn't blind us to the upside of improvement. When unemployment falls below 5 percent, we begin to see these gaps shrink, and that is all to the good.

Figure 10. Jobseekers per job opening by industry, 2018Q2 and 2021Q3

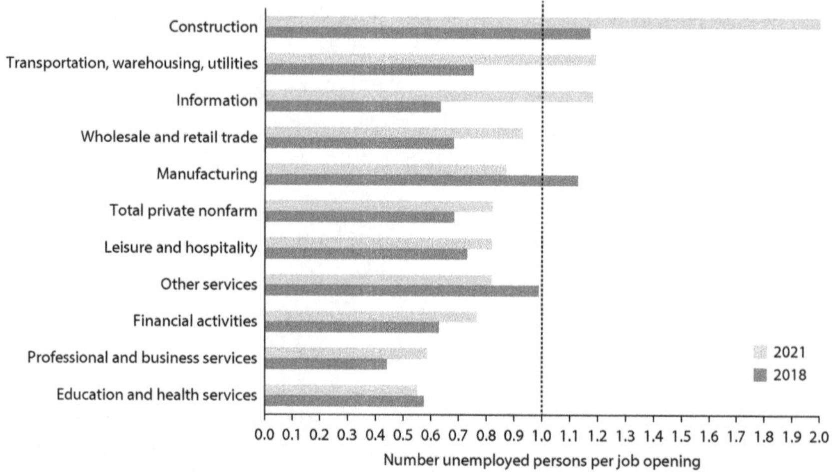

Source: US Bureau of Labor Statistics, Unemployment Level—Nonagriculture, Private Wage and Salary Workers, Thousands of Persons, Quarterly, Not Seasonally Adjusted and Industry Totals + Job Openings: Total Private, Level in Thousands, Quarterly, Not Seasonally Adjusted and Industry Totals from FRED, Federal Reserve Bank of St. Louis.

Finally, labor market dynamics affect workers differently depending on their occupation and industry.[73] By the second quarter of 2018, job openings outnumbered unemployed workers in all industries except construction and manufacturing, and even those industries were at twenty-year lows in unemployment relative to vacancy rates.[74] The economic tailspin of 2020 sent unemployment rates skyrocketing across industries, and the unevenness of the recovery is evident in figure 10. For every two unemployed construction workers, one construction job opening is available. Transportation and information services both remain relatively slack. Job openings outnumber jobseekers across every other sector of the economy.[75] Demand for education and health services workers is especially high relative to unemployment in these sectors, likely due to a combination of the full reopening of schools across the nation combined with increased demand for COVID-19–driven health care (e.g., vaccinations and testing).[76]

In the context of a tight labor market, employment dynamics differ across industry and occupation. If tight labor markets benefit high-paying jobs first, we can expect to find the working poor and the unemployed benefiting last. A shortage of engineers or computer programmers may drive up wages for highly educated employees, with little impact on those in the service sector. The distribution of work opportunities is also important for policy decisions: if the occupations that benefit from tight labor markets require specific kinds of skills, federal and local governments can better allocate resources to support worker entry into those fields.

Defining a tight labor market is a complex task—indeed, macro-economists at the Federal Reserve and elsewhere have debated the right set of metrics for identifying labor market slack for decades. Structural factors such as the shifts in the earnings distribution and changes in the labor force participation rate have complicated efforts to identify clear indicators. But, as we've seen in this chapter, a handful of key periods between the 1960s and the present stand out as times when a range of indicators pointed in the direction of labor demand outpacing labor supply at a national level. A tight labor market isn't merely a recovery, as many recoveries lead only to standard rates of unemployment. If we consider three types of labor markets—recessions, recoveries, and tight labor markets—those tight labor market periods, where unemployment comes close to the conventional wisdom of 5 percent or lower, we see that these periods are unusual and highly consequential.

The sustained high-pressure period of the 1960s was followed by a long stretch of less-impressive labor market recoveries where unemployment rates dipped below 5 percent for a year or two—in the late 1970s, then again in the 1980s. It was not until the second half of the 1990s that the United States enjoyed another sustained period like this. Our most recent shot at sustained tight labor markets was interrupted by the arrival of COVID-19 on US shores, but it picked right back up again remarkably quickly and—as this book went to press—appears on course to break more records. Whether a tight labor market on a national level translates into genuine opportunity for a given worker depends heavily on local conditions and they vary a great deal. Opportunities also vary by a workers' industry and work experience: whether or not an individual is able to gain traction may depend on whether her past work experience, skills, or social networks connect her to a job in an industry experiencing high levels of labor demand. We've also seen that tight labor markets have the potential to create opportunities for Black and other workers of color. This is due in part to the fact that the most opportunity accrues to those at the bottom, where these workers remain overrepresented due to the enduring legacy of racism and persistent discrimination.

It makes good sense that so much research and policy attention has been focused on the ramifications of economic downturns for the most vulnerable Americans. Yet the United States has had multiple periods of economic growth accompanied by labor markets brimming with the promise of expanded opportunity. In times of exceptionally tight labor markets, where the unemployment rate approaches or dips below 4.5 percent, we see signs that doors begin to open for workers and would-be workers living in poverty. Do people living on the margins manage to walk across the threshold and maintain gainful employment? Do they see their earnings and incomes improve, and, if so, do those improvements last? We now turn to those questions.

2 What Lasts? Durable Effects of Tight Labor Markets

Opening jobs to more people and seeing those jobs pay better wages—these are unequivocal benefits of tight labor markets, especially for the poor. But do the opportunities afforded by these positive conditions translate into *durable* change for the better? The structure of the US labor market has evolved. Have the opportunities that it creates for meaningful mobility in workers' lives altered as well? There are few studies that take a long historical view, which is what we need to answer this question or to situate our most recent experience with unprecedented tight labor markets—the lowest unemployment in fifty years—against the backdrop of the past.

The Panel Study of Income Dynamics (PSID), the longest running longitudinal household survey in the world, is a unique dataset that allows us to explore these questions by following the same workers across multiple business cycles.[1] The data are widely used by researchers and policy analysts seeking to understand questions that require following individuals over time.[2] The study began in 1968 with a nationally representative sample of more than eighteen thousand individuals living in five thousand families in the United States, and information on those respondents and their descendants has been collected continuously for more than five decades. The most recent complete survey year available is 2019 and reflects data from 2017 due to the retrospective structure of the survey.

The PSID collects rich information on individuals' economic lives, including employment, earnings, and hours worked as well as demographic data including race, gender, education, age, and the state in which they live. The survey allows us to follow cohorts of prime-age workers (ages twenty-five to fifty-four) across the ups-and-downs of a business cycle. We can observe not only how a tight labor market shapes employment and earnings but also whether that opportunity endures as conditions begin to unravel. And, because the PSID data spans such an impressively long duration, we can look at different periods of US history to see whether tight labor markets have consistent effects or whether the relationship between labor market conditions and individual outcomes have changed over time.

To ensure we take local economic context into consideration, we combine individual-level data on workers' lives from the PSID with state-level data on local economic conditions from the Current Population Survey (CPS) of the US Bureau of Labor Statistics. This allows us to ensure that we are assessing workers' labor market opportunities in the context of their regional markets, rather than relying on national figures. As discussed in chapter 1, regional labor markets create important context for workers' opportunities, especially for economically vulnerable workers who are less likely to move across state lines for a new job.[3] As a result, we use empirical techniques that situate individual workers and jobseekers in the context of their regional economies in all that follows. The state-level unemployment data from the CPS are available beginning in the 1980s, which allows us to examine the business cycles of the 1980s, 1990s, and 2000s in our analysis.[4]

We use two distinct analytic approaches to examine how tight labor markets shape opportunities for workers. First, we explore whether falling local unemployment results in positive changes in individuals' employment and earnings. Our methods are inspired by an analysis of the long-term negative effects of the Great Recession—we flip the script to see whether there are long-term positive effects of tight labor markets, and for whom.[5] To assess whether the cyclical relationship between tightening labor markets and workers' outcomes has evolved as the structure of the US economy has changed over the past four decades, we look at each business cycle separately, and we follow individuals from the trough through the peak of the national business cycle as defined by the National Bureau of Economic Research (NBER).

However, the positive benefits of tight labor markets are not simply the inverse of slack labor markets. *Very* low unemployment merits focused attention, because employers and would-be workers may behave differently when labor markets are especially tight. Moreover, periods of low unemployment that last for many months may create different forms of opportunity than those that evaporate more quickly. In theory, tight labor markets that are *both* intense and durable are likely to produce the most transformative changes, relative to those that are neither particularly strong nor particularly lengthy. To answer these questions, we use an analytic approach developed by Julie Hotchkiss and Robert Moore.[6] We pool workers across the entire sample, from 1980 through 2019, so that we can focus in on subgroup differences and disentangle the impact of duration versus intensity.

We use state unemployment rates as the basis for our empirical definitions of tight regional markets throughout, for several reasons. First, the unemployment rate is a widely accepted indicator of labor market strength and tracks other metrics over time, as discussed in chapter 1. Second, the unemployment rate is consistently available at a state level for many decades, unlike other relevant metrics such as the ratio comparing jobseekers to job openings. We rely on state-level indicators because, as described earlier, regional labor market conditions are decidedly more important than national-level conditions for individual workers—especially economically vulnerable workers who are less likely to pick up and relocate for a job. We describe how we operationalize the concept of tight labor markets using these individual-place-year specific data in additional detail in the presentation of each of the analytic exercises below, and we direct readers interested in the data and the details of the technical analysis to Appendix 1, the methodological appendix for chapter 2.

How did tight labor markets shape employment trajectories over the ebb and flow of the business cycles of the 1980s, the 1990s, and the early 2000s? Our key predictor of interest is the change in a given individual's state unemployment rate during the expansionary period of the business circle, which serves as a proxy for the intensity of labor market tightness.

Our key outcome of interest is the *durability* of that individual's probability of employment. In other words, we are not simply interested in whether an individual is more likely to be employed as their local labor market improves. Rather, we are looking for evidence of long-term positive effects: does the traction that an individual gains in a tight labor market endure over time, and for how long?

Our results confirm the intuition that tight labor markets boost the probability that an individual is working even as the economy begins to contract.[7] This finding holds even after we control for the effects of age, industry, and prior earnings (for full results, see Appendix 2, the analysis results for chapter 2, table 1). For the 1980s, a 1 percentage point decline in a worker's state unemployment rate predicts 9 percent higher odds that they remain employed on the brink of the downturn of the early 1990s than it would been had the labor market not tightened. For the 1990s, a 1 percentage point decline in a worker's state unemployment rate predicts 13 percent higher odds that they remain employed on the eve of the 2001 recession than had the labor market not tightened. While results for the expansionary period of the early 2000s are not statistically significant, they are directionally consistent with a story of tighter labor markets providing an enduring lift for employment prospects across the business cycle.[8] These are meaningful differences. Take a worker in Massachusetts, where unemployment rates fell from 7 percent in 1983 to 4 percent in 1989. That labor market tightening meant that a given worker's odds of remaining employed on the eve of the business cycle downturn in 1992 were 27 percent higher than their odds of employment in the absence of the tightening labor market. The tight labor markets of the 1990s, when unemployment rates in Massachusetts fell from 9 percent in 1992 to 3 percent in 2000, translated into 78 percent higher odds that a given individual was employed on the eve of the 2001 recession.

However, not all tight labor markets generate the same degree of lift. The only episode that generated opportunity powerful enough to "stick" through the entire business cycle—not only when labor markets were tight but also as they began to weaken—was the boom period of President Clinton's administration, between 1992 and 2000. The impact of falling unemployment during the Roaring 1990s endured through the following recession. Residents of states that experienced tight labor markets in that boom period retained a higher probability of employment not only as the labor market barreled toward the 2001 recession but throughout the ups-and-downs of the early 2000s straight up until the eve of the Great Recession in 2007. Specifically, a 1 percentage point decrease in an individual's state unemployment rate in the Roaring 1990s translates into 14 percent higher odds that a worker remained employed in 2007.

Looking again at the specific example of Massachusetts provides meaningful context. For Bay State residents the tight labor market of the 1990s translated into 98 percent higher odds of remaining employed on the brink of the Great Recession in 2007 as compared to the counterfactual where unemployment rates remained elevated. We know that individuals in low-wage jobs face high odds of job loss when labor markets sour. But does the relative strength of the tight labor market in which a low-wage worker finds a job shape their chances of holding onto employment as through the economy's ups-and-downs in the years to come? In short: yes, albeit weakly. Once again, the Roaring 1990s stand out as a period of particular interest. A 1 percentage point decrease in a low-wage worker's state unemployment rate during the 1990s translates into 17 percent higher odds that they were employed on the eve of the 2001 recession. Considering the Massachusetts example again: the most disadvantaged workers' odds of employment on the eve of the 2001 recession were 102 percent higher, thanks to the tightening labor markets of the Roaring 1990s.

Other tight labor markets, in the 1980s and 2000s, are directionally consistent (i.e., positive), but they do not reach conventional levels of statistical significance. The variation in the power of the lift provided by tight labor markets across the past four decades is an indicator that tight labor markets are not all created equal; the tight labor markets of the 1990s offered unique benefits to low-wage workers. We will come back to this point later. Just as the tight labor markets of the 1990s had more powerful effects for those in the bottom of the wage distribution, they also had uniquely powerful effects on employment for Black as compared with white workers.[9] Every 1 percentage point decrease in their state's unemployment rate raised a Black worker's employment odds by 40 percent in the 1990s. The impact of tightening labor markets on Black employment trajectories in the Roaring 1990s is among the strongest of our results and a powerful signal that very low unemployment ignites opportunity for those who have historically faced barriers. The power of tight labor markets to create opportunity for Black workers is especially crucial given the disproportionate burden that these same workers face during downturns.[10]

We also see significant and large gender differences in the power of tight labor markets to create employment opportunity. The increase in women's labor force participation and earnings over the past half century has played a key role in bolstering family incomes, and female-headed households remain overrepresented among families living below the poverty line. Accordingly, the impact of tight labor markets on women's employment trajectories is of particular interest. Our results illustrate the role that very low levels of unemployment can play in fostering durable employment for women: for every percentage point decrease in her state's unemployment rate in the 1990s, a woman's odds of enduring employment increased by 22 percent in the 1990s and by 26 percent in the 2000s.

Labor market slack is particularly hard on young workers. Landing a first job in a weak economy effectively scars young workers for life.[11] They face enduring consequences over the course of their careers in the form of lower probabilities of employment and lower earnings. Do tight labor markets reverse this picture? That was the case in the 1990s, which stand out as powerful engines of employment opportunity: eighteen- to twenty-four-year-olds' odds of remaining employed over the course of the business cycle were 47 percent higher for each 1 percentage point drop in their local unemployment rate. We do not see statistically significant results for young workers in any of the other tight labor markets, once again indicating that the Roaring 1990s were unique.

For prime-age workers (ages twenty-five to fifty-four), falling unemployment rates predicted enduring employment in all three periods, though the results from the 2000s do not reach statistically significant levels. The strongest results for prime-age workers are in the 1990s period: a 1 percentage point decrease in local unemployment rates boosts the odds of employment on the eve of the 2001 by 13 percent. Moreover, those results endure through the 2000s: a 1 percentage point decrease in an individual's local unemployment rates in the 1990s raised their odds of employment on the eve of the Great Recession by 15 percent.

In sum, five main conclusions emerge from this first analysis:

1. Tight labor markets predict durable employment. The tighter an individual's local labor market during an expansionary period, the higher the odds of that same individual remaining in employed when the economy unravels. While this finding may seem intuitive, it need not be the case that a *given worker* enjoys the salutary effects of labor market recoveries. Because our data allows us to follow individuals across time, we are able to identify the way in which context can create opportunity.

2. Not all tight labor markets are created equal. The hot markets of the 1990s generated significantly more opportunity for those at the bottom of the economic ladder than those of the 1990s or 2000s.[12]

3. Tight labor markets also boost employment opportunity for Black workers. Again, the tight labor markets of the 1990s stand out as an especially powerful force for Black individuals than were the other high-pressure periods.

4. The impact of tight labor markets on women's employment has grown progressively more powerful over time, relative to the impacts of high-pressure environments on men's employment.

5. Just as bad labor markets can induce "scarring" for those beginning their careers in bad times, tight labor markets can create enduring opportunities for younger workers.

LONG AND STRONG

The benefits of tight labor markets represent the inverse lesson from the vast literature documenting the negative effects of labor market slack. But this is not the whole story: new kinds of opportunities open when the labor market becomes *especially* tight. What does that mean? We draw on the analytic approach of economists Julie Hotchkiss and Robert Moore to examine the effect of labor markets by intensity and duration.[13] We replicate their approach using the PSID, which allows us to capture the second half of the expansionary period following the Great Recession—including the period of accelerated labor market tightening that occurred after 2014 and before the COVID-19 crash in 2020. Because the most recent wave of the PSID was collected through 2019, we can extend the analysis to capture more of the extraordinary period of tightness in the labor market.

In the prior analysis we define tight labor markets in terms of decreasing regional unemployment rates. In this analysis we use a state-level indicator that defines tight labor markets in relation to the national average long-term unemployment rate, which results in a continuous variable that ranges from 0 to 17 (for technical details see Appendix 1, the methodological appendix for chapter 2). This approach allows us to examine the overall effects of tight labor markets as well as to distinguish between the *intensity* (i.e., the magnitude of the differences between the actual and long-term unemployment rates) and *duration* (i.e., the number of years for which the high-pressure environment persists) of tight labor markets. We generate estimates that distinguish between these two dimensions of high-pressure markets and look at a wider range of labor market outcomes, including employment (as captured by both the probability of unemployment and labor force participation rates), earnings, and hours. Unlike the analysis presented above, which focuses on understanding the variation in the effects of tight labor markets across three distinct business cycles, here we pool the entire sample across years. We still follow individuals across time, but the time periods themselves are no longer a focus of the reported results. The resulting pooled longitudinal sample is much larger and therefore allows us to look more carefully across a wide range of labor market outcomes by subgroup, including wage quintiles, race, gender, and age. We also decompose the effects of the duration versus the intensity of tight labor markets for each of these subgroups.

We begin by looking at the total effects of tight labor markets—that is, the combined effects of both intensity and duration (for detailed results, see tables 2a and 2b of Appendix 2, the analysis results for this chapter). Does exposure to high-pressure markets provide a modicum of protection against the negative consequences of future labor market contractions? The main overall effect of high-pressure labor markets is lower unemployment rates during the following recession. On average, across the full sample, exposure to a weak labor market meant workers spent more weeks unemployed (0.364), received lower hourly wages (-0.129), and worked fewer hours weekly (-0.222, though not statistically significant). Exposure to a high-pressure labor market, by contrast, mitigates these impacts significantly: a one unit increase in exposure to a high-pressure labor market minimizes unemployment duration by 0.0122 weeks and raises hourly pay by 0.5 percent.[14] To be clear, tight labor markets do not completely insulate workers from the negative consequences of downturns—to expect as much would fly in the face of what we know about the punishing impact of recessions, particularly for the most vulnerable. The important takeaway is that tight labor markets can provide a small but potentially meaningful buffering effect.

We also see key racial differences in how tight labor markets impact labor market opportunities. High rates of unemployment strongly increase Black workers' unemployment rates (0.58 versus 0.269 for whites). But exposure to a high-pressure labor market prior to a downturn provides a statistically significant protective effect for Black workers' unemployment duration (-0.318) and for hourly wages (0.0045).[15] Hot economies also provide more of a buffer to younger workers, as compared with older workers. Exposure to a high-pressure labor market reduces weeks of unemployment by 0.266 for eighteen- to twenty-four-year-olds (as compared to 0.0157 for twenty-five- to thirty-four-year-olds, and 0.0161 for thirty-five- to forty-four-year-olds). Younger workers also enjoy significant and relatively strong hourly wage gains relative to older workers. Exposure to a high-pressure labor market results in a statistically significant 0.7 percent increase in hourly pay for eighteen- to twenty-four-year-olds, as compared to an 0.048 percent increase for workers between the ages of twenty-five and forty-four. The relationship for workers ages forty-five to sixty-four is also positive but is not statistically significant.

Our analysis also includes evidence of protective effects of tight labor markets for workers with low levels of formal education, which economists often use as a proxy for skill and, in turn, wage prospects. Exposure to a high-pressure labor market in the wake of a downturn reduces weeks of unemployment by 0.054 for workers with less than a high school degree; workers with a high school diploma or more education see no protective effects from prior exposure to a tight labor market. These are critically important results, as they signal that tight labor markets may provide unique opportunities for workers with the lowest levels of formal advantage. However, the least-educated workers see no meaningful protective effects for hourly pay or weekly hour worked, while more educated workers appear to enjoy gains on both outcomes as a result of exposure to high-pressure markets.

Next, we look specifically at workers with a history of low earnings (for full results, see tables 3a and 3b of Appendix 2, the analysis results for this chapter). The protective impact of tight labor markets endures for these workers: when labor markets contract, exposure to a tight labor market reduces the duration of unemployment (-0.0176) and increases hourly wages by 0.66 percent for this group. These results are small but statistically significant. For example, a worker earning the federal minimum wage, which has been pegged at $7.25 per hour in real dollars since 2009, would have seen their pay go up by $0.05 per hour. For those working full-time (forty hours per week), this increase translates into an extra $2 per week. While this is not a huge bump, it's not nothing, especially for those living paycheck-to-paycheck. The protective effects of tight labor markets for low-wage Black workers' unemployment durations are even larger (-0.0411) and substantially larger than those for white workers (-0.0131). Young low-wage workers (ages eighteen to twenty-four) also see relatively large protective effects from exposure to tight labor markets as compared with older workers, for both unemployment duration and for hourly pay.

We now turn to the decomposition results, which allow us to distinguish between the effects of the duration of a tight labor market (how long do the good times last?) versus the intensity of a tight labor market (just how good are the good times?) (For full results, see tables 4a and 4b of Appendix 2, the analysis results for this chapter). For the full sample it is the duration of exposure to tight labor markets that counts rather than the intensity of labor market tightness. Longer periods spent in tight labor markets provide a stronger buffering effect against the negative consequences of subsequent downturns than do shorter periods of exposure to very tight labor markets. Unemployment duration is reduced by 0.0228 weeks and increases hourly pay by 0.49 percent in subsequent downturns. The exposure effects of the *intensity* of tight labor markets are not statistically significant across any of our measures of labor market outcomes for the full sample.

The story changes when we drill down into the results for key groups of interest. The effects of duration and intensity vary in important ways for Black workers as compared to the sample as a whole. Exposure to long-lasting periods of tight labor markets reduce the duration of unemployment for Black workers when the economy heads south (-0.2099). However, if we hold the duration of exposure constant and instead focus on the intensity of the tight labor market (i.e., just how low is unemployment?), Black unemployment duration in the subsequent downturn is actually *higher* (0.7702).

Although this finding may seem counterintuitive, a simple explanation is most likely behind it: intensely tight labor markets (i.e., very low unemployment rates) may draw Black workers off the sidelines and into the labor market in search of work, which will raise the unemployment rate for the "right" reasons. When those tight markets don't endure, the pool of unemployed Black jobseekers remains elevated and shows up as higher unemployment duration in our results. We view this as an indication of the power that tight labor markets have to pull previously marginalized workers off the sidelines and into the game.

We see similar results for the protective role of duration versus intensity on Black workers' weekly hours when the labor market heads south: duration of exposure to a tight labor market has a positive effect on weekly hours worked (0.229), while the intensity of the tight labor market has a negative effect (-0.889) for Black workers. These findings are consistent with models of labor market discrimination that show Black workers facing disproportionate losses when labor markets unravel. If intensely tight labor markets mean that employers are more likely to "submerge" their biases and hire Black workers who they might have otherwise deemed unhirable, those same Black workers may be the first to see their hours cut back as the labor market deteriorates. The sweet spot that will genuinely improve the lives of Black workers are tight labor markets that are both strong *and* long-lasting—a combination that the United States has rarely seen due to policy choices and inflationary fears. Our results are consistent along these same lines for workers who have less than a high school diploma. Taken together, these results suggest that long-lasting, very tight labor markets can have powerful, transformative impacts on the lives of workers. In sum, we offer up three central insights based on this analysis:

1. Exposure to tight labor markets provides a protective effect against the duration of unemployment and the erosion of hourly wages when labor markets unravel.

2. These findings hold even for individuals with a history of low wages and may be particularly important for lower-wage Black workers, those without a high school diploma, and younger workers.

3. Understanding the effect of tight labor markets requires distinguishing between intensity (magnitude) and duration (time). Longer periods of exposure to tight labor markets provide a stronger buffering effect against the negative consequences of subsequent downturns than do shorter periods of exposure to very tight labor markets.

CONCLUSION

Economists have written about the "scarring" effects of recessions on young people just getting started on their careers. We have shown the mirror opposite: young workers who launch their work lives in robust labor markets see lasting positive effects on their employment probabilities. We also see the uneven effects of tight labor markets across groups of workers. Tight labor markets provide a boost to Black workers but not enough to close Black-white wage gaps.[16]

Distinguishing between the effects of the duration of a tight labor market and the intensity of a tight labor market yields important clues as to what matters most, and for which groups. An individual's probability of employment is largely driven by the *duration* of the boom market—the length of the high-pressure economy matters far more than the relative strength of the labor market at any given point in time, so long as the market is tight. But other key indicators of labor market success—earnings and labor force participation rates—are more strongly influenced by just how tight a labor market actually is, not how long the tightness lasts. Taken together, these findings suggest that long-lasting, very high-pressure labor markets have the power to truly transform the lives of those struggling to get a foothold on ladders to opportunity.

Last, and perhaps most important, each episode of low unemployment bears its own hallmarks for vulnerable workers. The hot labor market of the 1990s appears to have created uniquely positive labor market outcomes for workers at the bottom of the wage distribution. That era was more powerful in creating and sustaining opportunity than the tight markets of the 1980s or the 2000s. Low unemployment in the 2000s and the tight labor markets of the 2017–20 period generated positive labor market outcomes for these workers but not as much as the Roaring 1990s.

Given the run-up in wage and income inequality that began in the 1980s, which has accelerated over the past forty years, we should not be especially surprised to see that those in the top half of the wage distribution reaped more benefits from tight labor markets than those at the bottom. A wide range of structural changes in the economy took hold in the 1980s, accelerated through the 2000s, and persist through the present.[17] Wage and income stagnation, growing inequality in wages and incomes, expanded trade and technological advances, eroding labor standards, the declining power of unions, corporate consolidation and the resulting increase in the power of large firms to set industrywide compensation norms have created a powerful force pushing down employment and compensation in the bottom half of the income distribution.[18] Tight labor markets still provide a boost to those at the bottom—just not enough of a boost to mitigate the wage and income *inequalities* that stem from powerful structural forces that transcend the business cycle.

Quantitative analyses can only tell us so much about the ways that low unemployment opens opportunities for individuals struggling to gain economic security, and whether they endure enough to allow workers to pull themselves up into the "missing class" of lower-middle-class workers about which one of us (Katherine Newman) has written extensively.[19] Most important, survey respondents at the very bottom of the economic ladder are notoriously difficult to track over time, which means that the sample size necessary for truly robust analysis of their mobility trajectories at the fine-grained level that we aim for is nearly impossible. Survey data is also limited in the details of workers' job quality, the nature of their actual work, and their job search behavior. For all these reasons we turn to qualitative research to dig in deeper in chapter 3.

3 Matching Up: How Employers Adapt to Tight Labor Markets

How do tight labor markets create benefits for workers, from more jobs to better jobs? The path runs through employers. Facing tight labor markets, employers have to put in extra effort to find workers. This might involve improving the quality of jobs, offering higher wages or better employment conditions. Alternatively, employers must search farther afield, tapping candidates that might have been overlooked when applicants were plentiful. Across industries, hiring managers feel the pressure and have to adapt, developing new strategies that add up to better prospects for workers.

These openings mean everything to poor Americans, the vast majority of whom work for a living.[1] In normal economic times, millions of Americans subsist below the poverty line even when they are on the job year-round and full-time. They face barriers to entry and ceilings—glass and otherwise—to upward mobility. Despite a notable decline in overt prejudice since the Civil Rights movement, race nonetheless remains a roadblock in many parts of the labor market.[2] In field experiments white applicants receive 50 percent more callbacks than identical Black applicants.[3] The influence of discrimination can be hard to detect, driven instead by less visible forces like implicit bias as and statistical discrimination.[4] More than thirty years ago, Joleen Kirschenman and Kathryn Neckerman interviewed nearly two hundred employers in the Chicago area and found widespread bias against Black job candidates. In the influential paper "We'd Love to Hire Them, But...," Kirschenman and Neckerman documented how employers explained that their hesitance to hire Black applicants was not based on race but rather on inferences that link race to social class, which is "less easy to observe" and correlated—in the minds of employers—with a lack of skills and work ethic.[5] Racial inequality in employment has been amplified by mass incarceration.[6]

It is easy to overlook minority applicants, or women, or young people who lack experience when long lines of jobseekers are knocking on the door. How do employer search and hiring practices change when that pool dries up?

FINDING A MATCH

At its best, managers tell us, finding new employees is something of a crapshoot. Weak signals abound. Sorting out the good prospects from the trouble cases is never foolproof. Randy Stefanski learned that lesson the hard way, many times over. After more than forty-five years in the waste recycling business, Randy has brought generations of new workers into an industry that is far from glamorous. The jobs he has on offer require a strong back, tolerance for dirt and sweat, and the ability to maneuver hulking, unwieldy trucks through the back lots of factories and construction sites. Although he has a pretty good idea what he is looking for in a new worker, Randy has a hard time assessing whether the candidate across the desk is a good bet or a disaster-in-waiting.

In Randy's early years, waste management was physically taxing, grunge work. Despite that, since trash has always been with us—in good times and bad—the business has given Randy more stability than many working-class men could expect. "I'm from a small town in central Massachusetts," he explained. "I pretty much went to school there and never went to college. Got out of high school... got into retail management and did that for a couple years and made real good money. Had a real good career going in, but in the meantime, my Dad had bought a small rubbish business and he started growing it and he asked me to go to work for him." A blue-collar guy of Stefanski's generation didn't say no to his father or turn up his nose at a family business, especially one that promised a future. "I just got married and had a child on the way," he said. "So, I got into this business that was roughly...forty-four years ago. I worked for [my dad] for ten years, he built a pretty successful company...a little smaller than midsize, and he ended up selling to one of the large companies. The second largest in the world, BFI back in the days, and I did about thirty-two years with them."

Within that time span, the waste business became the recycling industry we know today, and BFI, the big conglomerate that bought out Randy's family business, built the first material recovery facility in the Commonwealth of Massachusetts. Randy became the general manager of this behemoth—a sixty-five-thousand-square-foot facility, full of recycling equipment: "You would bring all your curbside recyclables, your bottles, your glass, your newspaper, your cardboard. [We] would take the stuff in and separate it and then bail it and then ship it out to be remanufactured." Randy was able to parlay his experience into several municipal jobs handling solid waste and by-products of construction demolition into materials that can be remanufactured. He has been working in Roxbury, Massachusetts, for more than five years now. Along the way he has been responsible for stocking this company—and all of the firms he has worked for over his lifetime—with workers. "I've been dealing with drivers, laborers, heavy equipment operators, mechanics, office staff, sales staff...for at least the last thirty-five years of my career."

Stefanski knows what he's talking about when it comes to recruitment. But by his own admission, that isn't very much. It's very difficult, he says, to pick out the people who are dependable and agreeable. Sitting across the table from a job applicant, he calls on working assumptions: men who look you in the eye are better bets than those who stare at the table. A guy with experience driving a sixteen-wheeler isn't going to require a lot of training to do it again. The woman with references that say good things about her work ethic will show up rather than "sick out," while those without the backup recommendations probably won't. But these signals rarely tell the whole story. If they did, success would come his way more often. Instead, Randy claims, hiring is hit and miss.

You can take a candidate with the best résumé. Great references. Bring them in. It's still a 50-50 proposition, you know, 50 percent of them are going to make it and turn out to be what you wanted, or you can get them to where you want to be. And the other 50 percent, that you thought were going to be dynamite, turn out to have issues . . . issues you can't overcome.

Whether it be timeliness or constantly calling in [sick], or always having an excuse not to perform the task at hand. Even though you try to coach them and do things to get their attention, and hopefully try to change them, with performance correction notices and so on. It doesn't happen.

And it isn't just the entry level that is hard to evaluate. Stefanski notes that he has similar problems when hiring new middle managers. You can hire sure bets that turn out to be disasters; you can also find diamonds in the rough.

I've had certain management positions that reported to me that you thought you were a home run. And after two months you're all of a sudden [thinking], "Oh no. I gotta do something 'cause this isn't working."

[Then you find someone] you didn't expect a whole lot out of . . . and that individual turns around to be not only one of your best employees but somebody who's promotable! [You're] saying, "Look, I never thought this would happen."

Why is the matching process so hard? Randy chalks it up to the inadequacies of the interview process—it just doesn't produce reliable information. "You can never ask enough questions. . . . You don't always know that individuals are being truthful with you through the interview process. . . . Hopefully you have enough time, if you bring a candidate in and you have enough things into place to support that candidate to nurture them and to grow [it will turn out alright]."

It is not always in the interest of a jobseeker to be completely straightforward about their background, particularly if there are elements that are sure to end their chances, even for jobs they think they can do. Hence while employers signal what they are looking for through job ads, electronic notices, and word-of-mouth, applicants shade their biographies hoping to create the impression of a good match, even when the unvarnished truth might indicate something else. If the matching process is hard during normal times, tight labor markets add more complexity, especially for hiring managers.[7] Historic low interest rates in 2018–20 were a boon to the construction industry, which had struggled to recover after the Great Recession of 2008.[8] During the fall of 2019, buildings were rising all over Boston. Contracts for the removal of construction debris (cement, iron, glass, wood beams, and electrical lines) followed. Randy needed workers if he was going to capitalize on the work coming to his firm, just at the time when everyone who was experienced was already snapped up.

And as unemployment fell to historic lows, the applications that began arriving in Randy's in-box were not like the candidates he was accustomed to. They had no experience in waste management; they applied for jobs driving heavy trucks even though they lacked the required commercial driver's licenses. They were unaware that a license was even needed, which told Randy that these candidates knew nearly nothing about his industry. It's particularly hard to recruit skilled workers when the work environment is unpleasant. "There's not a lot of good mechanics out there," Randy notes, "and the ones that are really good are working in a nice clean environment and they're working a nice easy day shift and they're being paid a lot of dollars." To find workers for his "dusty, dirty industry," Randy had to be willing to take "a lesser employee as far as experience" and hope that "they want to grow" into the role.

On top of this, Stefanski found it harder to hold on to the workers he already had. Quit rates rose as his workers realized they could find something better.[9] The more often they jumped ship, the more energy Randy had to devote to replenishing his workforce. Some industries can work around the pressures of tight labor markets by becoming more capital-intensive or automated.[10] Randy has already been down that road. Loads that used to be carried with hand trucks are now processed by giant forklifts. Lots of recycling materials are tagged with bar codes rather than logged by hand. But when all is said and done, Randy still needs people to drive trucks out to construction sites, and they have to know what to do when they get there. If they don't show up, an entire building site may need to shut down and wait for the debris to be moved out of the way. Delays costs money and can lose Randy a customer. So although waste recycling is not brain surgery, it's not nothing, he says. Finding people who can reliably take care of the job is hard when more desirable jobs are snapping up the men and women he needs.

EMPLOYER STRATEGIES

The first move in the face of low labor supply is to cast a wider net. Charles Meyer is very familiar with expanding search strategies because he has long worked for low-wage firms located in high-rent regions of Boston. Suburban hotels in high-income communities like Newton and Lexington were particularly difficult to staff, he says. Entry-level workers—housekeepers, groundskeepers, parking monitors, and the like—are in demand. Charles has been a hiring manager for catering and restaurant operations for several of these establishments, which means he has been on the hunt for minimum-wage workers in some of the most expensive communities in the region. Because the suburbs are off the public transportation grid, Charles has had to search for that rare breed: low-wage workers with cars.

Other kinds of employers struggle as well.[11] For example, continuing-care homes for the elderly are often located in the suburbs, where land is less expensive, making them difficult to for jobseekers to access, even if the fit is good. It was hard for Charles to find workers for his hotels, even when unemployment was high and workers were more desperate. As the labor market tightened, his outreach skills were put to the test. "When you're looking at 2.5 percent unemployment, and you don't pay competitively, and your benefits aren't competitive," he says, "you really have to get creative. And you've got background checks, and you've got drug tests, and you need workers 24/7. So, yeah, I have a huge distribution list that I send out to. It's probably 120-plus people." Charles builds this distribution list and amplifies it through contacts with intermediary agencies, public and private schools, and virtually any other networking opportunity he can connect with. Regulatory constraints (like drug tests) will eliminate people, so the trick is to grow that list as much as he can and hope it brings in enough traffic to yield at least some of the staff he needs to hire.

One source of new workers are referrals from employees Charles already knows, which is especially valuable when employees and new recruits can commute together. Managers offer bounties to the employees on the payroll to encourage them to bring in people who might be good candidates. Mike Petrini, the hiring manager at Boston's Lovin' Loaves, tried this approach out and found that current employees were good at finding new workers for him:

It's not groundbreaking but [employee referrals] have a really high success rate. [Our current employees] are able to talk about what the job actually is a lot better than, you know, a job posting does. So we played with the different incentives on that. We've talked it up a lot. That was pretty successful, we filled a fairly regular schedule of in-person hiring events that are at one of our locations, and we kind of flip back and forth between Boston and Cambridge, get the word out.

In addition to employee referrals, employers cast a wider net using online tools. The past twenty years has seen the growth of high-volume electronic job boards like Craigslist, Monster, and Indeed.com, which yield a steady supply of applicants.[12] Online job boards appeal to different streams of jobseekers and are utilized by employers to help target their ads to the right audience. When Mike is looking for a chef, for example, he will turn to Indeed if he can't find what he's looking for from employee referrals: "In this area anyways...everyone pretty much lives and dies by Indeed....It's not a high-volume funnel. But it tends to be a really high quality. So you tend to get...[applications] you're going to be looking at [closely]. With Craigslist, you'll get two great applications in a stack of two hundred."

In very tight labor markets using the internet broadens the search strategy to snare more people, but a smaller proportion of them will be qualified for the jobs. Still, electronic job boards are good for employers like the Sullivan's Market grocery store chain because they can set up a search using terms that capture specific skills and to screen for people who are qualified.[13] "With the search engine Indeed," assistant store manager Ken McAdams explains, "we can put in 'We need meat cutters'—a very specific job." He continues:

[For that] you need to have training. You need to have a little bit of experience doing it. So that enabled us to kind of branch out a little bit more and just say, "This is what we're looking for. Anybody that has this training, we'd be happy to speak with you."...Before [we used Indeed], it was a lot of people were applying and a lot of it wasn't sticking....It was just like a broad range of people that we couldn't identify easily if they were the right person for the job. Indeed and Monster, they just focused more on a specific person and talk to that person.

When workers are scarce, employers lower the bar, entertaining applicants whom they wouldn't have considered when unemployment was higher. There are two ways to think about the implications of relaxing job requirements. One is that credentialism runs wild in slack labor markets, ratcheting up qualifications well beyond what is genuinely needed to do a job. Today, for instance, most administrative assistants have a college or two-year degree; fifty years ago, virtually none of them did because it was a job for (mainly) women, most of whom did not attend college.[14] From one perspective, little has changed about the skills needed to do the work.[15] But a market that favored employers enabled them to demand degrees, and hence they did. Managers may well have scored talent that was more capable than the job required and gained productivity in the bargain. But since high school graduates could have managed the load, it was not the skill requirements that set the bar but a "taste" for cultural capital and employer power that sent credentialism into overdrive.[16]

Alternatively, one might imagine that skills really *are* critical to setting that threshold, but that in tight labor markets employers will loosen the entry-level criteria and make up for the gap by investing in internal training to bring new hires up to par. Our research suggests these are not mutually exclusive alternatives. Both forces—the downward drift of job requirements and investment in internal training—are at work in tight labor markets. Alicia Sasser Modestino, an economist at Northeastern University who studies skill requirements, adds some important national context to this observation. She has shown that the same jobs are advertised with much more demanding qualifications in regions of the United States that have high unemployment rates than in the zones with tight labor markets.[17]

GROWING YOUR OWN

"If the unemployment rate is high," Randy explains, "you have a better chance of getting a more qualified person." And when it is low? "It's very hard to get qualified individuals, so instead of an A player, you settle for a C or D player." When Randy sends workers out on the road to valued customers, he cannot afford to let Mr. C or D mess up. Accordingly, even if these newcomers might be able to manage, Randy ramps up the internal investment in training and spends more time and money bringing these recent recruits up to speed. He tasks experienced workers to work with new recruits, showing them how to lower the scoops on the back of the trucks and maneuver the debris into the hold. Inexperienced workers spend several weeks riding along with the veterans on the trucks and helping out before they assume responsibility for jobs on their own. Randy's approach aligns with economic theories developed nearly fifty years ago suggesting that low unemployment will lead employers to absorb more of the cost of training but to invest more in training that is specific to their organization, rather than in general training that workers can take to other employers.[18]

Stefanski moved even farther in the direction of absorbing costs and tailoring training to his workforce. Some of his heavy equipment operators are from Cape Verde. They could master the equipment used on the job but couldn't pass the necessary licensing exams in English. He says:

> They had great work ethics, but some of them had a communication issue because they were not great with English.... But they... were here every day and wanted to succeed.... We put them through our classes [in Portuguese], and get them their license, and then put them up there with the guys who have been doing it for a long time to train them. And slowly bring them along.... That was something creative that we had to do because we couldn't get the candidates that we needed in here because... unemployment is really low.

Charles Meyer moved from the hotel business, where he took charge of catering, to Boston's Logan Airport, where he is responsible for refilling supplies for airlines. His workers manage vehicles out on the periphery of the runways and the interstices of the tarmac where the planes are parked. They fill up pallets loaded with food and drink, then lift them mechanically into airplanes twenty feet in the air for unloading. By law, his staff must have special licenses. When unemployment is high because the economy is depressed, airlines typically run fewer planes and hence need a smaller staff. Under those conditions Charles can find people who meet the entry requirements. But as Boston hit the 3 percent unemployment mark in the fall of 2019, Charles couldn't find anyone who already had the right license. "Federal law is pretty clear," he notes. "If a truck is 26,001 pounds or more, it requires a CDL Class B license." Supplying the larger jetliners requires trucks that big. Charles's immediate predecessor on the job tried to bring in drivers who weren't legally qualified. That caused a mountain of trouble. As Charles explains:

> North Gate here at Logan ... gives you access to the airfield. Prior to my starting [this job], a driver was at North Gate to swipe his badge and get checked in. And his brakes failed, and he crashed into the gate. And so the police came. Everybody came. They did the accident reports. And he didn't have a Class B. So then the state police parked themselves outside of our parking lot and pulled every single driver and cited and fined. And it became a whole huge thing.

That "whole huge thing" could shut a firm down completely. Charles's company had to do something to ensure this episode was not repeated. Labor market conditions were not optimal for finding people who had those licenses already; the company had to grow its own. "We're the lowest-paying employer in the city [so we have a hard time getting people]," Charles says. "So what we ended up doing ... is we hired the former head of DOT compliance for the state police. We put together our own CDL [commercial driver's license] training program. [Since then,] I've never hired a CDL driver from the outside. I've exclusively trained and promoted my own from within. Drivers now go through a qualification process that combines time they put in on their own and training that the firm provides internally."

Multiplied thousands of times across firms, this process represents an important adaptation to tight labor markets: what was once an externally acquired credential is now produced on the inside, which means workers who once would have been eliminated can now be hired, and the cost of their training is now largely on the employer's tab.[19] Internal training is a high art in other countries that have routinely absorbed the cost of developing human capital for skilled jobs.[20] The German apprenticeship system, for example, pays young people preparing for more than 350 occupations for three years while they alternate between vocational high schools and the shop floor. They train under the watchful eye of master teachers who are veterans of the labor process in small groups of four or five apprentices. This system is a boon to industries that require highly skilled workers in auto factories or steel mills. But it applies as well to fairly low-skilled jobs like cleaners who maintain bus stops.

When asked why the United States hasn't adopted a similar model, the usual response from employers is that they don't want to invest in training that workers can use to get a job in someone else's company. Germans do not have the same mind-set: they fully understand that an apprentice may jump ship and take the skills that Company A paid for when they go to work for Company B. Most of the time, apprentices go to work for the firm in which they train, but when that doesn't happen, no one seems particularly bothered. They figure that what goes around will come around and do not spend time lamenting the "free rider" problem. It helps that the German system is underwritten by taxes, coordinated with national unions, and undergirded by substantial support within the school system.

American employers are more wary of investing in training that workers can use to move to another firm. But in tight labor markets, that risk is unavoidable. Those airport workers that Charles Meyer has trained now have skills—and Class B driver's licenses—that are entirely portable. Randy's Cape Verdean employees can make excellent use of the hoisting licenses they have in any firm that requires them, Randy's investment notwithstanding. Tight labor markets in a capitalist economy like ours force employers to cover the costs, but it doesn't prevent workers from moving along to a better job. And since a worker can more easily increase their wages by moving from one employer to another than by moving up within a single firm, the risk of the free rider problem is real, especially in a growing economy where tight labor markets lead to poaching.[21]

In highly regulated parts of the economy, employers are somewhat more constrained. Health care is a good example, especially in Boston, where the industry has grown dramatically. The combination of low wages, licensing regulations, and booming demand put hospitals and clinics in a bind. The answer? Loosen up by hiring people who are just short of being fully qualified and classify them into job titles that don't trigger these requirements. Over time, these new recruits will acquire full credentials. But months can go by when they are doing at least some work that would not normally be permitted. "For the most part," a local hospital manager explained, "we had a practice of not hiring new[ly] grad[uated] nurses." The manager continued:

> The only new grads we tended to hire were those who were in those [lower ranking assistant] roles [who were part of a] pilot training program,

because they've been working while they were earning their degree on the floor. So they had that experience and exposure. But we made an exception [when unemployment was very low] because of the need.

We did hire people who hadn't gotten their licenses, but they were eligible to get their license. That's what I remember. And I don't know if there was something being coordinated with the certification folks.... We did hire people that we normally wouldn't hire who weren't either fully certified, but they were about to get their certification, or they had it, but they had no experience.

NEW LITMUS TESTS

Low unemployment creates golden opportunities for workers who have been on the sidelines of the labor market. When markets are tight, employers look again at people who otherwise would have been passed by. But how do they pick and choose among pools of jobseekers that don't come in the familiar package? Randy found he needed new litmus tests. What guidelines can he turn to in selecting from among formally unqualified applicants? For jobs that lack any kind of cachet, which is most of the jobs in the waste industry, Randy has found it worthwhile to ask himself, *Does this person really need the job? How hard up are they?*

Mike Petrini of Lovin' Loaves sees it the same way. He always goes for the person who can't afford to lose the position because they are on their own with the bills. "People that need a job are more reliable.... They're going to [sick] out less because they need that money from that shift. They stick around longer." He says:

> I've worked with many great people that were doing a part-time gig or doing something because they wanted some extra money or saving some for something or whatever. But at the end of the day, they don't need it to pay rent. If you don't need it to pay rent, then [other] priorities can get in the way.... Maybe you prioritize a nice sunny day at the beach and [call in to say] "Oh I'm sick." Totally throws a wrench, especially in the restaurant industry there's not a lot of slack [if you suddenly need]... extra people.

People who have experienced long-term unemployment more than meet Petrini's test: they are desperate for work. They have jobs only because employers have fewer choices and hence they are relieved that they are, at last, among the chosen. These jobseekers are all too aware that theirs is a fragile victory and are therefore eager to hold on to what they have. Some Chicago employers report they are pleasantly surprised to discover that formerly incarcerated people will "go the extra mile," showing up when asked on weekends, fighting their way through snowstorms, beyond what their more convention counterparts will do.[22] Precarity drives marginal recruits to want to underline their reliability, even if the work they are asked to do is low-skilled and unpleasant. In looser labor markets, however, that job could easily go to someone without the mark of a criminal record.[23]

Since we cannot count on tight labor markets lasting, it would be comforting to think that the stereotypes that block easy entry into the labor market will bend with experience. So, do bosses change their expectations of workers from stigmatized groups when they are exposed to this work ethic? Do managers come to think they were wrong to block returning citizens at the front door? This is a critical question for which we have only limited answers.[24] Whether bosses conclude that "Jim" is great, a standout from a category that is still problematic, or begin to rethink the whole category to which Jim belongs, depends on how long labor shortages last. The longer they endure, the more managers are exposed to marginal workers. One Jim may be an exception; a dozen starts to feel more like a reason to change one's mind about, for example, single moms or returning citizens now reentering the labor force after a long hiatus.

We found some evidence that employers do turn this corner after they have some experience with stigmatized workers. Ken McAdams, a regional hiring manager for the Sullivan's Market grocery chain, recalls that for a time the company had a program for inmates of a women's prison, which proved to be a positive experience and one that they would repeat. Mike Petrini has hired people out of Hope House, a "sober home" in the Boston area. It wasn't his first choice, but tight labor markets forced him in that direction; he was surprised how well it worked out. "There were a couple people that were hired that were in a sober home," he recalls. "They had a few issues here and there, but in general, were really reliable, really great. They were between a rock and a hard place and really needed a job."

Randy Stefanski also connected with Hope House during an earlier period of low unemployment. He took this step when he discovered that his company already had a solid worker, Greg, who had come out of Hope

House years before. Over time, Greg turned out to be quite adept at learning new technologies and generally making himself useful. To Randy's surprise, Greg became a star employee, a model worker, and hungry to master new skills. "Greg learned to diagnose repairs that needed to be done, was able to go online and see how to do the repair because a lot of our equipment's Caterpillar," Randy recalls. "And he actually grew himself into a decent mechanic, went to some welding school. He's got a welding certificate. And turned out to be a decent employee, still has some issues, nothing to do with, you know, drugs or alcohol, and he's been clean and sober for six or eight years now." Given this experience, Randy kept up his ties to Hope House in case he could find more Gregs, and he sought out other potential workers with rocky backgrounds, meeting with the Suffolk County Sheriff's Office to see if there were ways to work with the local prison. The mere fact that Randy's company was open to recruiting workers from that venue says something important. Working with people like Greg can change an employer's mind about who might make for a good worker. Randy's willingness to give marginal workers this much of a chance tells us that tight labor markets have some profoundly important consequences for pulling at least some of the lost and damaged back on track.

Broader social norms play an important role as well. As a society, we have started to question the wisdom of prison expansion. The incarcerated population grew exponentially in the 1980s on the heels of the War on Drugs, and by 2000 more than two million Americans were locked up. As the public and policymakers began to recognize the costs of this policy— both human and financial—a new agenda began to emerge bent on reducing incarceration. Even many political conservatives, who have generally opted for a tough-on-crime approach, started to seek alternatives. In 2007, when the price tag of the prison system became an issue in Texas, the legislature proposed a $241 million package of programs that aimed to divert people away from incarceration. By 2019, Texas was closing prison facilities.[25] Changes in social policy can rearrange the moral landscape and put a different spin on the social profile of jobseekers emerging from behind bars.

Returning citizens are a special case of a broader category of people who "really need this job." The COVID-19 pandemic that began its sweep across the globe in 2020 created another. Frontline workers who could afford to quit often did so, to protect themselves and their families from infection. But many were not that fortunate and felt they had no choice but to keep working even when it meant exposure to a deadly disease. Minorities and immigrants in Queens, New York, were in just such a precarious position, which is why the rates of infection among them skyrocketed. They could not afford to lose those jobs, so they kept going to work and returned to crowded, multigenerational households, which was the perfect setting for a raging epidemic to continue on its deadly course. The same was true in many of Boston's poorest corners. As Allison Alabi, the director of Boston's chapter of Built to Soar, a labor market intermediary that places low-skilled workers, noted:

> A lot of our members who [were] living paycheck to paycheck, [were] not as actively worrying [about COVID-19] because they already [had] so much to worry about. . . . They couldn't have cared less about the guidelines that were being told to them because it just didn't feel possible. Whether it [was] for maintaining their own mental health or maintaining their employment or maintaining whatever it is that they pulled together as their foundation—the pandemic really wasn't their biggest concern but was absolutely impacting their lives.

There are clearly significant downsides to being desperate for work, including employee abuse, especially if the workers lack legal status. But that overwhelming need for a salary translates into a positive reputation for groups known to lack a backstop. It creates a litmus test—"Who really needs a job?"—that is particularly resonant during tight labor markets when other signals, like degrees or job experience, are not on offer.

Harvard University sociologist Sandra Susan Smith has written at length about this kind of threshold thinking. Smith identifies different "cultural logics" that jobholders use to determine whether or not to help a friend or family member get a job. About one-fifth of her survey respondents used a logic of "particularism," in which they decided whether or not to help based on their perception of how badly the jobseeker needed the job. According to these jobholders, "material need produced fidelity to work, because it was principally through work that one garnered the resources needed to feed, clothe, and shelter oneself and one's dependents."[26] Since they are privy to the private lives of acquaintances and relatives, they have some independent insight into whether they are truly desperate for a job and therefore likely to be reliable workers.

It is not hard to extrapolate from Smith's findings that equally qualified people will gain or lose in the search for crucial referrals or references because of circumstances extraneous to their formal qualifications. Katherine Newman found the same thing long ago when talking with fast-food workers who were constantly being asked by cousins and neighbors to help land a job at a chain she called "Burger Barn."[27] Employees demurred if the request was coming from someone who wasn't really desperate to work because an unreliable performance could jeopardize their own reputation in the eyes of a boss. Everyone remembers who recommended a bad worker, or so people believe. A yardstick of desperation is in play that is particularly important when tight labor markets soak up the obviously qualified and leave the playing field to people that employers cannot easily evaluate in conventional terms. It is a highly subjective game, though, because assessing how much someone "needs a job" without a fulsome biography leaves a lot of room for stereotypes. The rules of thumb Smith describes disadvantage people—especially men—who do not have families, compared to parents who have kids to support and therefore can be expected to "act responsibly."

And it is here that immigrants often gain ground when unemployment is very low. Sullivan's Market often has to source employees in a hurry. When the demand for service and delivery shoots up, they have an opportunity for record profits—assuming they can find the workers to keep the stores humming. Who do they turn to when that happens? Ken McAdams is unequivocal: his first choice is an immigrant, especially if the jobs on offer are entry level and do not require particular skills. If almost anyone can do the job, Ken wants someone newly arrived from overseas: "Albanian people that will say, 'I'll do anything you want,' and I find that those are some of the best workers that we have. Because they don't care what they do, they'll say, 'I'll clean the toilets for eight hours a day. Whatever you want, I gotcha. I'll do it.'"

JOB QUALITY: INCREASING WAGES, IMPROVING BENEFITS, MOVING SHIFTS

Low-wage workers rarely have the luxury of thinking about job quality. Scrambling at the bottom, especially when unemployment is high, they take what they can find and hope that over time, a better offer will come along. Tight labor markets do, however, provide them with opportunity to seek something better. They are, for once, in a position to bargain or shop around and find they can improve their lot in many ways. Firms that hire the working poor are often lodged in low-margin industries. They turn a profit, to be sure. But they are often locked in competition with other companies of the same kind and depend on providing customers with goods and services that are cheap, hence the drift toward offshore production for T-shirts and belts, basketballs, and bedsheets. Depressing labor costs is central to the way these companies operate unless circumstances force them to do otherwise. Indeed, during most recoveries low-wage workers are typically the last to see wage growth: while early declines in unemployment yield benefits for highly skilled workers, low-wage workers only see their wallets thicken once unemployment falls below 5 percent.

Yet, in the hot labor market of 2018–19, wages increased faster at the bottom than they had in decades, buttressed by the rapid spread of new $15 an hour minimum wages, whether voluntary or legislated.[28] This is a sure sign of a tight labor market. Higher up the skill ladder, it is understood that people are being paid for the human capital they bring to the firm. Competing for people with more education and job experience is part of the normal operation of the labor market. But when wages rise quickly at the bottom of the pyramid, we are looking at a different phenomenon. It happens when the need is so great that jobseekers with little to no relevant skill or experience find themselves the object of bidding wars. For example, when Charles Meyer was looking for housekeeping help for high-end hotels in the Boston suburbs, he encountered the perfect storm for entry-level labor: a community too expensive for workers to live in that was built around cars and highways, and had no public transportation. He tried everything he could to find people by casting a wide net. But when unemployment dropped to a fifty-year low, Charles had to improve the terms. "We made a strategic decision," Meyer explained, "to pay at least a dollar an hour over what the competition was paying when it came to housekeepers, dishwashers."

It sounds like a simple solution, but the ramifications can be complex. Randy wants to beat the other recycling firms in the area, but he has to keep one eye on the total wage bill because the rest of his employees, recruited under different conditions, are watching.[29] The wage scale is linked in their minds: if Randy pays a newbie more, he had better do the same for his more experienced workers. Up to a point, Randy doesn't mind, although keeping the payroll below a certain level is an important part of staying competitive in the recycling business. If the investment paid off in a long-term, stable workforce, he might even think of this as a smart move: a productive workforce is worth a lot. But Randy has his reservations about whether wages are a path to that kind of stability. Without gainsaying which came first—businesses treating workers in an instrumental way or worker loyalty eroding—he has certainly noticed that he cannot count on people staying put, even if he pays them well. "When I started, years and years ago," he remembers, "a lot of people wanted to make a career." Back then, he says:

> They were willing to come in at a lower level, learn the industry, had the opportunity to move up, whether it's in the management, of being one type of a driver and going from one type of system to another which would lead to more money [for] more experience. And through the years, you've seen that kind of wear away. If they work for the same company for ten years, that is a long time.

These more instrumental relations make Randy chafe at paying more just to land warm bodies, people who need a lot of training to be truly usable even in entry-level jobs. And when it forces the upward creep of his whole payroll to keep the rest of the workers satisfied, he can't chalk the effort up to a long-term investment in a good, stable workforce. It's just an accommodation to the moment that he has to make, whether he likes it or not.

Paychecks are not the only lure; benefits matter as well. Mike Petrini, the bakery hiring manager, thinks that workers care about whether their benefits come from recognized companies. Even though he can shave some expenses by moving to less expensive, unconventional benefit plans, Mike sticks with the vendors whose names signify quality. "What if I'm trying to really get someone and health insurance is something that's important to them," he says. "There's a difference between me saying we have Blue Cross Blue Shield and we have Neighborhood Health Plan." Mike knows this isn't the primary reason someone takes or refuses a job. But he thinks it makes a difference on the margin, and he often finds himself out there on that margin.

Job quality, especially for people with children, goes well beyond material considerations. Just as important is the structure of the workday. Shape-shifting work schedules shave the wage bill down, and in competitive industries it is quite common. Graveyard shifts, irregular hours, just-in-time work schedules, workers whose hours are cut short without warning, or the opposite—unexpected overtime—these are the indignities that low-wage workers face on a daily basis, especially when unemployment is high, and managers can easily replace someone who objects.[30] Tight labor markets should diminish this kind of employer behavior.[31] Workers with better options can quit those unstable jobs, and employers bear the costs of turnover. Survey data suggests this may be the last aspect of the work day to change.[32]

Our fieldwork revealed a greater willingness to adapt to this competitive dimension than the most comprehensive survey studies have shown.[33] One labor market intermediary recalls talking to a panicked employer who couldn't find enough workers to run his restaurant at lunchtime but was reluctant to change his normal shift schedule.

> So we said, "Just call us when you can't fill positions." Sure enough, they call us six months later, "We can't open a new restaurant because we can't find staff.... What are we going to do?" And we said, "Well, why don't you try shortening some hours so that moms can work during lunchtime rushes?" It's a very popular lunch. So they did that, and they were able to hire, and they were able to open.

There are limits, of course, to how radically companies can or will adapt. But we found some evidence of hiring managers altering schedules to keep people who might otherwise quit, paying more to those who endure the worst work schedules, and reshaping shifts altogether to become more competitive in the effort to attract the workforce they are after.

Besides improving wages, shaping work hours into more accommodating forms, and improving benefits to attract people in a competitive market, what else can employers do to solve their workforce problems in an environment of very low unemployment? They can try to reduce the need for new workers by providing more advancement opportunities for the people they have on the payroll and slow the quit rate. Job ladders that create opportunity for internal upward mobility incentivize people to stick with the job they have. Many years ago, labor economists writing about "dual labor markets" characterized the employment system as divided into two pieces.[34] The primary sector—unionized shops, big firms, high-wage industries—contained extensive job ladders and hence opportunities for promotion, especially for men and white workers, who dominate the favorable employment market. The secondary sector—which today we might loosely call the low-wage labor market—had a very different structure. Short job ladders or none at all, hence no opportunity for promotion, low wages, revolving doors of workers with short tenure, the absence of unions, women and minorities as the dominant workforce: these were the characteristics of the secondary sector. At the time, this literature assumed that jobs fell on one side or the other of this divide; they didn't morph over the line. Indeed, the primary and secondary sectors were sealed off and so was the workforce.

Of all the qualities of the secondary sector that "hurt," the absence of job ladders was perhaps the deepest cut. Workers were caught in an endless churn of short-term jobs that went nowhere. For the most part these were the only options available to the fast-food workers of Harlem that Katherine Newman studied for her book *No Shame in My Game: The Working Poor in the Inner City.* In the early 1990s there was little hope these workers would ever have more to look forward to. Yet when Newman went back to study the same people in what became a tight labor market during the late 1990s, the period of Bill Clinton's presidency, she found those same firms had morphed. There were now job ladders. Not extensive ones, but opportunities for managerial mobility just the same.[35]

The difference lay not in the nature of the jobs but in the surrounding economic context. Tight labor markets emerged in the 1990s as growth increased while inflation remained low. This "perfect weather" quickly led to a job boom, even in Harlem, where Newman's first wave of fieldwork saw fourteen workers apply for every job opening in the fast-food industry. By the end of the 1990s there were labor shortages *and* new "Burger Barn" restaurants opening up. The workers who started out on the shop floor in one location were promoted into management in the new restaurants. Workers who might have jumped ship for better jobs found themselves first in line for the better jobs opening up in another branch of the firm for which they were already working.

The health-care sector in Boston is a high-growth industry. And while it already has job ladders for people who are high-skilled, some firms are trying to provide similar opportunities to the entry-level workers in their hospitals. Support staff that are handling food services or custodial work are given the option of "upskilling" so that they can take on patient-facing jobs that are more important, better respected, and offer more options for further promotion. The point, according to hospital administrator Martha Dunlap, is to "move people out of what can consider to be dead-end jobs with low pay into jobs that have a clear career path." She says: "Individuals that go in and clean the patient rooms and [clean] the inpatient floors, they are learning how to become patient service associates.... You're working with the patient, but you're not a nurse, but you're working alongside a nurse and under their direction to help care for the patient."

As Martha explained, the "patient service associate" has long been a "stepping-stone for anyone interested in nursing." What is new is the recruitment into those roles: her hospital system is now actively looking to groom people who used to be considered out of bounds for clinical roles. "Our goal is for those individuals who are in those service worker roles," she says, " [to have] a career path so that they can potentially become a clinician, whether it's a nurse or some other type of caregiver that puts them in a professional job category." Although these initiatives were developed under tight labor markets, the hospital sector is generally able to recruit workers even in periods of low unemployment because it is among the most desirable of destinations for entry-level workers, has long been "CORI-friendly," and provides generous benefits akin to civil service jobs.[36]

Nonetheless, upskilling is becoming a major preoccupation of employers in the health professions because they face shortages of qualified workers as demand rises. Grooming people who are already part of the workplace family makes good sense since they are acclimated to the culture, already envision themselves as part of the workplace community, and have a reasonably clear view of the promotional opportunities that await. Job ladders are not abstract ideas but concrete opportunities visible on the many badges and uniforms of the modern hospital and the carefully constructed pathways from one level to the next. Moreover, as caring institutions, they generally embrace liberal values, which includes diversity and the integration of the skilled ranks of the workforce. Hospitals in Boston do not want workers of color confined to the ranks of housekeepers and meal delivery squads. They hope clinical employees will become more representative of the patients they serve and for this reason are investing heavily in educational programs that improve human capital and provide credentials that qualify their entry-level workers for better jobs.

Those same investments justify raising salaries. "We have a long-standing interest in ensuring that employees have a livable wage," Martha notes. "A couple of years ago, even before it became popular, we raised our minimum salaries to $15 an hour, for example. So there's always been an interest in lifting up this role group. There are no financial incentives that I'm aware of. . . . The goal is, . . . how can we do better?" Upskilling is becoming a national habit as firms discover that they cultivate loyalty and quality when they invest in human capital and internal mobility. They reap the benefits of employees who are already adapted to the culture of the organization and who are grateful for the opportunity to improve their lot in life, subsidized by the firm.

Employers are even supporting human capital development away from the workplace. Today, employers spend more than $22 billion a year in tuition assistance plans, a benefit that often provides financial support for workers and their family members to attend college.[37] A subset of that market is directed at low-skilled employees who are looking to enhance their skills. When Arizona State University created a college plan for Starbucks employees, for instance, it was a shot heard around the academic world, especially for online education, the preferred route to degrees and certificates for working adults. The Starbucks example has since been followed by Walmart, McDonald's, and many other employers known mainly for minimum wage, dead-end jobs. They are burnishing their image to be sure, but they are also slowing turnover in the workforce by providing benefits that are valued for the way they grease the wheels of upward mobility.

Boston's hospital sector invests heavily in tuition assistance and in some instances develops internal "schools" or academic programs in collaboration with universities to enrich the skillset of their frontline workers and make it possible for them to move up off the bottom of the labor market. Martha explains:

> We have the standard tuition reimbursement program, but we also have a grant that targets support staff, which, based on the numbers, are primarily diverse employees. It's money that can be used not just for tuition, but... to pay for a babysitter so they can go to school and those kinds of things. So it's a support grant program to help support our administrative support staff and service workers staff to go back to school.

These benefits make a big difference for workers who live paycheck to paycheck and most likely would not be able to afford more education if they had to pay for it. This includes a wide spectrum of frontline workers who come from disadvantaged backgrounds. As Martha explains:

> We always hired people with [criminal offender records] so that's nothing new for us. We have an English as a second language program, which has existed for many years, at least at least ten years. . . . We have a lot of immigrants who are in the service worker roles and one of the barriers for them has been their ability to speak and understand English. And so we created these beginner through advanced ESL program with the goal of, once individuals finish that program, we work with them to look for other job opportunities within the hospital.

The hospital tries not to focus just on the people who are obvious go-getters but also aims to ferret out the people who have potential that no one notices.

Educational programs qualify workers for better jobs, which is a boon for them. But they also enable the hospital to feed its own vast, internal labor market. It is costly, and can be cumbersome, especially in periods of low unemployment, to have to source such a large workforce, with thousands of openings at any one time. The hospital is such a large employer that they can use internal databases to find people—like those who have used the tuition assistance program—who might be qualified for an opening. These employees may also represent a more diverse group. As Martha says:

> Our workforce development arm is . . . responsible for all of our in-house training and also they manage the tuition reimbursement program. They'll often run reports of new grads . . . and try to match that up with what the

recruiters...to see do we have someone that just graduated with, I don't know, a bachelor's in health-care administration who might be open to considering a job opportunity? People will come and they'll say, "I just got my degree," and, "What can I do? What opportunities should I be looking for?" And these are, more often than not, diverse employees. And so I will make connections with them, with the recruiters and see if we can get them fast-tracked.

Theirs is both a civic commitment to diversity and equity and a functional convenience that cuts down on the need for external recruitment in favor of internal promotion. Anyone they can bring up from the inside doesn't need to be recruited or socialized into the workplace culture. They are already there. And while this is an ongoing program, developed and maintained through the business cycle, it is particularly useful when labor markets are tight. It is one of the reasons the hospital doesn't have a difficult time finding workers compared with other employers in the region.

CONCLUSION

When tight labor markets last, the adaptations that employers make to reel new workers in and hold on to the ones they have work to the employees' advantage. Wages, benefits, working conditions, investments in training, and options for upward mobility increase and the doors to opportunity open a bit wider than usual. These are not charity acts and while they grow when public benefits like unemployment insurance enable workers to look a bit longer for a better opportunity, they emerge without those buffers just because demand for workers has outstripped the supply. Firms have no choice: they cannot attract labor if they don't offer competitive conditions. Once in place, those benefits are hard—though not impossible—to shake.

4 Leaning on Intermediaries

Employers do their best to navigate tight labor markets by drawing on employee referrals and social media, job fairs, and other forms of outreach. They loosen job requirements, increase the attractiveness of the positions they have on offer by raising wages, adding to benefits, and beefing up internal training to compensate for the weaker credentials among workers they are choosing from.

These may sound like simple solutions. Yet hiring people who lack the usual credentials—education, experience, references, possibly even a home address—raises the hackles of managers, because they cannot rely on the usual frame of reference for judging who is likely to work out and who might be a walking disaster. Relying on "who really needs this job" may be hard to operationalize in an interview.[1] Fishing in waters that include people with criminal records, alcohol problems, and long-term unemployment profiles leads hiring managers to worry that they don't have very reliable ways of sorting out the good bets from the bad ones. Many prefer not to navigate the search process on their own. In 2018–19, with unemployment rates at a fifty-year low, many employers found they couldn't find the workers they needed no matter what they did on their own. They needed help. They found it by turning to organizations that connect workers—especially disadvantaged workers—with employers and support their entry into the labor market. These intermediaries provide a crucial bridge between marginalized populations and employers, and during tight labor markets—with their attendant economic expansions—they are often somewhat better funded than usual and prepared to provide valuable services that benefit workers and employers alike.

INTERMEDIARIES IN THE MIX

MIT labor economist David Autor defines labor market intermediaries as organizations that "interpose themselves between workers and firms to facilitate, inform, or regulate how workers are matched to firms."[2] Their existence dates back to the turn of the twentieth century when jobseekers were exploited by private labor contractors, leading reformers to advocate for public employment offices that matched employers and workers.[3] Nonprofit versions came later in US history but operated on a similar "honest broker" model.

There are many kinds of intermediaries today, ranging from for-profit temp agencies to electronic job boards, from union hiring halls to guilds and professional associations. Community and technical colleges sometimes dabble in the matching process, as do public agencies, nonprofits, religious organizations, and private industry councils. No one really knows how many labor market intermediaries there are in the United States, but the most recent efforts to tabulate them run into "many hundreds," with the most plentiful emerging where "state governments have incentivized the formation of sectoral partnerships."[4] They have become increasingly important in an economy characterized by high levels of labor mobility, frequent churning, and boom-and-bust cycles that see millions repeatedly searching for work.

A subset of these brokers is also dedicated to increasing human capital. These are the institutions of interest for our purposes since they are most concerned with people on the fringes of the labor market, especially those who for many different reasons are among the long-term unemployed. These labor market intermediaries have a long history. The War on Poverty, President Lyndon Johnson's effort to eliminate hardship and reverse the

trajectory of inner-city America and its poor rural counterparts, emphasized job training and placement. Before its advent, job training programs
were rare, especially programs focusing on the poor or racial minorities.[5]
In his 1964 Economic Report, Johnson outlined the need for more support for people who struggled to gain a foothold in the labor market.[6] He
would go on to expand the Manpower Development and Training Act and
launch new programs like the Jobs Corps that specifically targeted poor
and racial minority youth for education and job training.[7] Federal investment expanded under President Richard Nixon with the Comprehensive
Employment and Training Act but came to a halt when President Ronald
Reagan entered office.

During President Bill Clinton's administration the Welfare Reform
Act of 1996 began to pare back the role of public assistance by impos-
ing time limits and work requirements.[8] It also shifted the emphasis from
persistent support to "welfare-to-work," a regime that gave birth to many
agencies, often funded by the federal government, that were put in place
to cushion the blows that were expected when public assistance benefits
were taken away. These agencies funded diverse state and local programs
that either provided education and job training or directly connected
workers with job opportunities.[9]

Today, labor market intermediaries that are often the lineal descendants of those welfare-to-work programs facilitate economic mobility for
low-wage workers in multiple ways. Jobseekers who use intermediaries
are more likely to receive job offers and be hired than similar candidates
without these formal connections.[10] Aside from job placement, intermediaries can support the development of low-wage workers' skills by, for
instance, facilitating meaningful increases in literacy.[11] Where for-profit
intermediaries typically connect workers with jobs without meaningfully
improving their longer-term economic outcomes, nonprofits often have a
broader mission to increase skill and speak to employer needs.[12]

HEARTWARD BOUND: POSITIONING THE HOMELESS JOBSEEKER

Labor market intermediaries run the gamut in the extent of support they
provide for jobseekers on the one hand and firms on the other. Employ-

ment agencies tend to be instrumental and impersonal, classic bureaucra-
cies with rules to administer and mechanisms to sustain distance between
clients and workers. Boston's Heartward Bound is at the other end of the
spectrum. A residential facility for the unhoused for more than fifty years,
it runs job training programs in hospitality and culinary training. Heartward Bound trainees work in the city's hotel and restaurant industry and
are known to be well-prepared. While the organization must navigate the
delicate boundaries of personal involvement, their staff knows the residents well and works hard to support them.

Jack Wilkes is one of Heartward Bound's job placement specialists. He
is dedicated to doing what he can to move residents out of homelessness
through gainful employment. His clients have hit bottom by the time they
arrive at Heartward Bound. Most are longtime unemployed; some have
come from behind bars. The most stable of Heartward Bound's residents
have low-wage jobs that simply don't pay enough for them to be able to
afford Boston's sky-high rents. Instead, they live at Heartward Bound for
a time, going out to work every day, until they find a job with a paycheck
sufficient to cover a roof over their heads.

Jack's trainees have to mold themselves into conventional employees
when they have none of the structural supports needed to sustain the role.
They lack permanent addresses; they may have no form of identification
or bank account. If asked to produce a birth certificate, a passport, a utility
bill, or a driver's license—routinely required to join a payroll—they are
likely to come up empty-handed. Transportation to work, at least outside
of the city's transit system, is a problem because they rarely have cars.
Dressing for work—even in a casual work environment, but especially
in a professional office setting—is a problem, since their wardrobes are
threadbare. Even in the face of these disadvantages, the homeless deni-
zens of Heartward Bound cannot afford to break down or display the
stress that anyone would feel against this background. When Heartward
Bound jobseekers start to wobble, Jack steps into the breach. He will
track them down, rehearse interview strategies, find an appropriate tie or
jacket, and generally organize an off-track would-be-worker back onto the
straight-and-narrow.

Jack's job places him in between employers who want him to vet workers for them and often desperate jobseekers who need his help. Hiring
managers are more comfortable when Jack is there to serve as a buffer,

which is why demand for his services rise when labor markets tighten. There is something of an irony here: employers need Jack when workers have a *relatively* easy time finding jobs. However, Jack's particular population is never all that easy to place; they are just more likely to find a footing when firms have fewer choices. Hiring managers look to Jack to guarantee conventional behavior on the part of his clients, to backstop their daily attendance. Jack's cell phone is his constant companion; he uses it to follow his trainees from the time they get up in the morning, to the moment they arrive at work. Staying sober, staying focused, staying positive and agreeable: this is what Jack needs his clients to do, every day. Jack has the unenviable task of taking on responsibilities he cannot completely control.

A lot is riding on how well Jack manages that task. If he keeps these workers on the right path, employers will come back to him. Employers who have been disappointed will mean one less opportunity for another Heartward Bound resident who needs a job. To maximize the likelihood that an employer will continue to call, Jack must be able to identify those individuals living in the shelter that he believes will prove dependable and presentable. "I want to build a bridge every single time I meet someone," he says. "I look for common ground and I don't care what it is. I'll find it. I will find common ground and I will use that to spin it into an ongoing relationship where there's trust. They trust me, I'm not going to send . . . somebody that's unreliable."

In addition to satisfying the employers he has on tap, Jack also needs to find new opportunities. So he is a relentless networker: "I look at every single entity in Boston as an employer. I don't care what they do. I don't care what their product is or what their function is, all I know is, there's people working in there, making it go. Eleven thousand people are at Mass General [Hospital] making it work. So that means you got the head of brain surgery and you got the security guy." Jack cannot afford to let his own preferences get in the way. A setting that he personally finds off-putting could still be a place where a Heartward Bound resident could find employment. He explains:

> [Fancy] restaurants. I have not gone to these places, and many of them I never ever will. And frankly, I do have a chip on my shoulder sometimes

when I walk past a place like that and I see a Mercedes in the valet parking. But then I think to myself, I know that guy who is valet parking that car because I set him up for that job, and he gets good tips. Who am I to dismiss somebody else's employment? That's not me.

VPNE—the parking lot company—is a great employer in the city. They are at all the hospitals and [everywhere] that commerce is being done: restaurants, hotels . . . everywhere VPNE. And they're a good partner of ours. We got people in there. I didn't even know that company existed a few years ago.

He extends his network as widely as possible since he never knows when his contacts might lead to a placement.

Jack works hard to remain patient with employers who are not immediately responsive. That can be difficult when his anxious clients pepper him with questions about whether they have at last landed a job. "I want . . . to call [the employer] back and say 'What's going on?'" he explains. "Is [my client] still in queue with you? Is there something that you need from her? What's going on here?" But he cannot afford to be too pushy for fear of alienating someone whose goodwill he depends on.

Jack's jobseekers reap the benefits of his personal relationships; employers who trust Jack are more likely to trust his referrals. But he is only able to develop those ties when he can connect to them personally and develop a relationship that will ultimately transfer to one of his placements. If hiring decisions are unexpectedly stripped from local managers and transferred to a distant central office, the strength of Jack's recommendation wanes. He recalls: "I had an awful time with the local hospital when they told me, 'Oh, our hiring is all being done now by the home office outside of the city. So there's no local representative you can talk to.' Well, that's my lifeblood: local people that I can talk to."

Before that change a local supervisor could override HQ and decide to give someone a chance. "You know him on paper. We *know* the person," Jack says. "So we're going to override your [negative] recommendation. We're going to bring him in. . . . The guy at Heartward Bound is giving us the high sign and he's been working with [this person] for over six months. So who really knows the guy? The computer? The paper? The outside consultant in Canada? Give me a break."

BUILDING SELF-CONFIDENCE IN THE MARGINAL WORKER

Although Jack's most important task is to persuade a potential employer to take a chance on someone with a dicey biography, he must also face in the opposite direction and encourage a desperate person with a history of rejection to believe in themselves. Heartward Bound residents have been buffeted by some of the worst pressures society can throw at people. They have often been cast aside by their families, evicted from their homes, or survived long prison sentences. For most of these clients, failures come after years of disappointment in school and the work world. Before finding shelter at Heartward Bound, some of them have been living in their cars, eating out of food pantries, or reduced to panhandling. They know that residence in the shelter is conditional on their effort to improve their lot. Anxiety is palpable among them and for good reason.

With a thousand reasons for self-doubt in the background, intermediaries must reassure their job-seeking clients that "they can do this" and then pray they don't disappoint a potential employer by being late, dressing in shabby clothing, or taking a drink to calm their nerves. It's a drama for both sides, and Jack's own emotions—apprehension, disappointment, frustration, hopefulness, elation—are hard to hold at bay. One example Jack recalled:

> I worked on this job with [one female jobseeker] for more than two months. . . . She just started [the job], and all of a sudden they tell her, "You need a birth certificate to do [this job]." And she's like, "I don't even know where my birth certificate is. I had a backpack that was stolen." . . . She's been living out of a car. Most of us cannot imagine this kind of instability, but it plays an enormous role; it's devastating. It can be overcome, but many times people are exhausted. They feel like they're getting the crap kicked out of them, [especially when] the [hiring] process drags on for weeks.

It is one thing to bolster a nervous jobseeker; everyone feels anxious when so much is on the line. But when the candidate in question has a million reasons for self-doubt, it takes an experienced, devoted professional like Jack to talk them into a different mind-set. He explains:

> I'm a resiliency coach. I call people and I talk to them. I say, "Look, I know that this should only take a couple of days, it's going to take more than a

week. So you have to be patient. Please don't look at the clock. Look at the calendar. Give us time to make this work for you. Don't bug out." It's my job. So I'm trying to be as best at it as I can. I have to be a chilling factor. I have to be calming.

Small business owners are particularly challenging—especially restaurant owners. Driven, financially anxious, and oscillating between optimism and the doldrums, small business owners work 24/7 to keep their firms afloat. Even in good times, they often skate very close to the edge of survival. They fish in the waters of the low-wage labor force for a reason: these are the workers they can afford.

But they are looking for rare creatures—minimum wage employees who will knock themselves out during long shifts in hot kitchens. These jobs offer little in the way of intrinsic value and the monetary reward is modest. That combination of high demands and poor working conditions is almost engineered for disappointment. Jack commits Heartward Bound residents, graduates of their culinary training program, to these restaurant gigs, but he sometimes hears that they have disappointed the boss. "I sent one guy two trainees who were older gentlemen," he recalls. It didn't work out so well.

> The owner is like a firecracker…he's maybe forty or forty-five and these [workers] are a little bit older. They couldn't keep up with him. The minute they showed up to talk to him about an entry-level job like a dishwasher or a prep cook, this guy came on so strong, because it's [long been] his dream to have his own restaurant.…. You need to be driven when you have your own business like that. There's no way around it. He knows he's going to work eighteen-hour days, but he can't expect that of [other] people. They're like, "Look, [here] is my dream: I just want a job."

Jack has to hold back from his impulse to lecture employers like this. He must calibrate carefully how much power he has in the situation, taking into account how desperate the employer is for labor and how frantic the jobseeker is for a paycheck. When the placement works, when someone who has been out in the cold for years finally lands a job, Jack swells with pride over the victory. It nearly makes up for all the times when nothing worked out. "I placed a woman at Children's Hospital," he recalls. "[She] has the greatest personality you could imagine. She's always upbeat. She does the overnight shift, by the way. And when we got her that job, man

I wanted to ring that bell right off the wall. I knew that they would say to me afterwards, 'Man, you really got us a gem. She's exactly what we want.'"

Heartward Bound is committed to getting people back on their feet and into proper housing. The organization recognizes that providing people with the skills that will get them back into the labor force is a means to that end. It is also an avenue for restoring the dignity of residents in a society where working is both a way to cover the bills and a signal of moral worth.[13] Wanting to make a durable difference in the lives of the unhoused, Heartward Bound invested in training facilities for two industries that are in high demand in an affluent city: housekeeping and food service. "Food services is a twenty-four-week program and housekeeping is a sixteen-week program," explains Allen Browne, who organizes these efforts for Heartward Bound.

> The first eight weeks…is really structured around [generic] training: learning people skills, the soft skills, structure around coming into the operation on time, teamwork.…They also work about twenty hours in the kitchen and housekeeping areas side-by-side with our professional team members. So they're doing twenty hours of paid on-the-job training as well as ten hours of training. And again, that could be the ServSafe Certification, mindfulness, professionalism, financial literacy.

Heartward Bound's training regime differs from what employers might do in the way of training themselves. It is more broadly oriented toward adaptation to the work world, teaching people soft skills. It is more "school-like" and formal in its lesson structure than the "watch me and learn" approach that Randy Stefanski employs in his recycling business. Shelters like Heartward Bound are taking their trainees through a curriculum, one that they can describe to employers who want to know what the graduates of these programs have mastered.

Trainers try to instill in their "students," a sense of career trajectory, a way of elevating what they are learning to a dependable vocation. Visiting dignitaries, star chefs, hotel owners remind residents that the jobs for which they are training can lead to a true career. If a resident catches the eye of one of these visitors, it might be their lucky day. "We've seen instances of trainees forming relationships from those demos with a chef, and then later on that chef employed that person," says Allen Browne.

"We've had a few examples of that happening, where they go on to work for a chef who did a demo here." This emphasis on soft skills is particularly important in tight labor markets because, as many employers note, applicants on the margins may be especially problematic where these requirements are concerned. They have often been in dysfunctional settings and have lost their social bearings; they may have landed in a homeless shelter because they had trouble managing personal interactions. But when unemployment is at rock bottom and employers are looking to hire, employers are hoping intermediaries can remedy these gaps.

Jean Doyle, associate director of Workforce Development, has worked at Heartward Bound for several decades. She sees greater confidence emerging in her trainees who are listed in the Criminal Offender Record system (CORI) and the staff that works with them. Tight labor markets have given them hope. "Back in 2008," she recalls, "you would have had trainees...say 'Oh, I can't get a job. I have a CORI,' but I think there's maybe sort of like a mind-set shift where both trainees—returning citizens—as well as staff working with them are a little bit more confident because we are in a booming market right now."

IMMIGRANT BROKERS

Beacon Career Center (BCC) was born during the Great Depression with a mission to assist refugees and immigrants from Europe to find their way in a country that was struggling through one of its bleakest periods. Unemployment was at catastrophic levels—25 percent officially, although the true figures were much higher—and the depths of poverty and despair were unprecedented. We remember the era through haunting photographs of bedraggled men standing in lines that wrapped around city blocks waiting for meals at soup kitchens. Under these conditions immigrants were no longer welcome. They were routinely described as lying in wait to steal jobs that rightfully belong to people born in America. In the face of mass unemployment and social rejection, immigrant aid societies similar to BCC emerged in many urban centers. Like the settlement houses that preceded them in the nineteenth century, immigrant aid societies were staffed by co-religionists and ethnic brethren, volunteers, and members of the nascent social work profession, determined to assimilate these new arrivals, providing them with language classes and job opportunities.[14]

When World War II ended, Beacon Career Center pivoted to help refugees from many nations and GIs who needed assistance acclimating to civilian life. Today the organization serves a vibrant and (until recently) growing immigrant community in Boston. As its website proudly proclaims, BCC serves newcomers from "over 67 nations, speaking 59 languages." The center remains closely tied to religious communities, to which they turn for support. Business leaders of faith often open the doors of their companies to people trained by the organization, no matter what their religion or national origin. Given its longevity, the organization has seen business cycles come and go. Their clients have had to weather the expansion and contraction of the job market without being able to speak English or capitalize on their home country education or work experience. They must start all over again to earn certificates and degrees that will enable them to work in professions they have long practiced in their countries of origin.[15] Their families must do without, sometimes for years, while the parents retool.

Jacob Schimmel, the president and CEO of Beacon Career Center, came to the organization after many years in government service and a ten-year period with a nonprofit that leads research and policy conversations in workforce development. He led BCC as it built a strategy to train new immigrants for jobs in the burgeoning health-care sector. Hospitals and drugstore chains outsource their training needs to Schimmel's nonprofit. By specializing in one field, he has built a robust reputation for rigorous preparation that employers rely on with confidence. Health care is a highly regulated industry, requiring workers to have specific credentials before performing certain types of work. Outsourcing training means leaving to others (like BCC), the headaches associated with the credentialing process, which can become quite cumbersome and subject to backlogs. In 2020, during the COVID-19 pandemic, for example, thousands of nursing students were stuck in limbo, unable to complete their clinical training because hospitals were overwhelmed with work and could not provide the supervision students needed on hospital wards, pharmacy counters, nursing homes, and clinics. "For a few weeks," Jacob noted, "the pharmacy technician exam was down [so] you couldn't actually get certified."

BCC was similarly under strain, unable to secure clinical training from their usual sources. Instead, they pivoted to partnership with long-term care facilities and were able to continue filling the pipeline of immigrants eager to join the pharmacy and nursing professions. They negotiated workarounds with the largest area hospitals, enabling workers to start their careers under a different job title while they continued to complete their training and qualify for positions that require certification. These adaptations to a hot labor market had no precedent in BCC's experience but were responses to high demand among their long-standing employer partners.

BCC is a value-driven organization, and its commitment to immigrant clients was tested during economic transitions when the only jobs growing were in sectors where job quality was a problem. The "Amazon economy" has been growing for more than a decade.[16] Clearly there is opportunity in the shopping and shipping business. Warehouse jobs, delivery operations, packaging, and the like are bursting at the seams as consumers abandon brick-and-mortar stores in favor of the internet. The trouble is, the jobs that are growing tend to be low quality, starting with the salaries. "It just doesn't pay as well," Jacob says, shaking his head. "Look, it's better to earn $15 bucks an hour than trying to survive on unemployment insurance. But you know, if you were making $20 to $25 an hour in a union or even a nonunion hotel, that's a big drop in your wages. So . . . BCC has really shifted our focus from employment to job quality." He took the opportunity created by tight labor markets to develop a job-quality assessment tool, a composite of features that matters to workers and to communities. It was designed for employers to benchmark themselves and, in a competitive situation where they are bidding for labor, to understand how they stand relative to others in their industry.

Wages, hours, and schedules are primary concerns for workers. But so are health and safety, diversity, respect, and prospects for advancement. Jacob knows that when unemployment is low and hence workers have choices, employers need to think about what differentiates them from their competitors. "When people are going to work for you," he says, "you need to make it clear that you give a shit about [their well-being] and you thought about it. You've actually got some procedures in place. My team did a really good job, talking with the employer partners, where we have a close relationship where we can actually talk through some of these issues."

As labor markets tightened in 2021, BCC's tool began to attract attention. Municipalities like Denver and Baltimore wanted their employers to make use of it. Value-driven intermediaries like BCC can translate the clout that emerges when unemployment is very low into an organized effort to advantage labor, even in the absence of supportive legislation.[17] A health-care job fair that BCC organized offered a chance for employers to distinguish themselves from their competitors. Promoting their attention to health and safety protocols proved appealing. Each employer had a time slot to give a presentation about their organization because all of the jobseekers wanted to know about their protocols, Jacob explained. "We got to see...who was better at it than others, right. So, that was a pretty easy [example of job quality]."

Jacob noted growing attention to workplace diversity and equity policies. Public polling showed this to be a growing flash point. Employers felt a heightened need to account for the way they recruit, retain, and promote their workers. Employees of color and women in tech fields were particularly keen on this information since, under tight labor market conditions, choosing firms that will do right by them is an option. Jacob has been surprised—pleasantly—by the groundswell building in this direction. It wasn't what he expected, even if it is something he (and BCC supporters more generally) endorse: "If you had said to me, even a year ago, that whites in America would be actually open to the concept that Black Lives Matter, I would have said, 'You're out of your mind. Like, it's just not gonna happen. Not my lifetime.'" Jacob asks: "Will it last? Will it mean something? I really don't know." But for the moment tight labor markets created conditions in which jobseekers could be choosy, and his Black and Latinx immigrant trainees had options.

Because intermediaries sit astride so many hiring decisions, they have a more comprehensive understanding of the way labor markets move than any individual job hunter or employer could hope to have. In particular, they see that job qualifications are more sensitive to the unemployment rate than is commonly understood. When labor markets are loose, Jacob explains, hiring managers increase their expectations. "Why did [that escalation in job requirements] happen?" he explains. "Because hiring managers were flooded with people and résumés. They were literally trying to screen out 90 percent of the people [who were applying].... It takes time for employers to recognize that conditions on the ground have changed." Hiring managers are not particularly flexible when they have the upper hand; they stick with tried-and-true approaches until they just break down. "It's not like the unemployment rate changes and then the next week [employers shift their strategies]," Jacob says.

> The transition from the last recession to the very tight job market took like five years before companies really said like, 'Oh my god, like we can't get anybody and we're still acting as though we're trying to screen people out.' Hello! Like, maybe you should change your practices. But... companies are [not] that nimble that they see job market information, they see customer demand, they look at strategy, they match it all up and all of a sudden they change their HR systems. [No] I don't think I've ever seen that happen. I mean, it just moves very [slowly].... A year later I think that's more [likely]... at least that's what I've seen.

LIFTING UP COMMUNITIES

The largest and best-known labor market intermediaries serve jobseekers from across a region, without regard to where they live. But place-based organizations, founded with a broad antipoverty strategy in mind, rely on a "saturation" approach that tries to improve all facets of a neighborhood: its housing, schools, after-school care, adult education, banking, job training, and employment.[18] Nonprofit foundations like Robin Hood or the Harlem Empowerment Zone, both of which work to upgrade New York City neighborhoods in transition, often seek out place-based intermediaries to handle employment needs.

The Triangle Square Association is one such place-based organization; it is attempting that kind of "high dosage" approach to poverty alleviation in Dorchester, Roxbury, and Mattapan, three historically Black and poor communities of Boston.[19] All three neighborhoods are disadvantaged in terms of work opportunities: in 2020 they were among only seven of twenty-three neighborhoods in Boston with an employment rate below 90 percent. These areas have fewer local employers than more prosperous neighborhoods, which means residents have longer commute times than most other Boston dwellers.[20] In 1953 the meat-packing and food-processing companies that surrounded downtown Boston moved to the Triangle Square area when the city center was being groomed for tourism, especially the well-known Faneuil Hall retail development. Business activity increased in the Triangle Square neighborhoods in the 1960s and 1970s but without much investment in the infrastructure of roads or traffic management. "Out of sight, out of mind" seemed to be the philosophy of the mayor's office, an attitude that frustrated business owners in the neighborhood. In the mid-1970s a small group of local property owners and business leaders met at a local diner and decided to work together to pursue their common goals, especially business growth. Today the Triangle Square Association has 226 members looking to influence City Hall and to advance employment opportunities for residents of the area.

Anita Ramos is the director of the Triangle Square Jobs Initiative, which was launched in January 2020 and is supported by prominent Boston philanthropies. Anita's mission is to place residents of area with local employers. "[Our] district is sort of the...beating heart of [industrial] Boston," she explains. "All of our businesses [must be] comfortably near public transportation for employees and jobseekers from the neighborhoods of Dorchester, Roxbury, Mattapan. And I also recruit those jobseekers through relationships that I build with community-based partner organizations." The effort began with a data-driven assessment of the annual demand for employees. Anita determined that there are "roughly nine hundred open opportunities a year that they hire for within Triangle Square." Sixty-five community-based organizations refer jobseekers to the Triangle Square Initiative and sixty-eight employer partners post opening on its website.

Unlike Heartward Bound, which combines lodging and training, Triangle Square does not house its participants and focuses mainly on jobs that do not require new training. Human capital is not their issue.[21] Improving the Triangle Square neighborhood by reducing joblessness is. Anita explains: "We could connect to community partners that could source candidates for those jobs, up to maybe four hundred or five hundred of those nine hundred available opportunities that we were estimating a year. Those employers were in our network, dues-paying members of our association. We already had years' worth of relationships with them, a built-in community." Little is left to chance in joining jobseekers and businesses. Anita develops connections with neighborhood nonprofits, takes in their recommendations, and allows only the applicants they recommend to go forward with the application process. She scrutinizes every jobseeker to make sure she can stand behind them. As she explained, these are not "random people off the street." They are the people who have impressed someone along the pipeline that they are worthy of a referral: "All of them have to be affiliated with our partner organizations so that they are known to somebody and can be vetted and supported through the entire process of job readiness, résumé building, and searching and applying for jobs on our platform."

Anita attends to every person who meets these criteria, and she watches the listings Triangle Square employers contribute. Her job is to be sure that the match happens and that employers are excited about what she delivers. As she explains it:

> [Mine] is a very, very high touch sort of white-glove boutique approach to employment. It's a lot of hand-matching. I review every job that's posted on our platform. Most of the jobs I personally am posting myself employers will send them to me. But I'll post them.
>
> I'm able to see, oh, this job is looking for a UX web developer... I remember seeing a résumé come through that had those same skills listed. I can now reach out to that person and say, "Hey, are you still looking? This job came through. Make sure you apply for it." And apply quickly because I know that employers said they're hiring urgently.

If she doesn't get an instant reply, Anita can follow up and nudge the application along.

> [I make] sure that those connections are being made. I can reach out to the agency that that applicant came from and say, "Hey, I saw that Carlos had these skills. I encouraged him to apply, but you may want to also give him a nudge." And so everybody is involved, and then reaching back to the employer and say, "Hey, this agency referred this person Carlos, they said XYZ about him. He comes highly recommended." So it's a holistic approach.

Anita describes herself as the "auntie who works on the inside of the company you're trying to get into," except that she "works in every company, and I'm everybody's auntie." She says: "That's certainly what differentiates us from Indeed or LinkedIn or anything else where people are just sort of on their own. And I think, especially when you're talking about populations that need more support in these types of job searching and employment situations, and also from the employer side, I think what we're doing in a lot of situations, is challenging employers to think differently about their hiring practices." Aunties are never disinterested parties, and neither is Anita. She doesn't back away once one of her people is placed, especially since they are essentially next door in Triangle Square. She remains in contact with the employers and the workers in the neighborhood to nurture the relationship. This is no mean feat, with more than three hundred jobseekers on her radar at any given time and hundreds who have been successfully placed. When it works, the initiative not only improves the lives of the workers who have found work, but over time benefits the communities they come from by attacking the problem of joblessness. It is easier to do when labor markets are tight, critical when they are loose, but always appreciated by the workers and employers who benefit.

It may appear that this kind of "white glove" treatment would only be offered to candidates who are themselves conventional and highly skilled. But the purpose of the Triangle Square Jobs Initiative isn't to help jobseekers who really don't need assistance. While their population may include people with specialized skills, they are an antipoverty program—more like Heartward Bound than they might appear at first glance—looking to help people who could not easily find these jobs on their own. In essence, they are applying a "concierge approach" to people who have blemished records, who need someone to stand up for them so that they don't get the door slammed in their faces. Marginal workers, with blank spots in their biographies, are among the applicants Anita is looking to support. She explains:

> I talk to employers…challenging their thinking about hiring people…with gaps in their employment history…and people in recovery. People…maybe who lack some of the experience that employers may think they need for a certain role, and the difference between somebody who may lack some experience, but really be eager to learn and have a great work ethic and being able to advocate for those people.

Anita makes sure that applicants with gaps in their personal histories don't fall out of the queue, once she is personally convinced that they deserve this second chance. "Even though his résumé may have a gap, or he has a CORI, but [I point out] ... 'It was a long time ago and it was a minor offense. And I really think you'll be impressed by him. He's got a great work ethic.' [They say:] 'Absolutely, send him to me.' ... The stronger the relationship I build with employers, the more they trust when I have a recommendation of a person." Anita's approach to destigmatizing an applicant is to wrap the résumé in a narrative, to humanize the jobseeker, moving away from stereotypes that bask in generalities, toward the specifics of an individual. That stigma is not easily broken by an applicant; it takes an intermediary to do this work.

> [Employers see] that this résumé has gaps and that résumé doesn't. Why wouldn't [they] pick the one that doesn't? But when you can humanize it and actually say 'This is not two résumés. This is a person. And this is a great human being that's really eager to work hard for you and has all these wonderful human qualities and values and ... comes highly recommended,' It's easier to say, 'Yeah, I'll meet that person,' because someone I know and respect knows and respects this person. It's easier to take a chance.

Place-based intermediaries take an approach that is the opposite of an open free-for-all, which is often touted as the solution to discrimination. Where electronic job boards provide access to the multitudes, Anita sees that they leave those people who don't have the necessary resources on their own. Jobseekers she is trying to place will not survive that kind of competition; they need her closed shop, her neighborhood-focused approach, and her personal advocacy.

One of the hiring customs Anita most urgently wants to see change is the tendency to conflate applicants and the untoward aspects of the neighborhoods they come from. Employers are comfortable hiring people from areas that are safe and stable; they are leery of people who come from communities burdened by crime, lest they bring some of that trouble with them to the workplace.[22] Anita puts her reputation behind applicants from Mattapan and Dorchester who might otherwise be shut out because she can reassure employers that these are "good guys" they can trust. Sourcing employees locally has benefits beyond those that affect individual jobseekers. Employers can reduce poverty and joblessness in Triangle Square at the same time that they staff their enterprise. Otherwise, when a poor neighborhood abuts a city undergoing an economic boom, it is entirely possible for local poverty to decline without actually reducing poverty in the region at all. Gentrification moves the affluent into transitional neighborhoods and "cures" poverty just by replacing the poor with more privileged residents.

Boston risks exactly that outcome. It has become one of the country's most prosperous cities, with skyrocketing housing costs. Its go-go growth is spilling out beyond the suburbs and trendy neighborhoods of the city, engulfing communities like Triangle Square. White-collar and professional workers can migrate into these areas and still reach the downtown businesses on the subway. The Triangle Square Jobs Initiative is trying to stem that tide by advocating for "living wage" jobs that will enable some of these original residents to stay put. "I would love to see [us] grow," says Anita in one of her quiet moments. "We need to help as many people as we can get into work."

> More and more people need good paying, [high-] wage jobs, as we see our city gentrify and people get priced out of housing in these communities where they've lived for generations. [This] was one of the motivations for our initiative to connect people to jobs that pay a living wage so that they can afford to stay in the communities where they live and have jobs in the communities where they live.

To achieve that goal, the Triangle Square Initiative both advocates for higher wages and, where they can, puts muscle behind the talk. Anita simply refuses to post jobs that don't meet their criteria.

> Stop and Shop was hiring for cashiers and overnight stock . . . stockroom people. [But] cashiers were minimum wage and stock room, I think, was $13.75, which was just too low. . . . I won't post it on our platform. Full-time jobs need to [provide] benefits . . . Salaries need to be transparent . . . even if it's a range, or starting salary, or an estimated salary, based on skills and experience. Every single job post has to list salary information, so that people can [figure out], "Can I afford to apply for this job?"
>
> Because it may sound like the coolest job in the world, but if you can't afford to live on that, you deserve to know it before you waste your time

applying to it and going through a whole process or you may want to know like, "What am I going to need to go into this ready to negotiate?"

Anita tries to prepare her jobseekers to advocate for themselves, to take advantage of their desirability to push the employer to offer a better deal. As an intermediary in a tight labor market, she is also capitalizing on her value to firms—and the public nature of the Triangle Square Initiative—to pressure companies to up their game.

The dynamics of the economy may predispose—or dampen the ardor— for employing the marginal worker, a calculus shaped by supply and demand. But the politics of the moment matter as well. A spate of egregious police and vigilante murders of young, Black men that swept the country in 2020 raised awareness about inequality in the United States. Philanthropists like billionaire Laurene Powell Jobs and Mackenzie Scott responded with major commitments to improving education and social services; banks, brokerage houses, commercial real estate organizations, and universities committed to hiring a higher percentage of people of color; procurement operations were restructured by many big-spending companies to increase contracts with minority-owned businesses. The firms in the Triangle Square district felt the urgency of the moment, giving Anita the backing she needed to advocate for new policies. She recalls:

> Our city was built by the families that were here, that had money, that built our city, that built these businesses, and that's what it was. That's historical truth. What is exciting to me though in this moment is to see the generation that's probably my age, maybe a little bit younger, now taking over those businesses. They're saying 'I'm proud of our history [but] I want to do something different as I'm taking over my family business. I want my legacy as the owner or as the manager of this business to be that [change]. It's not just going to be our family [that prospers]. I want diversity.

It proved much easier to make good on that promise when labor markets tightened and employers were desperate for applicants. Anita could maintain her standards for listing "living-wage" opportunities and sourcing jobseekers from within Triangle Square who would have found it much harder to get a foot in the door in tepid labor markets.

GOVERNMENT AGENCIES AS INTERMEDIARIES

While nonprofit organizations dominate the intermediary services sector, following close on their heels are public agencies that provide employment matching services for the hard to employ. They are often funded by federal, state, or municipal budgets that promote work as a means of reducing reliance on the public purse. Andrew Walton is the director of a municipal agency that facilitates employment for those emerging from the county jails and state prisons. He and his staff help nearly three thousand people that return home to Boston every year, needing everything from identification documents to food, housing, tax preparation, health care, and employment. A relatively new agency, it puts on job fairs for private employers looking for workers and advocates with city agencies to ensure that civil service jobs are open to people with criminal records. "It's been a great ride so far," Andrew says, pushing back in his chair. "Just going from zero; there was nothing."

> We just knew what we knew. And we were able to supplement [our instincts] with the need to create relationships both in the community and internally throughout the city departments, then hold people accountable within the organization and ourselves, and then just provide advocacy, really. That's what we do. We provide advocacy. We are the air traffic controllers of the information for our returning citizens. And as information comes in, we can direct them to the different departments.

Andrew's organization pulls in private sector employers, city and state agencies, and even criminal justice institutions to create opportunities for employment. Temporary employment agencies, which find themselves with few people to place when labor markets tighten and most people have found jobs, know they can turn to this municipal office to find workers who need placements. Local unions—particularly those with municipal contracts—have been particularly eager to reach out to Walton and see to it that returning citizens have a crack at their jobs—high wage jobs, with good benefits packages. "January, February, March, April, those are—I call them—union entry day," Andrew notes. "They only put out applications once a year, and that's the time that they do it—during this timeframe. So individuals who are interested in the trades will contact this office and say, 'Hey, if you have some people, make sure you send them down.'"

Andrew has learned how to spot institutions whose values align with "second-chance thinking." He pushes them to take the next step and offer opportunities to returning citizens. High on this list are universities with academic research and activist programs connected to criminal justice reform. Andrew tries to make it just a little bit uncomfortable for those who espouse this worldview but refrain from actually hiring people with criminal records.

> [These] people are well intended; however, they have to look to themselves for the practices that are there. Colleges and universities are wonderful opportunities for individuals to be employed by because of many of the benefits. Benefit One, of course, is getting an education. Benefit Number Two is the exposure in an educational environment. Just being exposed to an environment where people want to learn how to learn. There's opportunities in the cafeterias; there's opportunity in groundskeeping. There's just multiple opportunities that a person can come in in an area where, we say there's "low-hanging fruit" [or a] "low-hanging entry threshold" and work themselves up.

Labor market conditions dictate who is likely to have a crack at particular occupations. Because that context shifts over time, different groups of people—defined by education, gender, race, and experience—will come to populate an occupation even when the responsibilities of the job or the skills required remain the same. Walton is very aware of that changing context. It has a profound impact on whether the returning citizens he advocates for will have a chance or be locked out. Employers don't change their minds along with the changing context, in his view. Some may hold their noses and consider people with criminal records, while others never will.

The difference, Walton thinks, is less a matter of revelation about second chances or a sudden recognition that formerly incarcerated people can be capable workers, than it is an adjustment to the market landscape. The stigma of criminal engagement is not just a matter of fear of violence or repeated illegal conduct. It is mixed up in the racial composition of the population behind bars. As decades of research on mass incarceration has shown, Black men are disproportionately represented in the prison population. Drug laws that subject cocaine sales to higher penalties when sold in the form of crack than in powder form; incompetent or overworked legal representation for poor people; the disruptive impact of fines and parole oversight—these factors have combined to make it far more likely that they will end up behind bars.

In a country with a history of profound inequality in the criminal justice system, the resulting social context fuses racial stereotypes with crime to create even more profound barriers to the labor market. Encouraging employers to offer a second chance is insisting that they blast past two compounding, reinforcing sets of prejudices. "The needs of the economy still can be... fulfilled in a racial polarizing way," Andrew explains. "So if the mind-set doesn't change, things will be the same." He has seen those durable mind-sets budged by the will of authority figures. Boston's mayor from 2014 to 2021, Marty Walsh (the US Secretary of Labor in President Joe Biden's administration), was an evangelist for second chances. Open about his own history of alcoholism and the possibilities of redemption, Mayor Walsh urged the city to be tolerant and supportive of returning citizens looking to reenter the workforce. "Institutions can change based on leadership," Andrew insisted.

> We changed the name to "returning citizens." Because we're not ex-felons. We're not ex-cons. We're not ex-anything. We are individuals who are coming back into society. We have been denied the right to vote, and denied the right to convene with our families, convene with our community. We were denied those rights when we were incarcerated, but as we move forward, we're citizens. And we expect from our community a certain level of connection, and our community can expect from us a certain level of behavior and connection as well. "Returning and restored citizens" is the mind-set that we rather use than "ex."

Changing the social perceptions of employers is only part of the battle. There are structural barriers to incorporating returning citizens into the work world. As Andrew says:

> Hands down, housing is an issue. . . . Prior to [this office] being involved in this work, the discharge plan for leaving prison was to send them to a shelter. [To] this mayor, this legislature—we have said that a shelter is not an option. . . . You got to come up with something better. [Because] when a person goes to a shelter, which is meant to be a temporary assignment, they have to be in line to get a bed assignment by 3:00 p.m. And they must be out of that shelter by 7:00 [a.m.]. And they cannot leave anything at the shelter.
> If they have to take their entire belongings with them every day to go to work and leave work early to come back to get a bed, that's extremely

problematic. And so many individuals can't sustain that schedule.... And employers began to say, "What is this?" And then judgment happens again. It's like "I'm homeless."... One of the strategies that people often have is to work enough to get a car so that they can live in their car. Which is sad.

The same growth that depresses unemployment, making it easier to land a position, also lights a fire in the rental market. Lack of affordable housing may even prevent returning citizens from leaving a prison halfway house in the first place. "When you're on parole or probation," Andrew explained, "the probation officer has to come out and approve the house that you're going to be living in. If you don't have an address, you don't get out. That's the catch-22. Even though you can get out, you can't get out." He says:

> We have partners who are in transitional housing and sober-living communities. But they require at least $180 to $225 a week. And they require a person to have something coming in the first week. Security deposits. Many times they don't have that. So we're currently exploring funding through our church partnerships to secure a bridge scholarship to provide individuals who are coming out and to give them at least thirty days of payment to a sober-living community, while they look for employment.

If they have that much stability, that razor-thin margin, Andrew's office can make the employment part of the equation work, especially in low-unemployment environments, where second chances are more plentiful. "We have good confidence that we can get someone employed within thirty days. Absolutely. If they stick to the plan." Their success rose sharply as labor markets in Boston tightened. Employers became more comfortable with the people Andrew was promoting because they had fewer choices.

INTERMEDIARIES IN DOWNTURNS

Tight labor markets make almost everything intermediaries do somewhat easier; as long as they can find firms who need workers. When the jobless rates are high, the opposite conditions apply. Now intermediaries need to upskill or train their clients to make them appealing in a buyer's market.

But every recession is a bit different, not only in who is engulfed first or hardest but in how much warning intermediaries have that a crisis is unfolding. The Great Recession of 2008 tore into the job market, for example, but it took a couple of years before it hit the absolute nadir.[23] As it unraveled the workforce, the Great Recession first impacted high-end professionals in banking, brokerage, and real estate before it trickled down eventually to the service sector. Men were more likely to be thrown out of work than women. The COVID-19 pandemic of 2020, by contrast, descended almost overnight. It tanked any industry that depended on face-to-face contact: travel, tourism, restaurants, and childcare. It landed like an unexpected tsunami on top of the Better Business Boston (BBB), a "school-to-career" intermediary, which went from empty job centers (since nearly everyone was working) in January 2020 to nearly 14 percent unemployment in Massachusetts, the worst in the nation, by March 2020. By then, job centers were empty because no one was willing to brave the possibility of infection, but thousands were unemployed and desperate.

Many of the workers who were turfed out during the Great Recession of 2008 were white-collar professionals accustomed to the technologies we use now to connect remotely. As Ryan Murphy, chairman of the BBB notes, workers in the service industries hit hard by COVID-19 were not used to these devices and platforms. He continues:

> This is very different in many respects from the Great Recession in that you had a lot of layoffs in financial services and other industries whose popula-tions actually probably could work through a virtual Career Center.... This [recession], it's a lot of in-person services, a lot of workers that are typically not used to office technology...Zooms and [Microsoft] Teams calls and that sort of thing.

The severe but short-lived recession of 2020 saw a different gender dynamic.[24] It differentially impacted industries with a predominantly fe-male labor force. Murphy noted: "The fact that it's two-thirds female.... Infrastructure investment and manufacturing subsidies aren't going to be the solution for those who are displaced."

The hospitality industry was particularly hard-hit in Boston. In June 2019 the opening of the Encore Hotel and Casino created thousands of entry-level jobs, so many that the demand upended the local labor market. People gave up other jobs readily for the Encore opportunity, which was paying much more for unskilled labor than almost anyone else. And then it all fell apart. As Linda Muldowney, another BBB leader, explained:

Encore had opened the hotel. They have one thousand rooms...and were thinking about opening [an additional] hotel across the street. BBB spent about a year working with Encore to get people from everywhere. Bilingual speakers, I mean they wanted everybody and anybody. And there was a lot of money that went into training and trying to source these people. And [they provided] English classes. [Encore was] paying $22 an hour to clean a room. So people gave up their two hospitality jobs, or delivery jobs to take these [openings]. And then the hotel shut down and the casino went on limited hours.

So you've got all these people who gave up what they had to take to take this wonderful opportunity. Who knows how long the casino will last? We had money to train people to be dealers and now they can't do anything with it. So it's just been this complete letdown.

The health-care industry saw a different dynamic. Any medical procedure that could be put off was canceled. That led to layoffs of administrative support staff and some physicians. But the need for hospital care was roaring as the pandemic deepened. Hence even in the middle of a record surge in unemployment in the second quarter of 2020, this sector was having trouble finding the skilled workers who could tend to these critically ill patients. The restaurant industry could absorb some of these people but not for jobs that paid anywhere near a genuine living wage.

Workers began shifting around, deploying their experience where there were better openings. And the training regime began to reflect those gyrations. People once bound for hotels and restaurants streamed toward hospitals and long-term care facilities, where they could claim a higher salary for the same skills. Jacob Schimmel, the CEO of Beacon Career Center, observed similar impacts as the labor market cratered and the immigrants who turned to BCC began coming back to the mothership as their jobs evaporated. Schimmel is a veteran of nearly forty years' worth of business cycles, which has taught him that each downturn is punishing in its own way. "The last recession which started soon after I took the BCC job thirteen years ago, really hit the financial services and the technology industry," he recalled. "This one [the 2020 recession]...initially just clobbered...anything having to do with what you would broadly describe as the hospitality industry.... Every hotel in the city closed, and every restaurant closed."

Boston is a mecca for the tourist trade and—even more important—business travel. The entire sector was in freefall from February 2020, the middle of our research fieldwork, to the end of the summer of 2021. Hotel occupancy was negligible. Business travel evaporated in favor of Zoom meetings from home offices and kitchen tables across the country. Airlines began to rebound in the spring of 2021 but only after nearly a year of brutally low travel. From Jacob's perspective, a long and painful period of restructuring should be expected before stability returns to travel-related businesses. "There's going to be restructuring in the hotel industry as well. It's sad because in Boston that industry is 50 percent unionized. In order to compete with the union hotels, even the nonunion hotels have had to up their game. They were paying living wages to people who lacked English and higher educational levels and we've lost that. And it's going to be a while before that comes back."

In other sectors, the low-wage labor force reaped advantages. Growth in the logistics or transportation business (e.g., Amazon) was nearly exponential during the pandemic, as consumers shifted almost entirely to online purchasing. For immigrant workers in the BCC system, Schimmel points out, the reemployment prospects created by the industry surge were critical:

> Since [COVID-19] started, we've reemployed about three hundred people. . . . The majority of folks who've lost their job, we've been able to get other jobs for, but they've been in different sectors. So kind of where you might imagine, right, grocery stores, distribution, like Amazon has grown like nobody's business, and any related company to remote distribution of groceries, of consumer goods. . . . It hasn't been 100 percent replacement by any means, but it's not been insubstantial.

Because BCC emerged from a religious and charitable history, it also pivoted quickly toward mobilizing relief funds from private sources as unemployment spread during the pandemic. Having done what they could to support emergency needs, BCC and other intermediaries turned to philanthropic donations to ramp up services in the face of an almost overwhelming need. As Schimmel explained:

> We've raised over $2 million for technology investment. And we've spent over a million already on the technology side, [to support remote access]. The philanthropic community has been amazingly responsive and supportive. . . . Our biggest foundation funders said, 'We'll convert your grant

to a general operating grant and we'll pay you now, the whole thing so you have cash on hand. We also qualified for a fairly large [federal Paycheck Protection Program] loan, which will convert to a grant also, we actually, we're actually this year we're in very strong financial state." By next year, I think it's going to be another story.

Place-based intermediaries like Triangle Square were not as well positioned to call on philanthropy for help. The industries for which Anita recruits workers came to a standstill, particularly the smaller family businesses. If they kept their doors open at all, it was only after freezing hiring, cutting wages, and bringing unpaid cousins and children to fill in on the shop floor. "We didn't have those employers to count on to provide jobs," Anita recalled. "So we had to really rethink our model and get creative and outreach to a more diverse pool of employers and kind of blow up the whole box, not just think outside of it." Hers was a difficult standard to maintain when the labor market fell apart. She was torn between helping people survive in 2020, during one of the most profound economic downturns in a hundred years, and trying to improve the structural conditions that contribute to persistent poverty by insisting on minimum standards of job quality. It's a slippery slope.

> Keeping to our values of not accepting jobs that were paying minimum wage... we initially started at $16 an hour or above, we lowered it to $14. We started only posting for full-time opportunities. [But] during the pandemic some people wanted part-time, so that it wouldn't throw off their unemployment benefits. So we did start posting some part-time opportunities as well. [We] pivoted from our initial model by request of both employers and jobseekers. So we went to things like some retail-type stores which weren't great, because they did have, they do offer low wages, but some of them had pandemic rates.

CONCLUSION

Employers and intermediary organizations make use of similar strategies in cultivating workers on the margins for opportunities that are going begging in tight labor markets. But for small employers, the training functions, the monitoring required to keep people "in line," and the cultivation of opportunities for upward mobility can be too arduous. This is why these small businesses find intermediaries so important when sourcing unfamiliar workers. Larger employers appreciate the chance to outsource training in soft skills among the hard-to-employ. Merely being able to depend on an external organization to do screening and provide a backbone to support workers if they start to falter is a boon to employers. Labor market intermediaries function as an ancillary to human resource departments, replacing some of the recruitment, training, and retention functions that matter, especially when an unfamiliar cadre of workers is employed, as happens far more often in tight labor markets. This division of labor works for hiring managers, jobseekers, and the nonprofit or public institutions that build the bridge between them.

Intermediaries have become essential organizing institutions, especially in the low-wage labor market but also in particular sectors like health care, where outsourcing training has become a modus operandi. Tight labor markets put a particularly high premium on intermediaries because they know this marginal population of jobseekers, either because they provide other vital services, including housing, or because they are linked to broader civic goals, like the resurrection of neighborhoods struggling with persistent unemployment. Arguably, the most interesting feature of intermediary work is the ability to pressure employers to boost job quality. Intermediaries can—and do—make more effort to find good workers for employers who are raising wages and providing benefits. They sideline hiring managers who are fishing to fill low-quality jobs. This is a form of collective bargaining, one that worker-focused intermediary organizations are excited to engage because they can deliver greater economic opportunity to their trainees.

Yet to absorb these responsibilities, as well as the "backup" services that relieve employers of some of the risks of unconventional hiring, intermediaries depend on a flow of funds that is not entirely reliable. These nonprofit entities rely on government and philanthropic support to enhance the services that make them successful, and those funding sources can lead to roller-coaster budgeting and service provision for a key set of labor market institutions. Employers, philanthropies, and government grant makers are generous to nonprofit intermediaries when workers are hard to find but all too often cut back on their largesse when the economy falters. Instead of seeing labor market intermediaries as a disposable service that can be ramped up and down according to conditions in the marketplace, we would do well to stabilize these organizations, so as to enable them to sustain the more robust model of their own workplace through thick and thin.

5 Entering from the Edge

Sam Conrad arrived at the office of Built to Soar, a labor market intermediary in Boston's city center, wearing the regulation Boston uniform: a gray zip-up hoodie and a Patriots cap. Standing six feet tall, a broad-shouldered white man with muscled, tattooed arms, Sam seems almost big enough to be a Patriots player himself. He works full-time in a job that pays a living wage. He has been promoted several times over by different companies.

This is a remarkable turn of events for Sam. Not long before this encounter in 2018, he was locked up in solitary confinement—a punishment he endured for five years—for violent acts committed behind bars. A long-time veteran of the Massachusetts prison system, Sam is one of the last people on earth who thought that he would be standing on his own two feet today. Yet he learned how to spot "the main chance," how to identify a crack in the wall that separates returning citizens from the labor market and go for it. He put in the hard work to impress employers who took a chance on a man with a criminal record.

But the opportunity itself—the fact that a hiring manager was desperate enough to hire a man with a long, serious, felony record—has something to do with the choices his employer did *not* have at the time. The competition to fill positions in a tight labor market drives employers to consider workers who might be overlooked in a time of greater labor supply. An epically tight labor market left very few people looking for the job that Sam took at the age of thirty-eight, when he freshly arrived on "the outside" after a twenty-year stint in prison. Understanding how workers move in from the margins is an important aspect of this sociological account of tight labor markets. When unemployment is low, these marginalized jobseekers are better able to spot opportunities, manage stigma, connect to intermediaries, and work against the headwind of stereotypes that limit their chances.

THE PAST

Sam grew up bouncing between several small western Massachusetts towns. His dad was a salesman and his mother a homemaker, but they divorced when Sam was nine. An angry, difficult kid, he was constantly acting out or running away. Early on, Sam was deemed a "Child in Need of Services," meaning his mother legally declared him out-of-control and in need of more supervision than she could provide. "I had a lot of behavior issues," he recalled.

> My parents were addicts, and they got clean. When they got divorced, they also got sober. And when they got sober is when they really got to see how many behavior issues I had because a lot of that stuff was softened up when they were using. So, they were able to see that I had a lot of behavior stuff—anger, ADHD. . . . So, I was put in some residential treatment programs.

Sam cycled between one foster care setting (and new high school) to home and back into foster care. Belligerent, disruptive, and visibly angry most of the time, Sam and his education suffered. Residential programs have poor reputations, but Sam fared better when surrounded by an edifice of someone else's making. His academic performance improved, perhaps because he wasn't in the principal's office all the time. He learned a sense of responsibility. But the success didn't stick when the structure fell away. Sam recalls:

My first job was [at] fourteen [years old]. I actually got a job, when I was at St. Vincent's [residential program], they gave me a janitorial job after school. I was on the books. So, that was actually my first job. I always forget about that. So, I worked there for probably a year. They hired me. They picked me out of the group of kids that were at the program.

So, it's not like everyone had a job.

No, I scored that. When I was in there, straight As. I had been there a couple years, I was used to it. Came home, with the regular high school, I just couldn't keep up. So, yeah, I got hired at McDonald's, Wendy's.... These are all around sixteen [years old]. I think even Burger King... Never long employments.

They were "never long" because Sam "wouldn't show up" and "couldn't keep up with the commitment"—not in school and not at work.

When he reached his full height, Sam felt that his belligerence was more threatening to those around him. His trouble was becoming their uneasiness. Neither school nor work could hold him, so he gave up on his education during his "second sophomore year." That was the beginning of the next bad chapter in his adolescent life. As he says: "So, I'm seventeen.... I started drinking, smoking pot. Mom kicked me out. I left her no choice, you know? In hindsight, she probably would do it differently, but I was seventeen, and I was just out of control. So I ended up basically going couch to couch." During this period Sam called on one of his more winning qualities: the ability to persuade hiring managers to take him on. This would seem an unlikely outcome, but in fact Sam had learned the fine art of job interviews from a classroom activity.

I had that advantage on a lot of people because I had these independent living and resourcing classes I took in these programs. So I actually rehearsed interviewing. So I was able to always—and I speak pretty much well publicly—so I was able to pretty much manipulate my way into jobs. I hate to say it like that, but that's the gist of it. So I didn't really have a hard time getting jobs."

It did not hurt that by this time in the late 1990s, the economy was in fine shape and labor markets were tight. At the tail end of the Clinton presidency, as Sam recalls: "It really wasn't hard to find work then.... The economy was really good. You're talkin' '98, '99. You open up the newspaper, there was all types of jobs in there." However, for a young man with a troubled educational history, the jobs on offer were not enough to pull above distress-level living standards. Sam could find work—he just couldn't find work that paid. He says:

> You never made enough money to live, especially as a kid. When you're eighteen, at that point, it wasn't going [cover the cost of] an apartment. . . . I was going couch to couch to friends' houses. I mean there was times I had to sleep outside and stuff. I think I went to a few shelters in that point. Hard to get a vehicle. I didn't have insurance for vehicles.

Entirely without a support structure, completely on his own, Sam could not make it on his earnings. And so began his career in robbery and his involvement with the adult criminal justice system. First arrested at age eighteen, he was in jail for thirty days, then remanded to a substance abuse program in western Massachusetts. A minimum-security facility, it urged inmates like Sam to continue with their education as a means of enhancing job opportunities and avoiding the long-term incarceration that is the fate of so many.

Unfortunately Sam was not able to stick to the straight and narrow when he got out of the facility. Whether it was his tendency to act out frustration or just the inadequacy of his earnings, he continued to indulge in street crime. A string of modest sentences followed: thirty, sixty, ninety days—seven times between the ages of eighteen and twenty-six. Finally he took a more serious turn, and "I caught an armed mass home invasion. And [for] that one, I went to state prison. . . . I was in maximum security for most of it." Sam recalls:

> When I was thrown into the state system, it became traumatic. You had to adjust to the level of violence and it became very racial. Worchester neighborhoods are intermingled, whereas Boston—especially '70s, '80s, '90s—was highly segregated. Charlestown, Somerville, Dorchester. . . . So when you get to state prison, it's so city- and racially oriented, and there's a lot of violence. . . . You have the Black Boston table, and you have the Black Worcester table, and you have the White Worcester table.

Racial divisions were dramatic; victims were everywhere. Sam had to learn the rules of survival and practice them even if they got him into deeper trouble.

You had to adjust to a level of violence that you're just not comfortable with, but it's kill or be killed. Not really. I mean, you *could* be killed. Not likely in state prison, but you could be hurt. A lot of the stuff I got in trouble with in there was just falling in line and having to do things that are considered necessary. Like say if you're sitting in the chow hall in prison and someone at your table is [hit] from behind, you all have to attack them and help him. So these are things that kept compiling, always happening. I ended up getting involved in a riot, a huge eleven-on-eleven fight in the gym that was white against Spanish. Half the kids on the Spanish side were my friends from Worcester. And we're like pushing away from each other, trying not to fight each other.

Having spent the better part of fifteen years behind bars already, Sam began to feel an overwhelming sense of hopelessness. His psychological balance was eroding; his temper was hard to control. Fighting to protect himself, whether he wanted to or not, began to get the better of him. All the acting out started to accumulate penalties and punishments. Sam was thrown into solitary confinement for assaulting prison guards. They returned the favor: "They beat the snot out of me all the time. They got shields, and you got nothing." What he got, in the end, was a long stint in solitary confinement.

With so much time on his hands, Sam began to dwell on how he had thrown so much of his life away, especially how his actions in prison had only increased his time behind bars. He realized he could have come out much earlier if he hadn't gotten sucked into the crazy-making atmosphere of inmate culture, which rewarded a tough-guy stance over keeping an eye on getting out. Sam started gathering himself up for the day he would leave prison altogether. "Around 2014 . . . I decided to make a conscious choice to try to get myself together," he says. "I needed to get sober and not be getting high. I had twenty years over my head when I came out on minimum. So, if I was to reoffend, I would go back to prison for twenty years minimum."

Three or four months before Sam's actual release, he met Allison Alabi, the director of Built to Soar, then a relatively new agency that functioned as both social work support structure and a labor market intermediary. The organization reaches out to inmates before their release date, conducting interviews and making plans for postrelease support. Sam was only the second person to participate, but the program helped him prepare for what was to come: "I needed help with small stuff. Regain my license, which I had to pay fines, take classes, driver retraining classes on top of I had to take the permit and license over because it was so long—the suspension I was on. I had my license since I was eighteen [years old], twenty years I didn't have a license. So, I had to retake everything."

Sam's experience in solitary confinement made him jumpy and hypersensitive, unable to focus, and he was diagnosed with post-traumatic stress disorder (PTSD). Built to Soar counselors let him know that the medical diagnosis qualified him for Supplemental Security Income (SSI), a public disability benefit. "[Built to Soar helped me] apply for and obtain SSI for a bridge to when I could be employed, you know what I mean? Just to have some type of income, just in case. Everybody says that you're not going to be able to do it, and I did it. I was able to apply, four months later I got SSI."

FINDING A JOB

If ever there were a challenging biography from which to launch a search for employment, Sam's would qualify. His is not the typical profile employers are looking for: behind bars for twenty years, six of them in solitary confinement, a record of violent crime, bad conduct in prison that kept him incarcerated for at least two years longer than was required at the outset, compounded by persistent drug addiction. And in more conventional labor markets, Sam would have had little chance of landing a job.[1]

But tight labor markets shift the odds. Typically during recessions, fewer than 20 percent of unemployed people find a job within one month, but these numbers double during periods of economic growth: in the high-growth period of the late 1990s, more than 30 percent of the unemployed found jobs within a month.[2] Low levels of unemployment clearly make a difference because employers cannot be as choosy as they might like.[3] Intermediaries like Built to Soar and Heartward Bound are architects of the second chance. In tight labor markets they rack up more success stories. Legislation that supports their efforts have helped as well. "Ban-the-box" policies prohibiting employers from asking job candidates about whether they have a criminal record prior to offering an interview is one of the most important. The goal of these laws, adopted in more than a dozen states since 2010, is to give candidates a chance to make a positive personal impression on employers. If they create a good impression before that biographical history is introduced, they have a better chance of being hired despite their criminal record.[4]

The combination of tight labor markets and ban-the-box practices has led to better outcomes. Between 2014 and 2017 the percentage of people on parole in New York state who were unemployed dropped by half, from 8 percent to 4 percent, and the rate of full-time employment nearly doubled, from just over 20 percent to nearly 40 percent.[5] Returning citizens were faring better in Massachusetts as well. In 2017, the year Sam was released from prison, unemployment in the Commonwealth was roughly 3.8 percent—a favorable spot relative to its long-term average of 5.6 percent. Job hunting was getting easier, even for people who had been out of work for years. Owing to his tenacity and these propitious conditions, Sam found work not long after his release. "I found a part-time job at Shaw's. Shaw's Supermarket. Not the best job, minimum wage, overnights, but it was down the street from my house." Paydirt on his very first interview.

Sam's prison reentry courses had prepared him for the Shaw's interview. His instructors discussed the complexities of raising a criminal record, especially when felonies are involved. They also taught him how to explain federal programs that can help to subsidize the wages of the formerly incarcerated, making it more attractive for employers to take them on. For instance, the Internal Revenue Service offers a Work Opportunity Tax Credit that subsidizes 40 percent of pay up to $6,000 for employees who are within one year of a criminal conviction or of being released from prison.[6] The federal government also provides a bonding program, which insures the employer against losses from theft or "dishonest acts" by employees who fall into qualifying groups, including those recently returning from prison.[7]

> In my Shaw's interview I said, 'Listen, this is the way it is. I live up the street in my grandfather's home. He lived in this town his entire life. He passed away. Me and my mother inherited the home. I'm a resident of [this community] now. I'm not going to lie to you, I served time in prison. I was an addict, I'm in recovery. I'm looking to work overnights.' I broke it down. I gave them the benefits of hiring me, and they hired me.

Sam understood that he needed to look for the rare overlap between a critical need for an employer and an absolute distaste among most job-seekers. As he learned while still behind bars, the overnight shift fits the bill. And in a tight labor market it is especially appropriate because other more conventional applicants do not have to settle for disagreeable jobs in the same way. Hence Sam faced less competition. As he recalls:

> I learned in that reentry class that overnight shifts have a really serious turn-over. If you hire six people for an overnight shift, they say one out of six will be there three months later. So I was told to target overnight shifts because nobody stays. It's a hard sleep schedule, but there's a shift differential, usu-ally. Unfortunately, Shaw's was like 50 cents, but some companies give you $2 to $3 more to work overnight for incentive to keep you to stay, because it's really hard.

Sam could have landed the job and then kicked back. That is what most of his coworkers were doing on the night shift. They hated the job and put in the bare-minimum effort. "Shaw's used to be a union [shop] in the '80s," Sam explains. "And then something happened, but they were still making union money. So they just never left because they're making 45 bucks an hour, and they're trying to get to their retirement. So they were just winging it."

Sam, by contrast, took the carpe diem approach. "I went in there with a 'take no prisoner' attitude," he recalls. "I was stocking [shelves], so I just went and just busted my ass. Because before, I'd been a horrible em-ployee—stole, didn't show up, not reliable. So I said [to myself], 'I'm going to switch that around.' So I went into Shaw's, and I'm working [hard] there [as if] I was making $3,000 an hour. I didn't care. I busted my ass." Management noticed. Despite his criminal history, his twenty years be-hind bars, and his drug treatment requirements, Sam was headed up the ladder. "Four months, never missed a day, killed it every night, gave 100 percent, they offered me the night manager position." He says:

> Night manager is like a $5-an-hour pay bump. So I went up to like $16.50. You run the night shift. You get a desk. It's a commitment, though. You are now a Shaw's manager, you're going to be there probably for twenty years or the rest of your life. So it's like, 'Damn!' [Look at me!] Everybody on the night shift was pissed. Because you had people who had been there twenty

to thirty years, and I'm the one offered the [promotion]. They were older. They kind of went at their own pace.... I think management was impressed to finally have somebody on the night shift that was going to work, try hard, not slack off, and get stuff done, which I did.

Sam was on a roll. Now that working hard was his new identity, he sought out more opportunities and found himself in demand—so much so that he ended up with one-and-a-half jobs.

A friend of mine worked at UTS [Universal Testing Services]... a concrete inspection company. [He recommended me for] an entry-level position as an ACI field technician.[8] You come in entry-level, you have to have your own vehicle and a driver's license, obviously, and they teach you the entire concrete and rebar testing format for a couple months. Then they put you through the school, and then you take the ACI test.

It can be very lucrative because you're paid to travel. If you work—some jobs could be an hour, you bill them for four, some jobs could be five hours, you bill them for eight. Not the best money at first. It's like $14 an hour, but your travel and stuff helps.

So, I had to make a choice: do I want to work at Shaw's, or go to this position? I ended up telling Shaw's, 'Listen, I'll work part-time the three nights you get deliveries. Tuesday, Thursday, Saturday.' And then I took on the full-time position at UTS.

Sam trained for more than a month to learn the ins and outs of testing concrete, making sure it was properly composed and set. Construction sites are obligated to arrange for quality control and as a result there is a steady stream of work in any region that is growing. "Quality control for concrete or rebar," he explains. That was his new role, and it took him all over the eastern United States. Although the job itself wasn't difficult, the schedule proved unsustainable, with sixty-hour workweeks becoming increasingly common. "Some days I'd be getting up at like 4 a.m. and then have to come home, sleep three hours, and go work an 11 to 7 or a 10 to 6. It wasn't going to work out, so I ended up having to leave Shaw's."

For the next two years, Sam worked for UTS, traveling five hundred to a thousand miles a week to different jobs, often working on three or four different jobs sites a day. It was an exhausting schedule, filled with more stress and distraction than his PTSD would easily accommodate. He decided to extract himself and find work he could do in one location.

In the end, a friend in the masonry business on Cape Cod found Sam an opportunity, again in a region where demand was high and skilled labor in short supply. Manual labor jobs tend to be CORI-friendly, and that is where he found work in abundance. Sam moved from one blue-collar job to another, finally landing a unionized position, again connected to construction, where a criminal record is not a barrier. "I got into the Roofer's Union. . . . The agent told me 'The Roofer's Union—if I hire twenty people today, in a year there'll be like two left.' So it's a big commitment going to union—sometimes six days a week. You gotta travel, you're gonna bust your ass for them, but they pay you excellent. That's the best you're gonna do—I was going to do—financially."

Access to union opportunities was a huge step forward for Sam. Returning citizens' access to union hiring halls has improved, thanks to reform-minded sheriffs and criminal justice experts. "I think half the unions, they were taking guys right out of Norfolk [prison]," Sam says. Sam's union job came with benefits: a pension and a reserve account he could draw on if work slowed down and he was laid off. He was able to access that reserve account four times a year, which helped to put a secure floor underneath him. The work was physically demanding, but he could not beat the hourly wage. Sam recalls:

> Your wage is still good after [all the deductions]. It's still like $28 an hour, to start. And then it just keeps rising. But it tops out at like the fifth year, but it's like, you could be making like $45 an hour. The thing is, can you hang? Can you stay that long? Can you work forty to sixty hours a week busting your ass? . . . It's just a lot of hard work. You're on top of high-rises like this building right here. You'd be doing the [University of Massachusetts] roof right now! And it's freezing. You'd be up there all day, so it was a little intimidating for me.

While the job wasn't perfect, Sam took satisfaction from his track record of continuous employment, a positive fate that was not what anyone expected for someone with such an inglorious background. But he could not crack every barrier. For example, jobs covered by federal contracts were off limits due to his criminal record. That was a keen disappointment because, in the Boston area, many of the best construction jobs are for labs that are government funded.

I put my résumé [on Indeed], and they saw that I had concrete inspection experience. So this woman contacted me, she said that there's a really good company in Cambridge. It would be a one-year contract, it'd be like $20 bucks an hour to start, and they need you to do concrete testing on site. It was some type of lab. It seemed like a really good opportunity. The hours were great. And she said if they decide to keep you on after a year, you get a 50 percent raise. And you become a permanent employee of the company. So it would've went up to $30 bucks an hour, and I would have been on everything—benefits, pension... [The interviewer for the temp agency] says, "Your résumé is perfect." So, set everything up, the interview was at 11:00 a.m. in Cambridge.

At 9:00 a.m. that day she called me and said that security at the place had run a CORI and she said, 'Please don't go to the interview. They don't even want you on the property with your record.'

It is deeply ironic that the answer to Sam's quest for stable employment that didn't involve physical exertion came about because of one of his biggest life mistakes: addiction. As the opioid crisis began to build, derailing white families and minority families alike, state agencies began to pour money into counseling and other forms of prevention and treatment. Who better to deal with oxycontin addicts than former users? Sam was perfect. Sam's hometown won a grant to train former addicts in case management, substance abuse, and prison reentry. Nonprofit organizations lined up to take the funds and began looking for people like Sam who could trade on their personal experience to help others with the same problem. "If you're affected by opioids... and you need a job," Sam marveled, "they will find you a job for a nonprofit."

Fifteen bucks an hour, interesting work? This was just the ticket. And Built to Soar, the organization that helped Sam when he was behind bars, was game to hire him and train him to help people just like himself. He reconnected with Allison, Built to Soar's director, and volunteered his time to show goodwill. With the supervision of a trained counselor, Sam went to work helping first one and then a second addict get past dependence. He says:

I was the core member, with these people helping me, now I'm helping other people. And then, Allison's like, "Listen, is this something you'd want to do? Work in this field?" And she's like, "I'll still hire you. It's free to me. The grant's paying for it." She's getting employees for free right now, until December of this year, and then they're gonna figure out what they're going to do.

Allison hired Sam to do some advertising for Built to Soar, to increase the visibility of their work and encourage more returning citizens to seek support for a life free of debilitating dependence. He tracked down a telemedia center in the downtown area and signed Built to Soar up for a membership available to nonprofit organizations. For $12 a month, Built to Soar is able to promote its work and Sam was able to launch a career in broadcasting, something he had always hoped to do as a sportscaster. "We have access to all the best stuff to do the [ads]. They'll help us put it out through them as well as our own newsletter, website, stuff like that. So this grant," he says, "it's given a lot of people a chance to come into an organization, work in the field, get the experience, and the organizations are obviously benefiting because it's free for employees for now."

Sam's journey—from twenty years in jail and prison to a full-time employee of Built to Soar—has been long and winding. That he has ended up, at least for the moment, with a job he enjoys and work he is proud of often seems like a miracle. To be sure, it is a story that benefited from Sam's first steps back into the labor market under conditions that, relatively speaking, favored a better outcome than he would likely have found had he emerged from prison in a period of higher unemployment.

Was his experience unique? Did Sam just luck out? No. A survey from the Society of Human Resource Management conducted during the tight labor market of 2018 found that three-quarters of HR managers had hired people with criminal records, and the majority rated the quality of their work as equal or superior to that of employees without records.[9] Accedo, a temporary staffing agency, reported that employers were relaxing qualifications in response to low unemployment: more than 50 percent reported reducing their requirements overall, and 35 percent reported being open to hiring workers with criminal records. According to Accedo, "this isn't something employers would have considered when unemployment rates were 6 percent, 7 percent or higher. So, it's really a dramatic shift that we've seen within the past twenty-four months."[10] These moves turn out to be good for employers. Workers with criminal records have higher retention and longer tenure—turnover was 12 percent lower on average—benefiting the companies that employ them.[11] More broadly, in the era of mass incarceration, when as many as one-in-three Americans have a criminal record, it's difficult to see how employers will meet their staffing needs without embracing returning citizens.[12] Researchers estimate that excluding these workers has a negative impact on GDP on the order of $80 billion per year.[13]

Workers like Sam are hardly on easy street. They can find themselves out in the cold if the winds shift in the labor market. His criminal record continues to disqualify him for some of the steadier jobs he would like to pursue. The labor market itself, particularly the conditions that prevail in blue-collar jobs, often leaves something to be desired. "People can find employment easier now than back ten fifteen years ago," he reflects. "But I don't think it's gainful. . . . Companies like McDonald's, they run you to the grave. You work there, you are busting your ass . . . but what are they paying people? What are they making? A lot of the stuff's unfair." Sam has been able to make a decent living, although his grant-funded position at a nonprofit labor market intermediary is not especially lucrative. "Like this job, $15 bucks an hour? Whatever. But it's something I love, so it makes it a lot easier. And $15 ain't so bad. It's really not. It's better than $12 or $11, you know?"

MELANIE'S MAIN CHANCE

Melanie Abbott has also mastered the art of finding work with a criminal record. "I'm the youngest of six siblings," she explains. While her brothers and sisters grew up in public housing projects, by the time Melanie was born, her parents had been able to buy a single-family home in a Black neighborhood of Dorchester. After years of struggle, they had arrived: "My [parents] thought of themselves as middle class. My mother was a school bus driver. My father had multiple small businesses: carpet cleaning, exterminating. He also sold dinners at times. So yeah, . . . we were always on the grind, as you would say. . . . The ethic in our house was everybody worked."

Melanie put those values into play as a young teen, working as a dishwasher in a school cafeteria where a friend of her family was the chef. She had odd jobs in banks and shops thereafter, always advantaged—as she told the story—by the middle-class dialect and manners she picked up when she attended school in the leafy neighborhood of Sudbury, where she was bussed as a participant in Boston's METCO program, which was created in the 1960s as part of the city's desegregation effort. "I can honestly say my last name will get me in the door because it's Abbott," Melanie recalls. "I had been on several interviews, and the person has come out and called the name, 'Melanie Abbott,' and they look across the room and I'm waving my hand and they look over me because you're not expecting to see a Black woman."

Melanie's life did not continue on a conventional path, though. She became a single mother at eighteen and was incarcerated in her mid-twenties. When she came out of prison at the age of twenty-eight, Melanie realized that she would have to rearrange her biography if she was going to find a job. When presenting herself to hiring managers, she took to downplaying—or sometimes hiding—her work experience and education, to appear closer to what she thought they were looking for. Melanie worried that if she disclosed the full range of her human capital, an interviewer could conclude Melanie was too high up the ladder to truly be interested in the job at hand. She might genuinely want the position, but no one was going to believe her unless her demeanor communicated personal qualities that were attractive.

> When I first got out and started looking for a job unemployment was low; they're always hiring.... Right, so it's not a problem getting the job; it's the kind of job, right. Getting the job ... I don't think has ever really been the problem. If you can sell [your story]. I mean you have to be able to be someone, or to appear ... to be someone, the [manager is] willing to be around for eight hours, or trust to be around for eight hours. You want to appear pleasant enough to do that and show that you can have the ability to do the job that you're showing up to do.

Melanie has heard from other returning citizens who have not been able to modulate this way and, as a result, they are jobless. "I know a couple of people who are experiencing [this]," she said, with a touch of anxiety. The only way to avoid this unfortunate outcome, she says, is to dumb down the credentials.

> You have to put yourself in the seat of the employer. And when you [as a jobseeker] say that you'll do anything ... that's not necessarily true, right? Because people want an employee that's going to be there for a while. So, this employer knows that if something else comes along, you're gone. Like

any [job] above this [level], right? . . . So it's just a waste of [their] time [as an employer] because by the time the paperwork dries you're out of there. . . . So don't apply. Or if you are, do not bring the MBA résumé [for a job that doesn't require an advanced degree]. Meet the job that you're showing up for, and only that job. Okay, so if you're just . . . going to a base-level job, have a base-level résumé.

Instead of reaping any benefits from higher education or professional work experience, Melanie explains, applicants must be careful not to over-shadow the interviewer. The decisionmaker on the other side of the table will take offense if the jobseeker seems socially or educationally superior.

You have to be mindful of your presentation because you can appear conde-scending. . . . You have to be self-aware, so that you can give off the impres-sion that will benefit you. Everything you do has to be about the result, and not how good it makes *you* feel. It may make you feel good to talk to someone, [as if you are on] their level, but if it doesn't benefit you, I don't advise it.

Applicants need to put hiring managers at ease, Melanie explains, es-pecially once a criminal background and prison time comes into the mix. Returning citizens must work overtime to calm managerial anxieties and try to normalize themselves, making it clear that they are not threatening. "In a calm manner, . . . [you need to] sell them what they're looking for," Melanie notes. And the rest? Leave it! She continues:

You may have all these other skills and everything but sometimes we can overwhelm an employer. And if you're overwhelming at an interview, how would you be on a daily basis?
 . . . A lot of people don't understand what it is, incarceration. For some people, I mean, they have a vision of what that is. Right? It might come with some unpredictability they feel, or some volatility. Or [they might think] someone else would [find out] and how would my customer or clients feel? Or other employees? . . . When we're sitting in that chair, we have a big responsibility to change the narrative about what postincarcerated people look like.

A staple item in the curriculum of prison pre-release programs takes inmates through the process of deciding how to divulge their criminal past. Melanie believes the best approach is to limit disclosure as much as possible, confine the potential damage to HR files that, she hopes, few people in the organizational chain of command consult. In other words: turn the problem into paperwork and assume the universal distaste for bureaucracy will leave that CORI gathering dust.

But how does a person account for a big blank spot in her résumé? How can they explain what they were doing with all that time? Melanie is clear that she should never lie. But she also recommends learning how to tell a version of the truth that sidesteps the stigmatizing damage of a prison term and embraces a middle-class concept: time out to "consider one's options." She explains: "When I was sitting across from [an interviewer], I would sometimes say that I was afforded an opportunity to step away from my life, not burdened with financial responsibility and reflect on some things and make some changes." She readily admits that this strategy is more likely to work for women than men, since women frequently step in and out of the workforce. "I can only think what people are imagining," she says with a slight smile, "because incarceration's not in the story yet. So they're automatically assuming there's some Prince Charming footing the bill, right?"

Melanie's strategy works better for people who can point to some tangible form of self-improvement following this period of introspection. That's how Melanie ended up going back to school after she was released from prison. And like many unemployed people who return to college to transition to a new career, Melanie went back to school to scrub her identity. She could honestly describe herself as an adult student, working hard to learn new skills after a vague hiatus. And this is not just for show; Melanie genuinely believes that more schooling makes a difference. Her advice to others in her situation is to be brutally clear with yourself about your virtues and your limitations, then find an educational program. As she explains it:

> Look at where you are, honestly, like your education level.... Find the high point in your [life], and if that's not enough to sustain you, then you need to work on what will. School right now is the way to go, I think, for anyone postincarceration.
>
> A lot of people who go into prison aren't job ready, right, so you don't necessarily come out job ready.... Those who go in, ill-equipped, who don't read very well, don't articulate very well. It doesn't get easier coming out.

Those are the things that need to be addressed first....A lot of people that I've run into who are just getting out, their language is still very street, and they don't turn it off very well. There's this disconnect [between] what a job or employer is looking for and how you're moving through the world.

A stint in school provides more education. But it also transforms the unemployed—whether returning citizen or not—from their undesirable status quo into the culturally positive identity of a student. School helped Melanie change the subject from that five-year gap that was prison. "I started applying [for work] immediately [after getting out]," she says, "but I really needed to get some filler for my résumé. I needed to enroll in college, so I can at least say I'm a student, right. So there's something that's there, it's tangible, I'm doing something."

That symbolic role shift, from the cultural identity of "ex-con" to that of "college student," helped Melanie land a job in a temp agency working as a customer service representative for a home security company. The job wasn't what she wanted long term, mainly because it didn't pay well and was repetitive work. But it was a start. And she knew exactly how to parlay that start into something a bit more elevated: "I fancied it up, I called myself a 'tech support, technician'...really pretty words. Then I added some organizations that I had been on the advisory board for... and those types of things, to pad the résumé." With these biographical embellishments—a job in hand, college enrollment—in good order, Melanie set her sights on better jobs in institutions that had made public commitments to open themselves to returning citizens.

"I interviewed for fifteen different positions," she recalls. "I did not give up." Her perseverance paid off. Melanie landed exactly the kind of job she had been hoping for, working in an administrative role in a local college. The job is secure, it pays reasonably well, and allows Melanie to spend her days doing work she enjoys among people who treat her with dignity and respect. She attributes this happy ending to her clear-eyed, strategic understanding of what one must do to repair a broken biography, as well as her tenacious personality.

I kept reworking that résumé and changing...because at first I had like customer service tech and things of that nature, but I did the language, and just didn't give up....I don't believe that I would have been able to get that position had I left that five-year block [blank on my résumé], had I not been employed, or had I not had said that I was a full-time student. Yeah, you have to be in the game to be in the game.

BARRIERS TO WORK

How large is the pool of jobseekers that sit on the margins of the labor market? It is not a small number. The most common reason for being excluded from job opportunities is prior unemployment—it is easier to get a job if you have a job.[14] And the longer someone remains unemployed, the harder it is to get back to work.[15] In interviews, recruiters list multiple barriers—age bias, success bias, underqualification bias—all of which keep people who are unemployed out of the workforce.[16] Returning citizens like Sam and Melanie are special cases in a much larger population of people who have less than the usual qualifications. Most prison inmates are more like Sam—poorly educated with few formally recognized skills—than they are like Melanie. If a job requires physical strength and stamina, as jobs in construction and salvage do, men are more likely to find their way in. But if the job requires computer skills, returning citizens are less likely to be equipped for them.

Conventional economic theories of human capital account easily for this kind of "deficit" explanation for unemployment. A low-skilled adult—someone with no formal credentials, no recent job experience, and no references—will drop to the bottom of the queue, whether or not they have been behind bars. If the job queue shrinks, as it does when labor markets are tight, employers' demand for workers rises, and people like Sam will have a better chance. But skill will be a limiting factor and rising high enough to earn a living wage will be a challenge. At least that's the theory. In practice, very skilled and highly educated people can be hard to place as well. Melanie was highly strategic in finding her place in the sociocultural order that shapes labor market opportunity—she realized that going back to college was an essential strategy for changing her public identity. But acquiring more education and elevated credentials doesn't always work, even in tight labor markets.

Mark Davies is a regular volunteer in the municipal office that advocates for the unemployed. He has had almost no luck finding conventional employment and hence has time on his hands and feels restless. Mark is the kind of man who is accustomed to being occupied; he craves the structure of a job to organize his day. Working in the municipal office provides that backbone. And while it doesn't pay him for his time, the mission-driven work wards off some of the frustration Mark feels after days of job searching that result in nothing more than the sound of doors slamming in his face. Unlike Sam, whose adolescence unfolded in what we used to call "reform school," Mark grew up in a much more stable household. Like Melanie, his family hails from Dorchester, a storied Boston neighborhood composed of triple-decker houses once filled with the Irish Catholic working class.

While a student at Northeastern University, then a commuter school of aspiring business students, Mark earned his way through college as a bartender in the Prudential Center, a fixture of the downtown commercial district. A fellow worker at the Ground—a bar popular with business types—had started a limousine service in the high-flying 1980s. Mark quit Northeastern, went to work full-time in the limo trade as a part-owner of the business, and rode the party economy of the 1980s until 1987, when he decided to sell the enterprise and return to school. Happily for Mark (and unhappily for the new owners of his limo business), the transaction cleared only two days ahead of the Black Monday stock market crash—and the end of limo-riding for many devastated financiers.

The proceeds of the sale went to paying Mark's Northeastern tuition, which was just as well since it turned out his parents were actually quite serious when they told him they would not cover the cost of college if he dropped out to run the limo company. Northeastern's co-op program, which enabled students to interweave paid employment with semesters of classes, made it possible for Mark to pay the rent. He worked for an accounting firm, and when he was filling out job applications while on the job, one of the firm's managing partners offered him a position. "I loved the work...and the people that I worked with," he says. Mark was on his way to a professional career. And although there were some ups and downs along the way, eventually Mark ended up with a good Boston accounting firm that was in the early stages of building up its client list and cementing a reputation as a relatively large regional firm of a hundred employees.

By 2002, Mark was senior enough to be named a partner in the firm. The celebration was not long-lived though, as a struggle broke out over whether the firm should merge with another company—something Mark thought was ill-advised. Rather than provoke a nasty internal battle, he reached an agreement to break free and bring all of the accountants in his practice group with him, along with their open cases. "I started my new firm in January of 2003," Mark recalls, "and, boy, it was great. It was so much fun. I ran the firm for about ten years, and we grew from three to thirty-six employees, and we worked all over the world."

Mark is not eager to review the circumstances of his fall from grace. He speaks vaguely of mistakes that were made during periods when he was on the road. Being away wasn't good for the company and didn't enhance his marriage either. Both began to fall apart and "things were done" as well as "things [he] did" that put the firm into a tailspin and forced Mark to sell off chunks of the practice. Mark left "[his] baby" in 2010 and turned to teaching to make a living. But an acrimonious divorce and a business careening downhill set the stage for his downfall. In December 2016, Mark was indicted for submitting a false tax return. It does not get much worse for a CPA.

> You don't mess with the Feds. They don't actually have to prove intent under the federal law and so my attorney just said, 'Listen, they're gonna put your accountant up on the stand and they're going to say, Look, you're a CPA, you should know better. You should've done this. You knew exactly what you were doing is what they're going to imply, and, your accountant, while he's already told them that you would never do … something like this intentionally, … they're going to have him up on the stand, they're going to ask him questions.' Ultimately my attorney convinced me that the best thing to do was to plead guilty.

Mark was mortified to be publicly deemed a fraud, especially within earshot of his fellow accountants. Many of them rallied around him; he provided the sentencing judge with sixty letters of support attesting to his philanthropy, community engagement, and future potential. Just about everyone he knew, with the exception of his ex-wife, swung behind him. Nonetheless, tax evasion is a crime, and Mark had to pay. He spent more than a year in jail, about seven weeks in home confinement with an electronic bracelet around his ankle, and a year on probation.

If education and experience were the main predictors of success in the search for employment, Sam should have taken a long time to land a job and Mark would have been snapped up in a hot minute. Instead, the reverse has been the case. Sam barely had time to unpack his bags before a roaring labor market generated a full-time job. Mark has searched everywhere and by every means—paper applications, online job boards, referrals by the municipal office, tips from friends—and has come up with almost nothing in the same low-unemployment environment. He has cobbled together some online tutoring jobs for Chinese students trying to master English and for accounting students needing pointers as they prepare for certification exams. But none of this could be called steady work.

Andrew Walton, the director of the municipal office that supports the formerly incarcerated, is pulling for Mark. He gives him as many leads as he can for jobs with the City of Boston, nonprofit positions, and the private sector opportunities he hears about. But they recognize that Mark is a living, breathing social contradiction: the well-educated felon. That anomaly seems to overwhelm hiring managers, even when they are searching high and low for workers. "Andrew likes to say to me 'Now you know what it feels like to be a Black man,'" Mark notes ruefully. "Because the door gets slammed in my face more often because they look at my résumé and they say, 'Here's a middle-aged, overeducated, nonaddict, privileged white guy.'...When somebody looks at my résumé, they say, 'Alright, here's a former CPA, a person who comes from academia, who comes from running an organization and building organizations.'"

Mark doesn't fit any of the categories on either side of the legal divide. He is no longer a respected professional with credentials to match, nor does he fit into the profile of a convict. Because he is strapped for cash, Mark applies diligently for every kind of job—from those for which he has the "right" education and experience to entry-level service jobs for which he is vastly overqualified. Because the ban-the-box policy prohibits hiring managers from asking about criminal records up front, he generally gets an interview. Indeed, Mark gets far enough that his spirits momentarily rise. But where Melanie has managed to parlay her additional education into a job she loves, for Mark the music stops right at the threshold.

Same things with the hospitals, Mass General, Brigham, Beth Israel. Deaconess. They all say that...they're "CORI-friendly." But their idea of "CORI-friendly" is food service, which frankly, if it gives me benefits and it puts me in a position then great. But I understand the hiring manager's concern: here's a guy who would like to take a just-above entry-level position. He's not gonna last very long.

At least initially the suspicion arises not from his criminal history, since at the early stages of an interview, employers are not aware that he has one. It derives from the disconnect between the job he is after and the educational qualifications and employment history on his résumé. The overshoot alerts the interviewer that something isn't quite right here.

Repeated failure to land anything has pushed Mark back to short-term, transactional work in the form of tutoring. He says:

So that actually worked out pretty well for a while. The challenge...is that it's cyclical. Kids all of a sudden realize that they're not doing really well in their accounting class and their final's coming up at the beginning of December and then realizing that they better get in gear. So it's really busy from November till the second week in December and then it dies down until classes start back up.

Since no one pays him for the down time, Mark had to look for other teaching opportunities. He found one through a local university program that specifically caters to students behind bars and returning citizens who, like Mark, are trying to launch themselves in new directions. Participants must have a GED or a high school diploma and are recommended via the offices of nonprofits and jail-based education programs that are trying to encourage further education. The Suffolk County Sheriff's Department recommends people for these positions, as does the Benedictine Fellowship's Care After program. The university enables these students to gain twelve credits of college courses at no charge, which is a significant pro-bono contribution.

Mark gets a small salary for teaching in this program, and he finds teaching rewarding. But it is piecework and does not cover the cost of living. What he needs is a full-time job with benefits—yet that type of employment is precisely what has proven out of reach, even though tight labor markets have opened doors for others who have less education or work experience. Most frustrating to Mark is the sharp contrast between the

public pronouncements of support for returning citizens and the lived realities of searching for work. "In these times today... everybody likes to say
they are... 'CORI friendly,'" Mark notes. "They [say they want to] stand up
for racial justice and social injustice, [and so forth], but it's all bullshit."

Are these liberals just disingenuous? Making welcoming noises without
any intention of following through? It is very hard for Mark to distinguish
those who are just offering lip service from those who really do try to help
but face a set of brick walls when they try to hire someone like Mark.

> People say stuff that they can't carry through. I interviewed with... an area
> hospital that maintained that they were CORI-friendly.... I sent my résumé
> off to the HR person, right away she calls and says, 'All right! Another per-
> son from Dorchester—I love it,' she said, 'I grew up in Dorchester!'... We
> were just talking about some small stuff and then she invited me in [for an
> interview].... This is October of last year. And so I sat down with her, had a
> very frank, transparent conversation. She was super supportive. I interview
> for the manager of internal audit position.... And then they squash it. And
> the reason they gave me was that at the time I was on probation, and you
> can't be on probation. They consider that you are still serving part of your
> sentence in their [in air-quotes] "CORI-friendly" program.

Taking this setback at face-value, Mark waited until he was officially
done with probation, six months later. He contacted the hospital HR department, leaning on the goodwill of a reference with some influence in
the organization to open doors.

> I contacted them again in May, they put a whole bunch more conditions on
> there. Made it nearly impossible for me to get. My friend Leslie at Human
> Resources, she said, "Look, about the only thing that you're going to qualify
> for, because you don't have health, you don't have health service or health
> administration experience positions," she said. "Basically, what they've set it
> up for is never going to be an entry-level position because of your qualifica-
> tions, your age, everything else."... She's being very frank with me. She said,
> "You know, you can push them off or... or you can work in food service."
> And she said, "but even that I'm not so sure."

MARGINALIZED WORKERS AND JOB QUEUES

Theoretically the labor market is structured as a ladder. At the bottom are
the least-complex jobs, positions that require no education or experience.

At the top are the brain surgeons and the rocket scientists. Workers are similarly arrayed on the ladder, from high school dropouts to postdoctoral scholars, complemented by job experience ranging from none to decades upon decades.

The internal dimensions of job queues—the way they cut off toward the top and the bottom—leaves thousands who could easily handle the work, out of the picture. The labor market is less a long ladder than a set of rubber bands with varying degrees of stretch. At the center of each band is a kind of "ideal" employee, the person a hiring manager has in mind for a position, who fits the sociological type. When unemployment is high, those bands have very little give because they don't have to stretch to find someone who fits the standard of the "ideal worker."[17] When relatively few people are pounding the pavement, the bands loosen up and stretch farther. But there are people, like Mark, who are simply past the point of accommodation, beyond the elasticity of that band. And while a criminal record will make it much harder—particularly an ethically loaded charge like tax evasion for a certified public accountant—it is important to recognize that more than that is standing between Mark and a job. He exemplifies a more general social anomaly: overqualified, burdened, and "over the hill."

Why was Melanie able to get this far while Mark has zeroed out? Is it because she is a woman—and therefore perhaps less likely to be saddled with the cultural baggage that a prison record loads on the back of a man? Is it because the sight of an educationally privileged white man violates racial stereotypes about who ends up in jail and hence marks Mark as far more deviant?[18] Or is it because Melanie had a plan to characterize herself in ways that matched the expectations on the other side of the table and stuck to it, while Mark lacked a similar strategy? Hard to say.

CONCLUSION

What we learn from these journeys toward employment is that people with damaged biographies—whether from long periods of unemployment or drug addiction—face steep odds against finding good jobs. But in tight labor markets, they are more likely to find work of some kind, because the demand is there and the supply is not, or at least not in as plentiful quantities as employers need. Even Mark is working—just not as much as he would like, not in the type of job he believes he is qualified to do, and for neither the wages nor the benefits that he enjoyed as a matter of course prior to his fall from grace. But we should not kid ourselves that upward mobility for those marked by incarceration and misfortune is an easy quest. Neither should we expect that when unemployment returns to "normal" levels, returning citizens are easily able to bust through the walls that a prison record erects around them.

It is only when unemployment dips *very* low that employers learn to look past these highly constraining stereotypes. That is what happened in Massachusetts and many other parts of the United States in 2018 through 2020. In North Carolina, when there were 2.5 jobseekers for every open position (compared to 3.8 jobseekers, which is more of an average benchmark), returning citizens saw an uptick in their employment rates and wages. In 2009, in the midst of the recession, only 30 percent of people in North Carolina who were released from prison found a job within the next year, but that number increased by 9 percentage points as the economy began to recover. By 2014, 39 percent of returning citizens were employed within a year.[19]

The farther out from the end of their prison sentences, the more likely North Carolina's returning citizens were to find work. But the overall numbers are still low and need to move up if we are to see the majority of these marginal applicants join the workforce and stay there. When they do, the results can be very positive. For example, military enlistees with criminal records are promoted especially quickly; call center workers with criminal records have longer tenure; and employers subject to ban-the-box see lower turnover.[20] In short, returning citizens, like other long-term unemployed jobseekers, can end up being a good bet for employers. Someone who gets a second chance knows how precarious that new life is, how easily they could have ended up out of luck. That is why so many go the extra mile, as Sam did back in his days on the night shift at Shaw's grocery store and Melanie has done in making a plan for her future. Looking around, Sam observed that the workers who had those jobs didn't particularly appreciate the opportunity and thought maybe they could do better. Sam knew he had something to prove, and he eclipsed all of them.

6 Declining Drama

In 2003, David Harding, then a doctoral student in sociology at Harvard, set out to understand how neighborhood conditions—joblessness, concentrated poverty, single-parent households—impacted the experience of adolescence in three Boston neighborhoods: Roxbury Crossing and Franklin, two high-poverty neighborhoods to the south of the city, and Lower Mills, a better-off predominantly Black community. Harding was looking to pin down a methodologically fraught and hence somewhat elusive force: neighborhood effects.[1] The concept is simple: how do poor individuals who are sociologically similar fare when they grow up in neighborhoods that differ in their composition? Above and beyond the struggles they encounter because of their own characteristics or family conditions, does it matter if they are surrounded by other households that are poor?

These questions are important because we want to know whether changes in a fundamental aspect of poor neighborhoods—the employment status of their residents—leads to other changes in the quality of a neighborhood's public life and the likely future trajectories of its residents. Harding was doing fieldwork at a point in time when unemployment was high and crime, especially violent crime, was a serious problem in Roxbury Crossing and Franklin. His book *Living the Drama* (2010) explores just how constricted the social worlds of adolescents was in those two neighborhoods when concentrated poverty and urban violence hemmed them in to the few places—blocks actually—where they could trust the people in their orbits.

Fast-forward some fifteen years, and we found these two communities significantly improved. The central question of this chapter is whether rising rates of employment in Franklin and Roxbury Crossing had anything to do with that positive outcome. If tight labor markets emerge in places where opportunity was sparse in the past and more people, especially more young men, are at work, does the atmosphere of their communities noticeably improve? Does residential stability increase? Do public spaces become less violent? Do young boys start to feel more at ease on the block, and thus less likely to gravitate toward older boys who protect but also entangle them in a negative spiral of illicit activity? Does crime go down because employment provides a substitutional income flow? Does violence decrease because strangers become increasingly willing to intervene when they see something amiss?

Neighborhoods can affect individuals' outcomes in several ways. They can shape their residents through socialization, as people learn the behaviors, styles, and languages of those who surround them.[2] Neighborhoods can also constrain people's opportunities. Underserved by institutions like schools and community organizations, residents of poor neighborhoods have less access to services. Cut off from more affluent communities, residents miss out on the opportunity to form the kind of social ties that might enable them to hear about job possibilities. Neighborhoods also affect individuals by virtue of the strength of internal solidarity, or what Harvard sociologist Robert Sampson calls "collective efficacy."[3]

Collective efficacy theory, rooted in research pioneered by James Coleman when describing schools, focuses on the impact of social networks, the ties that link people to others, carrying information, reinforcing social norms and values, and fostering cooperation, especially in times of need.[4] In Sampson's view, social capital consists of the actual or potential resources embedded in people's social relationships, and collective efficacy is the process of activating those relationships to generate a sense of trust and a bedrock of neighborhood stability.[5] Where people have something important to protect, something critical to invest in if they are to keep their surroundings livable, they will move to defend it if they have the right social resources. Sampson measured the strength of collective efficacy by asking survey respondents how likely they were to "intervene on behalf of the common good."[6] Would they interject, cautioning strangers about bad behavior, warning unrelated kids to stop acting out?

In Sampson's work it turned out that poverty per se did not predict willingness to step up: some poor communities were high in this kind of intervention behavior and others were low. But on average, crime subsided where collective efficacy was high. Ne'er-do-wells knew they would be denounced in neighborhoods defended by people willing to intervene with strangers and could get away with almost anything in zones that lacked these social expectations. But what drives collective efficacy? Sampson argues that it is strongest when residential stability (often via higher rates of homeownership) grows and declines with a growing proportion of female-headed households and concentrated poverty.[7] Like the literature on poverty more broadly, jobs are a crucial key to understanding dynamics of collective efficacy—but that employment story is often implicit, a prime mover in a long chain of conditions.

The factors associated with an increase in collective efficacy, and the benefits that flow from it, are all correlated with jobs: employment fosters stability, since households can afford rent or make the leap to homeownership. Stability increases the likelihood of interpersonal interaction and social trust, since people who stick around know their neighbors and watch out for them. More workers in a neighborhood means fewer idle people hang out on the streets—and fewer idle folks means less potential for trouble. Jobs (and the income they provide) reduce insecurity and tension—people are better able to pay their bills and worry less, which increases the likelihood they will have the emotional bandwidth to bond with neighbors and foster the well-being of their children. The factors that diminish collective efficacy are, conversely, correlated with a lack of employment opportunities: single parents with inadequate income, housing instability, idle men on the streets, and concentrated poverty all increase when jobs are not available.

POVERTY IN THREE BOSTON NEIGHBORHOODS

The problem of "concentrated poverty" came to the fore in the 1970s, when the suburbanization of white-collar jobs intersected with housing segregation to create a "spatial mismatch" that excluded low-wage work-ers in urban centers from the kind of high-quality, stable job opportuni-ties that might facilitate upward mobility.[8] "The concentration of poverty," Paul Jargowsky explained "[means the] poor not only have to cope with their [own] poverty but also that of those around them."[9] Between 1970 and 1990 the number of people living in neighborhoods where more than 40 percent of the households fell below the poverty line increased dra-matically, from nearly two million to nearly four million.[10] This kind of concentrated poverty has "an independent effect on social and economic outcomes of individuals" over and above their own characteristics—these impacts are known as neighborhood effects.[11] Higher rates of poverty in one's childhood neighborhood translate into lower social mobility over the life course, even when people move away from the place where they spent their childhood.[12]

Harding's contribution to the study of neighborhood effects several de-cades later focused on the ways in which growing up in poor and violent places influence the attitudes young men have toward school and roman-tic relationships. In *Living the Drama* he homed in on these outcomes because young people who experience difficulty in school and are then prone to dropping out, are at risk for a life of poverty since workers with-out a diploma suffer lifelong earnings losses. Romance (or perhaps just sexual relationships) between teens has its own consequences in the form of early pregnancy, which is also associated with long-term disadvantage for young parents and their children.

Harding was at pains to point out that poor neighborhoods are not cultural monoliths.[13] In this, he was swimming against the tide since por-traits of the "inner city" were rife with descriptions of social isolation and oppositional norms. The stereotypes drew portraits of kids who don't care about school, know nothing about the work world, are attracted to the drug trade, and have casual sexual relations all the time.

A more accurate representation of life in poor neighborhoods would have pointed to the many families leading conventional lives: working parents, kids who graduate from high school and go on to college, and churchgoing elders. Harding interviewed many parents who were quite traditional in their values and behavior and worked hard to protect their children from influences they regarded as negative. These examples of "upstanding" families were visible and known throughout the neighbor-hoods he studied. Accordingly, Harding argued, what is unique about neighborhoods of concentrated poverty is that they are zones of "cultural heterogeneity," where young people are presented with *conflicting* models of appropriate behavior. The problematic side of inner-city life is there and in greater concentration than in more middle-class communities. But even in the most rundown neighborhood, trouble is never there by itself. People choose, sometimes daily, between conflicting and competing tem-plates for social behavior.

Here Harding makes a critical observation about the conditions that expose young boys to more deviance and magnify its power. Violence is at the heart of the matter. Adolescents who live in poor communities that are plagued by guns and knives, assaults, and robberies, find their social worlds shrinking. Staying inside a tight-knit circle assures some degree of protection from the aggressive, threatening force of rivals. The more intense the violence, the smaller the geography within which a young man feels secure. It may come down to one block. Inside those vigilant, anxious cocoons, a young boy finds more sophisticated adolescent guard-ians. Those older boys keep watch, menace outsiders, and ward them off. Because they are older—often in their late teens and early twenties—the guardians are more practiced in behaviors that are not appropriate for their younger counterparts. Sexual experience is prevalent, prized, and the subject of much casual banter. To the degree the guardians are hanging on the corner, they are almost by definition less attached to school and employment. These "cool" older adolescents carry cultural weight. They model what the heart of adolescence is supposed to look like.

Their example stands in contrast to the more conventional men and women in the same communities who go to work every day: the plumb-ers and electricians, clerks and school teachers. But in those communi-ties where violence is an issue—which is, by no means, all poor neigh-borhoods—a young man's world contracts. He is spending time with his guardians and the presence or influence of more conventional role models is more contested and therefore weaker. The "corner boys" wield outsized influence.[14]

Contrast this portrait of adolescent life to typical Black middle-class neighborhoods in which physical violence from peers plays a minimal to nonexistent role in shaping daily life.[15] Young men can move about freely from home to school, from the local baseball field to the pizza shop. Setting aside the troubling rise in police shootings, which is a crisis for Black teens, middle-class boys do not have to look over their shoulders constantly or are less likely to worry about whether they might be gunned down by gang members a block from home.[16] That freedom means that more affluent Black youth can associate with whomever they please, subject to the usual competitive landscape of adolescence. Their lives are geographically fluid and filled with social discretion. In general, middle-class adolescents, no matter what their race, cleave to age-bounded friendship groups. High school seniors turn their noses up at freshmen; juniors are miles ahead of sophomores in social currency. Every year conveys advantage, and while dating relationships breach these age boundaries—as they do in later life as men typically marry slightly younger women—for middle-class teens, even a year makes a difference in who could be a friend.

While the sexual exploits and general social cachet of an older boy carries weight in both settings, the degree of daily contact is significantly different. In a neighborhood beset by violence, an eleven-year-old boy is likely to keep company with sixteen- and seventeen-year-olds, a pattern that would be almost unthinkable in an affluent neighborhood. Harding found that these age heterogeneous ties made a huge difference in shaping social norms: young boys know well what lies ahead years before they could be involved in relations with the opposite sex. They can see, by example, the scorn for school common among dropouts. In Lower Mills, the more affluent Black community Harding studied, adolescent boys stuck to their age peers and were not exposed to these influences any more than everyone sees in television or social media. But in Franklin and Roxbury Crossing, which were notoriously gang-ridden communities in the past, young boys and older boys were in each other's business every day. That, Harding concluded, creates a transmission belt for behavior that multiplies the risk of bad outcomes.

These are conditional or probabilistic possibilities. Some parents in Franklin pull their children indoors and forbid them to hang on the corner; they take them to church; and empower grandmothers to keep them in check while their mothers and fathers are at work. Some Roxbury Crossing families enrolled their children in after-school programs and sought out the most positive mentors they could find to help young men stay the course. Indeed, Harding found that many parents responded to his neighborhood flyer asking to interview young boys because they wanted their sons to spend time with a Harvard graduate student. That opportunity doesn't happen often in these poor neighborhoods. Hoping for a positive influence, these parents seized the day.

But other families cannot exercise this level of vigilance and cannot segregate young boys from the influences of older adolescents who both protect them and expose them to negative social influences that are beyond their years. There is variation and heterogeneity in role models everywhere—but there is also a higher likelihood of bad outcomes where violence tightens social circles, reduces the geography of social contacts, and hence increases the density of interaction between young boys and older ones who are hanging out, as opposed to the ones who are in high school or at work.

Harding could establish the veracity of these divergent pathways because he was able to interview boys and their parents or grandparent caretakers who shared certain individual characteristics (especially household income) but lived in neighborhoods that varied in the aggregate. All three of the communities Harding observed were predominantly Black, but that's where the similarities ended. In 2000, Roxbury Crossing had a high family poverty rate of 36 percent and Franklin was neck-and-neck, with 36 percent of the families below the poverty line. But Lower Mills was only 10 percent poor.

Not surprising, homeownership rates tracked family poverty. More than half of families in Lower Mills lived in homes that belonged to them. Only 6 percent of Roxbury Crossing families were homeowners. This matters for neighborhood stability as renters are a far more mobile population. When people stay put in a community, they invest in the physical appearance of their homes, create durable relations with their neighbors, are more likely to intervene when trouble arises on the street. They have something important to preserve, which has the added benefit of providing more security for residents. But neighborhoods of homeowners who live above the poverty line face fewer disturbances in the first place: they are lower in crime and in general disorder. Young people are not tightly constrained and do not need to seek protection from older adolescents. There simply isn't as much to be protected from.

Other features that differ between Harding's neighborhoods mattered as well. For example, 35 percent of Roxbury adults had less than a high school education; 38 percent of Franklin adults also lacked a diploma.[17] In Lower Mills, however, only 20 percent had not graduated from high school. Female-headed families were the norm in Roxbury (69 percent) and Franklin (65 percent). Over in Lower Mills, meanwhile, the comparable figure was 41 percent. Low levels of educational attainment and single-parent households are typical features of poor neighborhoods because they define the sociological conditions that lead to poverty. High school dropouts earn less over the lifetime and are locked out of professional jobs and the salaries that go with them.[18] Female-headed households, and households with single incomes generally, are at much higher risk of being poor.

Arguably, though, the most important feature that distinguishes poor neighborhoods from more advantaged communities is male joblessness.[19] Although many poor Americans work in jobs that pay too little to pull above the poverty line, without employment a man is almost destined to fall below it. And the families of jobless men are at great risk of poverty. The marked difference between Franklin and Roxbury on the one hand and Lower Mills on the other on this score were notable. In the 2000 census, for example, fully 45 percent of Franklin's adult men were without work; Roxbury Crossing was even worse: 51 percent were jobless. Over in Lower Mills, however, the figures were far less troubling: fewer than 30 percent of its men lacked employment. Median household income tracked these numbers. On average, Lower Mills households had twice the median income (nearly $44,000) than their counterparts in Roxbury Crossing ($15,371) and Franklin ($23,157).

The traditional literature on poverty closely connects joblessness to other neighborhood indicators, such as crime and single-parent households. Jobless men are said to make poor marriage partners, hence in communities where they are a large proportion of the population, single-parent households dominate.[20] Single parents are at much greater risk for income poverty and reliance on public assistance. Outcomes for children, from high-school graduation to teen pregnancy, are also more problematic. William Julius Wilson argued that the combination of social isolation—which Harding describes as a severe problem in Franklin (less so in Roxbury Crossing)—and joblessness means that young people growing up are not exposed to the conventional structure that the workday imposes on daily life.

This linkage has been contested, however. Indeed, Katherine Newman's *No Shame in My Game: The Working Poor in the Inner City* took issues with monolithic portraits of poor neighborhoods as chronically jobless. While 45 percent of Franklin's men were jobless (which is a huge problem), 55 percent were not. Who has a hold on the culture? On the values? On what kids see growing up? This is precisely the point that Harding made in insisting that we replace the classic monolithic model with one more closely characterized as a contested terrain. What kids see growing up is *both* models, but they experience much more of a tug of war—conventional behavior versus deviant behavior—and the burden is on them to choose and their families to try to shape those choices.

If we ask what makes joblessness so prevalent in poor neighborhoods, the answer comes back as another contested topic: is it structure or culture? Are men in Franklin or Roxbury Crossing out of work because they lack the desire or the skills to find employment? Or is the opportunity structure in front of them the culprit? In the early 1980s the Commonwealth of Massachusetts experienced a rapid tightening of its labor markets. It was a time of sustained economic growth, a remarkable recovery from a period of deindustrialization and high levels of unemployment. In 1975 the unemployment rate in the state was 12 percent; by 1981 it had dropped below 3 percent.[21] The "Massachusetts Miracle" inhaled thousands of people from the margins of the labor market.[22] As MIT Sloan School's Paul Osterman documented, young Black men, historically the least-favored jobseekers, found employment at record rates.[23] Latinx men flooded into the labor market as well.

The speed with which these employment effects rolled out casts doubt on the notion that culture is particularly important in explaining joblessness. Values, expectations, and social behavior do not change in the space of a few years. Skills can grow, of course. But as we learned in the chapter on employers, red-hot labor markets encourage employers to reduce the demands they make on jobseekers for education and experience. Competition gets so fraught that they turn to internal training to upskill their workers rather than depend on external institutions to provide the trained workers they need.

What tight labor markets do, fundamentally, is shift the opportunity structure in favor of workers, opening slots that were once closed to people who have been sitting on the margins of the work world.[24] That structural shift matters more than culture in an individual's life chances. Multiplying all those people times thousands, and we have neighborhoods that turn the corner away from deterioration and toward something of a renaissance. But they don't always stick. The positive conditions of the early 1980s were history twenty years later when Harding arrived to begin his fieldwork.

SOCIAL TRUST AND NEIGHBORHOOD STABILITY

In the earliest studies of "ghetto life," sociologists considered the atmospherics of public spaces, pointing to the power of class composition to shape the experience of walking down the street in poor communities. Ulf Hannerz, a Scandinavian researcher doing fieldwork in Washington, DC, in the 1960s, noted the tension in the air when racial segregation forced middle-class "mainstreamers" into close residential proximity with "swingers," their poor—and especially unmarried and young—neighbors and "street families." In his classic book *Soulside: Inquiries into Ghetto Culture and Community*, Hannerz describes the enmity that educated professionals had for the "swingers" who were hanging out, carrying alcohol in paper bags, smoking weed, and generally carrying on loudly.[25] No love lost here: class difference in the norms of public behavior created simmering strife.

The growth of the Black middle class from the 1960s onward, coupled with desegregation orders in schools and increasing pressures to prosecute racial discrimination in housing, led to the outmigration of the most affluent Black families and the growth of concentrated poverty among those left behind.[26] Of course, the outcomes were mixed, even for those who managed to leave. As Mary Pattillo's research in the 1990s in Chicago documented, often the class divide was resolved not by racial integration but by the emergence of nearly all-Black middle-class neighborhoods. In her book *Black Picket Fences*, Pattillo shows how the class heterogeneity in places like Soulside gave way to class homogeneity even when racial segregation persisted. Middle-class people living in the neighborhood Pattillo calls "Groveland" may have looked askance at the behavior of the next neighborhood over, but troubling behavior was now on the other side of a line. "Underclass" conduct might slip over that line from time to time, but it is marked as not belonging to the more conventional behavior expected in the Black community of Groveland.

But inside the poor neighborhoods, now bereft of the middle-class families once confined there by racial restrictions, street life was deteriorating. Without homeowners to look after their property, without the guiding influence of the "old heads" described so vividly by Eli Anderson in his research on Philadelphia ghettos, and with the rise of unemployment and the spread of the drug trade, social interaction in public became tense.[27] Social capital was eroding and, consequently, collective efficacy was weak.

But this erosion of collective efficacy did not impact every poor community. Mario Small examined how social capital can surge, even in a neighborhood where low-wage work and unemployment prevail. A graduate student at Harvard in the same era as Harding, Small studied Villa Victoria in Boston's South End, a Puerto Rican neighborhood that was threatened with displacement when urban renewal projects were proposed to clear the way for more upscale residential development.[28]

Most poor communities buckled under this kind of pressure and disappeared. Indeed, Herbert Gans's *Urban Villagers* recounts the total evaporation of Boston's West End, a working-class Catholic neighborhood that melted away in the face of urban renewal. Those urban villagers disappeared from the West End, but the residents of Villa Victoria stood their ground. They organized, protested, and created an incredible ruckus. And they won. This community of first- and second-generation Puerto Rican migrants, with very little formal education, defeated development interests and the community remained intact, even as the streets around them gentrified. This activism forged lasting social ties, burnished them in the heat of battle, and led to a network of leaders (and followers) who knew all too well what they had to protect. It was the external threat that activated social capital, and in turn, willingness to intervene when trouble is brewing on the streets. Looking back at Sampson's original maps of Chicago, a glimmer of the same observation is evident. Some of the highest levels of collective efficacy are found in the neighborhood of Hegewisch, which successfully resisted Mayor Richard Daley's proposal to build a third Chicago airport on that site.

The link between social capital, collective efficacy, and unemployment is not well-explored in any of these foundational books. Neighborhoods are often described by drawing on employment data, but the theoretical link is rarely made.[29] We know that poverty and employment are connected, but is social trust wedded to employment? As least as a first approximation, social capital is visibly tied to residential stability because it is hard to generate and maintain bonds and bridges when the parties are in constant flux. And residential stability is clearly enhanced by homeownership, which is in turn far more common in places where employment is high and steady. It makes sense that there is a chain from one to the other, but it is less often explored.

We can look at the data and see that, at the very least, where we have high levels of employment, there are vastly higher levels of owner-occupied housing. Homeownership is not the only route to residential stability, however. Being able to pay the rent will also ensure a degree of stability. In Lower Mills, 61 percent of the residents were living in the same place in 2000 as they had been in 1995. In the poorer neighborhoods Harding studied, people moved around more, though not dramatically so: 59 percent of Franklin residents were there five years earlier, and 55 percent in Roxbury Crossing were longtime residents. Whether residents regard public housing as a necessary curse or a welcome perk, it too can produce high levels of residential stability: it is too valuable to let go, hence once awarded, families try to hold on to it. But when combined with high levels of unemployment, the stability of public housing doesn't produce the same outcomes as the residential stability one finds on owner-occupied blocks. The combination of stability and employment means that public life in Lower Mills was more orderly, violence-free, and liberated from the tension and anxiety that pervades the other two areas Harding describes.

There are fewer idle young men hanging out in Lower Mills, hence the public atmosphere is calm and untroubled. To the extent that crime rates are driven by lack of conventional job opportunities, Harding saw more of it in Roxbury Crossing and Franklin. Violence itself was basically not an issue in Lower Mills, while it dominated the lives of young boys in the poorer neighborhoods, who were constantly having to look over their shoulders and worry about whether they would be assaulted while walking to the store or down the corridors of their high schools. Their daily lives are fraught with low-level (and sometimes high-level) fear and the vigilance they must exercise, particularly when not in the company of older boys who "have their backs," is exhausting.

DID A RISING TIDE LIFT THESE BOATS?

Roxbury Crossing

Roxbury Crossing was a high-poverty area in the early 2000s, when David Harding first began doing fieldwork there. "Located on the border of [Boston's] gentrifying South End and the historically Black neighborhood of Roxbury," Harding recounts, "it is a study in contrasts and transitions."

> Along Washington Street, gleaming bus shelters with digital kiosks for the new Silver Line bus rapid transit system reside in the shadows of deteriorating buildings with shabby and barren-looking storefronts. Yet Roxbury Crossing is only blocks from renovated South End brownstones and some of [Boston's] most chic restaurants. Newly renovated Northeastern University buildings are visible from "the bricks," the local public housing developments that have seen only minor updates since their construction in the 1940s and early 1950s. . . . Roxbury Crossing is home to a unique blend of public, private, and cooperative housing. The Whittier Street public housing development, constructed in 1953, is a cluster of medium-rise brick buildings set in a no-man's land between a busy four-lane thoroughfare and the grounds of two public high schools. After especially heavy rains, a putrid marsh appears around the development's cheery blue and gold Boston Housing Authority sign. The area in the center of the buildings, once a playground, is now a patch of dirt and concrete, all that remains of a renovation stopped midstream when funds dried up. Inside are overheated apartments with cinder-block walls and noisy, smelly stairwells.[30]

One feature of low-income neighborhoods that received a lot of attention, beginning with *The Truly Disadvantaged*, was social isolation. It's relevant to Harding's work because the influence of older boys on the normative orientations of their younger followers is strongest where other moderating forces lack the strength to break through. From Wilson's work on, though, the assumption has been that poor neighborhoods are almost by definition socially separated from the more fortunate, thus cutting off the development of social networks that carry vital information about jobs, schools, and the like. Concentrated poverty was also associated with organizational deserts: the absence of institutions that provide support, employment, and connections to the wider world of the city.[31]

But is every poor neighborhood socially isolated? Roxbury Crossing, Harding tells us, was not. It is adjacent to subway lines and a major bus terminal. There are universities and medical centers, public high schools and community colleges, and many nonprofit institutions that serve the residents. Of course, physical proximity to institutions is not the same thing as seamless access. For instance, a Boys & Girls Club—which play a key anchoring role as community institutions for parents and children in many of these neighborhoods—can be physically nearby and still socially out of reach. Roxbury Crossing differed from Franklin on this dimension. It was at least superficially loaded with institutional vitality, which was simultaneously a sign of the city of Boston creeping south and an indigenous florescence.

People from Cape Verde, Puerto Rico, the Dominican Republic, Haiti, Mexico, and many other sending nations have long been attracted to Boston's labor market opportunities. In the years of Harding's fieldwork in the early 2000s, that flow began to register in Roxbury. By 2020 this diversity was a point of pride for Michelle Davis, the executive director of a prominent social service agency. She explains: "Roxbury was a predominantly Black and brown neighborhood when I started, and I'll say, you know, pretty much Black and Latino, but Black encompasses, you know, African Americans, Caribbean Americans, people from South America, Central America. People from the African diaspora.... I see Roxbury as this whole melting pot of different cultures. People [might] think Black people are monolithic when we're not." Roxbury Crossing experienced increasing diversity or—from the perspective of many African American residents—a dilution of ethnic uniformity in favor of uneasy competition over scarce resources, especially housing, as Harding explained: "The once overwhelmingly Black neighborhood now has a large population of Latinos particularly in the two public housing developments where, between 1993 and 2003, the resident composition shifted from majority Black to majority Latino."[32]

Map 2. Map of Roxbury

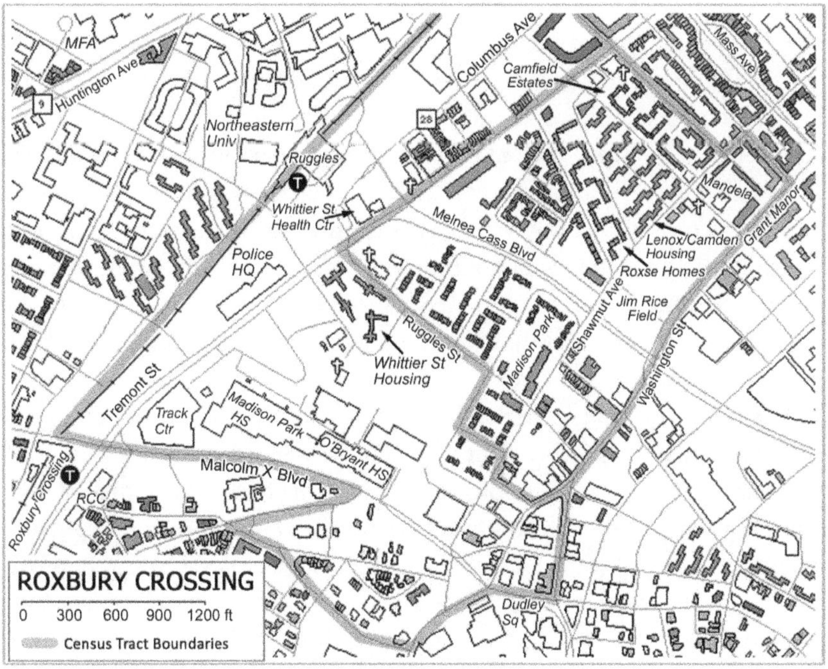

Source: Harding 2010.

In time, another symptom of urban growth began to register in Roxbury Crossing (map 2): the arrival of young, white, educated "pioneers" breaching Boston's traditionally high racial walls. Gentrification in Boston plays out on a stage backdropped by the city's role as the historical epicenter of resistance to school integration—especially during the angry controversies over school busing in the 1970s.[33] In the early 2000s white residents began moving south, propelled by overheated central city housing markets. As Harding noted, Roxbury Crossing was caught in a pincer movement: "Community activists see their neighborhoods as jeopardized both from gentrification, which threatens to displace residents from what is now highly valuable land near the center of a growing city, and from the violence and drugs that threaten to reverse the recent revitalization effort."[34]

In the years since Harding's work in the neighborhood, the composition of the residents has changed in some dramatic ways, including a sharp decline in the proportion of children, from 33 percent in 2000 to 19 percent in 2019, and a drop of one-third in the representation of Black residents, from 54 percent to 36 percent. The white population grew from a tiny minority in 2000 to one-fifth of residents in 2019. Despite these changes in the neighborhood's demographic composition, some characteristics have remained stable. Median household income in 2019 was roughly the same as it was in 2000, around $23,500 in 2020 dollars, although it took a dive in the post–Great Recession years from which it has since recovered. There is modest evidence of doubling-up: the rate at which grandparents are living in the household remains the same, at 3 percent, but there are substantially more household that include adult children: 12 percent today compared with only 3 percent in 2000.

Most notably, economic conditions have improved considerably: unemployment rates are down for men and women, and jobless rates—indicating the number of people out of the workforce—have dropped by more than 10 percentage points for nearly all groups, including men and women, Black and white adults; the decline for Hispanics was 6 percentage points. Reliance on public assistance declined, from 9 percent to 6 percent. Roxbury Crossing's residents were better educated; the community saw a sharp decline in the proportion over age twenty-five with less than a high school degree, from 35 percent to 23 percent, and a dramatic rise in the rate of college education. Associates degree holders jumped from 14 percent to 54 percent of the neighborhood, and 18 percent of residents have a four-year degree compared with only 10 percent in 2000.

But this good news is complicated by the rising cost of living in Roxbury Crossing. Although median incomes are level, the cost of housing has increased: only 63 percent pay less than $1,000 per month for housing today, compared with more than 90 percent in 2000. No doubt this helps to explain a dramatic increase in the presence of affluent families: only 4 percent earned more than $75,000 in 2000, compared with a striking 23 percent today. The very affluent population, earning more than $150,000, remains small, at 4 percent, but that is quadruple the size of their presence in the neighborhood in 2000. Is this evidence of gentrification, with wealthier people moving in and driving up the costs of housing for everyone else? Not necessarily. Census data suggests that at least some of these gains are accruing to people who already lived in the neighborhood:

a large and growing number of people report living in the same unit for more than five years, from 44 percent in 2000 to 67 percent in 2009 and 79 percent in 2019.

Franklin

If Roxbury was standing in the crosshairs of gentrification and urban displacement, Franklin was another story (map 3). Equally poor, Franklin's geography inclined it toward a more pronounced degree of social isolation, as Harding noted:

> The high poverty "Franklin" area is in the southwest corner of Dorchester on the Mattapan border. The geographic center of this area is the large open space that includes Franklin Field and Harambee Park. To the west is Franklin Park... and a buffer between Dorchester and the white parts of Jamaica Plain. Unlike Roxbury Crossing, Franklin is surrounded by other disadvantaged neighborhoods....
>
> Franklin has many signs of disorder and blight: trash-filled lots, boarded-up houses, abandoned cars, and dirty streets.... Young men loiter outside the local pizza joint and small grocery store.... Many small businesses line Blue Hill Avenue, and the residential areas are also dotted with small car repair and auto body shops, take outs and bodegas.[35]

Public housing developments in this area were built in the aftermath of the Second World War, as veterans came home to drastic housing shortages and the government responded by building publicly owned apartment buildings all over the country. In Franklin Field that construction was finally completed in 1954, and it was barely touched into the twenty-first century. Harding noted the struggle to find funding to improve the housing projects, mostly unsuccessful in his time:

> The Franklin Field housing development is a wide swath of low-rise brick buildings connected by winding streets and pedestrian pathways. The Franklin Hill housing development [is] located on the other side of Blue Hill Avenue. [Its] age is abundantly clear from the rusting clothesline poles relics of a previous era, that still occupy some parts of the main courtyard.... The Boston Housing Authority, which attempted to secure funding for redevelopment from HUD under the HOPE VI program in 2004, was unsuccessful in its bid.[36]

Map 3. Map of Franklin

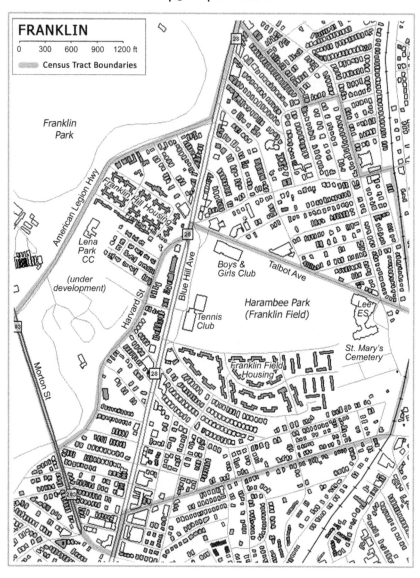

FRANKLIN

0   300   600   900   1200 ft

Census Tract Boundaries

Franklin
Park

American Legion Hwy

Franklin Hill Ave

Franklin Hill Housing

Lena
Park
CC

(under
development)

Harvard St

Blue Hill Ave

Morton St

28

28

28

203

Boys &
Girls Club

Talbot Ave

Tennis
Club

Harambee Park
(Franklin Field)

Franklin Field
Housing

Lee
ES

St. Mary's
Cemetery

Source: Harding 2010.

It was ultimately redeveloped, after Harding completed his fieldwork, and the 266 units were more connected to the surrounding neighborhood. Without a HOPE VI implementation grant, the redevelopment was funded by the Boston Redevelopment Authority, the City of Boston, and the Commonwealth of Massachusetts.

While Roxbury Crossing has seen a steady flow of Latinos and then white gentrifiers move into the area, Franklin's evolution moved in a different direction back in the late 1960s. In the three years between 1969 and 1971 these census tracts "changed rapidly from about 65 percent white to 90 percent Black." Franklin became a much poorer neighborhood. Isolation ripped through the social structure of the Franklin area, creating rival gangs—one centered in Franklin Field and the other up on Franklin Hill—that owned the turf on either side of the major thoroughfare that divided them. Drug wars, spurred by cheap and highly addictive crack cocaine, led the area to be labeled one of the most violent and dysfunctional communities in greater Boston, putting it on "the Boston police list of the city's worst 'hot spots' for violence."[37]

Franklin lacked the vibrancy and historical importance that Roxbury could boast. Major churches are anchored elsewhere. Public transportation is weak, leaving the residents less likely to find work opportunities in the city since accessing the subway is a chore. Even so, the neighborhood was starting to diversify, though not gentrify—during Harding's years. Because the housing in Franklin is inexpensive, immigrants began moving in during Harding's fieldwork years. As he wrote: "Haitians and West Indians are moving to the areas ... and Latinos are moving in from other parts of Dorchester and Roxbury."[38]

Social services, health clinics, and summer youth programs were all available and serving members of the Franklin community in the early 2000s. But the "youth centers supported by each housing development were closed after the Boston Housing Authority cut funding for teen centers across the city in 2002."[39] Although Roxbury and Franklin were both poor and largely Black communities in Harding's *Living the Drama*, Franklin was having a harder time sustaining the social institutions needed for a community to thrive. Like Roxbury, Franklin has seen some dramatic changes since 2000, but other things have remained the same. Most strikingly, the racial composition of the neighborhood has hardly budged: Black residents, who comprised 69 percent of Franklin in 2000, represent 68 percent of the neighborhood today; white people made up 1 percent of the neighborhood in 2000 and a mere 3 percent in 2019; and 25 percent of the neighborhood was Hispanic in both 2000 and 2019. Similarly, 19 percent of the households in Franklin in 2000 included married couples—the same rate we find in 2019.

But that consistency masks heterogeneity. The foreign-born population doubled, from 27 percent to 49 percent, in that same period, and the presence of adult children in the home tripled, from 5 percent to 15 percent. The presence of affluent families jumped by 20 percentage points, from 8 percent to 28 percent, and the presence of the very-affluent increased eightfold, from 1 percent to 8 percent—or one in twelve. The proportion of residents receiving public assistance fell by half, from 15 percent to 7 percent. And the presence of older people in the neighborhood nearly doubled, with the population over sixty-five growing from 6 percent to 11 percent.

Like Roxbury, Franklin saw promising changes in education and employment. The proportion of people over twenty-five with less than a high school degree fell from more than one-third to just one-fifth, and rates of associate's and bachelor's degrees increased substantially, although not to the same extent as in Roxbury. Unemployment declined for men, women, Black, white, and Hispanic jobseekers, dropping anywhere from 3 percentage points, for Black residents, to a dramatic 16 percentage points for white residents. Joblessness also declined dramatically, falling from at or above 50 percent for women, Black, and white residents to 40 percent and under for each of these groups. Also like Roxbury, Franklin's median income barely budged: it was $34,847 in 2000 and $36,542 in 2019, in 2020 dollars, compared with substantial income growth in Boston overall, where median incomes rose from around $59,500 to nearly $72,000 in 2020 dollars during the same period. And although rents increased substantially in Franklin—97 percent of residents paid less than $1,000 a month in 2000, compared with a mere 40 percent in 2019—the neighborhood is also exhibiting remarkable stability, with 80 percent of residents in 2019 reporting that they moved into their unit more than five years earlier.

CHARTING CHANGE FROM THE GROUND UP

Numbers tell us a lot, but they are not the whole story. In particular, descriptive statistics do not give us much purchase on the pathways between data points or the consequences of changing demographics. Most of all, they say nothing about how residents perceive change, attribute causality (whether they are right or not), or navigate the consequences. The leadership of nonprofit organizations and community centers in these two neighborhoods were particularly valuable sources of information for us as they were in Harding's *Living the Drama*. Many nonprofit directors had been in place for more than twenty years—and were more than willing to deliver their perspective of social change across the previous two decades. From these leaders we gained access to families living in these two communities now, and while few of them had a twenty-year longitudinal perspective, they are keen observers of the past decade, including the most recent period in which labor markets tightened up.

We learned from all these sources how multifaceted the social changes sweeping these neighborhoods has been. Growth in employment opportunities, they told us, played a key role in changing the social landscape of Roxbury Crossing and Franklin. But these trends unfolded alongside local migrations spurred by growing housing costs in central Boston and government-funded urban renewal programs that rearranged who lived where and broke up old social networks—some of which were none too savory—and introduced new interracial and intra-racial dynamics that were just on the horizon at the end of Harding's fieldwork.

Some might argue that this was all orchestrated in advance by city planning commissions that could see that real estate markets starting to broil in Boston's downtown and that began gearing up urban renewal projects, with the support of the federal government, to clear the way for gentrification.[40] Others would claim the opposite: that the evils of racial and economic segregation were understood by the policy descendants of the Great Society who seized the opportunity to enact a progressive agenda and set about creating conditions that would lift up poor, violent neighborhoods.[41] The two perspectives are not mutually exclusive, and the truth of the matter is not particularly consequential for our purposes.

What is important is that the ups and downs of the Boston labor market were interlaced with parallel transformations in the urban architecture and class composition of these neighborhoods.

Michelle Davis, introduced earlier in this chapter, has lived in Boston her entire life. Born in Roxbury, she spent her teen years in nearby Mattapan, when it was an almost entirely African American world. She is a pillar of the community, having served for twenty years as the executive director of a local after school club. Generations of Roxbury children have come of age under her watchful eye. Located in Roxbury's heart—Nubian Square—the club hosts one of the few swimming pools in the area and is a favorite choice for after-school programs, childcare for young children, and social activities for everyone in the neighborhood. Over the years Michelle has seen Roxbury cycle through terrible times—gangs duking it out in the housing projects, murder rates through the roof, children mugged on their way to school—and better times when these marks of despair began to wane, and people could come out from behind their protective shields. Her club has been an island of sanity and security for the community, no matter what the conditions on the street.

If asked what enabled Roxbury to turn the corner the first time—from the bad old days of gangbangers and street crime to a calmer, more stable existence—Michelle points to the transformation brought about by an ambitious redevelopment plan at Orchard Park, one of the city's most distressed housing developments.[42] A federal urban renewal grant envisioned a root-and-branch makeover through a HOPE VI grant from the Department of Housing and Urban Development. The story of its implementation, as told by the Boston Housing Authority (BHA), is instructive:

> Orchard Park was considered one of the most severely distressed developments in the BHA's portfolio. Its buildings were dilapidated, its name synonymous with crime, and its residents were isolated from everything around them. In fact, the distress at Orchard Park had spread into the surrounding neighborhoods and they, too, had fallen into a state of disrepair and abandonment.
>
> In 1996, Orchard Park was awarded a HOPE VI grant which provided an extraordinary opportunity to change the very nature of the neighborhood. The revitalization of Orchard Park was a catalyst for reuniting the disparate parts of Lower Roxbury, turning Orchard Park into a synergistic part of the community.[43]

In addition, the program includes a new school that has required a joint planning process between the BHA and the Boston School and Parks and Recreation Departments. The Boston School Department designed a new K–8 school, which was developed on a portion of the original public housing site. The school design and the new public streets contributed to the need to reconfigure the existing park.[44]

Apart from the promise of new dwellings that would replace the public housing that had deteriorated beyond salvation, the HOPE VI redevelopment process involved temporarily relocating the residents.[45] As Michelle explained, the displaced residents had several options:

> HOPE VI was supposed to do two things. One was to revitalize distressed public housing and give people in public housing an opportunity to get in the [private] housing market with Section 8 vouchers. For them to have choice. Because they knew they were going to have to displace so many people to renovate that, they did relocation offsite.
>
> So you had the option of returning [to Orchard Park] or the option of taking a Section 8 .... You're talking about—like three years, a little less than three years, and you're talking about a thousand families. You're talking about a lot of people that [BHA] needed to place [so that they could] excavate the whole site.
>
> And so they gave people the option of taking a Section 8 and never returning, or taking a Section 8 and that let us place you on relocation for you to return back.

The sorting process that saw some people stick and some depart was not random. As Michelle explained, it was the "underemployed, uneducated" who "lost their chances to come back" when the redevelopment was completed. Throwing a thousand families into the housing market was bound to upend the social organization of the Orchard Park community. As Michelle saw it, that was not necessarily a bad outcome. Upheaval on this scale had a way of encouraging the people she wanted on the block to stay, and jettisoning others whom she was glad to see get lost. According to Michelle, the people who left the neighborhood were the ones who "didn't pay, they got busted with drugs, [or] ... something [else]." Stable citizens, the working poor, the churchgoing folk—these were the neighbors who moved back in when the construction dust settled. And what they found on their return, was not only a safer neighborhood but a standard of living that was a distinct improvement. Dilapidated buildings with stinking hallways were replaced by new construction and appliances that worked.

Franklin's urban renewal projects had the same impact. Dolores Frank was one of the returnees in Franklin. A bus driver for more than twenty years, Dolores has been on disability since 2007 and manages on her pension. Decked out in a pink, zip-up sweatshirt, she uses a cane to get around these days. Dolores has a keen recall of what happened when the Franklin Hill projects came down. She was relocated to another BHA facility while she waited for the remodeling to finish and returned with her two daughters in tow when it was all over. The change was dramatic. "[When we lived here before]," she recalled, "it was so much shooting and gangs up here. It was unbelievable."

> I seen so many kids get shot right out in the front of my doorway, in the park, in the car. I know four sets of family that lost loved ones up here. It was terrible. It was terrible.
>
> When I first moved in here, I was so scared. The first day—my daughter was six years old when I moved in here. And when I came on the first day, you know, Boston housing...didn't give me no shade, didn't give me no blinds. So I had to put a sheet up to my window the first night that I moved in here. And let me tell you, it was frightening. It was frightening, all the noise.

Dolores returned to her old neighborhood—now completely transformed—in 2006. The old high-rise apartment buildings had been razed. In their place were lovely townhouses that she thought could have been set down in white suburbs. Never had she imagined she would be able to live in a place like this.

> So beautiful, oh my god. Just to see the place, you know...I would ride around with some friends of mine, and I would come along [and was just amazed].
>
> There was nobody hanging outside selling no drugs. No shooting. You would see, just by looking at it, like I said, I would come up here way before they even finish it to take a look at what how the process was coming....'06, I think it was '06 and I came up to see how it was being brought up. And it was fantastic. Fantastic.

The improvement Dolores noticed did not owe itself entirely to lovely new buildings. It stemmed from a policy that made it hard for troubled people to move back into the neighborhood when the renovation was complete. A police officer stationed in Dolores's neighborhood remembered that the disappearance of "the problem people" was a deliberate strategy to improve the quality of life in Franklin. As the officer said:

> Between 2005 and 2009. They started rebuilding so they used to be a lot of problems up there. And then when they kind of went to apartment style, condo style, they were like, okay, I think they took the opportunity to be like, "All right, we'll move you and it will rebuild." But then at the end of the day, like, "Yeah, y'all not coming back."
> *Do you think the rebuilding help that area?*
> Yeah, definitely.

The repopulation of the neighborhood increased the proportion of adults who were working or, like Dolores, were drawing on a pension that resulted from many years of steady work. It diminished the percentage of people who were not employed.

SOCIAL CONTROL

Stepping in to deter a fight on the street or calm the waters of a loud argument is a hallmark of a neighborhood that is rich in social efficacy. Stable neighborhoods, places where people know and trust each other, are more likely to exercise this kind of social control. And when intervention leads to peace, it encourages residents to sit together out on the stoop, greet a passerby, or go out shopping after dark. When residents of Roxbury and Franklin think about how their communities have changed over time, they focus attention on this upswing in safety and calm. It is not a perfect setting, and young people in both communities can still point to tensions that erupt from time to time among rivals who are still attached in some way to neighborhoods. Indeed, in October of 2022, one of the community's most revered Black leaders in education, Jean McGuire, by then ninety-one years old, was knifed in Franklin Park while walking her dog in the evening.[46] However, these destabilizing events happen far less often than they once did.

Crime rates in Roxbury and Franklin—as in Boston as a whole—have declined dramatically since the early 2000s. Our analysis of Boston Police

Department data shows that in Roxbury the incidence of robbery dropped from around 7.5 per 1,000 residents in 2003 to 1.5 per 1,000 in 2018, while assaults were cut down by more than two-thirds, from 13.5 per 1,000 residents to just 3.8. Similar declines were seen in Franklin: a decline in the frequency of robberies from around 6 per 1,000 to less than 1 per 1,000 and of assaults from more than 13 per 1,000 to somewhere in the 2 to 3 per 1,000 range. Perhaps most strikingly, murders in Franklin went from 4 in 2003 and 8 in 2004, to just 1 per year in 2015 and 2018.

Brittney and Megan, both longtime employees of another community after-school club, have observed the changes these quantitative data capture at close range. Brittney works for an outpost that serves primarily young residents of the public housing block. She has been involved with the organization since she was middle-schooler herself, coming back to work there after college. She has worked her way up to the role of director, a position she has had for twelve years. Megan has been with the organization for twenty years and has worked at her current placement for half of that time. She lives in the Franklin Hill area, a forty-minute walk from the after-school club.

The club sits on the main floor of the ten-story apartment complex on the east side of the facility and shares its common space with residents when they request it for events. There's a locked computer room and bathrooms reminiscent of middle school, replete with signs directing the kids to use soap and refrain from flushing paper towels. It serves kids up to the age of twelve, taking care of thirty to fifty children a day. "We provide a space for after-school activities," Brittney explains. "Our kids are rolling so they come in anytime between 2:00 and 6:00, 1:00 and 6:00, depending on the day and they're offered the opportunity to do their homework, use computers, play in the game room, the pool, the wi-fi, Legos. We do art projects; we do events on holidays and stuff like that."

Brittney and Megan have watched street violence ebb and flow, paying close attention because the atmosphere is so consequential for the young children they are supposed to keep safe. But Brittney testified to the improvements in the atmosphere of Franklin Hill. Residents have developed more confidence in the formal mechanisms of dispute resolution, she explained. Once the renovation was complete, there were institutions to turn to that they saw as legitimate and effective. "There's less incidents of violence here," she explained, "because the residents don't take things into their own hands." For instance, she said, "they deal with the management of the estate, go through the management.... Twenty years ago, you would've seen community neighbors just out there screaming at each other." In the past that screaming easily escalated into something more deadly. Instead, as the neighborhood settled into its renovated life, Brittney explained:

> [R]esidents started going to management for help instead of being in court settling a dispute that happened in your house that got taken outside.... And there's always a [private security company] presence even [and they] have an office up there. There's always a car up there. Whenever it gets late, they're there. They have more assistance. I think honestly, they just care more about the neighborhood so if you care more, you're going to put more into it. It's so well maintained over here.

As tensions declined and with it the violence that had once been a mainstay, Franklin residents started to think of their community as a place worthy of preservation. Adults go to work just as they do in more affluent communities, trusting nonprofit organizations and schools to watch over their children. The streets are no longer inhabited by unoccupied teens and unemployed adults with nothing to do. "The residents, they feel good, man," Megan affirmed. Safer streets have meant more latitude to take the children outside for activities, rather than being forced inside to avoid street violence. That freedom means a lot to Brittney because she can give the kids the chance to explore that would have been challenging in the past.

> During the summer we use the pool at Blue Hill. So we walk the kids down.... There's now parks popping up everywhere. And it's really good because now it's somewhere constructive for the kids to go instead of like, "We're going to just walk around." Like no, we have the option [to take them to] a big play area over there near Blue Hill, in between the Tennis Center and Blue Hill Boys & Girls Club.

They can visit basketball courts and Franklin Park, which was formerly a no-man's-land beset by gang violence. The liberty to "walk all over the neighborhood" is the antithesis of the restricted space Harding described during his fieldwork, when violence was out of control and moving even a block from one's home turf would have been dangerous.

"Ten years ago," Brittney remarked, "you wouldn't be able to take your kids just walking out in the neighborhood.... It would be like "No, we're staying inside today." So it's become a safer space for the kids just to be out in the summer. You always see someone outside. Even in the winter, you know, you will see some kids outside." And Franklin's kids have gone well beyond leaving fear behind. They have moved right up to broadcasting the pleasure and enjoyment that comes with being part of their community. Michelle can see it in their eyes, but she hears it in snatches of conversation between ten-year-olds:

> They're just so proud of their neighborhood. [They say], "Yeah, this is where I live."
>
> And the other kids who don't live here, who are bused in from school before they're picked up [by their parents], they're like, "Oh, I didn't know this [was a good place]." And [our kids] are like, "Oh, yeah, and I can tell you there's a park over there. And then you got to go to the store over here because they have the best slushie." . . . They promote their neighborhood.
>
> . . . That makes me feel good that they're like comfortable enough to be in their neighborhood and just be like, "Oh yeah, I know that person. That person my mom's friend. Oh, this is my aunt. Or we go to school together."
>
> I like that little community-based feel to it like, so it's like, you're just one big family. You're not really worried if something happens; I know you'll say something. Even when kids have problems with other kids coming off the bus like "Oh, this boy was yelling at me off the bus" another kid from the neighborhood who used to go here came over [and] it's like "Yep, he lives in that apartment over." So it's really nice.

This is not the Franklin Hill of old, where children were stuck indoors because their families were afraid for their safety and reluctant to tell outsiders where they lived. It is no longer a place where people are reluctant to step in and quell a dispute. It has become a place where trouble is more occasional than ubiquitous. Public space has become more inviting. Pleasant interaction and expression of care among residents has become something closer to second nature—not entirely free of the tensions that were so dominant in the past but a definite improvement. When Megan describes Franklin, she touches on the relationship between safety and social capital:

> I would describe the neighborhood as still up-and-coming with some residual side effects from years past where like they're still a little bit violent but not as much. There's certain times I wouldn't want to walk here still. . . . And it's a lot more positivity going around.

People say "Hi" to you on the street now, stuff like [that]. Or they'll acknowledge you.... The other day I dropped something, someone was like, "Hey, you dropped something!" Years ago, they would've just walked down the street.... People are more friendly in general these days. [In] years past, walking through here, you didn't want to ruffle people's feathers by saying things to the wrong person. Even "Hi" can be a bad thing to the wrong person on the wrong day. So you know, stuff like that.... I feel the more positive vibe in the atmosphere.... [But] yeah, people still expect [violence].

Brittney agreed, acknowledging that the public reputation of Franklin may not have caught up to the improvement residents experience:

I feel like now it's more welcoming. Even sometimes when people are like, "Oh, how is it over there?" I'm like, "It's, it's good," you know.

They still expect bad things, and they act like they're expecting the worst, but it's actually calm. There's not really any problems that wouldn't happen in another neighborhood.... It has, like, a overall safe bubble because most of the people who are here know each other. And even just with working with some of the families, you'll be walking down the street and someone's like, "Oh, hey, aren't you so and so?" I'm like, "Oh, hey, how you doing?" It's like Megan said, it's more friendly. People are not as standoffish.... From where it was, this neighborhood is really, really good.

Alice Gates is in her early forties. She is Black, and her family has been in Boston for a few generations. But Alice's mother moved her to Haiti when she was little. Alice moved back to Roxbury in 1993 to take a place in Brandeis University's transitional year program. After graduating, she lived with her mother's cousin for a number of years and eventually bought a condo in Roxbury. Today she is a civil servant in a public housing office and works as a shopper for a grocery delivery company for extra cash. Alice is a keen observer of the changes that have swept Roxbury from the time she bought her home in 2006. Back in the day, she didn't know her neighbors, but over time she became more interested in becoming friends. "I understood how living in community should feel like ... [b]eing safe, being comfortable, being able to share resources, if needed. So because that's what I thought it should be like, I definitely started to be more friendly, started to be more friendly first."

As the economy improved around her, Alice could feel a change in the neighborhood and she "started having more conversations with people, smiling more, helping people shovel [snow]." Alice and her neighbors started to take a more active role in protecting people when things went south in the streets. She recalled:

> A couple years ago, two men, in Dudley, actually, were walking. This woman was walking [with me] to take the bus, and two guys at the intersection were like arguing and getting heated. She and I both, as small as I am . . . were just like "No, guys, c'mon, just chill everybody!" But that's my personality, to just kinda jump in and try to make peace. [Intervening] is just a habit, it's just a habit. I come from a line of people who are like that apparently, my grandmother, my grandmother's sister, my great-grandfather, people who would stand up and fight, activists.

People who know each other, trust each other, and acknowledge one another's presence through superficial greetings create a sense of safety and stability that eluded Roxbury Crossing in the past. And the result is both concrete and immediate: people can walk outside without being afraid and children can roam a bit more freely, relaxing some of the vigilance that caregivers had to exercise in the past.

The change is also psychological: it lifts the community's estimation of its own value. Living in a scary, no-man's-land makes residents feel that they are of no consequence to anyone, that they have been abandoned by the world. Living in a place that is vibrant and safe reinforces the opposite sentiment. "Fifteen years ago, this [place] would have been like, filthy," Brittney explains. "You can look out the window now and you don't see filth, you don't see graffiti, you don't, you don't have the despair in your heart just looking out the window. Like you feel like you want to go outside and go to the store."

Fatima Burgess has lived through similar changes in Roxbury. Fatima's thoughtful comments and deliberate effort to speak up help to make her seem older than her mid-thirties. She wears a sky-blue headscarf around a face framed by glasses. She was born on Dudley Street but moved to Dorchester in 2017 after enduring eviction, and homelessness. She eventually settled down, and she and her family live with her mother in a co-op apartment complex. After many years of struggle and intermittent unemployment, she has a job as a social worker and her life today is stable. Fatima's husband has a job now in security but has a disability that means he cycles in and out of work. He receives Supplemental Security Income

(SSI) benefits to help weather the spells when his disability means he can't work, but SSI means he has a low ceiling on his earnings.

When she thinks back about growing up in Roxbury, Fatima gravitates back to the commercial center and transportation node of the community, Dudley Square. Thirty years ago, when Fatima was a child, it was a forbidding zone of street conflict but also a place that couldn't be avoided since it is the location of the main bus terminal. "Dudley was always an area that I couldn't go alone," she remembered. "My mom was always very concerned about the area. Eventually I did start to kind of go alone 'cause that's the only way for me to get to school. But [my mother always warned me]. . . 'Don't go by yourself. . . . Be vigilant. Be aware.' You would always see [drugged-out addicts]." But that was the Dudley Square of yesterday. Over the past decade, as Roxbury has become more affluent and less segregated, its central district—renamed Nubian Square—has become a vibrant place of cultural and commercial activity. The change has been so dramatic that people like Fatima find it almost hard to believe.

Alongside the renovation of Roxbury Crossing and Franklin came other signs of revitalization. Michelle Davis, the director of the after-school club, remembers when she had to travel out of her own neighborhood to do the simplest chores. Today the services she needs are just outside her door. As Michelle recalls:

> It was a bank desert, and now you see all of this renaissance investment. Bank of America [is] here, and Citizens and One United. Now there's Chase. There's Berkshire Bank. There's a Eastern Bank. The city, they have a Roxbury master plan to eliminate all of these vacant plots of land. It's just been sitting vacant for decades, to now be put into use. We have all these new, sort of, hip things. We have Mission Hill. . . . All of the supermarkets have been renovated, [but] we had a food desert twenty years ago. And so you see the community coming back to its heyday.

Alongside these retail investments came the loan funding to rehabilitate buildings that have long stood in disrepair. Michelle contrasts the period when Harding did his field research for *Living the Drama* with what she sees on the streets of Roxbury Crossing today. "Nineteen years ago," she says, "there were a lot of vacant buildings, vacant lots. People couldn't get loans to, you know, rehab. And so, as incomes went up in the neighborhood, families have more income, for those who were moving along in the economic spectrum. You saw their houses. So you see, like, real nice houses."

Long-term residents look outside their windows and see the visible signs of neighborhood improvement: safer streets, more commercial establishments to serve their needs. They also look inside, to what change over time has done for them as individuals, especially when it comes to work opportunities. Jonathan, whose friends call him Jay, lives with his grandmother near Franklin Park. He was a little kid back when Harding first began visiting the neighborhood. Today Jay is in his early twenties and a high school graduate. He stands about six feet tall and sports a buzz cut, which he explains is less expensive than dreads and still leaves him looking polished.

Jay finished school at exactly the point when unemployment rates dropped through the floorboards and dramatic labor shortages emerged in Boston, especially in the service sector. Accordingly, he has had a robust work history. He has a union job at Logan Airport, after having a restaurant position at Five Guys, a cashier job at the Boston Aquarium, and working for a short stint at Shake Shack. Jay has never had real trouble finding work. That said, he realized early on that even when jobs are plenty, it takes connections to land one, especially a desirable one. "You can apply to like a hundred different jobs tonight, but you're not gonna get hired or interviewed overnight." He continues:

> Some places you do but like now, like nowadays, you have to have somebody to like, "Yeah but this is my friend." Like, if you don't get that referral, you can't get a job. Like before this airport job, after I started working at Five Guys, I didn't have a job for like a good three months. And I applied to so many jobs. I noticed people getting the job that I applied to and I was like "How do you even get in there?" And he . . . was like "Yeah, well my sister works there or my best friend work there or something." But it was never like "Oh they gave me a call back." Like I went to a lot of places and I interviewed and like they gave me like that good hope like "Oh yeah, I might get the job, you know, Imma call you back." And you never get that phone back.

Stephen agrees that friends are key to finding work. Nineteen years old, Stephen, who goes by Rey, lives with his mother and older brother in Franklin Hill. Having been mugged and beaten by Franklin Field boys at the age of thirteen, he joined a gang for protection and dropped out. Now finishing up in an alternative school, he is working in a pizza shop and as a stand manager at a local sports stadium, a job he landed as part of a student employment program.

It is widely known that connections matter, so much so that good citizens in a position to be helpful as referrals look out for the people they know and try to "hook them up." That is particularly true when the economy slows, as Gillian discovered during the 2008 recession. A minister at a local Baptist church, Gillian is a leader who has taken on responsibility to provide meals, clothes, and support to the unhoused in the notorious Melnea Cass Boulevard area, which has gained a reputation for concentrated homelessness and drug addiction. Gillian is now divorced, and her children are grown, but she has remained a Roxbury stalwart through her own personal thick and thin. She remembers the Great Recession and the COVID-19 recession, two times when it became problematic for her Roxbury neighbors to find jobs. Since Gillian was positioned to know about openings, she used her connections to help them find their footing.

Gillian's day job involves running an after-school program in the largely white town of Newton. One of Boston's most affluent suburbs, with many dual-earner families, Newton seems to have a never-ending need for after-school counselors, a demand that has become much harder to fill as unemployment declined. Gillian took the opportunity of those openings to place a number of her neighbors who were badly in need of jobs. They were, by her own admission, hard to place because they lacked experience and credentials. But she knew them, they knew her, and Newton had a need. That was enough of a connection to motivate Gillian. As she put it:

> I could fairly say that every single person that I offered a job was living in low-income housing in the projects. They were undereducated. They didn't have many opportunities, but because they were also members of my church and I knew them well, I knew their character. I knew their struggles, I thought they would be dependable. That's why I took some risk is what I'm basically saying, you know, and if you cause a bit of a ripple in, in the after-school program, because it was in a completely white community, so I literally was importing people of color into an all-white community, high, a very high-income community.

Gillian's job-seeking churchgoers were experiencing hard times in the Great Recession. They couldn't meet the needs of their families and the options immediately around them were thin—but in a rich suburb fewer than 10 miles away, there was more opportunity. She says:

> They had dreams, you know, they wanted to buy a car. Just basic things that they were trying to achieve that's really how I chose who would come and work with me because the need was so great. In one [case], the guy was doing construction work, he had gotten laid off. Another person had gotten fired. Another person was just having a difficult time finding employment because of low skills.

It took some courage for Gillian to place Black workers in a white world, and she knew it would cause some ripples. But this was her duty:

> There was some dissatisfaction among the [Newton] parents who were paying to have the kids in the program to have so many people of color on the team, but I felt it was my responsibility as a human, you know, to be able if I have the power to help somebody, I am going to help them. So I didn't look at it from the point of view that I was hiring a person of color, I felt that I was hiring a person in need, you know, but it became a much bigger issue than that.

It is not news that social networks are important in employment. As Sandra Susan Smith has pointed out in several of her books on the topic, jobseekers need promoters, and those advocates need to have trust in those they are putting forward.[47] But it helps if tight labor markets provide people who can help—cousins, friends, church contacts—with options. And, as Mark Granovetter showed decades ago, in his classic book, *Getting a Job*, those information nodes need to have a ready supply of job opportunities to transmit to their contacts.[48] Tight labor markets create a bolus of those listings, but for Rey or Jay to get to them, they need the networks.

PRICED OUT

The same forces that fueled Boston's emergence as a tech city powered the explosive cost of housing and the rising specter of gentrification. Alongside San Francisco and New York, Boston became one of the most expensive cities in the nation. Where was that young, highly skilled, and relatively affluent—but not rich enough—crop of workers going to live? They began pushing out of the city center and into adjacent neighborhoods, particularly those that are well-served by public transportation. Roxbury Crossing was especially inviting, both because of its historical significance as the epicenter of Boston's Black community and because residents can hop the "T" and be in downtown Boston or the thriving Seaport district (home to so many tech companies) in just a few minutes. Franklin is not quite as well served, but it is close enough to have attracted new residents who are more middle class.

Kate moved to Roxbury in September 1988. She was the deputy director of a sports club that has been in the area for decades. Her reflections on Roxbury's history are those of someone who hails from the upper crust, the Black elite. The block she lived on was home to all Black homeowners, but it has changed over the years.[49] Kate is a mother of a college-aged son and is now divorced. A stately woman, she is a body-talker, moving her hands and leaning in or out to make a point. "When I played tennis [in the neighborhood]," she says, "like when my son was coming up, you know, twenty plus or minus years ago, my whole tennis team was African American women." She recalls:

> It was the most empowering: African American professional women. It was like Black from head to toe, all of the teams. And they were these super-duper, inspirational, brilliant Black women. They were engineers. They were doctors. They were owners of their own businesses, a lot of entrepreneurs [and] leaders in nonprofit organizations [or] graphic designers. They inspired me, like, I want to be like you.

Kate reveled in the success stories that surrounded her and in the culturally dominant presence of Roxbury's African Americans. It was her first "all-Black environment," she says. And her specific corner of it was full of professionals: "My neighbors were lawyers, were doctors, were great new people with multiple degrees, very educated police officers, and they really cared about the neighborhood." But as portraits of Harlem's "Sugar Hill" or Chicago's upscale Black enclaves make clear, Black elites could not easily wall themselves off from the difficulties of poorer neighbors. "We were surrounded on all sides by like the projects," remembers Kate. "So you have this juxtaposition of, you know, folks from projects to these homeowners who live in the neighborhood."

Kate thinks back with fondness to treasured aspects of life in Roxbury. Although its public reputation was driven by discouraging crime statistics, she found the community stimulating and stately.

> My memories are of waking up every morning for like twenty-five years and being able to run up the street...past that Museum of African American History and Culture that's at the intersection of Walnut....And my path up to Franklin Park, which is absolutely beautiful. It's a jewel and a gem. It has the Franklin Park Zoo where I, you know, bought a membership and took my son throughout his childhood. In the summertime, there was always a festival at the park. Every single weekend, there would be like, a West Indian festival, Dominican festival, a Haitian festival, you know. [I] had lots of friends in the community, lots of connection to people always. And then as my son was growing up, you know, he had access to the YMCA and to church and to a good education.

But to secure that excellent education, Kate had to put him in private school and pay for the privilege. He mixed with kids of all colors coming up. "I tried to keep him grounded in his Blackness by, you know, having him enroll in programs at the YMCA and [get] involved in church activity. So he would see people who kind of reflected who he was, and then try to balance that with a good education."

For Kate, seeing Black people in positions of influence and authority, at work and in community institutions, was an important reason to remain in Roxbury. It reinforced racial solidarity and helped to ensure that Black voices would be heard in Boston as issues of public importance were debated—from the quality of Boston Public Schools to controls on the behavior of the police where the lives of young Black men like her child were concerned. She was proud of Roxbury's heritage, the center of Black Boston's history, home to both Martin Luther King and Malcolm X in their Boston days. Despite its problems with crime, there was much here to glory in.

Gentrification, which emerged as more young white professionals began moving south to escape Boston's high housing prices, began to chip away at that social history. In the 2000s, Roxbury slowly began to return to the multiracial status it had enjoyed at the turn of the previous century, when the Irish built Hibernian Hall, a social club and dance hall, and the Jews constructed the Blue Hill Avenue Synagogue. In this repeated cycle of racial turnover, Roxbury is no longer the segregated Black enclave that Kate treasured for its cultural flavor. The neighborhood was improving economically and providing more amenities, greater safety. But it was also less hers.

Elisha Wells has seen it all as well. Raised in a segregated Black neighborhood of Brooklyn, she moved to Boston after finishing college. Her voice carries that distinctive New York accent to this day, but she feels Bostonian through and through. She wears an elegant ensemble with assurance around a homeless shelter on a main thoroughfare, where she serves as the development officer. The house caters to women and their children and has a day-care center on the interior and multiple rooms to support the adults. Elisha has given a lot of thought to how the declining proportion of Black people in Roxbury has begun to influence the community's visible power structures. As a nonprofit leader herself, she would like to see Black Bostonians consulted more often about what the community needs, given more authority over the budget the city allocates to service agencies, and deferred to as spokespeople for the residents. But she sees the opposite tendency developing, which bothers her. "When you talk about healthy communities," Elisha asks, "who are your leaders?"

> When you look at your health centers, your churches, your public officials, are they people of color? Who's running your agencies? Who's running your businesses? Mostly, it's white people. And it's hard to get a sense that you are empowered to run your life, or to even dream about running a business.... I think in this city, if you look at the nonprofit organizations, which a lot of our families come in contact with, they're not led by people of color. I can go to a meeting of shelter directors and it's all white, with the exception of maybe myself and my boss.

When people can't identify with the leadership in their midst, Elisha thinks their confidence starts to erode. They start to feel more dependent, less able to seize the day. She explains:

> What message does [a preponderance of whites in roles of authority] send to a community? In certain cities your organization doesn't have any credibility if you do not have representation on your board and in your leadership. Not who's at the front desk, who's answering the phones, who's at a lower place in the structure, but who's actually making the decisions? It's

very rare in this city. And do you as a young person feel empowered to go downtown and do anything? Ask for a job? That might be a little bit of a reach.

George Young is a Black police officer who has patrolled Roxbury for many years and offers similar observations on the evolution of power in the neighborhood. His concern is less the executives of the nonprofits and more the formal power of political office. A community that isn't able to put its own into positions of visibility and authority is letting others speak for them. "When you look at voting trends throughout the city," he says, "this [community] still tends to be one of the lowest voting [areas]. They talk about the city of Boston as being a majority-minority city; when you look at voting trends, we're still not where we should be. We now have more people of color in political power, but we still have to do better in terms of increasing our numbers."

This lack of political voice means that the community gets less than their fair share of resources, even when those needs are profound. As Michelle Davis noted: "The fact that, you know, 02119, 02118, 02120, 022121 zip codes means you were trapped in an oppressive educational system. Children in Roxbury go to every system possible because people didn't want to be defined by their zip code and being trapped in an educational system that was going to . . . keep them in poverty." Roxbury families should not have to flee the public school system to access quality education, Michelle argues. Loss of voice leads to exits rather than pressure for reform.

The weakness of African American political power was driven home in the fall of 2021, when a historic Democratic primary saw the loss of an opportunity for the first Black leader to be elected mayor.[50] Three talented Black candidates, drawn from the city council and the executive branch, competed to make it to the general election, but none of them succeeded, in part because Black voters were split among them and supporters of progressive causes were dispersed among too many candidates. Low voter turnout in the city's Black neighborhoods contributed to the defeat. It was a major disappointment for a city that has seen the proportion of its population that is Black grow. Optimists pointed out that the combined vote for Black candidates was higher than anyone else. Pessimists noted that nonetheless there was to be no Black mayor come 2022.

Sergeant Young recognizes that the absence of clout means that the community is unable to claim its fair share of the public purse:

> I don't think as a whole we've created enough political power that we can push politicians along and make them do some of the things that we want them to do.... Obviously there's a little bit more wealth in this community. How that's dispersed is questionable. And the other piece is, I always tell people you need economic power.... People of color need educational empowerment, need economic empowerment, and political empowerment. There are enough people of color who are doing well, who are well-educated. I don't think as a whole we've created enough political power that we can push politicians along and make them do some of the things that we want them to do.

Elite competition for scarce political resources matters to the professional class. But they are not the only ones who experience racial succession as problematic.

Rey, the young Black man who works at the stadium, also bridles at some of the tension that follows from the influx of people his family regards as competitors. The conflict is most pronounced across the lines that separate Blacks and Latinx neighbors and was an issue that was beginning to pick up steam back when Harding did his research. Competition for public housing—and for the scarce attention of managers in the "bricks"—is one arena where the tension is most pronounced. Rey argues that management doesn't give Black people the respect or service they deserve. "If you don't have the money to pay your rent," he says, "they'll be quick to kick you [out], leave you on the street. But that's only for like Black people. I don't think they really be like that with Spanish people." Rey explains:

> They be giving Spanish people like some time. They treat Black people clearly different here. Like me and my mom was supposed to have a normal apartment when we first came here. They moved us into a bricks. And we were like "Yo, we was supposed to get a townhouse. We was supposed to get a back and front yard." But now they gave it to a Spanish person, told us [to just] hold on. It took us like eight more years just get another apartment. And they promised us four years. Four years turned to five, five to six, six turned to seven, seven turn into eight. I'm like "Yo, why y'all lie to us for?" And then we still have yet to move into one of these houses.

Eventually Rey and his mother were moved to a better place. But they were angry about its condition and interpreted the disarray as a comment on what housing officials think Black people deserved: not much. As Rey explained:

> They moved us to different side of the bricks; they gave us a little yard. But guess what? Every Spanish person they move, they fix up the whole yard. But now that my Black family moved into one of these, you see what they all look like? [Gestures to a littered yard.] We cleaned it up more. When they gave it to us, they had glass everywhere from the last Spanish people lived there. They gave us this house dirty. Like, yeah, they painted up a little bit but, like, literally, the shower, I don't know what was wrong with it, but like even the shower had like the tub was literally messed up. There were stains on the floor.... I don't know how stains got down there, but it was like yellow stains in the bathroom.... I know for sure they don't do that for the Spanish people.

Rey's mother draws a straight line between their Black selves and the disdain of the Boston Housing Authority. When asked whether contacting BHA would result in attention to these defects, she was adamant. "They're not going to do nothing about it," she said emphatically. The bureaucracy is now staffed by Latinx bureaucrats, Rey notes. And he believes that's why his family's complaints would go nowhere:

> I'm pretty sure most of Black people's didn't contact BHA. But they don't know what else to do.
> *But why wouldn't BHA do something about it?*
> Because they're full of Spanish people too, literally. Like my mom, she'd be going up to those meetings. If you notice, a lot of Black people is one who's running these meetings going. But we get treated so terribly. And then they talk behind on our backs when some of us, we try to learn Spanish on purpose, just so we could just know what's really going on around here.

Rey, who came by his nickname to signal acceptance among his Spanish-speaking peers, has tried to fit in with them. He's made an effort to learn Spanish, inside school and on the streets. But mostly he has been trying to adapt to get what he and his mother need to live better. "You need to have a Spanish name if you wanna be treated Spanish," he says. "You gotta—you gotta be one of them."

CONCLUSION

In the early 2000s parents and adolescent kids in Franklin and Roxbury Crossing needed stability and safety, and that—for the most part—they have achieved since Harding's day. It is now possible for families like theirs to enjoy their neighborhood without constant fear of violent crime. They can shop in stores that weren't there in the past. They may have to wend their way around runners and dog walkers, the pastimes of their new middle-class neighbors, but that is a modest price to pay for the peace of mind that they enjoy compared to the old days.

As is likely true for most urban neighborhoods, the sources of change are multiple and difficult to tease apart. In particular, the role of tight labor markets is hard to isolate amidst the many other streams of improvement. The census data tells us that labor force participation is up, unemployment (especially for women) is down. Median income has recovered from its postrecession plunge, and reliance on public benefits is accordingly lower. The history of urban renewal tells us that social engineering through urban renewal also played a role in the prospects of both neighborhoods. Whatever its source, rising income created the conditions that attracted commercial infrastructure and made both places more convenient to live in.

Yet the improvement has come at a cost: the sense that these communities belonged to their original African American residents has diminished. They are less dominant, and the leadership of important institutions has migrated out of their hands. People like Elisha or Kate are not arguing for the return of the bad old days when children could not play outside and gunshots rang out across their front porches. They would like to believe, however, that the improvements didn't have to translate into cultural or political dispossession.

Even more important, they would like the improvement to make it possible for Black residents to remain in the community and enjoy its elevation. Some surely have, as the census figures on residential stability make clear: a growing proportion of residents moved to the area more than five years earlier and an increasing share of the housing units are occupied by owners, who are more likely to stay for the long term. But there are others who are no longer in place and that includes people who were not troublemakers. Rather, they were the Roxbury and Franklin residents who simply couldn't afford the rising cost of housing, as the proportion of residents paying less than $1,000 per month plunged from more than 90 percent to 63 percent in Roxbury and just 40 percent in Franklin. Incomes that have stayed roughly flat, compared to 2000, simply can't keep pace. This has led to demographic shifts: more white residents and fewer Black residents in Roxbury and a major increase in the proportion of affluent families in both neighborhoods.

The same forces that drive tight labor markets—principally economic growth—also spur an ever-escalating cost of living. As we learned in chapter 1, these trends are almost inexorably tied together. Whether this constitutes a hamster wheel, in which costs run ahead of improving wages, or an opportunity for people to jump off that wheel and actually get ahead is a matter of public policies and local dynamics.

7 Family and Fortune

Brittney Martin has seen many families in her decade as the director of an after-school program in the Franklin neighborhood. Brittney's organization serves up to fifty elementary- and middle-school-aged children daily, from a centrally located space on the main floor of a mid-rise building in one of Franklin's larger housing developments. Residents of the ten-story tower and the tidy townhouse-style units in the complex count on the club for after-school homework help, art, tutoring, and, in many cases, free dinner.

At the height of the pre-COVID-19 labor market boom, the parents of those children were on the job for many hours. "They're working their butts off," Brittney noted at the time: "I think they are working a ton. And some people have multiple jobs.... Sometimes they may not say it, but you can tell they're just drained [from work]."[1]

> Parents tell me, "Oh, I just got off a fourteen-hour shift. I'm exhausted. I still have to pick up [my child], and then I gotta go to sleep for a little bit, and start all over again tomorrow." It makes me so mad—it's just crazy. It's sad when you have kids but you can hardly see them because you're at work all day, you're working even more time [now that jobs are plentiful], and you get home exhausted.

In his seminal 1965 report on the "Negro Family," Daniel Patrick Moynihan, then assistant secretary of labor, declared that Black families were trapped in "the tangle of pathology" that did not include working multiple shifts. Instead, the report put the national spotlight on poor Black families mired in persistent, ubiquitous unemployment, the marginalization of men from kin and the economy, and concomitant reliance on public benefits.[2] Contrary to contemporary memories of Moynihan, he actually took expanded economic opportunity for Black workers seriously: indeed, in his role as an adviser to President Lyndon B. Johnson's War on Poverty, Moynihan argued for jobs, vocational training, and educational programs as the most powerful response to the problem of poverty in the Black community.

Moynihan saw a connection between labor market opportunity and family stability, arguing that a lack of access to jobs and an inability to provide meaningful support for a family would ultimately alienate Black men from their roles as husbands and fathers, which would in turn destabilize Black families.[3] Ultimately, however, Moynihan—and the press that covered him—focused on the "disintegration" of the Black family as a central cause of persistent poverty, joblessness, and low rates of upward economic mobility for Black communities. Decades of research following on his observations have sought to build the empirical case for the importance of traditional marriage in generating economic stability.[4]

Since the 1970s, scholars have returned repeatedly to the question of how poor women form ideas about the kind of relationships they want to have with men, including the fathers of their children. Although marriage rates have declined, they have done so unevenly. People with more education continue to marry at similar rates to those of decades past, but marriage rates among the less educated have dropped, and single mothers bear the burden of raising the next generation.[5] Underlying these patterns of family formation, and underneath the emotionally loaded nature of "marriage markets," lies the invisible—or not so invisible—hand of the labor market. Men who have unstable jobs or erratic employment do not appear to the women in their world to be good bets for matrimony. Noncustodial fathers contribute to their children's needs, often in the form of goods or cash that is provided outside the formal child-support system.[6] However, incarceration and child support debt are bound up in "feedback loops of disadvantage" that make it harder for men to reintegrate postincarceration.[7] When fathers fall behind on child support, they also distance themselves emotionally from their kids. Money matters, but so does the parental bond, and when one goes south, the other does as well.[8]

Pundits and policymakers have wondered why unmarried women have children when the burdens of raising them on inadequate income and the variable attention of noncustodial fathers complicates their lives. That was the question posed by Kathryn Edin and Maria Kefalas, who gathered the stories of more than 150 single mothers to understand their decisions to forge ahead with having kids.[9] Contrary to popular explanations—including women's greater economic independence—they found that the dynamics William Julius Wilson identified in *The Truly Disadvantaged*: a decline in marriageable men coincided with women's rising standards for the type of man they would be willing to marry.[10] Gainful employment was at the top of that list of qualities they expect in husbands but was often out of reach for the men in their lives. Supporting children on their own was often difficult for single mothers, whether they were employed or relied on social benefits.[11] However, that was often preferable to putting up with men who would not carry their weight. Mothers were not prepared to forego the emotional pleasures that parents experience simply because the men in their lives were not reliable providers.[12]

How central is the relationship between economic stability and marriage? Has Wilson's core claim stood the test of time?[13] The benefits of employment to parents and children are substantial. But the recent tight labor markets have coincided with important changes in Americans' ideas about family. Where scholars once thought that more employment would increase the rate of marriage, and therefore reduce family poverty, instead we find that marriage has become less relevant to many families, even when those resources are readily available. We may see an improvement in families' economic circumstances, but it might not come in the form that was once expected.

FAMILY LIFE IN FRANKLIN AND ROXBURY

Franklin Hill would be familiar to students of the "urban ghetto" that Moynihan and his followers worried about. Poverty is common, as are nontraditional families. More than a quarter (27 percent) of families in

Franklin Hill have incomes below the federal poverty line, according to Census data from 2019.[14] Median household incomes in the neighborhood were roughly $36,500 (in 2020 dollars), well below the national median household income of $67,521. Among families with children, 33 percent are headed by a single mother. Multigenerational households are also common: 15 percent of Franklin Hill's adults over age eighteen live with their parents. Franklin Hill is a predominantly Black and brown community; 68 percent of all residents identify as Black, 25 percent identify as Hispanic, 3 percent as "other." Nearly half (49 percent) of Franklin Hill's residents are foreign-born.

From an economic perspective, however, Franklin Hill looks nothing like the "tangle of pathology" that Moynihan sought to unravel. The vast majority of Franklin Hill's residents are in the labor force. Two-thirds of the men and women over the age of sixteen who live in the neighborhood are either working or looking for work. And they have done well: 90 percent of women and 89 percent of men in Franklin Hill who are in the labor force were employed as of 2019.

It hasn't always been that way. When David Harding interviewed Franklin Hill residents, and even more in 2009 as the tidal wave of the Great Recession swept thousands of jobs away, those numbers were lower: 82 percent of women and 80 percent of men in the labor force were employed.[15] But the community began to recover as the economy emerged from those dark days. Between 2015 and 2019 the number of people employed rose at a steady rate. What didn't change much were patterns of family organization. Single-parent households still compose a significant part of the community. This would seem at odds with the assumptions of the sociological literature on the family that posits unemployment as the primary driver behind the absence of marriage. What are we to make, then, of the relationship between labor market opportunity and household structure, in light of the empirical evidence on the ground in Franklin Hill? Is marriage a key component of family economic security and upward mobility for those living in poverty? Or does marriage no longer matter as much to these families? Most important for our purposes is the economic opportunity created by tight labor markets sufficient to underwrite stronger, more stable families with or without the wedding ring?

The relationship between the economic opportunities created by tight labor markets and family structure is not at all straightforward. Marriage still offers obvious prospective benefits: two potential earners to help boost family incomes; two adults to provide care and enrichment to children and elders; and the emotional benefits of mutual support and love that stems from a devoted, long-term partnership. And for decades, politicians on the right have championed policies that promote marriage, arguing that it is a key causal force underlying economic well-being.

Yet marriage is no longer the only assured way to meet the need for economic stability and provisions for children. The culture of the country has changed in ways that reduce the salience of marriage, except among the most privileged classes. This is not to say marriage is irrelevant. We know that it confers a great degree of economic security and boosts the prospects of children beyond the life chances of kids from single-parent households or cohabitating partners. But when parents start to earn more, experience more stable shift schedules, and gain benefits they never had before, they can do more to contribute to the well-being of their children whether marriage is part of the picture or not. Plentiful work creates pathways to stability.

However, it is not a panacea, largely because tight labor markets are not forever. They weaken eventually and, as we saw in chapter 1, only in one business cycle over the past seventy years have the benefits of extremely low unemployment carried over through the next trough. It is their less-than-permanent nature that renders better days less consequential for household structure than it is for parental behavior. Wage growth and occupational mobility make a positive difference but are often insufficient to enable a total escape from the pressures and uncertainties that accompany near-poverty.

What tight labor markets make possible is a shift among parents' contributions to their children's well-being that comes closer to realizing their normative judgments about, for example, what a loving father should do for his kids—regardless of his relationship to their mother. For millions of Americans at the bottom of the social structure, record levels of employment, better benefits, and rising wages impact the quality of life even when they do not revolutionize household structure. This mix of realities—shifts in the role of marriage in the lives of the poor, complex multigenerational households, and new economic uncertainties created by increased labor market income—mean that our old frameworks for understanding the relationship between family structure and economic well-being are badly in need of updating. Long-standing paradigms that put a primacy on marriage as the lynchpin simply don't match the realities of the lives of those struggling to make it at the margins. Understanding the space in between improvement and perfection is the mission of this chapter.

THE DECLINING SIGNIFICANCE OF MARRIAGE

Alicia Wells has seen her neighborhood change a lot over the past fifteen years, but she hasn't seen much change at all when it comes to marriage and family formation. She explains: "Black women don't get married. I don't think [that's] changed." Alicia's observations are matched by the Census data for the neighborhood, which shows fairly stable trends in family structure. On the one hand, the absence of a relationship between the labor market boom and marriage rates for the low-income residents of Franklin Hills is surprising, in light of decades of social science research that suggests that economic opportunity and family formation are strongly related. On the other hand, however, the fact that marriage is simply not on the radar screen for so many residents of Franklin Hills is consistent with the fact that marriage is still regarded as a long-term partnership requiring enduring stability and security—something that families struggling to make a living have little reason to expect, even in the midst of a tight labor market where work is (for a time) more plentiful and more bountiful.

In Gary Becker's classic economic model, marriage is the means by which partners increase material well-being through specialization.[16] Men's wages in married couples provided critical support for the household and for the cost of childrearing. Even in two-parent working households, fathers' wages theoretically provide continued support while mothers are out of the labor force caring for children, or, increasingly, for elders.[17] Dual-income households are more reliably able to remain above the poverty line, and, in theory, have the potential to insure against volatility in earnings by increasing or decreasing time at work when a partner's earnings fluctuate. Decades of research shows that children who grow up in single-mother and cohabitating households fare worse than children who grow up in married-couple households on a wide variety of cognitive, behavioral, and health outcomes, especially because these internal safety nets are too thin to withstand shocks.[18]

Yet the economic role of the family has changed dramatically over the past half century. As economists Shelly Lundberg and Robert Pollak note, "long-term marriage combined with childrearing is no longer near-universal adult experience, and the intense gender specialization that characterized the traditional nuclear family of the 1950s now seems archaic."[19] Moreover, many of the "production complementarities" have been beside the point among Black families for generations.[20] Black women and Black men both had "market value" as enslaved people, and Black women have always worked at substantially higher rates than white women.[21] Although fewer than 18 percent of all women worked for pay in the late nineteenth century, labor force participation rates for Black women hovered around 40 percent until the Great Depression and rose consistently starting in the 1940s.[22] Both Black men and Black women faced severe constraints on maximizing their true productivity in the labor market under Jim Crow, and they continue to face disadvantages in the labor market today due to persistent discrimination—often implicit but sometimes outright and explicit—and structural racism.[23]

In the decades following the publication of the Moynihan Report, researchers focusing on the "problem" of Black single motherhood cemented the idea of a "culture of poverty" in the sociological imagination.[24] Proponents of the approach followed Moynihan's lead in arguing that groups that are marginalized develop distinctive cultural patterns as a way of coping with their disadvantage—which entrench them in poverty. In *The Truly Disadvantaged,* for instance, William Julius Wilson carefully acknowledges the complex origins of the persistently poor Black "underclass" that received sociological scrutiny beginning in the 1960s but insists that destructive social norms diffuse and are reinforced across generations. Whatever their origins, they take on a life of their own.

Whether and how to "correct" cultures viewed as "deviant" has generated reams of research and commentary that splits into two main factions. Conservative policymakers seized on Moynihan's observations of the high rate of welfare reliance by Black families, especially Black women, to justify a drastic shrinkage of the federal safety net in favor of self-help, cultural change, and marriage promotion. Welfare supports without qualification, they argued, allowed women to rely on "handouts" rather than marriage as a source of familial stability. President George W. Bush's 2001 Healthy Marriage Initiative is a case in point: more than $600 million in federal spending between 2001 and 2011 was devoted to "responsible fatherhood and healthy marriage programs to reverse the rise in father absence and its subsequent impact on children."[25]

But sociologists have long argued that culture and economic opportunity are fundamentally linked and have pushed for a focus on promoting labor market opportunity—especially for men. Wilson and Kathryn Neckerman argued that understanding Black "family instability" requires remedies for male joblessness. It is unemployment that makes Black men "unmarriageable."[26] If society wants to promote marriage, it should do everything possible to provide Black men with jobs and conventional family formation will follow. Katherine Newman argued—along similar lines—that if the country really wanted to put the brakes on teen pregnancy, it should flood poor neighborhoods with jobs for young women. Employment provides its own incentives for avoiding pregnancy.[27]

No matter which side of the political equation is ascendant, one thing is quite clear: the increase in public spending aimed at promoting traditional marriage between 2000 and 2010 and the concurrent rollback of traditional welfare benefits did absolutely nothing to encourage marital bliss. Marriage rates continued to decline steadily during this period, from 46 percent to 34 percent.[28] The job strategy never really materialized either and the proposition Wilson and Neckerman raised—that improving employment rates for Black men would lead to a resurgence of marriage— has never been proven. But tight labor markets may offer an opportunity to "test" this idea, to the extent that they raise the employment rates and wages of Black men. But even this begs some critical questions: How much better does the job picture have to be? How much higher do wages have to rise? How durable do those changes need to be to make a serious difference for families? And is marriage the solution it once was anyway?

Economists Betsey Stevenson and Justin Wolfers raise the last of these questions in noting that "the family is not a static institution," and the marriage model that Gary Becker spelled out a generation ago is increasingly irrelevant.[29] Labor-saving technology (e.g., dishwashers) and the development of service industries (e.g., grocery delivery services) allow much of what was once provided by specialized homemakers to be purchased in the market. The accessibility of birth control and abortion—at least for the fifty years before the Supreme Court decided against *Roe*—have affected the consequences of sexual relations inside and outside of marriage, while changes in divorce law have altered the terms of the marital contract.

Perhaps most important, the upswing in the number of working mothers means that household production specialization has either declined or changed in meaning.[30] Women across all racial groups increased their labor force participation from 1970 through 2000, interrupted by a brief dip for Black and Hispanic women in the 1990s. White women caught up to Black women in the early 1990s, and Black and white women's labor force participation both peaked at around 80 percent in 2000, before declining steadily to 77 percent in 2016.[31] These trends have coincided with a decline in marriage rates and with the erosion of men's wages and labor force participation rates. The shifts are particularly pronounced among people with low incomes, but they are not confined to Black families.

"Marriage gaps"—the difference between the percentage of families comprised of married couples at the bottom versus the top of the income distribution—are closely related to levels of economic inequality in a society.[32] Indeed, this is the second time in history when the marriage gap has grown during a period of high economic inequality; the first occurred in Gilded Age of the late nineteenth century, when the United States had no welfare system in place. We are living through the second period— beginning in the late 2000s and continuing through the present. In this contemporary period, non-college-educated adults between the ages of twenty and thirty-four are once again having children in fragile cohabitating relationships even as teenage childbearing has declined sharply.[33] Kathryn Edin and Maria Kefalas explain why, based on their ethnographic interviews: women put childbearing ahead of marriage because they simply do not believe that a stable, supportive marriage is achievable given the economic circumstances they face.[34]

The marriage gap persists because tying the knot remains profoundly important to Americans perched on the uppermost rungs of the economic ladder: 80 percent of thirty-three- to forty-four-year-olds in the top income quintile were currently married in 2018, compared to just 38 percent of families in the bottom income quintile.[35] That stability has persisted over forty years for the fortunate as marriage rates declined sharply for those in the bottom half of the pyramid between the late 1970s and the late 1990s and have remained relatively flat since then. Although we hear more about falling marriage among Black Americans, in fact these trends hold across racial groups, though levels look somewhat different. Thirty-three- to forty-four-year-old non-Hispanic whites have married at consistently higher rates than Blacks and Hispanics for the entire 1979–2018 period, regardless of where they sit on the economic ladder. But, just like those of Black and Hispanic people, white Americans' marriage rates have declined for those on the bottom rungs—and have stayed stable and high at the top.[36]

In his 2012 bestseller *Coming Apart,* conservative firebrand Charles Murray argues that the top 20 percent of the population has "regained its moorings" and returned to traditional values (i.e., marriage followed by childbearing), while the rest—including the large swaths of "white America" on the lower rungs of the economic ladder—are trapped by a culture of "indolence, self-indulgence, and fail[ure]" to understand the "founding virtues," including marriage.[37] Economic conditions explain more than 20 percent of the decline in marriage for *both* Black and white men between 1969 and 2013.[38]

Although we think of families as micro-worlds bound by emotion, their formation is responsive to economic and organizational changes that have little to do with love.[39] For example, men who join labor unions are more likely to marry than comparable peers who are not union members; the increased income, regularity and stability of employment, and fringe benefits that come with union membership create that platform of stability that is necessary to contemplate permanent relationships.[40] Jennifer Lundquist has studied marriage and fertility among enlisted soldiers, who benefit from steady work and good benefits. She finds that under these circumstances there is no Black-white marriage gap, and Black enlisted military members have lower divorce rates than their white counterparts.[41] But the advantages conferred by unionization or military benefits place both of these "conditions" way out on the positive end of the stability spectrum, to a degree matched only by the very high incomes of the middle and upper-middle class.

Sociological research helps make sense of the persistence of single-headed female households and low rates of marriage in Franklin, even in the context of a booming labor market. Marriage is still viewed as a permanent, long-term decision.[42] Tight labor markets come and go, and the employment opportunities that they create—while important for household income—do not generate the degree of prosperity needed to boost families into the steady working class. This does not mean they are unimportant. Rather, moving people from the unemployment lines to jobs, from below to poverty line into the near-poor group that Katherine Newman and Victor Tan Chen identified in their book, *The Missing Class*, matters.[43]

Tight labor markets help to improve the quality of life, enabling parents to take care of their children's needs more robustly, and protects them against eviction, spiraling indebtedness, and bad credit—at least as long as the good times last. For young people who land entry-level jobs that provide them with college tuition, working parents who are now provided sick leave or vacation pay, the benefits of very low unemployment are crucial to families in Roxbury Crossing and Franklin. These virtues are not sufficient to turn these communities into havens for the traditional nuclear family and hence do not materially alter long-term decisions about the structure and formation of households. Moreover, they do not eviscerate either the practical or sentimental value of other kinds of relationships, including multigenerational arrangements that bind grandparents and adult children (and cousins, nieces, and nephews) for survival. Nonetheless, rising employment and income enable men to "do the right thing" by their children, even if they are not living in the same household.

THE NEW FATHERHOOD

Marriage is not part of the social equation for many households in Roxbury Crossing and Franklin. But fatherhood is, as it is all over the United States. Nationwide, the share of fathers who stay home full-time with children under age eighteen increased from 4 percent in 1989 to 7 percent in 2016, and fathers made up 17 percent of all stay-at-home parents in 2016 compared with 10 percent in 1989.[44] Nearly a quarter of stay-at-home fathers in 2016 reported that they were at home specifically to take care of children full-time, up from just 4 percent in 1989.[45] Fathers are now just as likely as mothers to say that parenting is extremely important to their identity, and—perhaps surprisingly—dads are more likely than moms to report that parenting is both rewarding and enjoyable.[46]

The disadvantages that accrue to children who grow up living with a single parent (typically mothers) stem from both economic deprivation and from the stress associated with the experience of family disruption.[47] When jobs are more plentiful, however, these pressures are moderated— in part because noncustodial parents (typically fathers) are better able to provide financial support to their children when their wages increase.

Child support payments serve as one key indicator of noncustodial parents' ability to contribute economically to their children's households.[48] When a parent lives with a child, they automatically share their income with that child. But when children live apart from a parent, that noncustodial parent's financial obligations to the child become less clear. Court-ordered child support is designed to serve as a key mechanism for protecting children against the financial consequences of growing up in a single-parent household.[49]

When we conduct a simple analysis comparing the ratio of child support paid to child support owed, we find the expected inverse relationship with tight labor markets—but only when labor markets are very tight. Child support paid as a share of child support owed increases when the unemployment rates is at or below 5 percent, but it does not reach levels of statistical significance until unemployment rates are at or below 4 percent. In very tight labor markets, defined as those where unemployment rates are at or below 4 percent, noncustodial parents are better able to fulfill their child support obligations.[50]

Specifically, when unemployment rates are at or below 4 percent, households with children receive 16.5 percent more of the child support that they're owed. To illustrate this effect, take 2018—the most recent year for which we have data. The average child support payment was $5,518.76, and the average family received about 86 percent of the amount they were owed. But "average" can obscure important differences, and our analysis shows substantial variation between areas with tight labor markets (unemployment at or below 4 percent) and areas with labor market that were not so tight. In tight labor markets, families received an average of 94 percent of the child support they were owed. In areas where unemployment rates were above 4 percent, the amount received as was 82.5 percent. That support gap adds up to a 12 percentage point difference correlated with very tight labor markets. The boost that tight labor markets provide to men's ability to successfully work and earn translates into additional nonfinancial benefits for their children and their children's mothers.[51] Engaged, involved fatherhood and successful coparenting no longer requires a marriage contract as a prerequisite; unmarried partners, both those who live together and those who do not, are able to work as a team on behalf of their children. When both parents have stable work and more resources, those relationships are more successful.[52]

Megan sees this every day in her work at the after-school club. "Even if [the children] don't have parents that live together, [those parents'] coparenting is astronomical, I feel. Some of these parents are such good coparents that you don't even know that their child doesn't live together with both of them. They're so well-adjusted." She explains that much of this is due to generational changes in what fatherhood means, regardless of whether or not the father and mother are or have ever been a "formal" couple. Megan continues:

> Fathers are more recognized in this generation. Their rights are more prevalent, and they want to be part of the family.... Moms are willing to accept that help, and work with the dad.... [F]amilies are tighter, more sustainable even if the parents aren't together.... All the rethinking about a fathers' role ... has changed the dynamics about how coparenting has come about.

Brittney agrees. "I feel like an old lady, but this generation is different. The new generation is so based on interaction, communication in some way, so there's no possible way for something to happen without everyone knowing.... [The parents] are in constant contact, even if the mom is the one with the kid, or vice versa. There is still that open communication." She adds that it's not about the money for men—it's about the quality of relationships: "Men don't just say 'I'll just provide the money.'... It's like, 'No, I want to spend time with my kids.'... It's more interaction than just standing in the background."

Ahmad Costen has never been married to his daughter's mother, but they coparent. He notes that "sometimes it's easy, sometimes it's hard," which is a familiar refrain to anyone who parents children—whether married or not. Ahmad is a good example of the thoughtful next-generation father that Brittney and Megan are talking about. He explains:

> At first, [coparenting] was tough, because when a woman goes through the postpartum experience, her emotions change. And she'll take that out on dad, sometimes. If you don't know how to handle that, it can be tough, really challenging. And so once I learned to understand how she was feeling, how she was reacting, then it stops bothering you, nothing really bothers you. If a problem happens, you just deal with it.

Ahmad sees many friends and coworkers who are going through similar experiences and has become a resource for fathers looking for advice on being an involved but noncustodial father. "A lot of people call me," he laughs. "People who work at it will be successful. But if you focus on anything other than the child, it will be challenging."

Ahmad views employment as a key to success for coparenting relationships, regardless of whether the partners are married, cohabitating, or still romantically involved. "[Employment] is very important. Very important. You have children, you both need to work." He sees the balance of parenting and work shifting, though. Ahmad observes that "it's becoming more and more common" for a mother to have a better, higher-paying job than the man: "There's a lot more women in college, and a lot of men, especially in the Black and Latino community, they're not in college." Plus, he notes, "women have been fighting for equal pay," so they're "doing better." The change in the gendered nature of work has impacted the gender dynamics of parenting, in ways that make it economically wise for fathers to be far more involved than they have been in the past. While marriage or cohabitation are not a prerequisite for a father's involvement to have a positive outcome on children, the quality of the relationships between parents is key.[53] Working together to raise a child across households helps keep nonresident fathers connected to their kids.[54]

COMPLEX FAMILIES, COMPLEX LIVES

When asked about whether marriage patterns have changed over the past decade, Roxbury resident Alice Gates is more certain about multigenerational families. "When I'm thinking family," she says, "I'm thinking the household. You have more intergenerational people living together.... Definitely, you have more younger folks living at home, for sure.... You have intergenerational [families], they're all bringing in their money and pooling their money together."

Alice's observations are supported by Census data, which show a rising number of adult children living at home with their parents in Roxbury, where she's lived for decades. The economic value of "doubling up," or living with relatives, is a crucial component of the "private safety net" for low-income families.[55] Sharing the cost of housing is an essential survival strategy, especially when times are tough or, as Katherine Newman shows in her book *The Accordion Family*, to subsidize the costs of further education for young adults who can cover tuition if they don't have to pay for housing.[56] In the wake of job loss, unemployed workers are three times more likely than their peers to move in with another family.[57] The Great Recession saw a significant uptick in the proportion of American households with more than two generations living together, since the labor market crisis was deeply intertwined with the collapse of the housing market.[58]

Indeed, for people living in poverty, complex "nontraditional" families are common. In her seminal 1975 book *All Our Kin*, anthropologist Carol Stack outlined a very different picture of Black female-headed households than was to be found in Moynihan's portrait. Stack's matriarchy is resilient, especially when women combine their networks into shared system of support (both economic and social) between households—drawing together both real and "fictive" kin.[59] Stack highlighted the importance of grandparents in the lives of low-income children, a finding echoed by more recent research.[60] Brittney Martin notes that she sees grandparents picking up their grandchildren in the evening regularly: "It's generational.... We see a lot of grandparents helping." Except, as it happens, it isn't generational; this adaptation has been with us for decades.

Pooling family resources matters in hard times, but it turns out to be critical even when times are good. Entry-level jobs in low-wage industries pay too little to cover basic expenses and that doesn't really change when labor markets tighten because the same forces push basic costs up. Housing is notoriously expensive in Boston. Few residents of Franklin or Roxbury Crossing find it easy to afford the rents. Sandy Jensen, who works for a sports club in Franklin, grew up in Dorchester and now lives in Mattapan. She's been at the club for twelve years, having worked previously in the corporate sector and then opened her own consulting company. She knows a lot about the community, the greater Boston area, and the people who visit the club. Even in the booming labor market in the spring of 2019, Sandy notes, "so many people in these areas struggle, even when the economy is good. People here struggle, no matter what. Boston [has] an incredibly high cost of living, [a]nd a scarcity of jobs for lower, unskilled workers that pay a living wage.... They're facing an incredible housing market, a rental market... it's a slippery slope and it's easy to find yourself completely losing your footing before you even realize it."

Although sharing housing costs is helpful, policies governing income limits for residents of public housing introduce some hurdles, especially when tight labor markets lead to rising wages. There are strict income limits to qualify for coveted subsidized housing and once they have secured this valuable benefit, residents must still be careful not to exceed the earnings ceiling. When incomes go up, a household's good fortune can threaten its hold on this essential support. Bashir Abdi, the director of a community development organization for East African youth in the Franklin neighborhood, runs up against the challenge of high housing costs daily in his work. "Housing, affordable housing, it became very much difficult," he explains:

> We have a young guy, second generation, who is happy to be graduating college and beginning his career as a young professional. [He] cannot really afford paying $2,000, $3,000 [per month, in rent] for an apartment. [He] cannot stay with [his] family in low-income [subsidized] housing, because if a person starts making more money, immediately, they [the Boston Housing Authority] will hike the family rent. But [young people] want to be close to the family, to help out, especially to help out with the younger sibling. But now they are pushed out to looking for a place to live outside of the Boston area, and that means that they are far, far away from the family.

Residents of the Franklin neighborhood echo Bashir's concerns. Rey, who lives with his mother in a subsidized apartment with a tidy yard in Franklin Hill says: "I feel like my mom kind of needs me here.... She got in a car accident, so I don't never like my mom walking. And if I'm not here, who's going to help? But the way we pay the rent in this family, like, they kind of need me to help out. But everything goes up [if I graduate and work]."

One way around the challenge of increased income and housing availability is through formal caregiver relationships. Both the US Department of Housing and Urban Development and fair housing law require an allowance for live-in aides to assists disabled tenants. For subsidized housing tenants who are disabled, elderly (defined as sixty-two or older), and near-elderly (defined as fifty or older), the earnings of live-in aides do not count against income limits for residents, and that aide can be a family member, neighbor, or friend. Doubling up through personal care assistant (PCA) relationships is not uncommon in Franklin Hill—not only because it allows for the pooling of earnings without the pressure of income limits, but because many of the aging residents of the housing complex are truly in need of help with basic daily tasks such as cooking, cleaning, and errands.

Dolores Frank is a case in point. She moved to the Franklin Hill public housing complex in 1999, relocated to a different site while her community was under redevelopment. Dolores relies on a cane to move around, but even so, her gait is a painfully short shuffle-step. Her nephew, who is in his mid-fifties, lives with her as a live-in personal care assistant. Because the nephew is her official PCA, his earnings from the white-collar job he holds down at a university on the other side of the Charles River doesn't count toward the income limit for her subsidized housing unit. These caregiving arrangements provide a way to keep elderly and disabled individuals housed in communities rather than in institutional settings, but they also provide a way for kin and near-kin to work their way up in the labor market without risking their relative's housing stability.

RUNNING ON THE HAMSTER WHEEL

Low-income families are engaged in a constant balancing act—looking for an equilibrium between earnings, benefits, expenses, and, critically, time for meaningful family relationships that stretch across generations just as often as they involve romantic partnerships. While tight labor markets bring more opportunity to work and earn, they also introduce new uncertainties. They improve the income of households, often moving them up above the poverty line and into the "missing class" or the "near poor." If prices—especially rent—remained static, the increased income would pull families into more positive terrain. However, the same forces that push unemployment down often lead to the overheating of real estate markets and the exodus of more affluent urban pioneers from city centers into neighborhoods like Roxbury Crossing and Franklin.

Moreover, because the American welfare state has an aversion to subsidies, there is pressure to reduce them the instant a family crosses a fairly meager income threshold. This translates into a hamster wheel in which the families in Franklin and Roxbury Crossing are running harder, earning more, but unable to cement their gains and create either durable equity or comfortable margins. The metaphor of escape velocity comes to mind: when space rockets leave the earth, they have to speed up to free themselves of gravity. In poor neighborhoods, especially given the rules that govern public subsidies, it is hard to command that velocity and pull free of the hamster wheel. That leads to a sense of futility: if you do all the right things and it doesn't transform your circumstances, the frustration is almost as high as if there were no improvement in employment or earnings. What good is this doing me, residents want to know, if my family remains stuck and cannot capitalize on all this work? Can't the rules change so that we can make real progress?

Mahmud Hassan lives in Roxbury Crossing and comes from Somalia. In his culture, fealty to parents is important: girls stay home until they marry, and boys often do as well. But Mahmud hears the same story over and over again from Somali clients at his Roxbury Crossing community development agency. They say: "My brother brings home an income, and I bring home an income. Our combined income should mean that our parents' social status should be increasing. According to the [public policies] that are in place . . . if you're living in subsidized housing, we should increase your rent. . . . It's all, it's like, they move the [goal post]. So should we move out, as siblings, so that Mom and Dad don't get increased rent, so that they don't see their government checks cut and their EBT [food stamps] cut because we're here?"

"The system wants to undercut achievement," Mahmud observes. He describes a typical story from one of his clients:

My parents came into to this country. Yes, they're not educated, and they've had to take jobs considered menial—but they're essential. We've lived on a basic income, minimum wage, all our lives. Now I went to college, I am now, say, a certified public accountant. But I don't make too much, I make enough to improve my parents' lives a little bit, make sure the utilities are paid for. And maybe there's a little extra, so that we as a family can go out to dinner together, because that's improving your quality of life. But . . . what the system does, it looks at the individuals who are on the lease, and they'll say, Oh, hey, you earn $45,000 a year. . . . You should be able to afford living in an apartment, but you're not choosing to, you're choosing to take advantage of the system.

Earnings limits for public housing residents shape the choices made by young adults on the brink of the transition to adulthood. Rey, the former gang member who is now working toward his GED, explains:

Doing [illegal] stuff on the street, that don't count [because the authorities can't count it against his mother's subsidized rent, or her food stamps]. And that changes us, it changes our whole life, to be honest. It . . . makes us want to stay doing the [under-the-table, sometimes illegal] things we keep doing. And then the more you do it, the more you get into it. So, it's like, it's harder to leave. And then when you finally do leave, it's like you don't know if you meant for the streets now, or if you meant to do anything better, but you know, you're already good at doing one thing, doing stuff on the street. So it's like that's always gonna be everyone's backup plan. That's not always good, but you gotta have some way [to provide for yourself].

Mahmud puts it bluntly: "This is bias, this is bias against people of color especially. You keep someone in an underprivileged state so that they do not see any economic freedom." He notes that demands and expectations have only grown more intense: families are not able to save, because the rent in their subsidized housing—the only housing they're able to afford— continues to rise as their earnings go up, and families remain trapped on the hamster wheel.

Labor economists Rebecca Diamond and Enrico Moretti quantify the relationship between the cost of living and the standard of living experienced by residents in a given local labor market (measured by US Census–designated commuting zones).[61] Low-income families living in high cost-of-living areas have exceptionally low consumption levels as compared with those in low cost-of-living areas. Yet those high cost-of-living areas are precisely the places that have enjoyed phenomenally tight labor markets in recent years. The three local labor markets with the lowest relative rates of consumption for low-income households are San Diego, San Francisco, and San Jose, California—all three are areas with extremely low unemployment. Low-income families who live in the most affordable commuting zone in the United States enjoy a level of market-based consumption that is about 70 percent higher than families with the same income who live in the least affordable commuting zone.[62]

Even in boom times, wages for workers on the bottom rungs of the ladder remain too low to come anywhere near covering the cost of living in expensive cities like Boston—but moving to more affordable housing markets outside of the city places workers far away from the labor market they need to access and separates from the family relationships on which they depend to stay employed. Take Gary, for example, a forty-something man with a full-time job as a cook, who has been homeless and living in shelters for three years. He can't afford market rent, and he's been on the waiting list for a Section 8 housing voucher for a very long time.

Sgt. George Young moved to the Boston neighborhood of Mattapan when he was seven. He joined the police department after college and worked as social worker, prosecutor, and police officer. His strong Boston accent colors his account of family life in the areas he has patrolled for many years. A keen observer of the social scene, Young reflects on what he sees on the streets and among the residents for whom he provides public safety:

> There are a lot more job opportunities [now]. But...those job opportunities, are they going to the lowest sector of the population, those that don't have a bachelor's or a master's? And are they creating enough opportunity for those people so that they can have some form of upward mobility? Sure, you can absolutely get a job making $10, $12, $15 an hour. But in the city of Boston, even if you made $15, or even $20 an hour, alright? Working forty hours, you'd make $800 before taxes, after taxes let's say you make $600. Let's say you're a single person, and you're renting a one-bedroom. One bedroom in the city of Boston? You're not going to get that for less than $1200 to $1400, and then you gotta pay for gas, electric, cell phone, cable.... Ya gotta eat, ya gotta get around, ya gotta clothe yourself. Even if you're married, you're still barely making it.

The instability of work for low-wage earners, even in boom times, has ripple effects for family relationships up, down, and across the generations. Sandy Jensen notes that the combination of the precarity of work in the low-wage labor market coupled with the high cost of living means that families are living on a knife's edge. She elaborates:

> It's a very quick slide, to losing a job or even just having a sick child and being out of work for a couple of days. Suddenly, you're behind on your rent. And perhaps you're evicted, and you go into a shelter. What happens when you go into a shelter? You lose all your furniture, maybe. You lose all your belongings. And the shelter may have rules that are so restrictive that you lose your job, because you have to follow the shelter rules in terms of what time you can be there and who's able to be in the shelter with you.
>
> It can be a very small occurrence that suddenly knock you completely off your feet. And we haven't always paid attention to what that can do to a child. Instead, we're focused on the fact that this child is acting out in the classroom, and we're not recognizing the impact that this instability at home has on the way the child is behaving.

Mahmud Hassan argues that the COVID-19 pandemic exponentially increased these risks for multigenerational families, including the East African immigrants that his organization serves in Roxbury Crossing. "There's the challenge of me coming home with COVID, and the risk that I can infect my parents. And there's the challenge of me not being home when I'm needed most." Adult children in frontline jobs risked exposure to disease daily. Their living situations meant that they risked exposing elderly, fragile older parents. But their tight relationships meant that they do not want to leave—indeed, cannot leave—because they feel deep responsibility for their parents. While tight labor markets may create the opportunity for working more and earning more, that extra time at work means less time for family. Mahmud offers a telling story about a client who immigrated to the United States from Haiti:

> You watch the media, and they're talking all the time about "full employment, full employment, full employment." But I had a conversation with this fellow, he come here from Haiti about twelve years ago. And he said to me, "I'm done. I'm going back to Haiti." And I said, "Why?" And he said, "Listen, this place, I get more stress than anything else. . . . So even people may find a job, but happiness of your life, the improvement of your life conditions, your social life, it's just not really there."

"People are very much frustrated." Mahmud says. "People are very much worried. This [booming] economy, it is not really changing the minds of people in a positive way."

CONCLUSION

Of course, it can be difficult in these communities—and the country as a whole—to appreciate the catastrophic pressures brought about by the sharp recession that followed the COVID-19 pandemic. Even though the labor market bounced back quickly, especially compared with the Great Recession of 2008, ordinary people were put through a roller-coaster without precedent in this century. They saw the market move from high growth and low unemployment to the worst unemployment since the Great Depression of the 1930s, and back again to a period of labor shortages—all in the space of about sixteen months. These oscillations take their toll, most especially on people at the bottom. Accordingly, even when—setting aside the short-lived nonetheless painful downturn—times are relatively good, problems are afoot for families in Franklin and Roxbury Crossing.

None would exchange low unemployment for the opposite, but the benefits that flow to them in good times are not good enough to wrench them free of hardship. It just enhances their ability to struggle through it.

8 Policy Lessons from Tight Labor Markets

A record 4.4 million Americans quit their jobs in September [2021], as workers took advantage of the surge in job openings across the country.... That number is up from the previous record, set in August, when 4.3 million people quit their jobs.... Many businesses are so strapped to find and retain workers that they are dipping into budgets to offer higher pay and bonuses, creating the most worker-friendly labor market in recent history.

—Eli Rosenberg, 2021

Weekly jobless claims plunge to 199,000, the lowest level in more than 50 years.

—Eli Rosenberg, Taylor Telford, and Aaron Gregg, 2021

These are complicated times for employers and managers, but for workers the years 2018 to 2022 included the most promising labor market in decades. Able to demand improvements in almost every aspect of work—from wages to benefits to promotions—workers are finally able to make a difference for themselves and for their families. This remarkable turn of events has caught students of poverty flat-footed. No doubt the lack of attention to rock-bottom unemployment arises because this degree of good fortune happens episodically and often lapses back to less favorable circumstances in short order. Nonetheless, the premise of this book is that tight labor markets matter, especially for people at the bottom of the well, and most especially in a labor market long characterized by rampant inequality. They matter because when bargaining power accrues to workers in tight labor markets, fortunes change for the better for the truly disadvantaged. Moreover, the conditions that emerge under tight labor markets offer critical lessons for how we might see genuine, durable improvement in the fate of the nation's poor that last beyond these fortunate circumstances.

Public conversations about the macroeconomy can seem detached from the lives of everyday people. This disconnect is especially true for the individuals and families struggling to stay afloat in lives characterized by long-standing poverty. Yet macro conditions have real, tangible micro impacts. When labor demand outstrips labor supply, the tight labor markets that ensue can open meaningful new opportunities for work—even for those at the very bottom of the ladder.[1] Markets are not magical, contrary to much of the narrative around the virtues of American capitalism. Instead, markets—including labor markets—are the product of active choices made by policy leaders and employers. We can decide to ensure that the opportunities tight labor markets generate are available to workers and jobseekers who have long been forced to the margins, unable to secure dignified work that pays a livable wage. We can elect to apply the lessons learned from how tight labor markets make a difference and help to spur meaningful movement toward economic security and upward mobility.

Indeed, the consequences of record low unemployment hold myriad lessons for how a wide range of institutions can improve the lives of the American poor, even when what goes up eventually comes down. There are proactive steps that stakeholders can take to make good on the promise of an inclusive economy, one that endures even when the market inevitably contracts, and jobs become harder to find. And they point toward what needs to happen for workers who have gained a foothold during good times to continue their climb toward genuine economic stability over the long-haul.

Policies that matter are not the stuff of fantasy. We lived through them as the research for this book developed. Federal policymakers acted with remarkably speed in the darkest days of the COVID-19 pandemic (2020–22), the worst public health emergency in one hundred years, and the resulting policies helped buffer the consequences of the economic freefall by providing emergency patches to the holes in our social safety net. Workers who had previously been excluded from unemployment insurance—due to archaic state rules that denied this support to large swaths of the low-wage working population—were suddenly deemed eligible. The unemployment system offered critical extra weeks of benefits. Paid leave was made available to workers on an emergency basis, marking the first time in history that the United States had a national-level guarantee of wage insurance for workers who needed to take time away from work because of their own illness or that of a loved one. Access to in-kind benefits including health insurance (via expanded Medicaid access) and food assistance (via expanded access to the Supplemental Nutrition Assistance Program, or SNAP) provided millions of struggling families with necessary aid. A federal eviction moratorium protected low-income families all over the country from homelessness.

Families with incomes under \$75,000 received relief in the form of cash assistance via economic stimulus payments and expanded Earned Income Tax Credit (EITC).[2] Millions more families with children received an additional cash benefit in the form of an expanded child tax credit (CTC), which covered children over sixteen for the first time, increased the size of the credit per child, and was fully refundable, guaranteeing parents the full amount of the credit.[3] These interventions led to an unprecedented outcome: in the depths of a powerful recession, the worst since the 1930s, poverty *declined*.[4] The EITC and CTC lifted 9.6 million people out of poverty in 2021.[5] In particular, child poverty plummeted. Combined with the effects of the pandemic stimulus checks, policy interventions sliced the poverty rate in half for Black children, from 17.2 percent in 2020 to 8.3 percent in 2021.[6] Never before in the history of economic downturns did we see the fate of the poor improve. The lesson? We know how to move this needle.

Businesses—including many of the small businesses in the service industries hit hardest by 2021 recession—received support as well. Taking a page from the European playbook, which avoids the wastage that long-term unemployment visits on workers and industries, we paid firms to keep their people on the payroll, to increase the likelihood that they would be ready to return to work when the public health crisis was under control.[7] The tight labor markets that emerged in 2021–22 were fueled by these policies.[8] What a contrast to the long, slow, painful recovery from the Great Recession of 2008, when an underpowered policy response left millions of workers on the sidelines for years as the recovery evolved at a glacial pace.

This social policy expansion is not without its critics. As often happen when the welfare state enlarges, skeptical policymakers turn to arguments about "entitlement culture," suggesting that key income supports turn America's most vulnerable into weak, lazy individuals who accept handouts and forget the meaning of hard work. The evidence for this argument is scant. In a wide-ranging review on the impact of the EITC, Nada Eissa and Hilary Hoynes find that the refundable tax credit encourages those who are sitting on the sidelines to join the workforce, and that it does not reduce the number of hours clocked by eligible workers.[9] Among single mothers with less than a college degree, a $1,000 increase in EITC benefits leads to a 7.4 percentage point increase in employment and an 8.4 percentage point reduction in poverty.[10]

Early studies of guaranteed income programs, which offer a nonconditional cash transfer to eligible families, suggest that giving people who are poor a modest sum of money with no strings attached may actually *increase* work effort. Take the example of the Economic Empowerment Demonstration (SEED) initiative in Stockton, California, the nation's first mayor-led guaranteed income initiative. SEED offered 125 residents of low-income neighborhoods $500 a month for twenty-four months. The award is unconditional: no strings attached and no work requirement. Using a randomized control trial that compared SEED program participants with eligible applicants who were not randomly selected to participate, researchers Stacia West and Amy Castro Baker find large increases in employment for the former group compared to the latter. In February 2019, 28 percent of recipients were employed full-time; one year later, 40 percent enjoyed that status. In contrast, the control group saw a 5 percent increase in employment over the same period, from 32 percent in February 2019 to 37 percent in the next February.[11]

Our quantitative analysis of sixty years of data from the Panel Study of Income Dynamics (PSID) reinforces this narrative with new evidence: low-income families and workers of all colors readily seize the opportunity to work when it is available and especially when it pays a living wage. The employers, labor market intermediaries, and residents and community leaders in two of Boston's poorest neighborhoods who participated in our qualitative fieldwork tell compelling stories of hard work and persistence in good times—and a deep desire to climb the ladder of opportunity to be genuinely financially independent.

Our research also shows that the opportunities that arise, even in economic times that are advantageous to low-wage employees, may not pay off in *durable* security. They do make a huge difference. But when a family is staring up at opportunity from the vantage point of a deep well, the climb is long. And the structure of our social safety net is riddled with so many holes and cliff effects that finding a reliable foothold is a challenge. To do better, we need to reinvent social policies to underwrite the leap to greater security that tight labor markets ignite. Most critical, the support we currently provide is disconnected from ladders to opportunity. Marginalized workers and their families must balance their efforts to obtain and retain a job, while caring for their loved ones, and nurturing and sustaining meaningful relationships with their chosen families and communities. Those who do move ahead—and there are many more of them when labor markets are robust—find themselves trapped on a hamster wheel where policy rules and employer practices make it nearly impossible to get ahead and stay there.

And yet the progress is real. If it could be consolidated so low-income families can stabilize, accrue equity, and create a margin or buffer against potential hardship, the entire country would benefit. We can repair the safety net, to ensure that an economic shock—regardless of its cause—is not a catastrophic loss. We can connect the safety net to ladders of opportunity, ladders that allow workers to reach higher, starting from a newfound place of stability. If we invest in the training necessary for workers to take advantage of labor market opportunity, and reward employers who make these investments on their own, we will reap the benefits of that increase in human capital. When stable platforms replace precarious tightropes, neighborhoods become safer, families—married or not—are able to do more for themselves, while the community organizations they turn to can concentrate on helping the neighborhoods around them flourish. These are not impossible dreams. To varying degrees, we have seen them unfold in Roxbury Crossing and Franklin over the past twenty years, although their hold on better days remains tenuous without the investments needed to make them permanent.

In this chapter we lay out a vision for what this might look like, based on what we have learned about the power of tight labor markets—and their limitations. We start with the (perhaps obvious) argument in favor of a continued focus on full employment as a key policy goal for macroeconomic policymakers. We then pull back to summarize how tight labor markets fuel opportunity for disadvantaged workers and offer policy recommendations for recreating these conditions during the downturns when the underlying economy is not as favorable to workers. We conclude by reminding ourselves that rose-colored glasses are not good lenses for understanding the realities on the ground: workers and families continue to struggle to keep their balance and gain momentum even in the context of tight labor markets. We need a sober look at how we might make the improvements in their lives more durable.

WHY FULL EMPLOYMENT?

The Federal Reserve's dual mandate of price stability and full employment has been in place for decades. Yet enormous untapped potential remains for making good on the promise of full employment as a true priority for US economic policy. Twenty years ago, economists Dean Baker and Jared Bernstein noted that the second half of the 1990s represented the first time in three decades that the labor market had hummed along at or near this target. Consistent with what we have seen in our analyses, Baker and Bernstein argue: "While many worthy social programs can improve on market outcomes, there is no better way to lift the living standards of all working families than through full employment in the labor market."[12]

We could not agree more. But they argued that the time had come for a new definition of full employment for federal monetary policymakers: a more comprehensive view that moves beyond tying full employment's definition to stable prices and instead moves toward defining it as the level at which additional demand in the economy will not create more jobs. For too long, they suggested, policymakers have overweighted concerns about inflation and runaway prices and underweighted the role that full employment plays in generating benefits for workers and businesses. When unemployment goes down to historically low levels, the drumbeat of concern over inflation and the attendant ills of rising prices tends to grow louder. In 2021–22 consumer prices rose to the highest rates since 2008, and analysts worried that the record-high levels of government support combined with the Federal Reserve's low interest rate policies were elevating the risk of rising inflation.[13] Public opinion polls suggested a gloomy consumer outlook despite record-tight labor markets and rising wages.[14] This is not an unusual conversation: inflation is a worry whenever the economy runs hot and if a more robust safety net, designed to attack recessions, has been part of the landscape, calls to rescind supports for families often follow.

As this book went to press, inflation continued to spiral upward in the wake of enduring supply chain disruptions from COVID-19's continued global effects as well as the Russian invasion of Ukraine and severe global weather events precipitated by rapid climate change. Many economists viewed the spike in prices as temporary when inflation began creeping upward soon after the economy reopened in earnest after the initial pandemic shock.[15] Yet rising prices have persisted across multiple spending categories, including essentials such as food, housing, fuel, and utilities, and inflation's bite is eating into family budgets.[16] In an effort to stabilize prices, the Federal Reserve began pushing interest rates upward (i.e., making borrowing more expensive), as Board Chair Jerome Powell worried: "Without price stability, the economy does not work for anyone. In particular, without price stability, we will not achieve a sustained period of strong labor market conditions that benefit all."[17]

Tight monetary policy is *designed* to raise unemployment. When asked how he would know that the Fed's response was having its intended effects, Chair Powell responded that "we'll want to see movements in the labor market return to a better balance between supply and demand," as a precursor to the ultimately goal of returning inflation to the Federal Reserve's annual target of 2 percent.[18] The underlying idea is that higher interest rates will increase the cost of borrowing and hence reduce employers' demand for workers. As firms pull back on hiring (and potentially begin laying workers off), labor's bargaining power erodes, which in turn puts downward pressure on wages and pushes unemployment rates up. Consumers pull back on spending, and prices stabilize.

While the goal is a "soft landing" that eases inflationary pressures without severe negative spillover effects into the labor market, a growing chorus of experts believe this path may not materialize. Prices have continued to increase despite repeated interest rate hikes.[19] Indeed, economist and former US Treasury secretary Larry Summers argues that an increase in joblessness is a necessary precondition for price stability. "We need five years of unemployment above 5 percent to contain inflation," he cautioned.[20]

Yet tight labor markets do not necessarily translate into inflationary pressures. The remarkable low-unemployment periods of the Clinton era were not accompanied by troubling price increases, and workers at the bottom of the earnings ladder saw real benefits. The Clinton boom was applauded for high growth rates, low unemployment, and virtually nonexistent inflation. In the current context, it is not at all clear that wage increases are driving inflation. While wages have risen at historically high rates, workers' take-home pay increases continue to lag price increases.[21] A more plausible account of persistent inflation is the global pressure on supply chains due to the 2022 Russian invasion of Ukraine, as well as soaring corporate profits resulting from reduced industry competition in key industries including food and fuel.

Economists Mike Konczal and Niko Lusiani have argued that corporate consolidation and the resulting pricing power accruing to a small number of firms is behind both the rise in corporate profits and the upward pressure on prices.[22] Tightening monetary policy in order to raise unemployment rates will not get to the root of either of these issues. Instead, infrastructure investments designed to ease supply chain pressures combined with more robust competition policy (including anti-trust and anti-trust enforcement) may be sharper tools for fixing the inflation problem, which is both quite real and seriously damaging to the poor.

Tight labor markets in 2019 through 2022 reshaped opportunity for workers, pulling many off the sidelines and into the labor market. For some, upward mobility translated into real and durable social mobility. For others, the change meant exchanging a life of nonworking poverty to one of working poverty. Working poverty is no one's end goal. But when someone moves from society's margins into the workforce, they are better positioned to seek the next job that may come closer to economic stability. Employers will be more likely to recognize a track record and offer jobs that pay better to hold on to their workforce. In the current period, benefits are relatively plentiful, job ladders are sprouting, and paid leave, health insurance, and retirement accounts are on the docket for workers who never had any such thing in the past and doubtless wouldn't except for the pressures that tight labor markets produce.

The combination of the bargaining power enjoyed by workers as a result of tight labor markets, the shifts in employer hiring and training practices that resulted, the federal policy response to COVID-19, and the racial awakening of spring 2020 resulted in a host of new supports for workers that provided stepping-stones onto this promising pathway.

People with little formal education, those ensnared in the criminal justice system, and individuals with a history of substance abuse and other mental health struggles have all benefited from these changes. Taken together, the incentive to hire and maintain talent when labor is scarce can create transformative opportunity for those who have been historically disadvantaged by structural forces such as race and gender discrimination as well. Tight labor markets generate upward pressure on wages, even—indeed, especially—at the bottom.

One of the most important consequences of tight labor markets is an uptick in labor productivity for the economy as a whole.[23] When wages rise, employers restructure jobs to maximize productivity.[24] As we discuss elsewhere in this chapter, this restructuring can expedite automation in ways that have implications for the future of work for all of us, most especially those on the bottom rungs of the ladder. Advances in technology, especially artificial intelligence, matter for the future of low-wage work too. Yet we have policy options available that allow for smoothing the fallout from technological change, so that it does not derail the potential for immense progress that would stem from a full-throated prioritization of full employment.

In utilizing macro tools, including monetary policy, policymakers need to look beyond aggregate economic statistics and account for the distribution of opportunity across earnings groups, across family incomes, across gender, and, critically, across racial groups. Topline employment and unemployment rates mask significant disparities brewing beneath the sur-face, and these disparities are reflections of the lived experiences of many of the nation's most disadvantaged workers and jobseekers. For example, Black workers—especially Black women—have endured unemployment rates far higher than those of their white peers. Economist Janelle Jones suggests that if those who have been systematically excluded and exploited can thrive, the economy (including the labor market) would be working for all. She makes a compelling argument for centering Black women as the canaries in the coalmine, given the long history of their exploitation.[25] Any consideration of full employment needs to be calibrated to the lives of the least fortunate, to genuinely make a difference.

Nonetheless, we need not rely on the Federal Reserve alone to shape opportunity in the labor market. Indeed, our research has given us im-portant insights into how tight labor markets create opportunity in the lives of America's most disadvantaged. These lessons can be translated into practical insights that can be applied by employers, workforce inter-mediaries, policymakers, and workers themselves—regardless of whether the labor market is on fire or in a slouch. Moreover, a compelling body of research suggests that investing in these kinds of policies and programs is not only good for the most vulnerable workers and families in our midst but for our economy as a whole.[26] Bolstering labor force participation, raising wages, and supporting upward mobility are key elements of a healthy, growing, inclusive economy.

WHAT CAN WE LEARN FROM TIGHT LABOR MARKETS?

Our fieldwork in two of Boston's poorest neighborhoods, along with quantitative analysis of half a century of longitudinal data, shows us what can happen when work is plentiful. Employers change their behavior in concrete ways that create real opportunities for individuals who have struggled at the margins. Workers who seize the opportunities provided see measurable changes in their economic and family lives. Intermedi-aries, including community organizations of a variety of different types, play a key matchmaking role between employers and workers. Neighbor-hoods and families reflect the benefits these opportunities make possible, becoming safer and more stable. The following lessons summarize what we learned:

1. Employers are more willing to take risks on nontraditional, formerly marginalized workers.

2. Employers absorb more of the cost of training workers to do the job.

3. Employers increase the quality of the jobs on offer.

4. Workforce intermediaries take on heightened importance, because of their ability to supply employers with vetted entry-level candidates—and their ability to provide disadvantaged workers with coaching, mentorship, and access to supports that boost a low-wage workers' job performance.

5. Low-income workers seize on the opportunities provided by a booming labor market.

6. Low-income workers see improvements, thanks to employment opportunity. But persistently low wages, the high cost of essentials such as housing and childcare, and the resulting inability to save for the inevitable rainy day mean that precarity remains for many.

WHAT ELSE DO WE NEED TO DO?

If we are to make good on the promise of a more "inclusive capitalism," we need to encourage, incentivize, or regulate markets to expand the employer practices that become commonplace in tight labor markets. Many so-called "high road" firms have long-standing programs in place that do exactly this because they have found it to be good for business—paying a living wage, hiring "nontraditional" workers from the local community, providing generous benefits including health insurance and paid time off can all lead to higher rates of productivity, lower labor turnover, and more market share in communities that increasingly look askance at exploitative labor practices.[27]

In the wake of the racial reckoning that followed the murder of George Floyd and the wave of protests and activism around the nation in 2020, corporate initiatives designed to boost the hiring of workers of color caught fire.[28] And business-driven efforts to focus on skills rather than credentials in hiring, and to build career ladders through both on-the-job and outside training, are thriving.[29] Whether these voluntary efforts endure when the labor market cools off and hiring becomes less of a competitive game is the key question for public policy. Our research implies a clear set of policy and practice options for leaders who want to move the needle toward economic security and opportunity in the lives of low-income workers, families, and communities. Tight labor markets create these conditions, but policymakers and employers can make active choices to replicate these same outcomes, regardless of the unemployment rate.

Rewrite Regulatory Policies to Ensure That the Labor Market Generates Higher-Quality Jobs

INCREASE THE MINIMUM WAGE

Tight labor markets increase the likelihood that an employer will provide higher wages, even to workers at the bottom. But when unemployment rises again, the incentive to keep them high is greatly diminished. If we want to ensure that workers will see wages rise in the absence of tight labor markets, our best bet is to keep the minimum wage moving up at a regular pace, with a substantial boost to revive its relative purchasing power and then pegging it to inflation. A vast literature suggests that boosting the minimum wage provides needed additional income to workers at minimal aggregate cost to employers. Deliberate efforts to increase wages at the bottom disproportionately benefit Black workers. For instance, the extension of the minimum wage to predominantly Black occupations under the 1966 Fair Labor Standards Act closed the racial wage gap entirely in industries that were affected by the new regulations.[30] Similarly, recent minimum wage increases have boosted Black workers' wages disproportionately, due to the overconcentration of Black workers in low-wage jobs bound by the minimum wage.[31]

Increasing wages does not "kill jobs," even when the labor market is sagging.[32] Yet the federal minimum wage has remained at $7.25 an hour since 2009, the longest that Congress has allowed the wage floor to remain unchanged since the regulatory standard was first established in 1938.[33] In inflation-adjusted terms, today's federal minimum wage is in fact worth a dollar *less* than it was in 1950.[34] Cities (and some states) around the nation have experimented with progressively higher minimum wages. While some economists continue to argue that raising the minimum wage is a mistake, they have become a minority. When the Nobel Prize (in 2021) goes to the author of a key study showing that increasing the minimum wage does not raise unemployment, the case is largely closed.[35] We can and should increase the minimum wage at the federal level so that workers benefit regardless of where they live.[36]

ENCOURAGE FAIR SCHEDULING PRACTICES

We expected to find that tight labor markets would incentivize employers to reduce irregular shifts because those jobs would be so undesirable that workers would desert them. We recounted some examples of this tendency from our fieldwork. However, survey data from the Shift Project at Harvard University shows that these pressures are not as powerful as other impacts of tight labor markets.[37] Employers seem to be resistant to giving up the benefits of just-in-time scheduling more than they are to raising wages. Hence the tight labor market of 2021–22 generated additional pay for just-in-time shifts (i.e., last-minute new hours) or "clopenings" (working until closing on a late shift followed by an opening shift early the next morning) more than they did changes in the organization of work, even in the face of high quit rates.

For workers who are living paycheck-to-paycheck, control over their time is especially important because they don't have the money to buy the time of others. A well-paid, highly educated worker can afford to cover childcare for an infant, but a low-wage worker who is still on the waiting list for subsidized childcare cannot.[38] As a result, many low-wage workers face time constraints above and beyond those of their higher-paid colleagues—yet they are also subject to far more unstable, unpredictable schedules.[39] A growing body of evidence suggests that employers investing in fair scheduling practices (stability and predictability as well as more equally shared control over schedules between manager and workers) see economic benefits in the form of increased productivity and ultimately lower labor costs.[40]

While employer practice may eventually change as more evidence on the win-wins of fair scheduling practices are broadly understood, regulatory policies designed to facilitate fair scheduling practices are needed to level the playing field and speed adoption. Cities around the United States—along with the state of Oregon—have begun experimenting with policies that guarantee workers a right to flexible and/or predictable scheduling. They are placing workers and employers on a more level playing field when it comes to determining how to meet each other's needs regarding time and work—and time for the rest of life. This kind of control is a key element of a quality job, and we know from a growing body of research that it pays off for both workers and employers. Workers enjoy stronger, more stable family relationships, better physical and mental health, and higher levels of labor force attachment and earnings mobility. And employers are rewarded with a healthier, more productive, more loyal workforce.[41]

DEVELOP A COHERENT SYSTEM OF PUBLIC, UNIVERSALLY ACCESSIBLE, PORTABLE BENEFITS FOR WORKERS

Highly educated workers in demand in the postindustrial information economy have long enjoyed far higher levels of access to so-called "fringe" benefits such as paid family and medical leave, employer-subsidized health insurance, transportation subsidies, and, in some cases, on-site childcare or benefits to reimburse for childcare expenses. Low-wage workers also have babies and need time off to recuperate from childbirth and to bond with their newest family members. Those babies have doctor's appointments that require a parent's presence. They grow up into children who get sick and need their parents' attention and time. Low-wage workers have parents and other loved ones who need care as they grow old. Low-wage workers fall ill themselves and need time away from work to receive treatment and recuperate.

Indeed, low-wage workers are more likely than higher-paid workers to grapple with these challenges, both because of the deep and enduring connections between poverty, trauma, and mental and physical health and, as the pandemic has shown, because of the dangerous and dirty jobs that low-wage workers often fill.[42] Providing access to benefits such as health insurance and paid leave can fuel labor force attachment over the long term, which in turn boosts earnings.[43] Paid leave policies can also result in increased retention and reduced labor turnover, which boost productivity for employers.[44] All of these improvements did, in fact, gather force in the tight labor markets of 2018–19 and 2021–22 simply because adding these benefits attracted workers in a period when they were scarce. Competition spurred these improvements.

In slack labor markets policy is required to keep the economy moving in the right direction. The Affordable Care Act (ACA) took a significant step toward removing the responsibility of providing health insurance from the shoulders of American employers. It recognized that employers would never voluntarily provide affordable, quality insurance to low-wage workers and many smaller employers just couldn't afford to cover their workers, even in boom times. While the ACA was imperfect in its reach and its impact on coverage, quality, and affordability, it represents a historic moment by recognizing a broader role for government in ensuring access to basic social protections. Indeed, one of the most trenchant critiques of the ACA was that the enabling legislation set the onset of its benefits some four years beyond the enactment of Obamacare, leaving more room for opposition to grow before the advantages registered in American households. These improvements at scale cannot come too soon.

Proposals for similar expansions to social insurance exist for paid family and medical leave. The most promising federal proposals build on successful examples that are up and running in a growing number of states.[45] For instance, the FAMILY Act (sponsored by 36 US senators, and accompanied by a matching bill with 206 cosponsors in the House) would set up a federally-run program that collects a very small payroll tax from workers (including both those with W-2s as well as "contract" workers and self-employed).[46] In turn, the program guarantees progressive wage replacement for a specified number of weeks when a program enrollee needs time off from work to care for a new baby, to recover from their own major illness or health event, or to provide care for an ill loved one.

These benefits are not simply "nice" things to do for workers. They are a critical set of supports that allow for continued labor force participation, even when the inevitabilities of life get in the way. They have the potential to supercharge mobility by giving those low-wage workers who get a foot on the ladder the opportunity to hang on while they manage their lives outside of work. Moreover, updated public benefits can help level the playing field between different types of employers, regardless of the health of the labor market—small businesses, entrepreneurs, gig workers, and others in the "1099 economy" are perennially disadvantaged by their relatively small scale, even when markets are tight, yet we know that these are all important on-ramps to labor market opportunity for low- and middle-wage workers.[47]

Tight labor markets provide crucial boosts to family incomes, but those increased earnings are rarely sufficient for workers to move from living paycheck-to-paycheck into the middle class, or even the "missing class" of the near-poor. Many continue to need a combination of public support and earned income to make ends meet—but too many of the public supports are based on eligibility rules that phase out or disqualify them entirely once they see their earnings begin to rise. Workers find themselves on a hamster wheel, as they run faster and climb higher, only to find they may have jeopardized critical resources (like a roof over their heads) or forced family members out of the house to avoid that fate.

The "spoils" of tight labor markets mean that folks who are doing exactly what society has long been telling them to do—get a job, bring home the bacon—face the perverse consequence of losing critical income and benefit support well before their labor market earnings enable them to meet the cost of living. Experts refer to this as the "benefit cliff" problem, which applies to not only housing vouchers like Section 8 but also Supplemental Nutrition Assistance Program (food stamps), Medicaid, the State Children's Health Insurance Program (SCHIP), and many other means-tested programs. As Alex Ruder, an expert on benefit cliffs for the Atlanta Federal Reserve's Community and Economic Development team puts it: "Workforce development programs are aimed at increasing income. As income goes up, families are likely to lose public assistance. The benefits cliff specifically means that loss in public assistance makes you economically worse off than you were before you increased your income."[48]

Instead of supporting the working poor as they try to elevate themselves out of poverty and into stability they can count on, America's social policies pull the rug out and ensure that they remain perpetually vulnerable. This makes no sense. It is far more useful to support their climb and boost them over that threshold and into, for example, a savings account or a down payment on an apartment. Policies that recognize the overwhelming desire of America's working poor to achieve stability and carve out their corner of the American dream would relax those benefit thresholds and enable families to create a cushion and use it to acquire assets they can rely on. One option is to use a more sophisticated measure of family balance sheets than simple cut-offs or phase-outs based on family income or earnings for determining program eligibility. Local measures of "self-sufficiency" take into account the full family balance sheet—that is, not just earnings and income but also the cost of living including the true cost of market rate housing, transportation, childcare, health care, and so on.[49] Benefits programs could target eligibility standards and phase-outs of benefits to a self-sufficiency standard in lieu of earnings, and in turn provide an extended runway for workers and families working their ways up and out of poverty.

Small pilot experiments are currently in the works, to examine whether alternative approaches to benefits cliffs might work.[50] For instance, the Families' Ascent to Economic Security (FATES) pilot in Orange County, Florida, would target parents who are at or near the childcare subsidy benefits cliff. FATES aims to phase out the childcare subsidy gradually after parents (1) enroll in education and training, (2) obtain an occupation with higher wages than their starting place, and (3) cross the childcare eligibility threshold. FATES enables participants who would otherwise lose the childcare subsidy to instead pay half the childcare costs in the first year following the loss of the subsidy, 75 percent of the costs in the second year, and 100 percent from the third year on to any additional years. Modeling from the Federal Reserve Bank of Atlanta suggests that the FATES approach would support low-wage workers who are climbing the wage ladder, by calibrating the phase-out of childcare subsidies more carefully to the increased wages over time.[51] The Atlanta Fed team has also developed a free forecasting tool—the Career Ladder Identifier and Financial Forecaster (CLIFF)—that allows individuals to map out how public assistance losses intersect with local in-demand career pathways.[52]

Benefits cliffs do not reduce the work effort of those teetering on the edge of a cut-off; instead, residents of Roxbury Crossing and Franklin struggle to come up with workarounds such as under-the-table work, underreporting of income, and, in some cases, simply leaping off the cliff.[53] Continued efforts to smooth benefit cliffs through more creative policy approaches to eligibility and phase-outs is a critical next step for social policy in the United States.

PROVIDE CONSISTENT PUBLIC FUNDS TO INTERMEDIARIES

While middle- and upper-middle-class workers and their families have social networks with myriad ties to the labor market and trusted references, workers struggling on the margins rarely do.[54] Workforce intermediaries play a critical role in developing trusted relationships with employers as well as with the low-income populations that they serve, facilitating matches between jobs and workers and providing the support and encouragement that disadvantaged workers navigating new and unfamiliar workplace cultures and expectations need to continue to succeed.

Yet these programs face a constant ebb and flow of support. Public funding is rarely sufficient and often dries up when the public coffers run low in recession. Many of these intermediaries rely on employer contributions, but employers are most enthusiastic about the services that they provide when *they* need them most—that is, when the labor market is tight. Insecure funding means that intermediaries are only able to operate at full capacity episodically—especially because the most effective intermediaries are based on a relational, whole-person approach that requires persistent, long-term commitments. Employer networks and relationships with hiring managers don't come into being overnight. Job readiness training, wraparound supports, and trusting relationships with low-income individuals take time and resources to develop and maintain.

Boosting public support for workforce intermediaries could provide badly needed consistency for this critical yet underappreciated set of labor market institutions. Making that support countercyclical could be an efficient way to spend public dollars. In slack labor markets employers have their pick of potential workers and are therefore less invested in relying on these intermediaries and less likely to help support them with private contributions. This is precisely when public investments are most needed, to allow for the continuity of relationships that make the most successful intermediaries so valuable when the market tightens up and employers come flocking to them looking for help. Generating a true public-private partnership that considers the ways that labor market conditions shape incentives would be a massive step forward.

The United States invests far less in workforce development and training efforts than our global competitors and has increasingly shifted toward a work-first model that offers little in the way of worker support or funding for training.[55] The result has been a patchwork of intermediaries that are often underresourced and unable to offer the "whole person" approach taken by successful programs like Boston's Heartward Bound. By shifting our approach to when and how we spend public funds on workforce development, and when we expect employers to boost their contributions, we have the potential to shore up a critical and often underappreciated element of the pathway to opportunity.

SUPPORT WORKFORCE DEVELOPMENT THAT WORKS

Even in the tightest of labor markets, there will be ceilings on upward mobility within certain industries. Katherine Newman spent years following the lives of low-income workers in Harlem's "Burger Barns," and while the Roaring 1990s created opportunities for some experienced workers to move up into management positions, there was never sufficient growth to accommodate all of the would-be upwardly mobiles in this workforce.[56]

In the absence of strategies to connect workers in low-wage industries to opportunities in higher-paying industries, including high-growth industries with internal career ladders, mobility out of low-wage work will remain elusive for too many. Workforce intermediaries that take a collaborative, cross-industry approach focused on matching workers to jobs both *within* and *across* industries and occupations have the potential to generate transformative change for individuals who might otherwise end up stuck in a dead-end job. They are likely to find more traction in tight labor markets, but since talent matters, it is worth supporting as a general human capital strategy. An approach along these lines would blend two of the highest-impact workforce development strategies with the emerging set of data-driven tools for matching workers to promising new employment opportunities. Sectoral employment workforce development strategies are industry-driven and include multiple employers from one sector. Employers help shape program design and training, and programs offer a continuum of services—from "soft skills" workforce readiness to initial job placement to coaching and mentoring to support a worker's progress up a well-defined career pathway within the given sector.[57]

Heartward Bound is an example of a successful sectoral training program for the culinary industry in Boston. WorkAdvance, which operates programs across the country focused on growth sectors in local economies (e.g., information technology and environmental remediation in New York City, health care and manufacturing in Northeast Ohio), is another.[58] Both programs succeed when labor markets are tight and employers are willing to look at people who are not a perfect fit for the jobs on offer. Sectoral training approaches are remarkably effective at improving both employment and earnings outcomes for participants—but they lack a formal way of sourcing workers who have shown promise in other sectors where opportunities for growth are far more limited.

Similarly, career pathway approaches to workforce development focus on cultivating well-articulated sequences of quality education and training offerings and supportive services in a given industry or occupation.[59] Current federal law—both the Workforce Innovation and Opportunity Act of 2014 and the Carl D. Perkins Career and Technical Education Act of 2018—encourage career pathways as an important workforce development strategy for building workers' skills and meeting employer demand. The Logistics Education and Pathways (LEAP) program in Atlanta is an example of a career pathways program. Run by Georgia Tech's Supply Chain and Logistics Institute, LEAP targets veterans, youth, and under-represented minorities in Georgia and provides training in supply chain and logistics at progressively more advanced levels for program participants. Industry representatives consult on the curriculum, and a local organization that manages concession stands provides on-the-job training for participants.[60]

Sectoral training and career pathways approaches have the potential to support workers, but they fall short in a few important ways. First, most programs remain largely focused on getting disadvantaged individuals onto the first rung of the ladder.[61] And then they stop. Second, the quality of the employer networks *and* the relational trust between case managers and program participants vary widely across programs. Third, while the focus on sectoral/industry-specific career ladders is important, these programs offer little for workers who have found their way into a low-wage job in a low-growth, low-ceiling industry. Building on these approaches requires creative solutions that not only help workers find solid footing on the bottom rung, but also facilitate moving across industries or sectors into higher-paying positions with the opportunity for upward mobility and provide necessary training and support.

Local consortia that weave together networks of employers from multiple industries have the potential to create breakthrough opportunities for workers who have shown promise in their entry-level jobs but have nowhere to go from there.[62] While a successful janitor in a hospital setting may have the opportunity to be part of a career pathways program for health-care workers, what about the hard-working custodian at the local pizza shop? Place-based strategies that build out referral networks to connect workers to opportunities could create genuine transformations in the lives of those stuck at the bottom.

A variety of new data tools exist to help workforce development professionals build out these approaches. For instance, the Workforce of the Future Initiative at the Brookings Institution uses network analysis to identify place-specific, earnings-enhancing occupational transitions for low-wage workers.[63] The Occupational Mobility Explorer from a team of community development researchers at the Cleveland and Philadelphia Federal Reserve analyzes the skills that employers request in the thirty-three largest US metropolitan areas and identifies opportunities for workers to transfer those skills from a low-wage occupation to a higher-wage occupation in the same labor market.[64] Local workforce development practitioners could use these tools to develop approaches that blend occupational mobility with sectoral, career-pathways programming to generate transformative opportunities for mobility up and out of dead-end jobs for low-wage workers.

INCENTIVIZE EMPLOYERS TO OFFER ON-THE-JOB TRAINING

In tight labor markets employers do not have the luxury of waiting for the just-right candidate, and they are more willing to offer on-the-job training. Figuring out how to encourage on-the-job training in the absence of clear labor market incentives is a critical policy challenge. Job training requirements have risen over time, which implies that on-the-job experience has increased in value.[65] Yet this type of training is infrequent and largely concentrated on higher-wage, higher-skill workers. Moreover, the share of workers receiving on-the-job training decreased between the mid-1990s and the mid-2000s, from 13.1 percent in 1996 to 8.4 percent in 2008.[66]

We should be humbled by the examples of Austria, Germany, and Switzerland, countries that have long invested in robust technical training and apprenticeship for young people. More than half of the students in those countries are enrolled in high-powered vocational high schools that combine rigorous education with shop-floor experience.[67] Over a three-year period German students alternate between the classroom and the workplace, training under *meisters* who develop the skills they need to be productive employees. Germany boasts the best trained workforce in the world and that is no accident. But it also sees its teenagers earning a handsome wage throughout their apprenticeships, starting at the age of sixteen.

German employers do not worry about the "free rider" problem. While the vast majority end up hiring their own apprentices, they don't fret if their trainees end up working elsewhere. Why? Employers are not in this enterprise alone. The system is richly supported by tax dollars, unions, and the public education system itself. They are right to realize that if they lose a particular trainee, they will pick up another. And the whole country basks in the glory of a talented workforce that has fueled its prosperity. As Katherine Newman and Hella Winston have shown, there is no barrier to importing a similar system to the United States: South Carolina has already done so, largely to attract German and Japanese car companies that demanded the kind of trained labor force they were used to having in their own countries.[68]

The United States is not going to transform into a full-fledged social-democratic nation anytime soon. But we do have policy tools at our disposal to attempt to jumpstart on-the-job training as a more consistent element of work in the United States. Apprenticeships—including federally registered apprentices via the US Department of Labor—are one such option, as they offer work-based learning in an employment context, combined with support and classroom instruction. Employers are key; an employer must create the opportunity before the apprenticeship materializes. Research in both the United States and Europe shows strong returns to apprenticeship investments for both employers and for workers.[69]

Tax credits for businesses that offer on-the-job training for disadvantaged, low-wage workers are a second policy option. The United States already engages in variety of tax credit–based strategies to incentive employers' engagement with disadvantaged workers. Examples include the federal Work Opportunity Tax Credit, which provides a tax credit to employers who invest in jobseekers who have faced persistent barriers to employment and Empowerment Zone tax credit opportunities for businesses who offer jobs in economically distressed places. Several states provide tax incentives for employers' investments in training, including Connecticut, Georgia, Kentucky, Mississippi, Rhode Island, and Virginia, with incentives ranging from 5 percent to 50 percent of training expenses. None of these state programs are limited to on-the-job training only. All of them cover a broad range of employer-subsidized training expenses (including tuition reimbursement in a variety of institutional settings), and none are limited to specific sectors of the workforce.[70] The Investing in American Workers Act of 2021, introduced by a bipartisan group of members of Congress, proposes a federal tax credit designed to incentivize training tied to recognized postsecondary credentials for lower- and moderate-income workers.[71]

Tax incentives come at the risk of subsidizing employers for expenses that they would incur regardless of whether the credit was available. For this reason and in light of the variety of other avenues for offering disadvantaged workers with training and experience, the tax credit approach is less appealing. That said, a countercyclical credit (i.e., a credit available only in periods of labor market slack or phased in/out depending on the level of slack in the labor market) that offered carefully targeted tax credits could help jumpstart on-the-job training at times when employers are least likely to need to invest.

BOOST TUITION ASSISTANCE PROGRAMS

Traditionally human capital is enhanced through training and conventional education. Low-wage workers are often on the sidelines because they lack both. We would be remiss if we did not focus some attention on how we open up the gates of higher-education institutions so that people who benefit from tight labor markets can solidify their hold on better jobs with more conventional credentials. Many of the ideas proposed above knit together on-the-job training with more traditional "classroom" based training and programs that require educational institutions for expertise and support. All of them are designed to boost demand for employers and workers for these types of services. Yet they will only work if the educational institutions that supply the training are well-funded as well.

The United States has engaged in a decades-long rollback of support for the public educational institutions that serve as the backbone of career and technical education (both credentialing and BAs), in no small part because these institutions depend on state dollars, and states face severe budget constraints at precisely the times when educational institutions are most valuable: in down times.[72] The ups and downs of funding, even the influx of funds in boom times, make it difficult to build high-impact, sustainable educational programming. Rethinking both the levels and consistency of funding flows into public higher education is critical for ensuring that the workforce development system can supply the high-quality, high-impact training opportunities that are necessary for supporting workers in their journey into the labor market and up the economic ladder.

Yet higher education has been too distant from the world of work. Unless we prepare young people and returning adults with the opportunity to master skills of immediate use—in addition to their more conventional degrees—students will find it difficult to transition into the labor market unless they have privileged parents who can make that possible. Tight labor markets improve their chances, but when unemployment rises, we need alternative mechanisms for bridging the gap between education and the job market.

UMass Boston, a majority-minority university that is over 50 percent Pell Grant recipients and 60 percent first-generation students, inaugurated the Professional Apprenticeship and Career Experience program (PACE) to address this gap. PACE provided students with paid training opportunities on campus—in information technology, lab science, accounting, and other areas—that qualified participants to move into "industry clusters" composed of employers in high-growth sectors in Boston. Computer science majors, accounting students, and English lit majors with writing talent could get campus positions (and the references that came out of them) that provided experience to complement their classroom studies. PACE enabled students to give up jobs that provided income but no professional credentials in favor of campus jobs that did both, positioning them for good jobs in high-paying industries. Young people whose families could not provide them with contacts for internships or job openings of the kind their more privileged counterparts enjoy could turn to the university to build that bridge. Programs of this kind retain the best of education for its own sake with the need to prepare for the world beyond the university and launch into professions that can ensure a higher standard of living.

THE FUTURE OF WORK, THE FUTURE OF WORKERS

The lessons of tight labor markets provide many reasons to feel reasonably optimistic about the future of work in the United States. Decades of research in the social sciences has studied the downside of the business cycle. Our focus on the upside offers a new perspective on the transformative power of labor market opportunity for those who have long been marginalized. It also illustrates the limits of tight labor markets in the context of the complicated policy landscape in the United States, especially in a political economy where runaway inequality means that even workers who gain a strong foothold on the bottom rung still face immense challenges.

For starters, inequality in the United States means that each rung on the ladder is much farther apart than it was in the post–World War II period. High levels of economic inequality are strongly correlated with low rates of mobility.[73] So long as the structure of opportunity continues to be distorted in this fashion, the climb out of poverty is likely to be difficult. The policy ideas sketched out in this chapter provide a roadmap for thinking about how to build those ladders from the bottom-up, even in the context of persistent inequality. Tight labor markets can reshape the entire earnings distribution, as strong employer demand for workers means that even the lowest-wage workers see their paychecks grow.[74] Economists Arin Dube, David Autor, and Annie McGrew find additional support for the role of tight labor markets in reducing labor market inequality by boosting wages at the bottom in 2020–22, as well as a critical role for increases in state minimum wages between 2015 and 2020.[75] We leave it to other experts to weigh in on whether and how we ought to approach the problem from the top down.

Two last challenges deserve a few words: automation and immigration. While we cannot do full justice to the complexities of these forces, no book on tight labor markets is complete without raising them.

Automation

Upward pressure on the cost of labor creates incentives for employers to automate as much as possible. This is true regardless of the source of the pressure on labor costs, whether through the labor scarcity or increased worker bargaining power in the form of collective bargaining or pro-worker labor law. And while technology still requires humans to develop and operate, it shifts the skill levels required, eliminating routinized jobs and expanding higher-skilled occupations.

Economists have documented this dynamic repeatedly over the past several decades, illustrating in particular how automation technologies have played a role in the hollowing-out of the middle rungs of labor market ladders.[76] The pace of automation is expected to accelerate in the coming decades, particularly in light of rapid advances in applications of artificial intelligence (AI).[77] Firms whose work is compatible with current AI capabilities replace some human-performed tasks with technology while simultaneously generating new tasks accompanied by new skill demands. The share of jobs currently impacted by AI is too small to meaningfully change the overall shape of wages or employment in the US labor market as a whole.[78] However, each new industrial robot killed, on average, 3.3 jobs in America between 1990 and 2007.[79]

The tension between technological process and workers' well-being is not new. In 1907, New York City's lamplighters went on strike. Manhattan's twenty-five thousand gaslight lamps stayed dark, and the only lights left on the island were on the handful of Central Park transverse roads that had recently been equipped with electric lights. Edison's invention of the lightbulb ended the five-hundred-year history of lamplighters. Over a century earlier, during the British industrial revolution that began in the late eighteenth century, the jobs of adult craftsman were replaced by machines (and child labor), and real wages fell for those at the bottom of the ladder—leading Friedrich Engels to conclude that machine-owning industrialists "[grew] rich the misery of the mass of wage earners."[80] The contemporary debate over the newest wave of technological innovation's impact on labor market opportunity reflects similar concerns. Writing in the *New York Times*, economist David Deming notes: "Americans are worried that technology will soon replace much of the work done by human, and they are right to be."[81]

However, the impacts of technological change are not ultimately out of our control as a society. The impact of automation on workers' lives is shaped by policy decisions. Recent technological advances are indeed changing the opportunity structure of the labor market, creating more opportunity at the top and bottom. Jobs that were once middle-wage, family-sustaining occupations have disappeared, replaced by low-wage, low-quality work. But these jobs need not stay this way forever. In response to the dismal factory conditions of the nineteenth century, trade unions and new government regulations helped raise wages, improve working conditions, and boosted workplace safety. In Sweden, where automation has revolutionized the manufacturing industry into a high-tech operation, strong social protections for workers (including social insurance and active labor market programs such as high-quality training and retraining) mean that workers and union leaders have embraced automation as a pathway to a richer, more efficient, high-growth economy.[82] Many of the policy ideas that we have sketched out would go a long way toward shifting the United States into the win-win world that Sweden and other Scandinavian countries have begun to build.

Immigration

The two most recent examples of tight labor markets have occurred in the context of a second extraordinary contemporary policy moment: a near-complete closure of the United States borders to migrants. Immigration has long served as the pressure-release valve for labor shortages in the United States. When demand outpaces the supply of workers willing to take the jobs on offer from employers, immigrants have eagerly seized on the opportunity for a shot at the American Dream.[83] Yet periodically we slam those doors tight. In 2020 we saw a dramatic slowdown in the growth of foreign-born people living in the United States as well as a steady decrease in the number of Mexican-born US residents.[84]

Whether the slowdown in immigration, especially the declining migration of workers willing to step in to low-wage, low-quality jobs, has shaped the opportunities created by high-pressure labor markets remains an open question. Recent signs suggest this may indeed be the case, as industries that depend on foreign-born workers face high job vacancy rates and upward pressure on wages. For example, in health care and social assistance (including nursing homes), 17.2 percent of workers are foreign-born and 9 percent of jobs are vacant.[85] It is a pressing question, however, because the United States is an aging society with epically low birth rates. What began as a gradual, secular decline in baby-making, deepened during the Great Recession—just as it did during the Great Depression of the 1930s—and absolutely bottomed out in 2020–22. Families are shrinking and that translates, down the road, into aggravated worker shortages. In the absence of immigration, we could be looking at a United States that looks much more like Japan—a society that is aging rapidly—in the future. From a demographic perspective, and a productivity stance, that would not be good news. We have historically had a more open view of immigration than the Japanese, and it would behoove us to return to something closer to our roots as a society of newcomers.

The policy recommendations sketched out in this chapter, based on our observations of the power of tight labor markets, can remain potent in the face of new rounds of immigration. We can make good on the promise of America that has long been a beacon to all comers. So long as the regulatory and benefits policies apply to *all* workers, regardless of national origin, and so long as immigrants (regardless of citizenship status) are treated equally as workers, native-born employees should have nothing to fear from newcomers to our shores. So long as regulations and policies are enforced such that employers cannot get away with noncompliance, and workers are aware of their rights, we can leverage the power of tight labor markets on behalf of all workers—regardless of citizenship status.[86]

·　·　·　·　·

We began this book with a synopsis of how social science centers the role of unemployment as the genesis of poverty in the United States. It is appropriate to end with a reflection on where the analysis of tight labor markets should fit. Classic works, as well as most of the contemporary research in this field, focus—quite appropriately—on the scourge of unemployment and economic insecurity on the lives of the nation's poor and near-poor. We agree on the centrality of employment in shaping the daily lives and aspirations of those at the bottom of the economic pyramid, just as it organizes the lives of virtually everyone else, save the very rich. There is no substitute for steady work for underwriting the stability we all seek, especially in a country where the safety net has not been especially capacious.

We believe it is important for social scientists studying poor families, neighborhoods, schools, criminal justice agencies, and the like to pay more attention to the impact of labor market change on these settings. There is a powerful conditional element to the dynamics of poverty that is often missed when the assumption is that the weakness of opportunity is permanent and invariant. It isn't. That is not to say that tight labor markets have become the norm. But we have shown that over the decades of the twentieth and twenty-first century, they have happened often enough and lasted long enough to be consequential. Not revolutionary, but not nothing.

We need to train at least one eye on that unemployment rate and understand that it inflects essentially every social institution poverty scholars write about. Fathers behave differently when they have jobs and rising wages. Employers, who no doubt have their biases, approach jobseekers who bear a stigma with more openness when they have little choice if they are going to run a business. Accordingly, "We'd Love to Hire them, But..." (a powerful paper documenting the impact of statistical discrimination) turns out a bit differently when employers have to look to peripheral sources of labor.[87] They do hire "them." Neighborhoods plagued by violent crime look different when young men (and women) are earning money in the legitimate economy. The lesson is not one of Pollyanna confidence in a rosy future. Just because labor markets tighten and boost worker power, doesn't mean they stay that way. The point is one of conditional outcomes. Young boys in Franklin and Roxbury Crossing do not have to cower behind teenage "guardians" when violent crime declines in their neighborhoods. And that is a conditional outcome that rides, at least in part, on what the labor market generates in the way of opportunities.

We know that good fortune can, and often is, followed by downturns.

How do we find our way to the benefits—especially the social benefits that accrue in poor neighborhoods—of tight labor markets if they don't persist? To the extent that the social science literature on poverty and low-wage work has engaged with the idea of labor market institutions shaping the context of opportunity, the lens has been focused on unions as the key institutions for increasing worker bargaining power. Unions play a key role in raising workers' wages, improving job quality through more control over schedules and benefits, and creating pathways to upward mobility.[88] Indeed, the decline of unions in the private sector has been an important driving force behind the secular changes that we've seen in wages and benefits for workers in the bottom half of the income distribution.[89]

Yet given the sharp decline in union density, we need to complement collective bargaining with other tools. Even in today's historically weak union environment, tight labor markets have produced glimmers of genuine opportunity in the lives of previously marginalized workers. Worker organizing—including work stoppages where striking employees demanded higher wages and better benefits from employers—increased meaningfully during the tight labor markets of the 2018–19 period and then again during the tight labor markets of October and November 2021, a period nicknamed "Striketober" by labor advocates.[90] Policies designed to mimic the gains of organized labor in a prior era of union power are arguably achievable even in the context of today's relatively weak labor movement. How durable they are depends on the willingness of policymakers to enshrine some of the suggestions we make here—ideas that others have proposed to be sure—in the law.

It is in no one's interest for these improvements in the lives of the nation's poor to erode. Instead, it is in our collective interest to boost the momentum and ensure it clears entry-level jobs for new entrants whether native-born or new to the country. We can elect to take up the cause of the protections outlined here in the name of prosperity, in the recognition that they will help American workers at all levels, but especially at the bottom, continue the kind of ascent that tight labor markets make possible. The benefits are substantial—greater income stability in households, fewer people standing on the side lines of the work world, and neighborhoods that are safer and more vibrant.

Methodological Appendix
for Chapter 2

DATA

Data for this study come from the 1970–2019 waves of the Panel Study of
Income Dynamics (PSID). The PSID is a nationally representative household survey with rich information on the demographic, socioeconomic,
health, and other characteristics of survey respondents and their families.
Key for our analysis, it has detailed labor force status information over
time, information on family formation and composition, and information on individual and household income, earnings, and receipt of public and private transfers. Alongside other demographic data collected by
the PSID, this information allows us to examine trends in employment
and earnings across different phases of various economic cycles as well as
general trends across all observed cycles for different groups of adults as
defined by their age, race, gender, and educational background.

Since its inception, the PSID team has collected information from
about 82,000 people, including multiple generations of the same families.
Due to its initial oversample of poor families, the survey includes a large
subsample of Black Americans. The number of individuals and families
interviewed varies considerably across the years, ranging from 4,000 to

11,000 families in a given survey year and 17,000 to 32,000 individuals in a given survey year.

Given our focus on full economic cycles, we do not include the Latino oversample, which was added to the PSID in 1990 and then dropped in 1995. Our race/ethnicity variable is a categorical variable with three categories—non-Hispanic white, non-Hispanic Black, and other. All analyses stratified by race focus only on the first two categories, for which we have consistently sufficient sample sizes over time.

Our basic analytic sample is limited to working-age individuals, defined broadly to include those between the ages of 18 and 67, and it covers the period from 1970 through 2019. However, the actual analytic sample for each analysis may be limited further by either a shorter period of data collection for some key variables of interest or by the specific research question addressed. For example, our analysis of the effect of high-pressure labor market conditions on labor market outcomes during the following economic downturn (and subsequent new expansion) starts in 1977, the earliest year for which we were able to obtain state-level information for calculating high-pressure measure of labor market performance (explained in more detailed below). Similarly, for the analysis of each economic cycle we limited the sample to individuals who were continuously present in the sample during the years of the economic expansion ending with the peak year of the economic activity, as well as at the bottom (trough) following the downturn segment of the economic cycle.[1]

To build our analytic sample, we start with the user-friendly version of the PSID data available from the Cross-National Equivalent File (CNEF) for 1970–2015 period. We augment these data with the information from the original PSID survey to extend the concepts included in the CNEF to the two most recent waves of PSID (2017 and 2019) as well as to add a set of variables not available in the CNEF but important for our analysis (e.g., detailed labor force status information, poverty thresholds based on key personal and family characteristics including age, family size, and the number of persons under age 18). In addition to the fact that it simplifies the task of building the longitudinal analytic file, a major advantage of the CNEF data is that it includes a set of constructed variables that are not directly available in PSID but are relevant for our analysis such as various summary measures of income (e.g., pre- and post-government income, labor income, private and public transfers). We supplement individual-level data from PSID with state-level information on high-pressure labor-market exposure, which takes into account both the strength and duration of high-pressure period in each state and is constructed using national-level information on long-term unemployment rate from the Congressional Budget Office (CBO) and the timing of recessions from the National Bureau of Economic Research (NBER) as well as monthly Current Population Survey (CPS) data on employment status by state.

Methods

DESCRIPTIVE ANALYSIS

Our descriptive analysis (available from the authors upon request) starts with an overview of labor market trends, including employment, unemployment, and labor force participation, as well as hours worked, individual earnings (hourly and annual), household annual income, and public and private annual transfers for population ages 18–65 since 1970s.[2] In addition to the trends for the full sample, we also stratify them by age (18–24, 25–44, 45–54, and 55–65, as well as the combined category of all prime age [i.e., 25–54] individuals), race/ethnicity (non-Hispanic white and non-Hispanic Black), gender, education (less than high school degree, high school degree, more than high school degree), marital status (married/partnered versus unmarried/unpartnered), household size (one, two, three or more), presence of children under 18 in the household, and having household income below federal poverty level and, alternatively, 200 percent federal poverty level.

We next create multiple relative mobility measures, including quintile and decile transition matrices, inverse rank correlation, and inverse log-income correlation.[3] The first of these measures tracks the proportion of adults who change their earnings (or income) quintile (or decile) over one decade. Because the PSID data is collected biannually since 1997, we kept only every other year of data in earlier waves too. Furthermore, to decrease the possibility of an outlier year impacting the results and, more generally, smooth any possible transitory income changes as well as to decrease possible measurement error, we average two adjacent years of earnings (income) at both the beginning and the end of the observed period.

For example, to measure the change between 2001 and 2011, we compare averaged 2001–2003 value with the averaged 2011–2013 value. Moreover, our measure of transition is rescaled to acknowledge the fact that fully random mobility from a starting quintile (or decile) would result in one-fifth (or one-tenth) of individuals not changing their initial position. Accordingly, we rescale the observed mobility of 1-1/q, where q is the number of quantiles to be equal to 1. In the case of quintile transition, this suggests that 0.8 is rescaled as 1, and in the case of decile transition, 0.9 is rescaled as 1. In addition to tracking the mobility of all persons in the sample, we use this approach to track specifically the fraction of individuals who move from the lowest quintile (decile) of earnings or income to higher quintiles (deciles).

The second measure of relative mobility—inverse rank correlation—shows the level of correlation between the beginning-of-period and end-of-period positions. The rank correlation measure ranges from 1 (perfect correlation between beginning and end rank) to 0 (no relationship between the beginning and end rank—i.e., perfect relative mobility), and its inverse is consequently scaled from 0 to 1.

The final of the three measures of relative mobility, inverse log-income correlation, shows the level of correlation between the beginning-of-period and end-of-period log income. As for the inverse rank correlation measure, calculating the inverse of log-income correlation rescales it so that the measure ranges from 0 (perfect correlation—i.e., no income mobility) to one (no correlation—i.e., perfect income mobility).

The final aspect of the descriptive analysis focuses on examining transitions in employment, and family formation and fertility at different stages of economic cycles for individuals who are least well-off at the beginning of a cycle. More specifically, for each of the four economic cycles since 1970 for which we have full information on the downturn and expansion periods, we compare employment rates of individuals who are prime age (25–54) and in the bottom quintile of earnings (or, alternatively, below the 40th percentile of median individual earnings) at the beginning of the cycle (initial trough) with their subsequent employment rates at the peak of the expansion. We then further compare their employment rates at the peak of the expansion with the following trough of the cycle, tracking separately those whose earnings at the peak remained in the bottom quintile (or below the 40th percentile of median earnings) and those whose earnings surpassed these thresholds.[4]

INFERENTIAL ANALYSIS

To assess the impact of economic expansion on subsequent labor market trends, we conduct two complementary analyses that draw on the methodological approaches from the prior literature. First, we examine whether the period of expansion has positive impact on employment at the peak and, alternatively, the following trough of each economic cycle since the 1970s for which we have the full required information available. This analysis modifies the approach of Danny Yagan (2019), who analyzed the impact of the Great Recession on employment in 2015. The second analysis largely follows the approach of Julie Hotchkiss and Elijah Moore (2018), who analyzed the impact of high-pressure economy—that is, the economy with the unemployment rate below its long-run sustainable level on various labor market outcomes (unemployment, labor force participation, wages, and hours worked) over the following period of high unemployment, with the adjustments in our approach primarily driven by differences in datasets used for the analysis.

We first fit a logistic regression model of employment at the peak of an economic cycle as a function of the extent of the labor market improvement during the preceding expansion, with the following general form:

$$y_{i,tp} = \beta EXPANSION_{s(i,te)} + \theta_{g(i,te-1)} + \epsilon_{i,tp}$$

Where

- y denotes employment

- i denotes an individual

- tp denotes peak year

- te denotes the period of expansion (listing the beginning year of the expansion)

- $EXPANSION_{s(i,te)}$ denotes the percentage-point change in each state's (s) unemployment rate between the beginning (te) and end year of the expansion period of an economic cycle for each individual (i)

- $\theta_{g(i,te-1)}$ denotes fixed age-earnings effects for groups of g individuals define using the information from the survey wave directly preceding the beginning year of the expansion, and

- $\epsilon_{i,tp}$ is the error term for each individual.

The coefficient of interest is β, which represents a causal effect of one's employment level at the peak of the economic cycle as a function of an individual's state's magnitude of the decline in unemployment rate over the preceding period of expansion. Due to limited sample size, we define broad categories of fixed effects using the categorical variable of age (18–24, 25–34, 35–44, and 45–64) and quintiles of individual labor earnings. While our sample includes all age-eligible family members, we also run a model with a more elaborate fixed characteristics information that adds single-digit industry codes (which is the only level available in the publicly available version of PSID), but it is limited to survey respondents and their spouses only. The identifying assumption is that individuals are randomly (or near randomly) assigned across local areas with groups g. While the model explained here is for the employment at the peak following the expansion, we fit the same model for the following trough too. All the elements of this model other than the outcome variable remain unchanged.

Our second model largely relies on the approach developed by Hotchkiss and Moore (2018) to examine whether greater exposure to a high-pressure environment during an economic expansion moderates the labor market experience during the following high-unemployment period. It assesses the following model:

$$LMoutcome_{ist} = \alpha + \sum_{k=4}^{4} \{AGEi_i^k (\delta_{1k} + \delta_{2k} HU_t + \delta_{3k} HU_t HPsum_{sh})\}$$

$$+ \sum_{k=2}^{3} \{RACE_i^k (\beta_{1k} + \beta_{2k} HU_t + \beta_{3k} HU_t HPsum_{sh})\}$$

$$+ \sum_{k=2}^{4} \{EDUC_i^k (\varphi_{1k} + \varphi_{2k} HU_t + \varphi_{3k} HU_t HPsum_{sh})\}$$

$$+ MALE_i\{\theta_1 + \theta_2 HU_t + \theta_3 HU_t HPsum_{sh}\} + HU_t\{\rho_1 + \rho_2 HPsum_{sh}\}$$

$$+ \tau_t + \sigma_s + \varepsilon_{ist}$$

where labor market outcome for person i in state s in year t (*LMoutcome*) includes the share of time spent unemployed, the share of time spent in the labor force, real hourly pay, and weekly hours. The share of time unemployed or in the labor force are essentially constructed like a personal unemployment or labor force participation rate. To calculate them, we use information on labor-market participation from PSID that reports weeks spent employed or unemployed during the past year. Demographic characteristics in the model include age (18–24, 25–34, 35–44, and 45–64), race/ethnicity (non-Hispanic white, non-Hispanic Black, and other), years of education (less than 12, 12, more than 12 but less than 16, 16 or more), and sex (1 = male).[5] They enter the model on their own and are interacted with a high-unemployment dummy (*HU*), which equals one for each period (i.e., year) during which the unemployment rate in a state is above its long-term trend, as well as with a high-unemployment dummy modified by the total high-pressure exposure (*HPsum*) during the expansion period that immediately precedes the high-unemployment period. The model also includes time (τ_t) and state (σ_s) fixed effects.

The key aspect of this modeling approach is the construction of high-pressure labor market indicator by state. To do so, we use CBO's national (annual) long-term unemployment rate (LTUR), and adjust (i.e., shift) it up or down for each state by the difference between the average state unemployment rate (calculated using CPS monthly data) and average national LTUR over the whole observed period, summing up differences between state LTUR and actual unemployment rate in years in which the latter is lower as long as this happens during expansion period nationally as defined by NBER. The same calculation is repeated for every expansion period followed by a recession—that is, a complete economic cycle. This procedure can be summarized as follows:

$$HPsum_{sh} = \sum_{t=1}^{N} \{LTUR_s - UR_{tsh}\}$$

where N is equal to the number of years, t, during high pressure period, h, that the long-term unemployment rate for state, s, exceeds the current unemployment rate. *HPsum* enters the regression as a modifier for the impact of high-unemployment periods—that is, periods when the state's unemployment rate falls above the state's LTUR.

Since periods of high-pressure exposure are defined both in terms of intensity (i.e., magnitude of the difference between actual and long-term unemployment rate) and duration (i.e., time the high-pressure environment persists), the estimation model presented initially can be adjusted to explicitly account for these two elements:

$LMoutcome_{ist} =$

$$\alpha + \sum_{k=2}^{4} \{AGE_i^k(\delta_{1k} + \delta_{2k}HU_t + \delta_{3k}HU_tHPavg_{sh} + \delta_{4k}HU_tHPn_{sh})\}$$

$$+ \sum_{k=2}^{3} \{RACE_i^k(\beta_{1k} + \beta_{2k}HU_t + \beta_{3k}HU_tHPavg_{sh} + \beta_{4k}HU_tHPn_{sh})\}$$

$$+ \sum_{k=2}^{4} \{EDUC_i^k(\varphi_{1k} + \varphi_{2k}HU_t + \varphi_{3k}HU_tHPavg_{sh} + \varphi_{4k}HU_tHPn_{sh})\}$$

$$+ MALE_i \{\theta_1 + \theta_2HU_t + \theta_3HU_tHPavg_{sh} + \theta_4HU_tHPn_{sh}\}$$

$$+ HU_t \{\rho_1 + \rho_2HPavg_{sh} + \rho_3HPn_{sh}\} + \tau_t + \sigma_s + \pi_i + \varepsilon_{ist}$$

where *HPavg* represents intensity—that is, the average percentage point difference between the state's (*s*) long-term and actual unemployment rates during high-pressure period (*h*), while *HPn* represents duration, defined as the total number of years that the actual state unemployment rate is lower than its LTUR during high-pressure period.

For the model that examines how exposure to a high-pressure environment during an economic expansion impacts labor market outcomes during the subsequent high-unemployment period, both in its original and modified specification, we use person-year data from all complete economic cycles over the past four decades. We fit pooled ordinary least squares (OLS) and random effects regression to examine the four outcomes of interest. Given that we are observing the same group of individuals over time, this may favor the latter estimation approach, although the two largely provide consistent answers.

APPENDIX 2   Analysis Results for Chapter 2

Table 1.   Impacts of tight labor markets on employment durability across business cycles

	1983–1989 Expansion		1992–2000 Expansion		2002–2007 Expansion	
	Employed in 1992	Employed in 1999	Employed in 2001	Employed in 2007	Employed in 2011	Employed in 2019
Full sample						
Change in state unemployment rate during expansion	1.09^2	1.04	1.13^3	1.14^3	1.07	1
N	4,679	2,588	3,434	2,902	3,806	2,498
Bottom two quintiles						
Change in state unemployment rate during expansion	1.06	1.09^4	1.17^4	1.1	1.14	1.05
N	1,576	845	1,192	1,021	1,310	904

Table 1.   (continued)

	1983–1989 Expansion		1992–2000 Expansion		2002–2007 Expansion	
	Employed in 1992	Employed in 1999	Employed in 2001	Employed in 2007	Employed in 2011	Employed in 2019
18–24						
Change in state unemployment rate during expansion	0.98	0.99	1.47[3]	1.14	1.04	0.95
N	707	423	343	300	488	357
25–54						
Change in state unemployment rate during expansion	1.10[2]	1.04	1.13[4]	1.15[3]	1.1	1.01
N	3,666	2,165	2,912	2,602	3,063	2,141
Female						
Change in state unemployment rate during expansion	1.05[4]	1.04	1.22[2]	1.07	1.26[2]	1.09
N	2,405	1,332	1,827	1,548	1,909	1,296
Male						
Change in state unemployment rate during expansion	1.16[2]	1.03	0.98	1.24[3]	0.87[4]	0.92
N	2,274	1,256	1,607	1,354	1,897	1,202
Non-Hispanic white						
Change in state unemployment rate during expansion	1.09[3]	1.04	1.10[4]	1.13[3]	1.08	1
N	2,968	1,757	2,251	1,901	2,612	1,651
Non-Hispanic black						
Change in state unemployment rate during expansion	1.03	0.96	1.40[3]	0.99	0.94	0.97
N	1,545	725	1,014	865	879	640

	1983–1989 Expansion		1992–2000 Expansion		2002–2007 Expansion	
	Employed in 1992	Employed in 1999	Employed in 2001	Employed in 2007	Employed in 2011	Employed in 2019
Employed during preceding contraction	X		X		X	
Employed during expansion	X		X		X	
Age-earnings fixed effects	X	X	X	X	X	X

NOTE: [1] p < 0.001; [2] p < 0.01; [3] p < 0.05; [4] p < 0.1

Since PSID data are available only annually (and, more recently, biennially), we designate as years of economic expansion only those that have no quarters of decline in economic activity as defined by NBER, and otherwise designate the years as periods of economic contraction. Change in state unemployment measures difference in the state unemployment rate at the beginning and end of the expansion period. Coefficients reported as odds ratios. Periods of preceding contraction for each of the three expansions, respectively, are 1981–1983, 1990–1992, and 2001. Age-earnings fixed effects are defined using individual characteristics from the year (i.e., survey wave) immediately preceding the beginning of the expansion period. X indicates that a given variable/set of variables is included in a model.

SOURCE: Authors' calculations using the Panel Study of Income Dynamics (1984–2019).

Table 2a.   Marginal effects of *high-pressure* exposure versus *high-unemployment* exposure on weeks unemployed and weeks in the labor force, full sample

	Weeks unemployed		Weeks in the labor force	
	Marginal effect of			
	HU exposure	HP exposure	HU exposure	HP exposure
Full sample	0.3644[1]	−0.0122[3]	0.022	−0.0471[3]
Age groups				
18–24	0.5375[1]	−0.0266[3]	0.196	−0.1234[3]
25–34	0.3922[1]	−0.0157[3]	−0.0831	−0.0371
35–44	0.3344[1]	−0.0161[3]	−0.0149	−0.0650[3]
45–64	0.2872[1]	0.001	0.0772	−0.0073
Race				
Non-Hispanic white	0.2689[1]	−0.0044	−0.0665	−0.0379[4]
Non-Hispanic Black	0.5803[1]	−0.0318[2]	0.3397	−0.1215[2]
Education (in years)				
< 12	0.9364[1]	−0.0540[2]	0.3184	−0.0991
12	0.3001[1]	−0.013	0.0071	−0.0671[3]
12–16	0.2123[1]	0.0069	−0.0563	−0.0311
16+	0.2561[1]	−0.0076	−0.0666	−0.0019
Sex				
Females	0.3726[1]	−0.0128[4]	0.0819	−0.0510[4]
Males	0.3550[1]	−0.0115[4]	−0.0463	−0.0426
N	225,548		225,548	

NOTE: [1] $p < 0.001$; [2] $p < 0.0$;, [3] $p < 0.05$; [4] $p < 0.1$

All regressions include year and state fixed effects. Sample is restricted to individuals who reported at least 44 weeks of total activity (employment, unemployment, and out of the labor force) during the year, and who had nonzero employment during expansionary periods and were present in the sample during the subsequent period of high unemployment. Additionally restricted to those with positive wage (for log real hourly pay model), and positive hours worked (for weekly hours model). SOURCE: Authors' calculations using the Panel Study of Income Dynamics (1984–2019).

Table 2b. Marginal effects of *high-pressure* exposure versus *high-unemployment* exposure on hourly pay and weekly hours, full sample

Log real hourly pay		Weekly hours	
Marginal effect of			
HU exposure	*HP exposure*	*HU exposure*	*HP exposure*
−0.0129[4]	0.0050[1]	−0.2217	−0.0094
−0.0161	0.0074[2]	−0.6084[4]	0.0173
−0.0108	0.0048[2]	−0.3186	0.0189
−0.0008	0.0048[2]	−0.0919	−0.0177
−0.0255[3]	0.0044[3]	−0.0867	−0.043
−0.0200[3]	0.0049[1]	−0.2385	−0.0023
0.0001	0.0045[3]	−0.354	−0.005
−0.0116	0.0019	−0.5127	0.0258
−0.0201[3]	0.0056[1]	−0.2292	−0.0485
0.0004	0.0034[4]	0.0884	−0.0361
−0.0168	0.0071[2]	−0.3956	0.06
−0.0270[2]	0.0081[1]	−0.0985	−0.0047
0.0012	0.002	−0.3445[3]	−0.0139
186,065		190,793	

NOTE: [1] p < 0.001; [2] p < 0.01; [3] p < 0.05; [4] p < 0.1

All regressions include year and state fixed effects. Sample is restricted to individuals who reported at least 44 weeks of total activity (employment, unemployment, and out of the labor force) during the year, and who had nonzero employment during expansionary periods and were present in the sample during the subsequent period of high unemployment. Additionally restricted to those with positive wage (for log real hourly pay model), and positive hours worked (for weekly hours model). SOURCE: Authors' calculations using the Panel Study of Income Dynamics (1984–2019).

Table 3a.   Marginal effects of *high-pressure* exposure versus *high-unemployment* exposure on weeks unemployed and weeks in the labor force, lower-wage workers only

	Weeks unemployed		Weeks in the labor force	
	Marginal effect of			
	HU exposure	HP exposure	HU exposure	HP exposure
Full sample	0.1802[3]	–0.0176[4]	0.1762	–0.0909[3]
Age groups				
18–24	0.2079[4]	–0.0262[4]	0.0519	–0.1187[4]
25–34	0.2505[3]	–0.0371[2]	0.1336	–0.042
35–44	0.2221[4]	–0.0111	0.2551	–0.1564[3]
45–64	0.0333	0.0122	0.3057	–0.0696
Race				
Non-Hispanic white	0.1946[3]	–0.0131	–0.0841	–0.025
Non-Hispanic Black	0.2721[3]	–0.0411[3]	0.3602	–0.1977[2]
Education (in years)				
< 12	0.4835[3]	–0.033	0.0166	–0.1283
12	0.1208	–0.0184	0.3253	–0.1525[2]
12–16	0.0126	–0.0047	0.2898	–0.0258
16+	0.1799	–0.0159	–0.3377	0.0597
Sex				
Females	0.119	–0.0118	0.0608	–0.1059[3]
Males	0.2957[2]	–0.0279[3]	0.3939	–0.064
N	51,983		51,983	

NOTE: [1] $p < 0.001$; [2] $p < 0.01$; [3] $p < 0.05$; [4] $p < 0.1$

Low-wage = bottom two wage quintiles. All regressions include year and state fixed effects. Sample is restricted to individuals who reported at least 44 weeks of total activity (employment, unemployment, and out of the labor force) during the year, and who had nonzero employment during expansionary periods and were present in the sample during the subsequent period of high unemployment. Additionally restricted to those with positive wage (for log real hourly pay model), and positive hours worked (for weekly hours model).

SOURCE: Authors' calculations using the Panel Study of Income Dynamics (1984–2019).

Table 3b.   Marginal effects of *high-pressure* exposure versus *high-unemployment* exposure on hourly pay and weekly hours, lower-wage workers only

Log real hourly pay		Weekly hours	
Marginal effect of			
HU exposure	HP exposure	HU exposure	HP exposure
−0.011	0.0066[1]	−0.1896	−0.1378[2]
−0.0026	0.0106[2]	−1.2498[2]	0.0196
−0.0087	0.0054	0.2221	−0.2389[2]
−0.0021	0.0047	0.8985[4]	−0.3432[1]
−0.0297	0.0047	−0.3494	−0.0636
−0.0368[3]	0.0086[1]	−0.1714	−0.1289[3]
0.0078	0.0060[4]	−0.451	−0.1629[3]
−0.0241	0.0072	−0.4321	−0.0974
−0.0258	0.0081[2]	−0.1503	−0.1943[2]
0.0058	0.0043	0.0313	−0.0826
0.0353	0.0052	−0.3505	−0.1157
−0.0317[3]	0.0077[2]	0.0686	−0.1250[3]
0.0286	0.0048	−0.6823	−0.1610[3]
51,139		51,139	

NOTE: [1] $p < 0.001$; [2] $p < 0.01$; [3] $p < 0.05$; [4] $p < 0.1$

Low-wage = bottom two wage quintiles. All regressions include year and state fixed effects. Sample is restricted to individuals who reported at least 44 weeks of total activity (employment, unemployment, and out of the labor force) during the year, and who had nonzero employment during expansionary periods and were present in the sample during the subsequent period of high unemployment. Additionally restricted to those with positive wage (for log real hourly pay model), and positive hours worked (for weekly hours model).

SOURCE: Authors' calculations using the Panel Study of Income Dynamics (1984–2019).

Table 4a.   Marginal effects of high-pressure *duration* versus high-pressure *intensity* on weeks unemployed and weeks in the labor force, full sample

	Weeks unemployed			Weeks in the labor force		
	Marginal effect of					
	HU exposure	HPD	HPI	HU exposure	HPD	HPI
Full sample	0.2995[1]	−0.0228[3]	0.0738	−0.03	−0.0521	0.0102
Age groups						
18–24	0.4891[1]	−0.0617[3]	0.1639	0.3732	0.0043	−0.8737[2]
25–34	0.2965[1]	−0.0711[1]	0.2797[2]	−0.4329[4]	0.2254[1]	−0.8196[1]
35–44	0.3058[1]	0.014	−0.1133	−0.0249	0.1597[3]	−0.9930[1]
45–64	0.2126[3]	0.0124	−0.0167	0.1708	−0.5217[1]	2.0424[1]
Race						
Non-Hispanic white	0.2039[1]	0.0528[1]	−0.2089[1]	−0.0358	−0.0208	−0.1836
Non-Hispanic Black	0.5333[1]	−0.2099[1]	0.7702[1]	0.3555	−0.3059[1]	0.7205[3]
Education (in years)						
< 12	0.8953[1]	−0.2359[1]	0.6663[1]	0.4876	−1.0703[1]	3.3312[1]
12	0.2476[2]	−0.0211	0.0695	0.4109[4]	−0.3279[1]	0.6480[2]
12–16	0.1221[4]	0.0296[4]	−0.0189	−0.2714	0.2382[1]	−0.8720[1]
16[4]	0.1825[2]	0.0409[2]	−0.1617[3]	−0.8687[2]	0.6672[1]	−1.9836[1]
Sex						
Females	0.3123[1]	−0.0323[3]	0.1031	−0.0049	−0.0894	0.163
Males	0.2850[1]	−0.012	0.0408	−0.0587	−0.0102	−0.1619
N		225,548			225,548	

NOTE: [1] $p < 0.001$; [2] $p < 0.01$; [3] $p < 0.05$; [4] $p < 0.1$
All regressions include year and state fixed effects. Sample is restricted to individuals who reported at least 44 weeks of total activity (employment, unemployment, and out of the labor force) during the year, and who had nonzero employment during expansionary periods and were present in the sample during the subsequent period of high unemployment. Additionally restricted to those with positive wage (for log real hourly pay model), and positive hours worked (for weekly hours model).
SOURCE: Authors' calculations using the Panel Study of Income Dynamics (1984–2019).

Table 4b. Marginal effects of high-pressure *duration* versus high-pressure *intensity* on hourly pay and weekly hours, full sample

	Log real hourly pay			Weekly hours		
	Marginal effect of					
	HU exposure	HPD	HPI	HU exposure	HPD	HPI
Full sample	−0.0225[2]	0.0049[3]	0.0125	−0.1941	0.0117	−0.1095
Age groups						
18–24	−0.0342	0.005	0.0321[4]	−0.8812[4]	0.1235	−0.125
25–34	−0.0117	0.0015	0.0157	−0.2412	0.012	−0.0621
35–44	−0.0126	0.0082[3]	0.0018	−0.1332	0.1259[4]	−0.5362[3]
45–64	−0.0388[3]	0.0056	0.0108	0.0788	−0.1375[4]	0.2301
Race						
Non-Hispanic white	−0.0283[2]	0.0089[2]	−0.0061	−0.1659	−0.0607	0.1719
Non-Hispanic Black	−0.0131	0.0016	0.0262[4]	−0.4385	0.2292[2]	−0.8899[2]
Education (in years)						
< 12	−0.0013	−0.0084	0.0274	−0.3875	0.0817	−0.3211
12	−0.0267[3]	−0.0008	0.0365[2]	−0.054	−0.0928	−0.0019
12–16	−0.0063	0.0037	0.0081	0.1883	−0.0088	−0.2492
16[4]	−0.0444[3]	0.0203[1]	−0.0243	−0.7298[3]	0.1548[4]	−0.0302
Sex						
Females	−0.0438[1]	0.0159[1]	−0.0116	−0.2204	0.2730[1]	−0.9896[1]
Males	−0.0013	−0.0060[4]	0.0364[1]	−0.1679	−0.2456[1]	0.7574[1]
N		186,065			190,793	

NOTE: [1] $p < 0.001$; [2] $p < 0.01$; [3] $p < 0.05$; [4] $p < 0.1$

All regressions include year and state fixed effects. Sample is restricted to individuals who reported at least 44 weeks of total activity (employment, unemployment, and out of the labor force) during the year, and who had nonzero employment during expansionary periods and were present in the sample during the subsequent period of high unemployment. Additionally restricted to those with positive wage (for log real hourly pay model), and positive hours worked (for weekly hours model).

SOURCE: Authors' calculations using the Panel Study of Income Dynamics (1984–2019).

APPENDIX 3 Demographic Information
for Chapters 6 and 7

The following tables summarize key demographic information for Roxbury and Franklin, in comparison to the broader City of Boston, based on US Census data from 2000 and subsequent years of the American Community Survey (ACS). More information about how these data were generated are available in Appendix 4, which addresses the spatial methodology, and Appendix 5, which provides details about the US Census data sources.

Table 5a.   Demographics, family structure, and income for Roxbury

	2000	2009	2015	2019
Total population	6,177	6,970	15,896	15,878
Population density	17,853	20,145	45,942	45,890
Individuals				
Male	46%	41%	48%	46%
Female	54%	59%	52%	54%
Age < 18	33%	32%	19%	19%
Age > 65	9%	8%	8%	9%
Black	54%	49%	38%	36%
White	8%	10%	23%	21%
Hispanic	32%	32%	29%	29%
Other race	7%	9%	11%	15%
Foreign-born	23%	21%	35%	34%
Families				
Family poverty[1]	38%	51%	32%	24%
Affluent families (income > $75,000)	4%	4%	16%	23%
Very affluent families (income > $150,000)	1%	1%	4%	4%
Female headed families[2]	49%	16%	15%	17%
Two-parent headed families[2]	19%	4%	6%	7%
Grandparents in household	3%	9%	2%	3%
Adult children (over 18) living with parents	3%	12%	11%	12%
Income				
Median household income (2000 adjusted)[3]	$15,688	$13,806	$16,612	$15,846
Median household income (2020 adjusted)[3]	$23,578	$20,750	$24,968	$23,817
Public assistance income	9%	12%	6%	6%
Monthly rent < $1000	91%	81%	66%	63%
Monthly rent $1000–$1999	7%	18%	26%	28%
Monthly rent > $2000	2%	2%	5%	4%

NOTE: [1]Family poverty = percent of all families that have income below the poverty line. [2]As a portion of all families with children. [3]Mean of median for each Census tract in neighborhood.
SOURCE: Authors' calculations using American Community Survey and Census data.

Table 5b.   Demographics, family structure, and income for Franklin

	2000	2009	2015	2019
Total population	11,900	10,985	23,493	248,34
Population density	21,835	20,156	43,106	45,567
Individuals				
Male	45%	46%	47%	45%
Female	55%	54%	53%	55%
Age < 18	38%	38%	27%	29%
Age > 65	6%	7%	9%	11%
Black	69%	62%	73%	68%
White	1%	3%	3%	3%
Hispanic	25%	31%	19%	25%
Other race	5%	4%	4%	3%
Foreign-born	27%	32%	49%	49%
Families				
Family poverty[1]	36%	34%	25%	27%
Affluent families (income > $75,000)	8%	11%	21%	28%
Very affluent families (income > $150,000)	1%	2%	4%	8%
Female headed families[2]	50%	16%	17%	18%
Two-parent headed families[2]	18%	6%	7%	7%
Grandparents in household	5%	5%	6%	6%
Adult children (over 18) living with parents	5%	17%	15%	15%
Income				
Median household income (2000 adjusted)[3]	$23,185	$21,349	$22,507	$24,313
Median household income (2020 adjusted)[3]	$34,847	$32,088	$33,827	$36,542
Public assistance income	15%	13%	10%	7%
Monthly rent < $1000	97%	70%	54%	40%
Monthly rent $1000–$1999	3%	30%	45%	53%
Monthly rent > $2000	0%	0%	1%	6%

NOTE: [1]Family poverty = percent of all families that have income below the poverty line. [2]As a portion of all families with children. [3]Mean of median for each Census tract in neighborhood.
SOURCE: Authors' calculations using American Community Survey and Census data.

Table 5c.   Demographics, family structure, and income for the City of Boston

	2000	2009	2015	2019
Total population	589,141	625,304	650,281	684,379
Population density	12,166	12,913	13,470	14,158
Individuals				
Male	48%	48%	48%	48%
Female	52%	52%	52%	52%
Age < 18	20%	18%	17%	15%
Age > 65	10%	10%	11%	11%
Black	24%	22%	23%	22%
White	50%	51%	46%	44%
Hispanic	14%	16%	19%	19%
Other race	12%	12%	13%	13%
Foreign-born	26%	27%	27%	28%
Families				
Family poverty[1]	15%	15%	17%	14%
Affluent families (income > $75,000)	23%	36%	39%	48%
Very affluent families (income > $150,000)	5%	11%	15%	22%
Female headed families[2]	23%	11%	12%	12%
Two-parent headed families[2]	27%	11%	11%	23%
Grandparents in household	2%	3%	3%	2%
Adult children (over 18) living with parents	16%	9%	9%	8%
Income				
Median household income (2000 adjusted)[3]	$39,629	$42,081	$40,536	$47,889
Median household income (2020 adjusted)[3]	$59,562	$63,234	$60,908	$71,968
Public assistance income	4%	4%	4%	3%
Monthly rent < $1000	75%	48%	38%	31%
Monthly rent $1000–$1999	22%	45%	46%	42%
Monthly rent > $2000	2%	7%	9%	12%

NOTE: [1]Family poverty = percent of all families that have income below the poverty line. [2]As a portion of all families with children. [3]Mean of median for each Census tract in neighborhood.
SOURCE: Authors' calculations using American Community Survey and Census data.

Table 6a.   Education and employment rates for Roxbury

	2000	2009	2015	2019
Education				
Less than high school degree	35	31	20	23
Associate's degree or higher	14	37	53	54
Four-year college degree or higher	10	18	28	28
Employment[1]				
Male employment	86	85	84	82
Male joblessness	49	39	40	38
Male unemployment	14	9	10	11
Female employment	89	81	88	91
Female joblessness	49	47	38	37
Female unemployment	11	10	7	5
Black employment	89	85	84	86
Black joblessness	52	56	38	39
Black unemployment	11	15	16	14
White employment	88	94	87	86
White joblessness	40	37	36	31
White unemployment	12	6	13	14
Hispanic employment	83	74	83	88
Hispanic joblessness	48	34	42	43
Hispanic unemployment	17	26	17	12
Employment sector				
Managerial/professional occupation	19	35	35	39
Service-sector occupation	32	36	33	33

NOTE: [1]Percentage of population over 16 years old, excluding armed forces.
SOURCE: Authors' calculations using American Community Survey and Census data.

Table 6b.   Education and employment rates for Franklin

	2000	2009	2015	2019
Education				
Less than high school degree	38	26	26	21
Associate's degree or higher	11	37	40	46
Four-year college degree or higher	7	8	11	16
Employment[1]				
Male employment	85	80	85	89
Male joblessness	41	34	32	33
Male unemployment	15	13	10	7
Female employment	87	82	83	90
Female joblessness	52	30	34	34
Female unemployment	13	13	11	6
Black employment	87	79	83	90
Black joblessness	48	34	32	32
Black unemployment	13	21	17	10
White employment	74	78	86	90
White joblessness	56	32	41	40
White unemployment	26	22	14	10
Hispanic employment	82	80	82	88
Hispanic joblessness	49	27	37	37
Hispanic unemployment	18	20	18	12
Employment sector				
Managerial/professional occupation	11	25	21	25
Service-sector occupation	30	46	40	41

NOTE: [1]Percentage of population over 16 years old, excluding armed forces.
SOURCE: Authors' calculations using American Community Survey and Census data.

Table 6c.   Education and employment rates for the City of Boston

	2000	2009	2015	2019
Education				
Less than high school degree	21	16	15	13
Associate's degree or higher	55	61	64	68
Four-year college degree or higher	36	43	45	50
Employment[1]				
Male employment	92	91	91	93
Male joblessness	32	28	29	28
Male unemployment	8	7	7	5
Female employment	93	92	92	94
Female joblessness	40	34	34	33
Female unemployment	7	5	5	4
Black employment	89	85	86	90
Black joblessness	41	36	34	32
Black unemployment	11	15	14	10
White employment	94	94	94	95
White joblessness	33	29	29	27
White unemployment	5	6	6	5
Hispanic employment	88	87	88	92
Hispanic joblessness	41	29	32	31
Hispanic unemployment	12	13	12	8
Employment sector				
Managerial/professional occupation	43	44	47	51
Service-sector occupation	18	31	30	28

NOTE: [1]Percentage of population over 16 years old, excluding armed forces.
SOURCE: Authors' calculations using American Community Survey and Census data.

Table 7.   Housing for Roxbury, Franklin, and the City of Boston

Housing	2000	2009	2015	2019
	Roxbury			
Median value of owner-occupied housing[1]				
adjusted dollars 2000	$133,900	$204,395	$177,005	$277,770
adjusted dollars 2020	$201,252	$307,140	$265,966	$417,438
Same residence for past year	55%[2]	79%	78%	84%
Owner occupied housing	6%	11%	13%	18%
Moved within 5 years	56%	33%	35%	21%
Moved more than 5 years ago	44%	67%	65%	79%
	Franklin			
Median value of owner-occupied housing[1]				
adjusted dollars 2000	$170,900	$287,759	$205,296	$235,952
adjusted dollars 2020	$256,863	$432,409	$308,477	$354,594
Same residence for past year	59%[2]	80%	84%	86%
Owner-occupied housing	22%	20%	28%	30%
Moved within 5 years	49%	36%	34%	20%
Moved more than 5 years ago	51%	64%	66%	80%
	Boston			
Median value of owner-occupied housing				
adjusted dollars 2000	$210,100	$324,639	$286,047	$365,364
adjusted dollars 2020	$315,780	$487,932	$429,928	$549,141
Same residence for past year	64.4%[2]	76.7%	79.1%	80.2%
Owner-occupied housing	47.8%	37.3%	34.3%	35.0%
Moved within 5 years	57.6%	36.8%	42.6%	32.2%
Moved more than 5 years ago	42.4%	63.2%	57.4%	67.8%

NOTE: [1]Mean of median for each census tract in neighborhood; [2]Same residence for past five years.

SOURCE: Authors' calculations using American Community Survey and Census data.

APPENDIX 4   Geographic Transformations
for Chapters 6 and 7

To understand how demographic characteristics have changed in specific neighborhoods over time, despite US Census boundary changes, we undertook a process to match our geographic areas of interest to the Census designations used in the past. This type of matching falls into a category of problem known as a modifiable areal unit problem (MAUP). Under MAUP, non-nested and changing boundaries over time lead to uncertainty as to how to compare the populations aggregated within a geographic feature (Goplerud 2015; Gotway and Young 2004). We employ the standard method of dasymetric mapping, which is the most accurate strategy (Amos, McDonald, and Watkins 2017). We employ dasymetric mapping with population weighted data to identify the change in boundaries over time, taking Census Block Group (CBG) data from non-2000 Census years and matching it the 2000 Census tracts of interest. We focus on four tracts in Suffolk County: tracts 00805, 00806, 00924, 01001.

Figure 11 demonstrates the process by which dasymetric mapping works. One takes a first level of geography, G_1, and spatially overlays it onto a second level of geography, G_2. Geographic dasymetric mapping would involve finding the geographic overlap and then assigning the proportionate geographic overlap from G_1 to G_2. However, such a method

Figure 11. Dasymetric mapping schematic

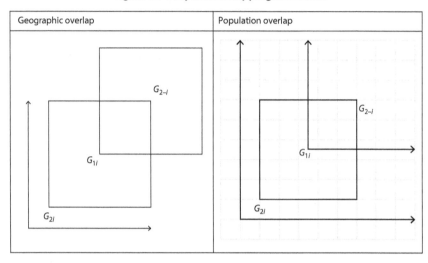

Note: G_1 represents the first layer of geography, and G_2 the second level. The grids present in the left figure for population overlap reflect the atomic grid provided by Census blocks, with each grid's weight dictated by the population present within the block.

Source: Illustration provided by Dr. John A. Curiel.

only works if the demographic variables of interest are spread uniformly across geography, which is unlikely in this case (Rao 2003). Dasymetric mapping with population weights minimizes the problem, as seen in the right panel of figure 11. One can overlay a grid of atomic census units (ACU) and find the three-way overlap between G_1, G_2, and the ACU. Only when G_1 and G_2 split an ACU are populations weighted geographically. Therefore population overlap minimizes assumptions and can effectively allocate split polygons present in a MAUP.

We use of the arealOverlapR package, a modified version employed by John Curiel and Tyler Steelman (2018) used to find the population overlap between different levels of geography.[1] Our inputs are the CBG data for the aforementioned Suffolk county tracts from 2000, overlaid onto the CBGs from the 1990 and 2010 US Censuses.[2] We incorporated 16 CBGs from the 2000 Suffolk county tracts, 37 unique CBGs from 2010, and 218 blocks from 2010. We created a crosswalk by which to weight the relevant demographics from the relevant Censuses and American Community Survey (ACS) years.

As specified in Appendix 3, we made use of CBG data where possible (from Social Explorer), and Tract data (often from the Census API). For the CBG tract-level data, we found the effective number of 2000 CBGs present in 2010 CBGs to average out at 1.094, a minimum of 1 and a maximum of 1.63. According to Steelman and Curiel (forthcoming), given that only five 2010 CBGs exceed a value of 1.33, 85 percent of the CBG matching will attain an accuracy rate above 90 percent. The five lower-bound tracts still exceed accuracy rates of 75 percent, which leads us to expect the areal interpolation matching to be sound.[3]

For the Census tract-to-tract crosswalk, we found the results to be largely the same. All but one Census tract from 2010 saw an effective number of splits under 1.06, with 11 of 16 tracts perfectly nested within 2000 Census tracts. The sole tract from 2010 substantively split, 080401, scored at 1.32. Census tract 080401 shared populations with the 2000 Census tracts of 805 and 806. This means that we can have near utmost certainty in the results for Census tracts 924 and 1001. While lesser accuracy exists for 2000 Census tracts 805 and 806, even the most split unit exceeds an accuracy rate of 90 percent. We therefore areal interpolate the post-2010 ACS data onto the 2000 Census boundaries in a manner that should not substantively impact the results (Steelman and Curiel, forthcoming).

APPENDIX 5   Census and American Community
Tables for Chapters 6 and 7

We pulled data from each US Census starting with the 2000 Census, followed by three of the five-year ACS data years: 2005–2009, 2011–2015, and 2015–2019. For the Census data extraction, we employed the R package "censusapi," to identify the relevant variables of interest by table name and then extract data.[1] For the individual and basic household-level variables, we made use of the Census Summary File 1. For family-level and socioeconomic (SES) variables, we drew from the Census Summary File 2, which went down to the tract level. These variable names are presented in Table 8, from a combination of the original Census names and the cleaned Social Explorer data.

For the ACS data we report the smallest level of precision available, using a combination of tract and CBG levels. We likewise used a combination of the Census API and Social Explorer data. Unlike the Census 2000 data, we had two areas of concern. First, the MAUP issue affects the ACS data following the new 2010 Census geographic CBG shapefiles. Second, a number of variables were associated with different table names or question wording. Therefore, table 9 reports the variable name, level data could be found, and category, in addition to noting where changes led to different names for the variables of interest.

We additionally pulled the above data for the Boston area. We pulled the data from the Census API and Social Explorer data. We aggregated to the level of place, using the FIPs code "07000" for this purpose.

Table 8.   US Census categories and table items

Item	*Table #*
Demographics	
White	P004_T072540_006^
Black	P004_T072540_007^
Hispanic	P004_T072540_003^
Other race	P004_T072540_008:0012^
Men	P008_T073308_003^
Women	P008_T073308_042^
Children (0–17)	P008_T073308_004:021 + P008_T073308_043:060^
Over 65	P008_T073308_036:041 + P008_T073308_075:080^
Foreign-born	P021_T074209_014^
Socioeconomic status by family	
Family poverty	P090_T074711_004 + P090_T074711_010^
Affluent families (income > $75,000)	P052_T075143_014:018^
Very affluent families (income > $150,000)	P052_T075143_017:018^
Female-headed families with children	P39_T080508_017^ P017_T075900_017^
Two-parent headed families with children	P39_T080508_004^ P017_T075900_004^
Married couples under age 25	PCT007045:047+PCT007032:034+PCT 007018:020+PCT007126:128+PCT007 113:115+PCT007099:101†
Married couples ages 25–29	PCT007048+PCT007035+PCT007021+ PCT007129+PCT007116+PCT007102†
Married couples over age 29	PCT007049:056+PCT007036:043+PCT 007022:029+PCT007130:37+PCT0071 17:124+PCT007103:110†
Socioeconomic status by household	
Median household income (inflation adjusted)	P053001†
Public assistance income	P064_T080908_003^
Grandparents in household	PCT008002†
Adult children (over 18) living with parents	(P027008 + PCT015012) P028004†
Unmarried partner households	PCT019005+ PCT019010 † PCT015011 +PCT015005†
Unmarried partner households with family (including children)	PCT015005†
Unmarried partner households without children	PCT015011†
Monthly rent costs	H054003:022†

Item	*Table #*

Socioeconomic status by individual

Managerial/professional occupation	P050010+P050057†
Service-sector occupation	P050023+P050070†
Less than high school degree	P037_T190229_004:011 + P037_T190229_021:028^
Associate's degree or higher	P037_T190229_015:019 + P037_T190229_032:036^
Four-year college degree or higher	P037_T190229_016:019 + P037_T190229_033:036^
Male employment	P043_T182732_007^
Male joblessness	P043_T182732_009^
Male unemployment	P043_T182732_008^
Female employment	P043_T182732_014^
Female joblessness	P043_T182732_016^
Female unemployment	P043_T182732_015^
Black employment	P0150B_T183943_007 + P0150B_T183943_014^
Black joblessness	P150B_T183943_009 + P150B_T183943_016^
Black unemployment	P0150B_T183943_008 + P0150B_T183943_015^
White employment	P0150A_T183759_007 + P0150A_T183943_014^
White joblessness	P150A_T183759_004 + P150A_T183759_011^
White unemployment	P0150A_T183759_008 + P0150A_T183943_015^
Hispanic employment	P0150H_T183808_007 + P0150H_T183808_014^
Hispanic joblessness	P150H_T183808_009 + P150H_T183808_016^
Hispanic unemployment	P0150H_T183808_008 + P0150H_T183808_015^

Residential characteristics

Owner-occupied housing	H11_T195018_003:004^ H010_T185123_002^
Same residence (moved within five years)	A10031_002*
Median value of owner-occupied housing	H085_T184800_002 (H004003)†

NOTE: † = Census API; * = Social Explorer; ^ = Census data page ("group #"_"table #"_"variable index"); *** = calculated by taking sum of (all households with children, all households with foster children) minus the number of total households with related children under 18.
SOURCE: Census.

Table 9. American Community Survey (ACS) categories and table items

Item	Table #	Level
Demographics		
White	A04001_003*	CBG
Black	A04001_004*	CBG
Hispanic	A04001_010*	CBG
Other race	A04001_005:A04001_009*	CBG
Men	A02001_002*	CBG
Women	A02001_003*	CBG
Children (0–17)	A01001_002:A01001_005*	CBG
Over 65	A01001_011:A01001_013*	CBG
Foreign-born	B05006_001E†	Tract
Socioeconomic status by family		
Family poverty	E13004_002:E13004_004/ E13004_001*	CBG
Affluent families (income > $75,000)	B19001B_013E:B19001B_017E*	CBG
Very affluent families (income > $150,000)	B19001B_016E:B19001B_017E*	CBG
Female-headed families with children	B11003016/(B11003003 + B11003010+B11003016)	Tract
Two-parent headed families with children	B11003003/(B11003003 + B11003010+B11003016)	Tract
Married couples under age 25	(B12002_020E:B12002_022E + B12002_113E:B12002_115E)/ B12002_001E*	Tract
Married couples ages 25–30	(B12002_023E + B12002_116E)/ B12002_001E*	Tract
Married couples over age 30	(B12002_024E:B12002_033E + B12002_117E:B12002_126E)/ B12002_001E*	Tract
Socioeconomic status by household		
Median household income (inflation adjusted)	A14006_001	CBG
Public assistance income	A10014_002	CBG
Grandparents in household	B10050_002E/B10050_001E†	CBG
Adult children (over 18) living with parents	(B09016_008E+B09016_031E) - (B09006_005E+B09006_002E)/ B09016_002E† (group B09019 replaces B09016 for 2015 onwards)	Tract
Unmarried partner households	(B09016_016E + B09016_030E)/ B09016_002E	Tract

Item	Table #	Level
Unmarried partner households with family (including children)	B09016_016E/B09016_002E† (NOTE: Absent for 2019)**	Tract
Unmarried partner households without children	B09016_030E / B09016_002E† (NOTE: Absent for 2019)**	Tract
Monthly rent costs ($0–999); ($1000–1999); ($2000+)	group (B25056)†	Tract

Socioeconomic status by individual

Item	Table #	Level
Managerial/professional occupation	A17008_002	CBG
Service-sector occupation	A17007B_004:A17007B_009 + A17007A_004:A17007A_009	CBG
Less than high school degree	A12001_002	CBG
Associate's degree or higher***	A12001_004:A12001_008	CBG
Four-year college degree or higher	A12001_005:A12001_008	CBG
Male employment	A17002A_005	Tract
Male joblessness	A17002A_007	Tract
Male unemployment	A17002A_006	Tract
Female employment	A17002B_005	Tract
Female joblessness	A17002B_007	Tract
Female unemployment	A17002B_006	Tract
Black employment	C23002B_007E+C23002B_012E+C23002B_020E+C23002B_025E/(C23002B_006E+C23002B_011E+C23002B_019E+C23002B_024E)	Tract
Black joblessness	C23002B_009E+C23002B_014E+C23002B_022E+C23002B_027E/(C23002B_001E)	Tract
Black unemployment	C23002B_008E+C23002B_013E+C23002B_021E+C23002B_026E/(C23002B_006E+C23002B_011E+C23002B_019E+C23002B_024E)	Tract
White employment	C23002A_007E+C23002A_012E+C23002A_020E+C23002A_025E/(C23002A_006E+C23002A_011E+C23002A_019E+C23002A_024E)	Tract
White joblessness	C23002A_009E+C23002A_014E+C23002A_022E+C23002A_027E/(C23002A_001E)	Tract
White unemployment	C23002A_008E+C23002A_013E+C23002A_021E+C23002A_026E/(C23002A_006E+C23002A_011E+C23002A_019E+C23002A_024E)	Tract

Table 9.   *(continued)* American Community Survey (ACS) categories and table items

Item	Table #	Level
Hispanic employment	C23002I_007E+C23002I_012E+C23 002I_020E+C23002I_025E/(C23002 I_006E+C23002I_011E+C23002I_0 19E+C23002I_024E)	Tract
Hispanic joblessness	C23002I_009E+C23002I_014E+C23 002I_022E+C23002I_027E/ (C23002I_001E)	Tract
Hispanic unemployment	C23002I_008E+C23002I_013E+C23 002I_021E+C23002I_026E/(C23002 I_006E+C23002I_011E+C23002I_0 19E+C23002I_024E)	Tract
Residential characteristics		
Owner-occupied housing	B25002_002E/B25002_001E	CBG
Same residence (moved within five years)	A10031_002 (+A10031_003 for 2019)	Tract
Median value of owner-occupied housing	A10036_001	CBG

NOTE: † = Census API; * = Social Explorer; ** = the data for unmarried by family is absent for the ACS 2015–2019; and *** = for the ACS the variable is "some college" as there is no associate's degree field in the table.
SOURCE: American Community Survey.

Personal and Institutional Acknowledgments

Since both authors have very demanding day jobs that are not built around academic research, we have institutions and individuals to thank, without whom this work would not have been possible.

The University of Massachusetts provided Katherine Newman with research support connected to what was then her home academic appointment on the Amherst campus. Chancellor Kumble Subbaswamy has always encouraged continuing scholarship, even for full-time leadership. Colleagues in the Office of the President, especially president Marty Meehan and the many people with whom Katherine worked as the system chancellor for academic programs, were steadfast in their encouragement. Special thanks go to Candyce Carragher, Carl Rust, Ismael Carreras, Preethi Lodha, Victor Owusu-Nantwi, and Bob Gamache, for their collegiality and dedication over the years we worked together.

The research for this book was undertaken mainly during Katherine's sojourn to the Boston campus of the university, where she served as interim chancellor from 2018 to 2020. Her many academic and administrative colleagues on that campus deserve mention, especially because it is a majority-minority campus whose students are an essential part of the story of social mobility, and whose families live in the neighborhoods that appear in this book.

The Urban Institute provided Elisabeth Jacobs with research support in her capacity as a senior fellow in the Center on Labor, Human Services and Populations (LHP), and as cofounder and then deputy director of WorkRise, a research-to-action network for jobs, workers, and mobility. Vice president Signe-Mary McKernan was a tireless advocate for Elisabeth's research time and budget, and senior vice presidents Kim Leary and Marge Turner, together with Urban's president Sarah Rosen Wartell, foster a vibrant research environment that is deeply grounded in policy and practice. WorkRise executive director Todd Greene and senior adviser Michael Deich generously supported a monthlong "book leave" at a key moment in the project. Countless Urban colleagues offered their expertise and inspiration, and the body of work generated by Urban scholars deeply informed Elisabeth's thinking from the earliest days of our work on the research. The Urban Institute is mission-driven to open minds, shape decisions, and offer solutions through economic and social policy research. We would like to think that *Moving the Needle* reflects that mission.

Katherine and Elisabeth first began working together at Harvard as participants in the Inequality and Social Policy (ISP) Program. The first book we wrote together, over ten years ago, was *Who Cares? Public Ambivalence and Government Activism from the New Deal to the Second Gilded Age*, which explored the history of public opinion about social policies designed to reduce poverty. That we have returned to collaborate on this project after many years of working in different realms says a lot about the institution where we first met. We both owe a tremendous debt to the many colleagues and students past and present of the ISP program, the Harvard Kennedy School, and the Department of Sociology.

Finally, a word about our families. Every book contains the authors' thanks to their loved ones and this volume is no different. But the ways in which the pandemic intersected our research and writing created special burdens for our partners and children. Like millions of Americans, we beat a retreat to home and worked remotely for more than two years as COVID-19 passed through our lives. We relied on our spouses to manage many burdens so that we could get back to the computer and keep writing.

Nothing happens in our lives as researchers, writers, or leaders that isn't made possible by their support.

Katherine rehearsed many of the ideas in this book with her husband of nearly fifty years, Paul Attewell, Distinguished Professor of Sociology at the Graduate Center of the City University of New York. Their oldest son Steven, now thirty-nine, teaches in the CUNY School of Labor and Urban Studies and added a historical dimension to much of the work here. Their younger son David, now thirty-three, is a postdoctoral scholar in comparative politics at the University of Zurich and from that distance offered valuable commentary on the ways other countries cope with the problems outlined here.

Elisabeth's husband, Sam Walsh, patiently listened as she thought out loud in their shared pandemic home office—and, despite his own demanding job, somehow managed to also provide hours of exceptional solo parenting to allow Elisabeth the nights-and-weekends research and writing time that a book project inevitably requires. Their daughter June, now twelve, asked great questions about the research and writing process, and constantly impresses with her sophisticated understanding of economics, society, and politics. Their son Miles, now nine, was a tireless cheerleader for the book and proudly describes Elisabeth as "a doctor, but not the hospital kind—she's a doctor who is trying to heal the world, like Martin Luther King was a doctor." While she is under no illusions that her work will come close to having the impact of Dr. King's, Miles is spot-on that we are doing our best to heal the world.

We are both grateful to Naomi Schneider and her staff at the University of California Press, who believed in the promise of this book and to the reviewers, including distinguished sociologist of the family, Andrew Cherlin, and Hilary Wething, assistant professor of public policy at Pennsylvania State University, who gave us such constructive feedback. To them and the many professional colleagues we leaned on in exploring the promise of tight labor markets, we offer our thanks.

Notes

1. The unemployment rate fell to 3.5 percent in 2019, which was the lowest unemployment in fifty years (Bureau of Labor Statistics 2020b). The tight labor market was accompanied by wage growth, especially for the lowest educated groups: workers with less than a high school degree saw their wages climb by 7.1 percent between 2018 and 2019, compared to a national average of 3.5 percent, and workers in industries including construction, transportation, and the service sector saw average wage growth over 5 percent (Bureau of Labor Statistics 2020b). Moreover, after years of stagnant wages, especially for low-wage workers, 2019 was the year wages started to climb. Wages grew fastest for those at the bottom of the distribution, driven both by minimum wage increases and tightening labor markets (Casselman 2019).

2. While the rapid recovery has surprised government officials and research-ers—with GDP showing full recovery by the second quarter of 2021—post-lockdown employment growth has been uneven, with some workers seeing a faster rebound than others. With many schools and daycares remaining closed into 2021, and childcare duties falling primarily on women, men were more likely to regain employment (Long and Van Dam 2021). There were also inequalities by race and educational attainment, with white and highly educated workers findings jobs more quickly than Black workers—especially Black women—and workers with less than a bachelor's degree (Long and Van Dam 2021).

3. Since the 1970s, the Black unemployment rate has ranged from 2 to 2.5 times that of the white unemployment rate (Ajilore 2020). Due to both racial discrimination and the correlation between race and educational attainment, Black job-seekers typically spend more time unemployed, taking longer to find a new job, than similar white jobseekers, and these gaps grow during economic downturns (Yu and Sun 2019).

4. The teen birthrate has been declining for thirty years, dropping by half between 2008 and 2018 (Livingston and Thomas 2019). While teen pregnancy was common and of great concern to policy scholars when Wilson was writing (in the 1970s and 1980s), the sharp declines—due to improved economic conditions as well as greater information about and access to contraception (Livingston and Thomas 2019)—has made teen pregnancy less of a social policy priority. In *A Different Shade of Gray: Mid-Life and beyond in the Inner City* (2003), Katherine Newman documents the marginalization of Black men over the life course and the increasing vulnerability that arises from their lack of social connections as they age.

5. Aeppli and Wilmers forthcoming; Autor and Dube 2022; Bivens 2021.

6. Not all women seek male partners, and vice versa, of course. Indeed, the share of Americans identifying as LBGTQ+ has steadily increased over the past several decades, in large part due to the diversification of sexual identification amongst younger Americans. Nonetheless, the vast majority (92.9 percent) of the US population identified as heterosexual as of 2021 (Jones 2022).

7. See also Bivens 2021 for effects on racial gaps in income and employment.

8. See Muro and You 2022.

CHAPTER 1

1. Henninger 2019.

2. "Employment fell by 21 percent in occupations in which telework is not feasible, compared with 8 percent in occupations in which telework is feasible. Over the same period the unemployment rate increased by 14 percentage points in occupations in which telework is not feasible, but only by 6 percentage points in occupations in which telework is feasible" (Dey et al. 2020; Gould and Shierholz 2020), and less than 10 percent of those with a high school education or less were teleworking between May 2020 and April 2021 (Gould and Kandra 2021).

3. These sectors "shrank by 11,131,666 jobs, or 38.2 percent as compared to their February 2020 peak. . . . For contrast, the workforce overall shrank by 24,691,596 jobs, or 15.6 percent compared to their February 2020 peak" (Dey and Loewenstein 2020). Retail trade specifically "shrank by 2,016,500 jobs, or 13.1 percent compared to their February 2020 peak" (Bureau of Labor Statistics 2020a).

4. Burning Glass Technologies 2020.

5. Cambon, Weber, and Chaney 2021.

6. Bureau of Labor Statistics 2021a; Bureau of Labor Statistics 2021e.

7. Burning Glass Technologies and Emsi merged in June 2021, so what was formerly Burning Glass became Emsi Burning Glass, and has since become a new entity called Lightcast.

8. Lohr 2021.

9. Lohr 2021.

10. Indeed.com, www.indeed.com/, accessed August 10, 2021.

11. Board of Governors of the Federal Reserve System 2020. In 1978, Congress passed the Full Employment and Balanced Growth Act, better known as the Humphrey-Hawkins Act, to specify explicit unemployment and inflation targets: within five years of passage, the unemployment rate should not exceed 3 percent for people twenty years or older, and inflation should be reduced to 3 percent or less, provided that inflation would not interfere with the employment goal. The legislation also specified that inflation be reduced to zero by 1988, providing that pursuing this goal would not interfere with the employment goal (see Steelman 2013). Under the leadership of Federal Reserve chair Paul Volcker the Bank pursued an aggressive suite of policies designed to reduce inflation. While inflation declined sharply between 1980 and 1983 (from 13 percent to 3 percent), unemployment rose substantially (from 7 percent to 10 percent). In 1983 joblessness was at its highest rate since the end of World War II, and the Federal Reserve came under scrutiny for ignoring the full employment half of its mandate.

The Fed stayed the course, and unemployment did eventually come down in the mid- to late 1980s. As a result, public discussion of full employment largely disappeared until the mid-1990s, when pressure to adopt a new formal inflation target reemerged. Opponents argued that doing so would reduce the Fed's discretion to achieve maximum sustainable employment. Vice chairman Alan Blinder noted that "we have a dual objective in the Federal Reserve Act now," referring to the twin goals of price stability and full employment (Steelman 2013). He introduced the concept to popular audiences, and since then the Fed has been charged by policymakers and the press with preserving price stability and maximizing employment.

Despite the popular acceptance of the Fed's dual mandate, the central bank's Federal Open Markets Committee (FOMC) did not explicitly reference employment in its policy goals until September 2010 (Steelman 2013; Thornton 2011). In January 2012 the FOMC adopted a specific inflation target of 2 percent while simultaneously noting the limits of the Fed's monetary policy tools in achieving a specific unemployment rate: "The maximum level of employment is largely determined by non-monetary factors that affect the structure and dynamics of the labor market. These factors may change over time and may not be directly measurable. Consequently, it would not be appropriate to specify a fixed goal for employment; rather, the Committee's policy decisions must be informed by assessments of the maximum level of employment, recognizing that such assessments are necessarily uncertain and subject to revision" (FOMC 2012; see also Steelman 2013). In August 2020 the FOMC amended its long-run goals and policy strategy by rephrasing the maximum employment portion of the dual mandate as "a broad-based and inclusive goal that is not directly measurable" (FOMC 2021).

12. Indeed, o percent long-run natural unemployment rate would be indicative of a completely inflexible labor market, where workers are unable to quit their current jobs in search of a better opportunity (Hobijn and Şahin 2021).

13. For more detail on the NAIRU (nonaccelerating inflation rate of unemployment) and the concept of the natural rate of unemployment, see Ball and Mankiw 2002.

14. Several other measures are important to assessing the health of the labor market: "labor force participation" and the "employment-to-population" ratio. The former is the sum of all workers who are employed or actively seeking employment, divided by the total noninstitutionalized civilian population. The employment-to-population ratio reflects the share of employed individuals in the total noninstitutionalized civilian population. These measures represent the outcomes of millions of decisions to either jump in to the labor market or sit it out. Poor people and others, including new mothers or retirees, who see wages rising and working conditions improve reenter the job market and push the labor force participation figures up, which in turn improves the employment-to-population ratio. To identify when a labor market is truly tight, then, we can't just rely on the garden variety unemployment rate: we need to know how comprehensively we are measuring the extent of opportunity for all those at least theoretically capable of working.

Figure 12 illustrates the total labor force participation rate for prime-age workers (ages twenty-five to fifty-four) as well as the labor force participation rates for prime-age workers living at or below the federal poverty line. In keeping with our focus on tight labor markets, the shaded areas of the figure indicate periods of very low unemployment. Most important is the uptick in labor force participation among the poorest workers at the back end of the tight labor markets of the Roaring '90s, which are indicative of the strength of tight labor markets to pull marginalized workers off the sidelines in search of work.

Employment-to-population ratios provide a useful complement to labor force participation rates, as they reflect the share of the population that is employed at a given point in time. Figure 13 illustrates two key points. First, the share of individuals living in poverty who are employed is substantially higher than conventional depictions of poverty would have us believe. Around half of the people living in poverty are working, and while that figure has gone up and down over the past four decades, it has not traveled the same dramatic secular journey as the employment rate for the broader working-age population. The differences here are likely due to the steep rise in women's work for families living well above the poverty line. Second, the tight labor markets of the 1990s stand out again as

Figure 12. Labor force participation rate by poverty status for 25- to 54-year-olds, 1976–2021

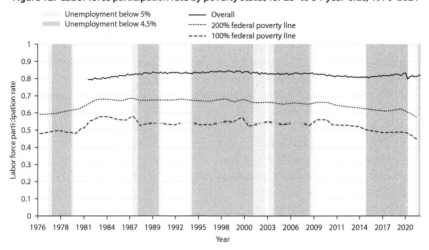

Note: The overall labor force participation rate is given as a quarterly average, while the labor force participation rate for those with incomes at 100% and 200% of the federal poverty line is given as an annual average.

Source: Sarah Flood, Miriam King, Renae Rodgers, Steven Ruggles, J. Robert Warren, and Michael Westberry, Integrated Public Use Microdata Series (IPUMS), Current Population Survey: Version 9.0 (dataset), Minneapolis, MN: IPUMS, 2021. Federal poverty line measure created using CPS and authors' own calculations.

Figure 13. Employment-to-population ratio by poverty status for 25- to 54-year-olds, 1976–2021

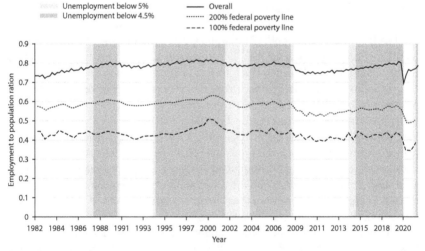

Note: The overall employment rate is given as a quarterly average, while the employment rate for those with incomes at 100% and 200% of the federal poverty line is given as an annual average.

Source: Sarah Flood, Miriam King, Renae Rodgers, Steven Ruggles, J. Robert Warren, and Michael Westberry, Integrated Public Use Microdata Series (IPUMS), Current Population Survey: Version 9.0 (dataset), Minneapolis, MN: IPUMS, 2021. Federal poverty line measure created using CPS and authors' own calculations.

a period of labor market opportunity for the poor, but it took substantial time before these groups achieved anything resembling take-off from the lift provided: employment-to-population ratios ticked upward for those living below the poverty threshold only after a sustained period of very low unemployment.

15. The data comes from the Current Population Survey (CPS) of the Bureau of Labor Statistics, a monthly survey of a nationally representative sample of American households.

16. Hoynes, Miller, and Schaller 2012.

17. Grusky, Western, and Wimer 2011.

18. Langdon, McMenamin, and Krolik 2002.

19. Walsh 1993.

20. Gardner 1994.

21. Okun 1973.

22. When unemployment is very low, workers feel more confident about quitting their jobs—either because they've already found new and better ones or because they anticipate finding new work easily, perhaps after a brief break between jobs. In the fall of 2019 more US workers quit their jobs than at any time since the US Bureau of Labor Statistics began collecting the data in 2001. While the quit rate following the Great Recession took nearly a decade to return to its pre-recession levels, the rebound from the COVID-19–driven crisis has been far swifter. In the second quarter of 2021, as the labor market continued its recovery from the pandemic, quits reached another historic high of 3.6 million. The Bureau of Labor Statistics began collecting data on job openings (vacancies), hiring, quits, and layoffs in December 2000 with the Job Openings and Labor Turnover Survey (JOLTS) (Figure 14). Prior to JOLTS, comparable data had never been collected in the United States. Alternate sources for vacancy data include the Conference Board's help-wanted advertising index, which measures the number of help-wanted advertisements in fifty-one major newspapers, but the reliability of this metric over time is unclear, as is the directional bias. The rise of the internet may have reduced firms' reliance on newspapers for advertising. However, newspaper market consolidation since the 1960s may have increased advertising in surviving newspapers, while Equal Employment Opportunity laws may have encouraged more firms to advertise job openings more extensively. As a result, we use the JOLTS data here rather than the Conference Board's index. For a comparison between the two datasets, see Shimer 2005.

Employers have complained loudly about rising quit rates, leading various private companies that track the job market to weigh in. Compdata, the consulting practice of Salary.com, analyzed data from nearly twenty-five thousand organizations of various sizes in the United States and found that employee quits increased from 13.5 percent in October 2017 to 14.2 percent in October 2018. Work Institute, a consulting firm in Tennessee, analyzed more than thirty-four thousand exit interviews and found that about 40 percent of employees who quit in 2017 did so within

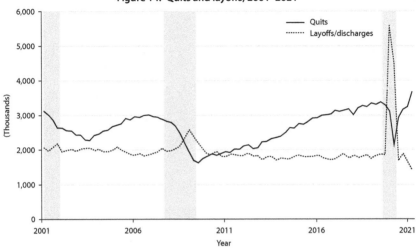

Figure 14. Quits and layoffs, 2001–2021

Note: Shaded areas indicate US recessions.

Source: US Bureau of Labor Statistics, Layoffs and Discharges: Total Nonfarm (JTSLDR) from FRED, Federal Reserve Bank of St. Louis.

twelve months of being hired. About half of those that left in the first year exited very quickly, within their first ninety days. The rise in first-year turnover is generally a sign of the robust job market, as employees recognize that they can easily go elsewhere if a given job doesn't meet their needs or expectations (Mauer 2011).

While there have been anecdotal reports of early retirements, people rethinking their career trajectories, abandonment of temporary "pandemic jobs," and federal stimulus payments providing the latitude to leave the labor market, the more plausible story is simply that when jobs are plentiful, workers understand they can quit their existing jobs to find better ones (Furman and Powell 2021). As figure 15 illustrates, job openings outpaced new hires in 2015. Openings once again began outpacing new hires in the third quarter of 2020, as the economy picked up speed. By the second quarter of 2021, they hit a historic high, indicating extraordinary levels of unmet demand from employers.

The jobseekers ratio captures the experience of looking for work by comparing the ratio of people actively looking for work to the number of job openings. Combining data on the number of unemployed people (from the BLS's CPS) and the number of job openings (from the BLS's JOLTS), allows for a "jobseekers ratio" that gives an estimate of the number of jobseekers for each job opening (figure 16). The lower that ratio falls, the tighter the labor market; numbers less than one indicate that the number of job openings was greater than the number of jobseekers. The severity of the Great Recession shows up in the record high number of unemployed workers per job: July 2009 saw nearly seven unemployed workers

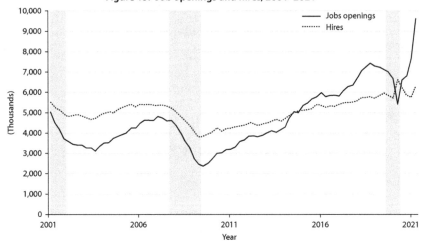

Figure 15. Job openings and hires, 2001–2021

Note: Shaded areas indicate US recessions.

Source: US Bureau of Labor Statistics, Job Openings: Total Nonfarm (JTSJOL) from FRED, Federal Reserve Bank of St. Louis.

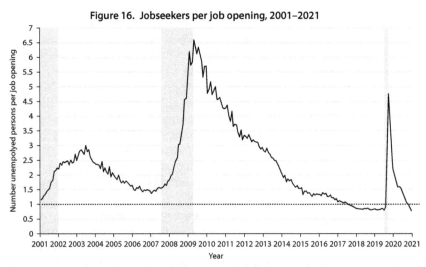

Figure 16. Jobseekers per job opening, 2001–2021

Note: Shaded areas indicate US recessions. Unemployment levels represent the average of the unemployment level for the current month and the subsequent month in the Current Population Survey to better line up with the job openings data from the Job Openings and Labor Turnover Survey.

Source: EPI analysis of Bureau of Labor Statistics Job Openings and Labor Turnover Survey and Current Population Survey.

for each job opening, and the recovery was slow. By this measure the labor market was extraordinarily tight from 2018 through 2020, a two-year period where job openings outnumbered jobseekers. The labor market has also had a remarkable bounce-back from the pandemic recession. In April 2020 there were 4.75 jobseekers for each job opening. A year later, in April 2021, the number of job openings was roughly equal to the number of jobseekers. By July 2021 things had reversed, and there were three job openings for every unemployed worker.

One point is worth keeping in mind: when unemployment falls, the quit rate typically rises. But this is not always the case. In 2021 the United States saw relatively slow decreases in unemployment in relation to the sharp increase in the quit rate. This mismatch—between quit rates and unemployment rates—is suggestive of the supply driven nature of the current shortfall from full employment. Since September 2020, the transition from unemployment to employment has been lower than that in the typical month. Normally one would expect the transition rate from unemployment to employment to increase as more jobs become available, as is the case as measured by job openings. The transition rate in 2021 was closer to what one would expect with a job openings rate of 3 percent, about half of the current openings rate. Based on the historical relationship between job openings and transitions from unemployment to employment, Furman and Powell (2021) predict that 34 percent of the unemployed in April 2021 should have transitioned to employment in May 2021, which would have resulted in one million more unemployed people finding jobs per month. There are several possible explanations for this change. The lingering pandemic, including the continued spread of the Delta variant, continued childcare supply shortages coupled with episodic school closures due to quarantines and illness, and the possibility that some people are taking additional time to rethink their lives more broadly may all be holding back the transition from unemployment to employment. While some speculated that the expansion and extension of unemployment benefits was creating a drag on the transition back to work for recipients, recent data utilizing the variation across states in the rollback of pandemic unemployment insurance extensions and expansions suggests that benefits availability was not a major driving force. For more, see Dube 2021; Coombs et al. 2021; Petrosky-Nadeau and Valletta 2021. These explanations taken together suggest the possibility of pent-up labor supply that could potentially be freed up to meet growing labor demand (Furman and Powell 2021).

23. Faberman et al. 2020.

24. For example, the Federal Reserve Board of San Francisco, uses a dashboard of twenty-six different indicators of the health of the labor market (Gilchrist and Hobijn 2021). The Federal Reserve Board of Governors similarly uses a dynamic factor model of nineteen different labor market indicators to generate the Labor Market Conditions Index (LMCI) (Chung et al. 2014). These composite models include a forest of metrics: unemployment and underemployment (e.g., the unem-

ployment rate, the labor force participation rate as measured by the employment-to-population ratio, and involuntary part-time unemployment), employment (e.g., private payroll employment, government employment, temporary help services employment), work weeks (e.g., average weekly hours of wage and/or production workers), wages, vacancies (e.g., help-wanted indices), hiring (e.g., the hiring rate), layoffs (e.g., the insured unemployment rate, job losers unemployed for less than five weeks), quits (e.g., the quit rate), and surveys of consumers' and businesses' perceptions (e.g., perceived job availability, hiring plans, and unfilled job openings).

25. For more detail, see "Useful Definitions" from the Economic Policy Institute, www.epi/newsroom/useful_definitions.

26. Mitchell 2013.

27. Trading Economics 2021.

28. Bureau of Labor Statistics 2021d.

29. Labor economists refer to this distinction as the "extensive margin" versus the "intensive margin" (i.e., how much). The extensive margin addresses "whether" questions (e.g., is a given individual working?). The intensive margin addresses "how much" questions (e.g., how many hours is a given individual working?).

30. Measuring underemployment is even less straightforward than measuring unemployment, because of the variation in definitions. For example, the underemployment rate calculations of the Bureau of Labor Statistics include three groups of people: unemployed individuals who are actively looking for work, employed individuals who work less full-time despite wanting full-time employment, and "marginally-attached" workers who are available and desire work but have stopped looking for a job. Several limitations make the official underemployment rate less useful than it seems. First, the measure does not include workers who have settled for a job that is below their skill or experience level. For example, an experienced machinist who finds work as a clerk at the local hardware store after the factory in her town closes is not captured in standard measures of underemployment. Currently no data exist that allow for the tracking of this expanded conceptual definition of underemployment.

31. Sometimes referred to as "part-time for economic reasons," involuntary part-time workers include those whose hours have been cut and those who are unable to find full-time work.

32. Golden and Kim 2020a.

33. In 2020, 14 percent of Latinx workers and 12 percent of Black workers were underemployed, as compared with 7 percent of white workers.

34. Women's rate of underemployment is 11 percent, compared with 7 percent for men.

35. Golden and Kim 2020b.

36. Valletta and van der List 2015; Henly and Lambert 2014; Lambert, Fugiel, and Henly 2014.

37. Kopczuk, Saez, and Song 2010; Mishel and Kandra 2020.

38. These include the Bureau of Labor Statistics monthly Employment Situation statistics (from the CPS of households) and JOLTS.

39. Geographic mobility has decreased steadily since the 1980s. As of 2009, a mere 1.6 percent of Americans moved from one state to another—half as many as in the postwar period—and only 3.7 percent moved from one county to another (Cooke 2011). The evidence points strongly to declining job changing as an important force behind the decrease in migration. Molloy, Smith, and Wozniak (2017) address leading explanations for the decline in internal migration in their research and find little empirical support for various alternatives to changes in labor market fluidity. For example, the aging of the US population could explain the decline in geographic mobility given that an individual's propensity to move declines with age. Both Molloy, Smith, and Wozniak (2017) and others (Cooke 2011; Kaplan and Shulhofer-Wohl 2017) find that aging explains very little of the secular decline in migration. While policymakers view population flows across regions as an important means of adjusting to local economic shocks, this kind of amelioration simply is not happening at the rate that it once did (Blanchard and Katz 1999).

40. Wozniak 2010; Levy et al. 2017.

41. Maps illustrating time-and-place variation in recent unemployment rate trajectories at a county level are available from the authors upon request. We use state-level data here for the purposes of analytic consistency. Specifically, the person-place-time specific metrics utilized in chapter 2 rely on data that is not consistently available across time and place at a more granular geographic level (e.g., county, MSA, or commuting zone).

42. The availability of job openings per jobseekers also varies dramatically across labor markets. These differences are evident across census regions, as depicted in figure 17. The directional movement is similar throughout the country across business cycles, but there are key regional differences in both the rate of change (represented by the relative slope of the various lines) and by the levels. Nonetheless, labor market recovery prior to the pandemic-induced economic crisis is evident in all four regions of the country. From late 2018 through the beginning of 2020, job openings outnumbered jobseekers in the Northeast, South, Midwest, and West. The labor market was back to remarkably tight levels in 2021, but the shape of the recovery looks different across regions.

43. Deloitte and the Manufacturing Institute 2018.

44. Scott as quoted in Ngo 2021.

45. Cappelli 2014.

46. Cappelli 2014.

47. Rampell 2014.

48. Hershbein and Kahn 2018; Modestino, Shoag, and Ballance 2016; Modestino, Shoag, and Ballance 2019.

49. National Center for Education Statistics 2019.

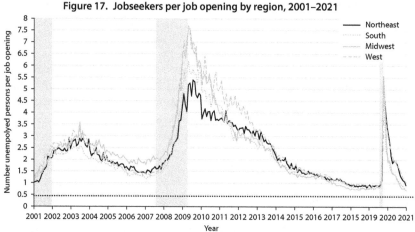

Figure 17. Jobseekers per job opening by region, 2001–2021

Note: Shaded areas indicate US recessions. Regions refer to United States Census regions.

Source: US Bureau of Labor Statistics, Job Openings: Total Nonfarm Unemployed Persons and Total Nonfarm Job Openings by Census Region, Monthly, Seasonally Adjusted, from FRED, Federal Reserve Bank of St. Louis.

50. Modestino, Shoag, and Ballance 2016.

51. Modestino, Shoag, and Ballance 2016.

52. Darity and Mason 1998; Bui, Famighetti, and Hamilton 2021.

53. Ross and Bateman 2019.

54. Cooper 2018.

55. Bivens 2021.

56. Quillian 2006.

57. Understanding the racial dynamics of the labor market—and the reasons *why* Black workers are overrepresented in low-wage jobs—requires a brief dive into the history of racial discrimination in the labor market in the United States as well as a summary of how the past is not yet behind us. The foundational insight on the intersection of race, employment, and inequality dates back to W.E.B. Du Bois's theory of the "racial wage." Du Bois posited that after the Civil War, with a population of newly freed Black workers in the labor market, employers actively deterred solidarity between Black and white workers by keeping wages low and offering white workers a "public and psychological wage" in the form of a superior social position (Du Bois 2013 [1935]). This practice led to a hardening of racial exclusion in the labor market over time. As Black workers migrated north in search of opportunity, they found themselves excluded from unions and exploited

by employers as strike-breakers in an effort to counter the growing power of labor unions (AFL-CIO 2017). Public policy compounded the disadvantages of Black workers by excluding occupations and industries that were majority-Black from the Social Security system and other basic labor protections (DeWitt 2010).

Even as formal barriers to employment slowly eroded, Black workers continued to face substantial obstacles, including individual-level discrimination and implicit bias as well as structural disadvantages. On an individual level, Black workers continue to navigate the personal biases of employers, which add up to produce widespread discrimination. Discrimination comes in many forms, including the most explicit "taste-based" discrimination, in which employers have a preference for certain types of workers (read: white), regardless of their productivity (Becker 1957). In recent years discrimination has become less overt in many cases, yet evidence from the field suggests it continues to be a major factor shaping employment outcomes (Quillian et al. 2017). More subtle forms of documented discrimination include implicit bias, where actors may not be aware of their discrimination (Banaji and Greenwald 2013), and statistical discrimination, where actors discriminate on the basis of beliefs about the statistical distribution of certain unobserved characteristics across social groups. Unobserved characteristics can include skills, education, or criminal records, for instance (Arrow 1973; Agan and Starr 2017). In addition, third-order inference may play a role in perpetuating discrimination: decisionmakers are influenced by their expectations about how their decisions may be judged or what valued others may prefer (Correll et al. 2017). Whether or not discrimination of all forms erodes when employers face a shortage of available workers is an empirical question that has not been thoroughly explored in the existing literature.

58. Bureau of Labor Statistics 2021c.

59. PayScale 2021.

60. Porter 2021.

61. Bayer and Charles 2017.

62. Western and Pettit (2005) find that accounting for incarceration raises the estimated Black-white wage gap by as much as 58 percent for Black men.

63. Thompson 2021.

64. In an analysis of the impact of tight labor markets on racial wage gaps, researchers from the Hamilton Project at the Brookings Institution utilize the gap between the noncyclical unemployment rate (the NAIRU, described earlier in this chapter) and the "real" unemployment rate as a measure of hot labor markets, defining a tight labor market as a period when unemployment rate falls below the NAIRU (Aaronson, Barnes, and Edelberg 2021). See also Aaronson et al. 2019.

65. Baert et al. 2015.

66. Aaronson et al. 2021.

67. Freeman 1990.

68. Freeman 1990: 18–19.

Figure 18. Jobseekers per job opening by industry, 2001–2021

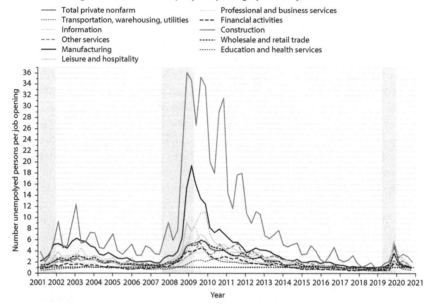

Note: Shaded areas indicate US recessions. Regions refer to United States Census regions.

Source: US Bureau of Labor Statistics, Unemployment Level—Nonagriculture, Private Wage and Salary Workers, Thousands of Persons, Quarterly, Not Seasonally Adjusted and Industry Totals + Job Openings: Total Private, Level in Thousands, Quarterly, Not Seasonally Adjusted and Industry Totals from FRED, Federal Reserve Bank of St. Louis.

69. Wilson and Rodgers 2016.

70. Disadvantaged workers are the first to lose in recession and the last to gain from a recovery (Freeman 2001).

71. Freeman 2001.

72. The authors note that the unemployment gap quickly reappeared once the pandemic recession hit, noting that "it would be very difficult to close the [racial] gaps based on strong macroeconomic performance alone." See also Aaronson, Barnes, and Edelberg 2021.

73. Figure 18 shows the jobseekers' ratio by industry since 2001, where unemployed workers are included in the industry group in which they last held a job. The ebb and flow of labor market tightness is clear across industries. The two-year period immediately before the COVID-19 crash is especially notable for widespread worker shortages, regardless of industry. Yet there are differences. For example, the number of unemployed construction workers has outpaced job openings at an elevated rate relative to other industries since 2001. Unemployment spread throughout construction in the wake of the Great Recession, due to the

Figure 19. Average wage growth by industry, 1998–2021

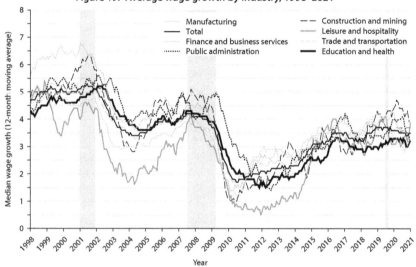

Note: Shaded areas indicate US recessions.

Source: US Bureau of Labor Statistics Current Population Survey and Federal Reserve Bank of Atlanta calculations. See the Federal Reserve Bank of Atlanta's Wage Tracker.

housing crisis and dramatic slow-down in home building; it took far longer to improve over the course of the recovery as compared with other industries. The housing crisis also reverberated through the manufacturing and transportation industries, though both recovered more swiftly.

74. Industry-level data is not available with seasonal adjustments, which explains both the bumpiness of the trend lines relative to the other pictures of the jobseekers' ratio. It also requires the use of consistent quarters for the purposes of comparison, to avoid noise from seasonal differences, especially in highly seasonally variable industries such as construction.

75. Wage growth rates are also uneven across industries (figure 19). When workers are unable (or unwilling) to transition, a tight labor market in one industry will not create opportunities for all workers seeking a leg up. Wages may grow in one industry while falling in another due to differing levels of labor demand relatively to labor supply. This is especially important for industries and occupations characterized by high rates of racial and gender segregation, where workers face barriers to entry to new industries due to discrimination or educational requirements.

76. Although labor shortages in health care and education have been developing for years, COVID-19 brought both of these to the fore (Associated Press 2021; Taube and Lipson 2021).

CHAPTER 2

1. For more information and access to the Panel Study of Income Dynamics (PSID) data, see http://psidonline.isr.umich.edu.

2. Recent years have seen an explosion of the use of administrative data for the exploration of questions of mobility, including restricted-use data from the Social Security Administration and the Internal Revenue Service. The best-known examples of this work come from Raj Chetty and his team (Chetty et al. 2014; Chetty et al. 2017; Chetty and Hendren 2018; Chetty et al. 2020). We use the PSID for two reasons. First, survey data like the PSID allow for respondents to self-identify in terms of race and other key demographic characteristics that administrative data do not include. They also include individuals who may be excluded from administrative data, especially those living on the margins who are less likely to have a consistent presence in government records. Second, the PSID are publicly available and therefore more easily accessed and replicable, as compared to administrative records from the US government that require lengthy application processes that are not easily navigable by all researchers.

3. Molloy, Smith, and Wozniak 2017.

4. Note that data limitations mean we are not able to examine the durability of the opportunities created in the tight labor markets of the 1960s. This is because the Bureau of Labor Statistics did not begin collecting state-level unemployment data until the 1980s, so we have cannot situate individuals in the context of their local labor markets prior to this period. Future research using alternative data sources would do well to explore the question of whether the booming labor markets of the postwar period created different patterns of opportunity for those living in poverty than did later periods, especially given the fact that economic inequality and wage stagnation were not yet overwhelmingly present.

5. For the first set of analyses, we bank off of Danny Yagan's (2019) analytic approach investigating whether the labor market effects of the Great Recession were "sticky" for individual workers and jobseekers. Did the severe downturn impact individuals' employment outcomes beyond the initial period of contraction? And how important were local labor markets (rather than national conditions) in this regard? Our central interest is the reverse of Yagan's—i.e., we are interested understanding whether tight labor markets create opportunities—so we reverse-engineer his approach. And we are interested in applying our analytic lens to look across the four most recent tight labor markets, rather than just the most recent data, so we extend the analysis to look at multiple business cycles. We use state-level unemployment data and compute year-to-year changes in state unemployment rates.

Thus tight labor markets are defined as a continuous variable, and each individual is assigned a state-year specific value. We include a host of fixed-effects, including age, earnings at last job, and industry of last job (where available), to control for individual-level differences and to isolate the effects of tight labor markets on our outcomes of interest. We focus specifically on employment versus nonemployment, which we define to include both those out of the labor market (nonparticipants) and those who are actively searching for work (unemployed). Finally, we pull apart the analysis to compare outcomes across various groups of interest, including (1) individuals who are living in low-income households at the beginning of the relevant tight labor market as compared to those living in higher-income households; (2) Black individuals as compared to white individuals; (3) men as compared to women; and (4) various age cohorts.

Note that Yagan's analyses rely on restricted-use administrative data with more detailed residential information than that included in the PSID, so his definitions of labor market shocks are based on commuting zone (CZ)-level unemployment rates. CZs are a more precise definition of local labor markets, but the PSID data does not allow us to drill down to this precise definition. Many other studies of the impact of the business cycle on individual-level outcomes rely on state-level economic data, and others rely on even less precise national-level data to draw general conclusions (see, for instance, Aaronson et al. 2019; Aaronson, Barnes, and Edelberg 2021; Bivens and Zipperer 2018; Hotchkiss and Moore 2018). Future research on this topic could extend our analysis to assess CZ-level local labor market effects, as a robustness check on our results. But we are confident that the state-level data that we use here are reasonably precise and thus stand by our results as a good indicator of the broader story of how tight labor markets shape opportunity.

6. Hotchkiss and Moore 2018.

7. Note that we do not find statistically significant results in the analysis of tight labor markets' durable effects on hours or earnings. Results from these additional modelling efforts are available from the authors upon request. These null findings are likely due to sample-size limitations, and we address this by using a pooled sample in the analyses later in the chapter.

8. The expansion of the early 2000s may not have resulted in significant results for a variety of reasons, including the shallow contraction in unemployment rates or a difference in the "quality" of unemployment along the lines of the various submerged portions of the Okun unemployment iceberg as discussed in chapter 1. Further exploration of this period is merited but beyond the scope of this research effort.

9. See also Bivens 2021 for the empirical and predicted effects on racial gaps in income and unemployment under varying degrees of labor market slack.

10. Many studies have demonstrated the disproportionate burden of economic misfortune by Black workers. In one excellent example, sociologists Elizabeth Wrigley-Field and Nathan Selzer (2020) find that Black workers are nearly always more likely than white workers to be laid off or "displaced" by involuntary, permanent layoffs. Between 1981 and 2017, for instance, Black men and women were 18 percent and 17 percent more likely than white men and women to be laid off,

respectively. Prior to the early 2000s, education was the best predictor of whether or not a worker would experience an involuntary layoff; regardless of race, college-degree holders were less likely to be displaced. By the early 2000s, however, the education advantage had disappeared. Black workers with college degrees are now more likely than white workers without college degrees to face a layoff. In other words, race is now the best predictor of whether or not an individual will face involuntary job-loss. Wrigley-Field and Selzer (2020) find that occupational and industry differences explain very little of the race gap. Instead, the decline in public sector employment for Black workers over the 1981–2017 period is a more powerful explanation.

11. Glen Edler Jr. documented the long-term effects of the Great Depression, following a cohort of more than 167 people born in 1920 and 1921. Using a life-course approach, he found that economic crisis had substantial scarring effects, confirmed by subsequent work in which he followed young cohorts (Elder 1998).

12. The jury is still out as to whether the tight labor market that we are in at the time of writing will endure, because the most recent available version of the PSID at the time of writing is from 2019.

13. Hotchkiss and Moore 2018.

14. Results for the effects on labor force participation and weekly hours worked are not statistically significant.

15. In contrast, the protective effect of exposure to a tight labor market for white workers' unemployment duration is far smaller (0.004) and not statistically significant.

16. Aaronson et al. 2019; Aaronson, Barnes, and Edelberg 2021; Hotchkiss and Moore 2018.

17. Bernstein 2018.

18. Piketty and Saez 2003; Alderson and Nielsen 2002. Eroding labor standards include the declining value of the minimum wage and the overtime salary threshold, the mismatch between legal definitions of employment relationships, and new forms of work generated by rapid advances in platform technology such as Uber and Instacart (e.g., Kirchner and Schüßler 2020). Also see Western and Rosenfeld 2011; Weil 2014; Wilmers 2018.

19. Newman and Chen 2008.

CHAPTER 3

1. In 2014 just over half (51.8 percent) of working-age poor people in the United States were employed for at least part of the previous year, excluding those who with disabilities or who were enrolled in school (Stevens and Pihl 2014).

2. Quillian 2006.

3. Bertrand and Mullainathan 2004; Pager, Western, and Bonikowski 2009.

4. Banaji and Greenwald 2013; Arrow 1973; Tilcsik 2021.

5. Kirschenman and Neckerman 1991: 209.

6. While the United States used incarceration sparingly in the postwar decades, the rate of imprisonment began to grow in the 1970s, and by 2000 the incarceration rate in the United States was "unparalleled in the economically developed countries" (Western 2006: 12). It was also disproportionately concentrated among poor Black men: those without a high school degree were more likely to have been to prison than not. While there are direct effects of incarceration on the psychological and social well-being of those sent to prison, the economic impact is magnified by the actions of employers. Extensive research shows that managers hesitate or outright refuse to hire formerly incarcerated applicants (Pager 2009). Nearly half of men released from prison remain unemployed a full year later (National Research Council 2014).

7. In economics and sociology, hiring is conceptualized as a matching process, where employers provide opportunities and workers have some choice among a set of opportunities (Logan 1996). But the system is far from ideal of perfectly competitive markets: labor markets, it is widely acknowledged, must be understood in the context of imperfect competition, where "frictions and idiosyncrasies" pertaining to information, preferences, and labor market institutions disrupt expected dynamics of supply and demand (Manning 2011). In economics the process of matching jobs and workers is a primarily an information problem. Jobs are conceptualized as alternatively an "experience good," where the match must be made to evaluate its quality, rather than a "pure search-good" or "inspection good," where the quality of the match can be observed prior to experiencing it (Jovanovic 1979). An imperfect match between the candidate and the job can still lead to successful employment, but the cost of training shifts from the worker, who paid to acquire the training outside the job, to the employer, who pays for the worker to be trained (Miller 1984).

8. Although it took nearly a decade for the construction industry to recover from the Great Recession, by 2018 there was enough construction activity that demand for labor vastly outstripped supply (Belmonte 2019), with nearly two openings for every jobseeker (Belmonte 2018).

9. The rate at which employees quit their jobs topped 2.5 percent in the spring of 2021 (Furman and Powell 2021). The quit rate was the product of rising wages as a result of increasing demand in the context of limited supply (Morath and Ip 2021). Businesses had to scale up to reopen after firing or furloughing employees during lockdowns, but many employees were reluctant to reenter the labor market, due to health or childcare concerns (Ember 2021). Employers who had difficultly recruiting offered higher wages (Rosenberg 2021b), which brought some unemployed workers back into the workforce but also stimulated a huge increase in quits, as employee sought out better opportunities (Weber 2021).

10. In the pre-pandemic tight labor market, for example, Boston's Encore casino announced that it would be replacing some of its fifty bartenders with machines

(Rosen 2020). Casinos are among the service-intensive industries that opted for automation in the context of record-low unemployment in 2018 and 2019. Further investment in technology during the pandemic, to reduce exposure and continue operations in the midst of lockdown, may accelerate automation in some industries (Casselman 2021).

11. A rich literature on poverty notes the important role of "spatial mismatch" between workers and jobs: the people who need jobs—often poor people living in dense urban centers—are geographically separated from the jobs that could help them rise out of poverty. This mismatch especially affects Black workers, whose housing options were substantially limited by housing discrimination (Kain 1992).

12. The percentage of all workers who researched jobs online doubled between 2005 and 2015, from 26 percent to 54 percent, and the rate was even higher among recent jobseekers, of whom 90 percent researched jobs and 84 percent applied for jobs online (Pew Research Center 2015).

13. A variety of tools make online job applications efficient for employers. For instance, Applicant Tracking Systems automatically scans resumes for required education or skills. But research suggests that, to date, online recruiting is not resulting in better matches: workers recruited online do not see higher wages or longer tenure than workers recruited through traditional means (Gürtzgen et al. 2021). This is because online recruitment leads to a broader pool, including more applicants who are qualified but also more who are unqualified.

14. As Lynn Peril (2011) documents, women in the 1960s typically had few job options beyond secretarial work. Most secretaries had no college degree, because fewer women pursued college education at the time, those who did often found that their job prospects were not improved: they were routinely passed over for professional jobs and limited to secretarial work like their high school–educated peers. Today, however, more than 90 percent of administrative assistants have some post–high school education, and more than 50 percent hold a bachelor's or two-year degree (International Association of Administrative Professionals 2019).

15. One caveat is that technological change has hollowed out many middle-income jobs through automation and routinization, driving down the number of workers in middle-wage occupations like secretaries. Ted Mouw and Arne Kalleberg (2010) document a "dramatic decline" in the number of secretaries between 1983 and 2002.

16. Theories of job queues suggest that employers will hire the most "desirable" worker available to them, regardless of whether all the skills that worker has are actually required for the job (Evans 2011). Supporting this theory, some research shows that economic downturns are often characterized by an increase in the employment of high-skilled workers in low-skilled jobs (Pollmann-Schult 2005).

17. Modestino and colleagues provide direct evidence that that employers "opportunistically" raise their education requirements when unemployment is high and labor markets are slack—and they have their pick of candidates—and

subsequently lower their education and experience requirements when labor markets tighten. During the Great Recession, for instance, they find that a 1 percentage point increase in unemployment was associated with a significant increase in the number of jobs requiring a college degree and more than two years of experience (0.5 and 0.8 percentage points, respectively), controlling for region and occupation (Modestino, Shoag, and Ballance 2019). By contrast, during the recovery a 1 percentage point decrease in unemployment was associated with a significant decrease in the educational and experience requirements of jobs, even within firm-job pairs (Modestino, Shoag, and Ballance 2016).

18. Employers provide less training when there are both more workers and more employers, and thus greater opportunities for employees to switch jobs (Brunello and Gambarotto 2007). Overall, the amount of training provided by employers declined substantially in the run-up to the Great Recession, between 2001 and 2009, despite low unemployment (Waddoups 2016).

19. Employers invest in training when job markets are tight. In theory, a rational employer would not pay to train a worker because that worker may leave at any time, taking their improved human capital with them (Brunello and Wruuck 2020). Consequently, economists mostly assume that employees bear the cost of any training they receive on the job, in the form of lower wages (Barron, Black, and Loewenstein 1989). But when the economy is strong, unemployment is low, and recruiting is more difficult, employers may pay for training, as the cost of filling vacancies (Fall 2019).

20. Newman and Winston 2016.

21. In recent decades the employment relationship has changed in a number of ways, but one shift stands out: where workers once moved up within companies, through "internal labor markets" (Dobbin et al. 1993; Doeringer and Piore 1971), today they are more likely to move between employers and employers are more likely to hire from outside (Cappelli 1999; Osterman 2014). Moving between employer is also associated with greater pay increases: although an internal promotion can come with a large pay increase, overall, job changers see more wage growth than people who stay within their firm ("ADP Workforce Vitality Report" n.d.).

22. One company that invested substantially in supporting "second chance" employees explained that they found that "the population we were hiring who had criminal backgrounds were our most loyal people" (Simon 2020). In fact, many employers find that workers with criminal records are a valuable investment (Mullaney 2018). Because people with criminal records often have fewer job opportunities, they may exert more effort to keep the job they have. The result, researchers and employers suggest, is that workers with criminal records are "more loyal" (Minor, Persico, and Weiss 2017; Simon 2019). Although they also face greater challenges, including fewer transportation options (Society for Human Resources

Management 2018), this population is more likely to exert effort to overcome these obstacles.

23. In a field experimental study Devah Pager (2003) found that applicants with criminal records are half as likely to receive a callback as identical applicants without a criminal record. Moreover, Pager found the effects of a criminal record also varied by race: Black men *without* a record were less likely to be called back than white men *with* a record, and Black men with a record received almost no opportunities. Since Pager's study was published, others have explored this phenomenon and confirmed similar patterns (Pager 2009; Pager, Western, and Bonikowski 2009), helping to drive a movement to "ban the box" indicating criminal records from job applications—a policy that has been adopted in 35 states and more than 150 cities (Avery and Lu 2020).

24. How does increasing employment opportunities for members of marginalized groups reconfigure the social beliefs that undergird discrimination? They evidence is mixed. An optimistic study in Norway found that employers' experiences with immigrants reshaped their future beliefs: whereas employers who lack experience with immigrant workers showed a tendency to be risk averse and discriminate against immigrant applicants, those who had positive experiences with immigrant workers showed a greater willingness to hire candidates from that group (Birkelund et al. 2020). But in the United States, researchers find much less reason for optimism. Devah Pager and Diana Karafin (2009) found that employers did not update their attitudes about Black workers in the wake of a positive experience—instead, they engaged in "subtyping," justifying the positive experience as a result of the fact that the Black employee belonged to some smaller, exceptional group of Black workers, and leaving their general negative stereotypes intact.

25. Michael Haugen (2017) profiles this shift in Texas policy in an article for *Veritas.*

26. Smith and Young 2017: 189. The authors identify two alternative cultural logics guiding the decision about whether to provide assistance: defensive individualism, in which jobholders decide whether to help depending on whether the jobseeker "really" wants a job, and matchmaking, in which jobholders decide whether to help depending on their perception of the fit between the job and the jobseeker.

27. Newman 2000.

28. Research shows that wage growth takes the longest to reach the poorest: only in extremely tight labor markets do low-wage workers see substantial gains (Aaronson et al. 2019; Freeman 2001). In 2019 wage growth was still modest, but new minimum wages—mandates by local and state governments or embraced voluntarily by employers—were helping encourage increasing benefits to low-wage workers (Gould 2020).

29. A large literature on "organizational justice" demonstrates that employees have strong beliefs about fairness and that violating those beliefs can negatively impact the performance of a firm (Colquitt et al. 2001). In particular, employees who

find out that they are paid less than their colleagues are more likely to reduce their productivity or quit (Breza, Kaur, and Shamdasani 2017; Card et al. 2012). Human resources scholars refer to this as the principle of internal equity, which suggests that workers should be paid equitably in comparison to their coworkers (Romanoff, Boehm, and Benson 1986). Although internal equity was once the foremost concern of compensation specialists, the salience of this factor for employers has declined since the 1980s (Adler 2021), although it remains important to workers.

30. Dan Clawson and Naomi Gerstel (2014) show that medical workers have different degrees of control over their schedule and how much unpredictability affects them, with the amount of control tied to occupational status as well as class and gender. Daniel Schneider and Kristen Harknett (2019) also examine scheduling instability, demonstrating a link to increased stress for children and parents and identifying other health outcomes.

31. Despite the extraordinarily tight labor market that emerged in 2021, researchers have found little improvement in the working conditions for service sector workers, especially when it comes to the availability of full-time hours and regular scheduling (Zundl et al. 2022).

32. Zundl et al. 2022

33. Research from the Shift Project (https://shift.hks.harvard.edu/), using surveys of workers matched to employers, finds little evidence that tight labor market brought on by COVID-19 has had an effect on job quality, to date (see Zundl et al. 2022).

34. Scholars of labor relations in the 1970s and 1980s wrote extensively about dual or segmented labor markets, positing this theory as an alternative to human capital explanations of inequality and unemployment (Doeringer and Piore 1975; Berger and Piore 1980). The theory emphasizes that the benefits of a job are not always a reward for prior investment in education and training; instead, better jobs often provide training, but those jobs are preferentially allocated to more privileged groups—namely, white men. Women and Black workers, being excluded from those better jobs, are forced into the secondary labor market that offers limited rewards and few opportunities for growth.

35. In *Chutes and Ladders*, Newman (2008) follows up with the workers she followed in her 2000 book, *No Shame in My Game*. She found that a substantial number have moved up, using their low-wage jobs as stepping-stones to better careers: nearly a quarter of the people interviewed saw their real wages increase, in the intervening years, by $5 per hour. They benefited from a tight labor market.

36. CORI is a widely used term of art for Criminal Offender Record Information, and "CORI-friendly" indicates employers and/or positions who are willing to hire those with CORIs. For instance, the national job search platform Indeed. com features a "CORI-friendly" filter for jobseekers (see www.indeed.com/q-Cori-Friendly-l-Massachusetts-jobs.html?vjk=04d31645054e727b).

37. More than 70 percent of US employers offer a tuition assistance program,

which constitute roughly 5 percent of all college and university tuition expenditures (Craig 2016).

CHAPTER 4

1. Sandra Smith and Kara Young (2017) show that some people make decisions about whether to help others find work on the basis of how serious they feel the person is about getting a job; the degree to which the person needs the job is taken to be an indicator of how reliable they will be as an employee. A similar standard is used by employers, as discussed in chapter 2. There is a crucial difference, however : a friend or relative who is deciding whether to help you find a job knows you well, but an employer only knows what you tell them or what they can observe. This makes it difficult for potential employers to assess the reliability of a candidate.

2. Autor 2009: 1.

3. Lee 2009.

4. Marschall 2021: 13.

5. Bailey and Danziger 2013.

6. "Economic Report of the President 1964" 1964.

7. Holzer 2013.

8. The 1996 Personal Responsibility and Work Opportunity Reconciliation Act aimed to encourage more poor Americans to enter the workforce. As Isabel Sawhill and Ron Haskins (2002) describe, the impetus was a widely held belief that the existing welfare system—which provided cash, food stamps, and Medicaid to the poor—contributed to "a decline in work by poor parents" and reduced the proportion of children in two-parent households. To encourage work, the reforms capped cash assistance to five years and required families to work—or prove that they were trying to work—to access public benefits (Sawhill and Haskins 2002). In place of cash assistance the government provided expanded benefits for the working poor, including the Earned Income Tax Credit and the child tax credit. These changes appeared successful during the fast-growing economy of the 1990s, but subsequent business cycles have shown that program use has become much more cyclical in the postreform era, meaning that poor families are hit harder by recessions than they might have been under the prior system (Bitler and Hoynes 2010).

9. Gueron and Hamilton 2002.

10. Fernandez 2010.

11. Pennell 2007; Patrick Hilton and Lambert 2015. See also Andersson, Holzer, and Lane 2005.

12. Benner, Leete, and Pastor 2007.

13. Many religious organizations that have taken up the employment intermediary role embrace it for the same reason: a belief that working is godly.

14. The settlement houses, exemplified by Jane Addams's Hull House in Chicago (Knight 2010), were the prototype for American nonprofit solutions to urban

poverty. Settlement houses arose in response to perceived declining urban conditions and growing immigration, and aimed to support and advocate for poor urban residents. But these efforts were also racialized, as settlement houses supported mostly European immigrants: with the growing population of African Americans and non-European immigrants in urban centers, many settlement houses shuttered or moved to whiter, more suburban neighborhoods (Koerin 2003).

15. Researchers have documented the extensive barriers facing immigrants with foreign credentials who hope to use those credentials in the US labor market, arguing that the United States would benefit—particularly in fields like medicine—from making it easier for immigrants' credentials to be recognized (Rabben 2013).

16. Amazon grew tenfold between 2010 and 2019 (Holmes 2019). But the most incredible gains were in the past two years. Amazon reaped huge rewards from the pandemic, as homebound families turned to the delivery service to provide groceries and household necessities. By April 2021 they had a global workforce of more than 1.2 million employees, which was 50 percent larger than a year prior (Weise 2021). Growth in the workforce, however, was vastly outpaced by a growth in profits, which increased more 200 percent, to 8.1 billion, between 2020 and 2021 (Weise 2021).

17. Intermediaries and other worker advocates are aware that the business cycle spells both advantages and disadvantages, with years of plenty followed by years of scarcity in which jobs openings are rare and often filled by overqualified works shut out from better opportunities (Modestino, Shoag, and Ballance 2019). Middle-class jobs—the kind that offer workers a sustainable path to economic mobility—are the most cyclical, especially susceptible to downturns that exacerbate the polarization of job quality (Foote and Ryan 2015). And it's not only the business cycle that threatens to undermine workers' gains: if labor becomes too costly, employers may invest in automation, shifting the balance of power (Casselman 2021).

18. The field of urban planning and development has long debated the relative merits of "place-based" as opposed to "people-based" approaches (Agnew 1984; Bolton 1992; Crane and Manville 2008). Experiments in place-based strategies like the Harlem Children's Zone have demonstrated efficacy in improving both educational attainment (Whitehurst and Croft 2010) and health (Spielman et al. 2006), although economists question the necessity of comprehensive community planning to producing these outcomes (Dobbie and Fryer 2011).

19. According to the Boston Planning and Development Agency's analysis of data from the American Community Survey from 2013 to 2017 (Boston Planning and Development Agency Research Division 2019), the three neighborhoods covered by the Triangle Square Association remain some of Boston's poorest. Each of the neighborhoods has a poverty rate over 20 percent, with Roxbury's poverty rate standing at 34 percent, among the top three highest neighborhood poverty

rates in Boston. Dorchester, which is 35 percent Black, 18 percent Hispanic, and 22 percent white, is the largest neighborhood in the city, home to nearly one in five Boston residents, and one in four of Boston's residents living under the poverty line. Both Roxbury and Mattapan are majority-Black: Roxbury is 52 percent Black, 30 percent Hispanic, and 10 percent white; and Mattapan is 73 percent Black, 15 percent Hispanic, and 6 percent white. Each of the neighborhoods has a high rate of single female heads of households: 28 percent in Dorchester and 33 percent in both Roxbury and Mattapan—twice the citywide rate of 16 percent.

20. Citywide, only 12 percent commute more than sixty minutes, while 17 percent of Dorchester residents, 13 percent of Roxbury residents, and 25 percent of Mattapan residents commute that far.

21. The one exception is the commercial driver's license, for which they do provide training.

22. Lincoln Quillian and Devah Pager (2001) found that perceptions of neighborhood crime were significantly associated with the percent of neighborhood residents who were young Black men, net of actual levels of crime. To the extent that employers discriminate against workers from neighborhoods that they perceive to be high crime (Kirschenman and Neckerman 1991), they thus not only discriminate against people who come from high-crime neighborhoods, but also against people who come from predominantly-Black neighborhoods, regardless of actual crime rates.

23. The Great Recession technically lasted from December 2007 to June 2009, but the unemployment did not reach its peak, over 10 percent, until 2010 (Kochhar 2020).

24. The gendered dynamic of the COVID-induced recession has been well-documented by researchers. The unemployment rate for women jumped by 12 percentage points between February 2020 and April 2020, compared with 10 points for men. Industries that could not easily switch to remote operations shed jobs, including predominantly low-wage sectors such as retail sales and hospitality. These industries employ a disproportionate number of low-wage women, which helps explain the gendered nature of job losses (Ross and Bateman 2019).

CHAPTER 5

1. Abraham et al. 2016; Kroft, Lange, and Notowidigdo 2013.

2. Nunn, Parsons, and Shambaugh 2019.

3. Even so, returning citizens are generally the last in line when employers engage in that search (Harding 2019). They are a special case among jobseekers who have been out of work for a long time because they bear the stigma of criminal justice involvement (Boshier and Johnson 1974) and are assumed to have lost skills over time (Western, Kling, and Weiman 2001). Their earnings take a hit (Mueller-Smith 2015) and their employment rates are as much as 25 percentage

points lower than the general population (Western, Kling, and Weiman 2001). This is not a function of age: within age categories formerly incarcerated jobseekers are unemployed at five times the rate of those with no prison record, even though they are more likely to be searching for work (Couloute and Kopf 2018).

4. In normal labor markets placing returning citizens is an uphill battle. Economist Harry Holzer (2013: 11) notes that "over 90% of employers surveyed are willing to consider filling their most recent job vacancy with a welfare recipient, while only about 40% are willing to consider doing so with an ex-offender." Consequently, researchers like Devah Pager have found that callback rates for workers with criminal records are dramatically lower than for applicants without a record: both white and Black applicants with criminal records are nearly half as likely to get a callback compared to applicants of the same race without records. Pager's research, reported in *Marked* (2009), is based on an audit study where matched Black and white men apply for jobs with real employers.

5. Kanno-Youngs 2018.

6. Internal Revenue Service 2021.

7. Federal Bonding Program 2021.

8. The American Concrete Institute (ACI) provided certification in concrete field testing (American Concrete Institute 2021).

9. Society for Human Resources Management 2018.

10. Moran 2019.

11. McNutt 2020; Atkinson and Lockwood 2016; ACLU, Trone Private Sector, and Education Advisory Council 2017.

12. Lee-Johnson 2020.

13. Bucknor and Barber 2016.

14. Faberman et al. 2017.

15. Bunker 2016.

16. Sharone 2021.

17. Researchers have identified a powerful image of "ideal workers" that is associated with a full-time employee who is typically a married male breadwinner who prioritizes work over family duties (Kelly et al. 2010).

18. Despite Mark's difficult journey, it must be acknowledged that whites are generally advantaged among returning citizens. Race and ex-offender status seem to interact in powerful ways in reducing the job market opportunities of Black men with criminal records, with Black offenders receiving fewer than one-seventh the number of offers received by white nonoffenders with comparable skills and experience. This is consistent with what has been observed in ethnographic work with employers (e.g., Kirschenman and Neckerman 1991; Moss and Tilly 2001), where they discuss their fears of violence among Black men relative to other groups of applicants. See also Holzer, Raphael, and Stoll 2003.

19. Berger-Gross 2018.

20. Couloute and Kopf 2018.

CHAPTER 6

1. Inspired by William Julius Wilson's *The Truly Disadvantaged* (1987), as vast literature has attempted to identify precisely how neighborhoods shape people's life outcomes, including their educational attainment, likelihood of experiencing poverty in adulthood, chances of being convicted of a crime, and choices about fertility and family formation. Yet this literature on "neighborhood effects" has had to grapple with significant methodological problems (Jencks and Mayer 1990). Namely, researchers have had to navigate the issue of "selection effects," in which the association between living in a particular neighborhood and experiencing a particular outcome may actually be explained by differences between the people who choose to live in that neighborhood and the rest of the population, rather than any influence the neighborhood exerts on its residents (Harding 2003).

2. Small and Newman 2001.

3. Sampson 1999.

4. Coleman 1988.

5. Using survey data from nearly nine thousand Chicago residents, Robert Sampson, Jeffrey Morenoff, and Felton Earls (1999) show how neighborhood-level characteristics, including concentrated disadvantage, residential stability, affluence, and density, either facilitate or constrain three key dimensions of collective efficacy: intergenerational closure, or the extent to which adults and children know one another; reciprocated exchange, or the prevalence of mutual support in the form of favors, lending items, or getting together socially; and social control of children, or the likelihood that a neighborhood would "do something" if a child were seen skipping school or disrespecting an adult.

6. Sampson, Raudenbush, and Earls 1997.

7. Sampson, Raudenbush, and Earls 1997.

8. Kain 1992.

9. Jargowsky 1997: 21.

10. Jargowsky 1997.

11. Jargowsky 1994: 4.

12. Chetty et al. 2018.

13. Recent research, in which Harding has played a central role, has emphasized heterogeneity and complexity in neighborhood effects (Harding et al. 2010; Sharkey and Faber 2014). It acknowledges that residents of poor neighborhood have different patterns of exposure to the factors that drive neighborhood effects, depending on how long they live in the neighborhood (Wodtke, Harding, and Elwert 2011); that neighborhoods exert effects at different geographic scales (Galster 2008); and that poor neighborhoods themselves often differ in a number of ways (Small and Feldman 2012; Small, Manduca, and Johnston 2018).

14. Whyte 1943.

15. For young Black men, including but not limited to those living in poor

neighborhoods, there is also the matter of exposure to violence from the police. Even for Black men and boys who have limited exposure to peer violence—either because they live in safer or richer neighborhoods or because they choose to steer clear of dangerous social situations—the possibility of encountering violence from police remains high. The disproportionate focus of policing on Black and brown men has been the focus of the national social movement Black Lives Matter as well as more local debates like the New York City policy of "stop and frisk."

16. GBD 2019 Police Violence US Subnational Collaborators 2021.

17. Individuals over the age of twenty-five.

18. Americans with less than a high school diploma see substantially lower median earnings and higher unemployment than more educated workers. According to data from the Bureau of Labor Statistics, 5.4 percent of people without a high school diploma are unemployed, compared to 3.7 percent of people with a high school diploma and only 2.2 percent of those with a bachelor's degree; the median salary for people without a high school diploma is under $31,000, compared to nearly $39,000 for those with a diploma and nearly $65,000 for those with a bachelor's degree (Stobierski 2020). Although it remains beneficial to have a high school degree today, the value of a high school degree has declined substantially, with the major differentiator in the labor market shifting from high school to college over the past thirty years (Fuentes and Leamer 2019).

19. "Male joblessness is the number of working age (16–59) employed males divided by the population of working-age men." This is different from unemployment, which factors in whether individuals are searching for work (Harding 2010: 254). The jobless numbers include large numbers of men who are no longer or were never searching for a job. We typically rely on the unemployment numbers in charting an area's economic health, but in many ways the jobless number is a better snapshot. Including people whom we might call "discouraged workers," those who looked for work but got nowhere, and captures the full dimensions of the employment desert that so many poor neighborhoods represent, especially when unemployment is high.

20. In *The Truly Disadvantaged*, Wilson (1987) argued that men who did not have jobs were not seen as marriageable, contributing to lower rates of marriage, higher rates of childbearing outside marriage, and lower family income overall. Research by Kathryn Edin and colleagues found that poor women usually want to marry but think that marriage should follow economic stability—childbearing, however, can happen at many points (Edin and Kefalas 2005). These factors, including Americans' reverence for marriage, desire for personal freedom, and economic inequality, have contributed to high rates of both marriage *and* divorce, cohabitation *and* separation, in what Andrew Cherlin (2010) terms the "marriage-go-round," with implications for economic stability and child development.

21. Butterfield 1988.

22. Massachusetts went from the among the states with the highest unemploy-

ment to the industrialized state with the lowest unemployment in the nation, in just a few years, through investment in the high-tech sector and public policy decisions (Lampe 1988). But some have questioned both the causes and the extent of economic growth, suggesting that government had little involvement and that the strong economic growth was set to rapidly disappear (Harrison and Kluver 1989).

23. Osterman 2001.

24. Autor 2021.

25. *Soulside* (Hannerz 1969) became a classic of urban ethnography. Published in 1969, it engaged with the policy debates centered on the Moynihan Report and the idea that poor Black families were held back by their own "culture of poverty" (Lewis 1959). Hannerz refuted these assessments by instead proposing culture as "largely situational" (Weszkalnys 2007). This more nuanced approach to culture would directly inform Ann Swidler's (1986) theorization of culture as a "toolkit" that actors use, both habitually and strategically, to respond to their environment. Swidler's conceptualization contributed to a more nuanced return to culture in the study of poverty in recent years (Small, Harding, and Lamont 2010).

26. Paul Jargowsky (1997) examined the issue of concentrated poverty, exploring the multiple mechanisms through which living among primarily poor people can affect one's outcomes, independent of their individual characteristics.

27. See Anderson 2000, 2003, 2013.

28. Small 2004.

29. Few have directly examined the link between employment and collective efficacy, but some have posited that the higher degree of social capital found in poor Latino neighborhoods, compared with similarly poor neighborhoods consisting primarily of other racial and ethnic groups, is due to the higher labor market involvement of Latinos (Burchfield and Silver 2013).

30. Harding 2010: 20.

31. Mario Small (2009) showed otherwise, demonstrating that the density of organizations serving even poor neighborhoods—including childcare centers and schools, churches, and grocery store—was much richer than most social scientists realized.

32. Harding 2010: 21.

33. In the 1970s, Boston became the focus of national attention when the public school system was required by the courts to desegregate the schools through busing. The effort led to protests and riots, calling sharp attention to the problem of racism in the North, which had long been seen in a favorable light compared with the more explicit racial policies of the American South. The episode has been the focus of major works of journalism and nonfiction, including J. Anthony Lukas's *Common Ground* (2012 [1985]).

34. Harding 2010: 22.

35. Harding 2010: 23.

36. Harding 2010: 24.

37. Harding 2010: 24.

38. Harding 2010: 25.

39. Harding 2010: 25.

40. Scholars of urban change have often drawn a link between policies of urban renewal and gentrification. In particular, scholars influenced by a Marxist perspective (Harvey 2001; Smith 1982) have argued that urban renewal clears the way and make an initial investment that allows the capitalist class to benefit at the expensive of the urban poor. Others, instead, argue that these are complex and multidimensional dynamics, in which every investment in urban infrastructure creates both costs and benefits, and that the benefits can be strategically directed toward the poor but more advantaged groups will often finds ways to reap the rewards (Rose 1984; Zuk et al. 2018). For a history of urban renewal programs in Boston, see Thomas O'Connor's *Building a New Boston* (1995).

41. Recent research adds nuance to the often-maligned policy of urban renewal by highlighting the origins of the policy as an alternative to the more drastic "slum clearance" approach (von Hoffman 2008); unpacking the complex connections between Black communities and urban renewal projects (Hock 2013); and identifying distinctions among different "generations" of urban renewal philosophies (Carmon 1999).

42. The Orchard Park development sits just a few blocks east from Roxbury Crossing.

43. These are the improvements the Boston Housing Authority (BHA n.d.) notes coming out of the urban renewal project:

- Complete redevelopment of the current site, via rehabilitation, demolition, and new construction, to create 331 high-quality housing units of a scope and scale reflective of neighborhood standards.

- Creation of 160 new housing units to link the Orchard Park site to the nearby and stable Mount Pleasant neighborhood. Housing will fill in vacant lots in this "transitional" area, drawing the strengths of the new Orchard Park and Mount Pleasant together.

- Reorganizing the site to create a typical family housing neighborhood and remove the "institutional" feel. All efforts have been made to combine various elements to create visual interest and identity.

- Relinking the development to the surrounding neighborhood by building new public streets and green spaces in accordance with the existing landscape.

44. Due to state law, the reconfiguration needed to be approved by home rule legislation that the BHA filed. Overall, the redevelopment impacted the original 16-acre site and an additional 4 acres in the surrounding neighborhood.

45. Because HOPE VI funding goes to redevelopment projects that usually involve demolishing old housing, these projects typically involve extensive relocation efforts, where current inhabitants are given the option of an alternative public housing unit or a Section 8 voucher to use in the private market. Returning to the

original, redeveloped HOPE VI housing usually involves passing various screening requirements regarding employment and criminal background.

46. Jean McGuire is the cofounder of the METCO, a voluntary school integration program that buses children of color from Boston to predominantly white suburban school districts, and the first Black woman elected to the Boston School Committee. Stabbed repeatedly in Franklin Park while walking her dog in October 2022, Franklin released a statement just days after her attack calling for her community to "stand together and continue working to empower our children" (Anderson 2022).

47. Smith 2007.

48. Granovetter 1974.

49. Five years ago, Kate moved to Rhode Island to be closer to her last job, but she has many years invested in Roxbury and plenty to say about how it has changed over time.

50. In 2021, in the midst of nationwide conversation about racial justice, Boston had the opportunity to elect its first Black mayor, with three Black candidates—two of whom were women—among the top contenders. But in the preliminary vote, the two Black women—councilor Andrea Campbell and acting mayor Kim Janey—came in third and fourth, while John Barros came in fifth. The loss was attributed to an inability to coalesce Black voters behind a common candidate (Ebbert 2021).

CHAPTER 7

1. Multiple jobholding is believed to be rising in the United States, with anywhere from 5 percent to 35 percent of workers employed in more than one job simultaneously (Campion, Caza, and Moss 2020). For some workers, multiple jobholding is beneficial, allowing them to build skills in a new occupation, but for others it's a survival strategy that increases stress and time at work while offering few benefits (Panos, Pouliakas, and Zangelidis 2014).

2. Moynihan 1965.

3. Herbert Gans (2011) argues that Moynihan undercut his intention to propose substantial increases in social spending in support of Black families by being relatively less forceful in his policy rhetoric and by framing the problem of poverty as a "cycle without proposing a break-in point [which] crippled the Report's potential contribution to national action."

4. Wilcox and Wang 2017.

5. Cherlin 2020; Karney 2021; Manning, Smock, and Fettro 2019.

6. Kane, Nelson, and Edin 2015.

7. Haney 2018.

8. Nepomnyaschy et al. 2021.

9. Edin and Kefalas 2005.

10. Wilson 1987.

11. Edin and Lein 1997.

12. The number of children living with only one parent rose continuously over the past fifty years, but the nature of those single parents has changed: fewer are single mothers and more are cohabitating (Livingston 2018). There has also been a dramatic decline in teen pregnancy (Office of Population Affairs 2021), contributing to a broader overall decline in birth rates across the United States (Kearney and Levine 2021).

13. These same patterns appear to hold today outside the US context. Using the case of trade shocks in the Chinese manufacturing sector, David Autor, David Dorn, and Gordon Hanson (2019) find that labor demand shocks do indeed predict significant declines in the fraction of young women that marry. But shocks that differentially impact male- and female-intensive employment sectors have opposing effects on marriage: less male employment leads to less marriage, while less female employment leads to more marriage. Of course, these are culturally dependent outcomes; they emerge where marriage is valued as a goal to strive for. This seems to have changed over time in the United States. When the fracking boom in the Midwest led to an explosion in the wages of blue-collar men, it led in turn to higher birth rates within *and* outside of marriage. But it had no significant effect on rates of marriage (Kearney and Wilson 2017). Marriage seems to have lost at least some of its luster, outside of the well-educated middle and upper-middle class across racial groups, where it remains high.

14. The most recent available data at the time of this writing was from 2019.

15. See Harding 2010. Labor force participation for Franklin residents ages sixteen and over has remained remarkably stable across the past decade, hovering at around two-thirds of the population of both men and women since 2009. Labor force participation rose sharply between 2000 and 2009, likely due to the displacement of former residents and the influx of new residents as a consequence of the demolition of a "traditional" 366-unit public housing development that was replaced with the 226-unit affordable rental housing development where the after-school club is located.

16. Becker 1973.

17. Despite increases in men's time and stated values regarding providing care to both children and elders, women still provide the vast majority of care in the United States (AEI-Brookings 2018).

18. For a comprehensive literature review on family structure and child outcomes, see Waldfogel, Craigie, and Brooks-Gunn 2010.

19. Lundberg and Pollak 2007: 4.

20. Between 1870 and at least 1980, Black women were substantially more likely than white women to participate in the labor force. For empirical evidence and a thoughtful discussion, see Boustan and Collins 2014; Goldin 1977.

21. Despite higher rates of labor market participation among Black women,

marriage was common for both Black and white women. Among Black women born in the late 1930s, only 11 percent would never marry, compared to 5 percent of white women born in the same period (Bennett, Bloom, and Craig 1989).

22. Costa 2000.

23. Black men and women were often excluded from labor market opportunities under Jim Crow, in many cases driving a move toward entrepreneurship (Wingfield 2008). At the same time, racial segregation contributed to and was reinforced by labor market segmentation, with racism keeping Black people, as well as women, out of the kind of good jobs that led to mobility and concentrating this workforce in low-skilled jobs, where a surfeit of workers would also keep wages low (Bonacich 1972). Racial discrimination remains prevalent in the labor market today. While employment discrimination is hard to measure directly (Quillian 2006), audit studies that use identical résumés but vary the name of the applicant, to sound stereotypically either Black or white, find that applicants with white-sounding names receive 50 percent more callbacks than applicants with stereotypically Black-sounding names (Bertrand and Mullainathan 2004).

24. Lewis 1969.

25. United States Congress House Committee on Education and the Workforce Subcommittee on 21st Century Competitiveness 2005, 10. See also Horn 2005; Manning, Brown, and Payne 2014.

26. Wilson and Neckerman 1987.

27. Newman 1995.

28. Manning, Brown, and Payne 2014.

29. Stevenson and Wolfers 2007; Becker 1973. Claudia Goldin (2021) argues that the issue of the gender pay gap is inextricably bound up with trade-offs that families face around care work and paid work, making the case that gender inequality in the distribution of household and care work, as well as workplace policies that reward overwork and penalize flexibility, have made it difficult to reduce gender pay inequality.

30. For instance, Deirdre Bloome, Derek Burk, and Leslie McCall (2019) show that women's dependency on men has declined dramatically. But while the relationship between men's and women's earnings is often measuring using a dependency ratio, which posits a "zero-sum" trade-off between partners, they find instead that women's substantially reduced dependency has entailed only modest increases in male dependency—increasingly both members of a couple are "self-reliant" through employment.

31. Black, Schanzenbach, and Breitwieser 2017. "

32. Cherlin 2010.

33. Cherlin 2010.

34. Edin and Kefalas 2005.

35. Note that the age of first marriage has increased over time. See, for example, Stevenson and Wolfers 2007. Richard Reeves and Christopher Pulliam (2020)

limit their study to individuals ages 33–44 to avoid the bias that the changing age of first marriage would introduce to their results. See also Cherlin 2014.

36. A growing body of literature offers strong support for the idea that economic opportunity shape family formation decisions, especially for men (Burstein 2007). For instance, Yu Xie and colleagues (2003) develop a metric designed to capture economic potential and find that men with higher economic potential are more likely to marry—although women's economic potential is unrelated to decisions about family formation and economic potential has no relationship to cohabitation. This is keeping with William Julius Wilson's marriageable men hypothesis of the early 1990s.

37. Murray 2012.

38. Schneider, Harknett, and Stimpson 2018.

39. Valerie Oppenheimer (1988) argues that uncertainty about one's long-term economic prospects impedes marriage formation, because marriage is expected to be a long-term commitment, a theory later echoed by the low-income women in ethnographer Kathy Edin's work (Edin and Kefalas 2005). In later research with coauthors, Oppenheimer provides an empirical assessment of the relationship between men's "career maturity," defined as the combined impact of a variety of indicators of men's educational attainment, work experience, annual earnings, type of work, and marriage (Oppenheimer, Kalmijn, and Lim 1997). Their findings suggest that the transition to a stable, "mature" career characterized by multiple years of stable earnings and employment is a key predictor of marriage and that less-educated, low-income men have seen their ability to achieve this sort of stability has eroded over time. In related work, Daniel Schneider and coauthors Kristen Harknett and Matthew Stimpson (2019) identify a strong relationship between job quality—jobs with standard work schedules and jobs that provide fringe benefits—and the likelihood of marriage for both men and women.

40. Interestingly, union membership has declined over time, implying that a resurgence of unions (or a new form of worker power that provides similar benefits in the form of a living wage, stable and secure employment, and benefits) has the potential to stabilize families. See also Schneider and Reich 2014.

41. Marriage and fertility rates among military women are higher than those of comparable civilian women, which Lundquist attributes to the strong pro-family policies in place for enlisted service members, including high-quality low-cost childcare and family housing (Lundquist and Smith 2005). See also Lundquist 2004, 2006.

42. Finally, a small body of research looks directly at economic context and individual decisions regarding family formation and fertility. Melissa Kearney and Riley Wilson (2017) investigate whether men's earning potential leads to an increase in marriage (and a decrease in nonmarital births) by exploiting the positive economic shock associated with the fracking boom of the 2000s. While local area fracking production increased male wages and employment for non-college-

educated men, marriage rates did not change—though birth rates increased for both married couples and unmarried women. David Autor and coauthors find that a decline in male labor market opportunity due to local trade shocks between 1990 and 2010 led to a decline in marriage, a rise in births to teen mothers, and an increase in the number of children being raised in single-parent households (Autor, Dorn, and Hanson 2019).

43. Newman and Chen 2008.

44. Pew Research Center 2019.

45. While stay-at-home mothers remain more common, they are increasingly less likely to be home by choice to care for family: 78 percent of stay-at-home mothers report that their main reason for being home was to care for family, compared with 86 percent in 1989 (Pew Research Center 2019).

46. Pew Research Center 2019.

47. McLanahan 1985.

48. In response to growing concerns over the consequences of changes in family structure, as reflected in the Moynihan Report, Congress began passing laws in the late 1970s designed to increase the amount of child support paid to children with a nonresident parent. In 1988 income withholding from earnings became automatic. As part of the welfare reform policies of the mid-1990s, states were incentivized to increase paternity establishment rates—a necessary precondition for child support. For more detail, see Case, Lin, and McLanahan 2003.

49. Case, Lin, and McLanahan 2003.

50. Utilizing the Current Population Survey (CPS) and the CPS Child Support Supplement to the CPS, both representative datasets from the US Census Bureau, we track child support receipt from 1992 (the first year the CPS began collecting specific information on child support) through 2019 (the most recently available data). Specifically, we create a ratio of child support received as a share of child support owed. Changes in child care policy mean that the share of noncustodial fathers who owe child support and the amount of child support owed vary in predictable ways over time; policies in the United States have deliberately attempted to increase both of these numbers. By looking at child support paid as a share of child support owed, we avoid the problems created by looking at absolutes and instead focus a narrow lens on whether noncustodial parents (mainly fathers) are better able to meet their obligations. We then look at the relationship between that ratio and the health of the labor market. We define a "tight" labor market using several different cut points for local unemployment rates, to understand just how tight the labor market needs to be to see shifts in noncustodial parents' ability to meet their child support obligations: at or below 5 percent, at or below 4.5 percent, and at or below 4 percent. We pool all respondents across the entire date range, to generate sufficient sample size.

51. Two major trends undergird much of the scholarship on low-income men in contemporary America: declining labor force participation and rising incarcera-

tion rates. First, the long-term fall in male labor force participation, particularly among those with less than a high school degree and/or those in the lowest wage bracket, is a well-documented empirical fact. Real hourly earnings for men ages 25–54 with no more than a high school degree declined by 18.2 percent between 1973 and 2015, while labor force participation rates for men ages 25–54 without a college degree has nose-dived. In the late 1960s nearly all 25- to 64-year-old men with no more than high school degree participated in the labor force; by 2015 this same group of men participated at a rate of 85.3 percent (Binder and Bound 2019).

Second, the fall in less-educated men's labor force participation rates has been accompanied by a massive increase in the share of men in the same group being incarcerated for some to all of their working years. Sociologists Bruce Western and Christopher Wildeman (2009) estimate that, as of 2007, a 30- to 34-year-old Black man without a high school degree had a nearly 70 percent chance of having been imprisoned at some point in his life thus far. The incarceration rate (defined as the number of inmates per 100,000 residents) increased from 220 in 1980 to 710 in 2012 (Kearney et al. 2014).

52. Positive father involvement has long been recognized as key to children's success. Indeed, part of Moynihan's motivation was widespread distress that fathers were no longer engaged in the lives of their families and children. Father absence has strong negative effects on children's outcomes as well—especially social-emotional adjustment, high school graduation rates, and adult mental health (McLanahan, Tach, and Schneider 2013). Positive father involvement in associated with children's higher academic achievement, higher levels of school readiness, stronger math and verbal skills, higher self-esteem, fewer behavior problems, and higher lives of social-emotional skill than among children who do not have caring, involved fathers (Flouri and Buchanan 2003; Mosley and Thomson 1995; Sarkadi et al. 2008; Volling and Belsky 1992; Yeung, Duncan, and Hill 2000).

Both employment and earnings are important factors predicting the quality of father-child and co-parenting relationships for nonresident fathers (Bronte-Tinker, Horowitz, and Carrano 2009). As ethnographers Katheryn Edin and Tim Nelson (2013) illustrate in *Doing the Best I Can: Fatherhood in the Inner City*, poverty and unemployment are sources of stress that undermine both fathers' and mothers' ability to engage in the high-quality, caring relationships that parenting demands. By providing an opportunity for more stable work and the confidence of higher earnings, tight labor markets open up the opportunity for unmarried fathers and mothers to build healthier, mutually supportive relationships.

53. Carlson, McLanahan, and Brooks-Gunn 2008; Hofferth, Stanhope, and Harris 2002; Pleck and Masciadrelli 2004.

54. Note that the causal arrow could theoretically go either direction there. Father involvement could predict positive coparenting in the future—or positive coparenting could predict future levels of father involvement. The most rigorous

efforts to assign causality find that positive coparenting predicts future father involvement, not vice versa. For a detailed review of the best causal evidence, see Carlson, McLanahan, and Brooks-Gunn 2008. To the extent that steady earnings encourage fathers to reconnect with their families, tight labor markets promote involved fatherhood (Schoppe-Sullivan et al. 2004).

55. Pilkauskas, Garfinkel, and McLanahan 2014.

56. Newman 2012.

57. Wiemers 2014.

58. Bitler and Hoynes 2015.

59. Stack 1975.

60. Pilkauskas and Dunifon 2016.

61. "Cost of living" is measured by place-specific weighted averages of local prices. "Standard of living" is measured by bank and credit card transaction data.

62. Diamond and Moretti 2021.

CHAPTER 8

Epigraphs: Rosenberg 2021a; and Rosenberg, Telford, and Gregg 2021.

1. Josh Bivens (2021) shows how tight labor markets have closed racial gaps in income and unemployment, and how lower levels of unemployment over the long term would have yielded dramatic declines in racial inequality. He uses this evidence to make the case for a federal government policy of sustained high-pressure labor markets.

2. US Department of the Treasury 2021b.

3. US Department of the Treasury 2021a.

4. DeParle 2021.

5. DePillis and DeParle 2022.

6. DePillis and DeParle 2022.

7. European countries have historically used wage subsidies to avert large-scale layoffs. Under wage subsidy programs, the state pays all or part of the wages for workers, even if those workers remain idle, to help workers and employers ride out a short-term crisis. This approach, which was effectively used in during the Great Recession, was deployed again across Europe during COVID-19 (Fairless and Hannon 2020).

8. Barnes, Bauer, and Edelberg 2021.

9. Eissa and Hoynes 2006.

10. Hoynes and Patel 2018.

11. West et al. 2021.

12. Bernstein and Baker 2003.

13. R. Miller 2021.

14. University of Michigan Surveys of Consumers 2021.

15. Horsley 2021.

16. Smialek 2022.

17. Powell 2022: 1.

18. Powell 2022.

19. Former US Treasury Secretary Robert Rubin, JP Morgan CEO Jamie Dimon, and others have weighed in to pour cold water on the probability of a soft landing in the current context (Watts 2022; Levitt 2022).

20. Summers quoted in *Slate* (Weissman 2022).

21. Callaci and Vaheesan 2022.

22. Konczal and Lusiani 2022.

23. The relationship between productivity and wages seems to vary over the business cycle, with early productivity gains many times not translating into increased wages for workers (Baker 2007). Few studies directly examine the effect of labor market demand on productivity. More people working is likely to increase the overall productivity of the economy, as measured in GDP (Ball, Leigh, and Loungani 2013). Although to the extent that the most skilled workers are the ones that remain employed when unemployment is high, decreases in unemployment are expected to reduce productivity, conditional on employment.

24. Bernstein and Baker 2003.

25. Jones 2020. See also Banks 2019.

26. Boushey 2019.

27. Somers 2019.

28. For example, see OneTen (www.oneten.org).

29. For example, see the Business Roundtable's Workforce Partnership Initiative (www.businessroundtable/wpi).

30. Derenoncourt and Montialoux 2021.

31. Much of the impact of expanded minimum-wage laws comes from spillover effects up the wage scale, rather than from an increase in starting wages (Wursten and Reich 2021). Other policy interventions impact the racial wage gap negatively. Industries and occupations dominated by Black workers (e.g., domestic work) have borne the brunt of New Deal era policies that established deep structural inequalities that persist today. When civil rights cases are brought to court, judges who dismiss those cases are letting the racial wage gap stand (Cunningham and Lopez 2021). When they rule in favor of the plaintiffs, the result is a victory for equality. In general, structural decisions that keep the racial wage gap in place are more common than those that help mitigate it (Wilkerson 2020).

32. Dube, Naidu, and Reich 2007; Cengiz et al. 2019; Romich et al. 2020.

33. CBO 2021.

34. K. Miller 2021.

35. Economist David Card was awarded the Sveriges Riksbank Prize in Economic Sciences in Memory of Alfred Nobel in 2021. Together with the late economist Alan Krueger (to whom this book is dedicated), Card's pathbreaking work on

the employment effects of the minimum wage was cited by the Nobel committee as a key contribution meriting the Nobel honor (NobelPrize.org 2021).

36. Some have argued against raising wage standards, pointing to potential negative impacts on employment (Neumark and Shirley 2021; Strain 2021). But the dominant perspective among economists has largely shifted away from concern about negative effects of minimum wage increases, estimating low overall negative impact of minimum wages on employment (Abraham and Kearney 2020) and toward support for a substantially higher federally mandated minimum, indexed going forward to inflation and to reflect the cost of living. Much of this work builds on techniques developed by David Card and Alan Krueger (1993; 1995), which leverage minimum wages changes as natural experiments.

37. Zundl et al. 2022.

38. Increased opportunity in other sectors combined with persistent low wages in the childcare industry have exacerbated an already grave shortage of childcare workers. As of September 2022, there were one hundred thousand fewer childcare workers than prior to the pandemic. Even as private sector employment fully rebounded over the summer of 2021, the childcare sector was 9.7 percent smaller in September 2022 than it was in February 2020 (Goldstein 2022). A full 98 percent of occupations pay more than those in childcare (McLean et al. 2021). The industry suffers from a classic market failure, as costs are passed on directly to families, and there are few options for efficiencies to cut costs. In the absence of new and sustained public investments, the care conundrum is likely to persist.

39. Howell and Kalleberg 2019; Osterman and Shulman 2011.

40. Kesavan et al. 2022.

41. Harknett, Schneider, and Irwin 2021; Schneider and Harknett 2021, 2019; Henly and Lambert 2014; Lambert and Haley 2021.

42. Press 2021.

43. Jacobs 2018.

44. Bartel et al. 2021.

45. Jacobs 2018.

46. The justification for a federal program over multiple state programs is twofold. First, a single federal program would create cost-saving administrative efficiencies compared to myriad state programs with their own rules, regulations, and eligibility guidelines. These administrative efficiencies would provide cost-savings to employers (many of whom operate in multistate environments), workers (including those who live and work in different states), and the government. Second, a federal program would provide equitable access regardless of the state in which a worker lives. For more, see Boushey and Jacobs 2018.

47. Internal Revenue Service 2022.

48. Ruder as quoted in Orrell 2021.

49. The United Way's ALICE measure (which stands for Asset Limited, Income Constrained, Employed) provides one way of conceptualizing what a self-

sufficiency standard might look like. ALICE households are those with earnings that place them above the federal poverty line (the threshold for most benefits programs) but less than the cost of living in their county. Phasing benefits out using the ALICE threshold in lieu of federal poverty levels could provide substantially more support for the working poor, allowing them to work and earn at a greater level of economic security, and potentially accruing savings in the meantime to have more of a financial cushion in down times. For more, see United Way 2020.

50. Altig et al. 2020.

51. Altig et al. 2020.

52. Federal Reserve Bank of Atlanta 2021.

53. Edin and Lein 1997.

54. Granovetter 1973; Smith and Young 2016.

55. "Investing in America's Workforce" 2019.

56. Newman 2000, 2008.

57. "Effective Practices in Sectoral Employment Programs" 2016.

58. Kazis and Molina 2016.

59. Eyster and Gebrekristos 2018.

60. Eyster and Gebrekristos 2018.

61. Eyster and Gebrekristos 2018.

62. In *No Shame in My Game*, Newman describes the potential for an employer consortium, which could recommend exceptional employees for new, better job opportunities within a network of employers who collaborated to facilitated upward development (Newman 2000: 286).

63. Escobari, Seyal, and Contreras 2021.

64. Demaria, Fee, and Wardrip 2000.

65. Cairo 2013.

66. Council of Economic Advisers 2015.

67. Newman and Winston 2016.

68. Newman and Winston 2016.

69. Hollenbeck 2008; Fersterer, Pischke, and Winter-Ebmer 2008; Lerman, Loprest, and Kuehn 2020; Reed et al. 2012.

70. Fitzpayne and Pollack 2018.

71. Warner 2021.

72. Yuen 2020.

73. Mazumder 2015; Chetty et al. 2017; Chetty and Hendren 2018; Jacobs and Hipple 2018; Chetty et al. 2020.

74. Aeppli and Wilmers forthcoming.

75. Autor and Dube 2022.

76. In the 1990s, Alan Krueger showed that workers who used computers on the job earn 10 percent to 15 percent higher wages than otherwise comparable workers, and the expansion of computer use in the 1980s accounts for between one-third and one-half of the increase in the rate of return to education over that

same period (Krueger 1993). His later work with David Autor and Larry Katz found that the increase in demand for college-educated workers was most intense in more computer-intensive industries (Autor, Katz, and Krueger 1998).

77. AI refers to what economist Daron Acemoglu and others have defined as "a collection of algorithms that act intelligently by recognizing and responding to their environment. AI algorithms process and identify patterns in vast amounts of unstructured data (for instance, speech data, text, or images), and this allows them to perceive their environment and take actions to achieve some specific goal" (Acemoglu and Restrepo 2020: 1). See also Russell 2019; West 2018.

78. Acemoglu and Restrepo 2020.

79. Acemoglu and Restrepo 2020.

80. Frey 2019.

81. Deming 2020.

82. Goodman 2017.

83. Borjas 2014; Card 2005; Peri 2014.

84. BBC 2020.

85. Hackman 2022.

86. There are lessons to be learned here from the struggles the European Union has had to contend with as they formulated policies for the gradual introduction of cross-border migrants from regions with lower wages to areas with greater opportunity, including regulatory control over the pace of migration.

87. Kirschenman and Neckerman 1991.

88. Rosenfeld 2021.

89. Card 2001; Fortin, Lemieux, and Lloyd 2021; Rosenfeld 2014; Western and Rosenfeld 2011.

90. Kallas, Grageda, and Friedman 2022.

APPENDIX 1

1. While we also examined results for the subsequent (i.e., new) peak of economic activity, this substantially constrains our sample, resulting in less dependable results. Furthermore, because of our age limitation on the sample and the usually long time that it takes from the beginning of the expansion in one cycle to the peak of the expansion of the following one (approximately 14-18 years focusing on economic cycles since mid-1970s), the age effect, that is, the aging of our sample, may dominate any other effects. This is particularly important for descriptive analyses, where we cannot effectively account it. Therefore, we focus on the relationship of labor market trends during the economic expansion on the labor market trends at the peak and trough of the same economic cycle.

2. For most variables we have information since 1970, but labor market indicators are consistently available since 1979.

3. Our analysis of relative mobility is inspired by the approach followed by

Katharine Bradbury (2016). We also focus on respondents and spouses ages 16–62 (or, more accurately, 16–50 at the beginning and 28–62 at the end of the transition period), although we track a more limited set of mobility measures over a partially different time period and focus primarily on a measure of gross individual earnings (and gross household income) as opposed to the income after federal and state taxes and inclusive of transfer receipt.

4. While we initially also examined the subsequent transition from the second trough to the next peak, we ultimately decided not to pursue this analysis for several reasons. First, because we are following the same group of individuals over time and the period between the initial trough and the second peak is much longer than the period between the initial trough and the second trough (14–18 years and 7–10 years, respectively), sample attrition becomes much more of a concern over a period of time that is effectively twice as long. Second, since we are conditioning our sample to be prime age at the initial trough and follow them over time, the impact of age effect on employment, which is not controlled for in the descriptive analysis, becomes an increasing concern the further away in time the points of interest are. In our case, all persons who are initially prime age are still of working age (and an overwhelming majority of prime age) within 7–10 years, but a nontrivial proportion of them ages past normal retirement age (and, especially, past prime-age working years) within 14–18 years, which is likely to skew our descriptive results substantially.

5. These year-of-education categories roughly correspond to less than high school degree, high school degree, more than high school degree but less than college degree, and college degree and above.

APPENDIX 4

1. Curiel 2021.

2. US Census Bureau, TIGER/Line Shapefiles, 2012, www.census.gov/geographies/mapping-files/2010/geo/tiger-line-file.html (accessed September 27, 2021).

3. The Census Block Groups from 2010 with an effective number of splits in excess of 1.33 are: 250250804012, 250250806012, 250250924005, 250251001006, and 250251001007.

APPENDIX 5

1. Recht 2020.

References

Aaronson, Stephanie R., Mary C. Daly, William L. Wascher, and David W. Wilcox. 2019. "Okun Revisited: Who Benefits Most from a Strong Economy." *Finance and Economics Discussion Series* (72): 1–80. https://doi.org/10.17016/FEDS.2019.072.

Aaronson, Stephanie R., Mitchell Barnes, and Wendy Edelberg. 2021. "A Hot Labor Market Won't Eliminate Racial and Ethnic Unemployment Gaps." *Brookings* (blog). September 2, 2021. www.brookings.edu/blog/up-front/2021/09/02/a-hot-labor-market-wont-eliminate-racial-and-ethnic-unemployment-gaps/.

Abraham, Katharine G., and Melissa S. Kearney. 2020. "Explaining the Decline in the US Employment-to-Population Ratio: A Review of the Evidence." *Journal of Economic Literature* 58 (3): 585–643. https://doi.org/10.1257/jel.20191480.

Abraham, Katharine G., Kristin Sandusky, John Haltiwanger, and James Spletzer. 2016. "The Consequences of Long Term Unemployment: Evidence from Matched Employer-Employee Data." SSRN Scholarly Paper ID 2839905. Social Science Research Network, Rochester, NY. https://doi.org/10.2139/ssrn.2839905.

Acemoglu, Daron, and Pascual Restrepo. 2020. "Robots and Jobs: Evidence from US Labor Markets." *Journal of Political Economy* 128 (6): 2188–44.

ACLU, Trone Private Sector, and Education Advisory Council. 2017. "Back to Business: How Hiring Formerly Incarcerated Job Seekers Benefits Your

Company." www.aclu.org/sites/default/files/field_document/060917-trone-re
portweb_0.pdf.

Adler, Laura. 2021. "From the Job's Worth to the Person's Price: The Transformation of Pay Practices since 1950." Yale School of Management.

"ADP Workforce Vitality Report." n.d. http://workforcereport.adp.com. Accessed
July 19, 2021.

AEI-Brookings. 2018. "The AEI-Brookings Working Group Report on Paid
Family and Medical Leave."

Aeppli, Clem, and Nathan Wilmers. Forthcoming. "Rapid Wage Growth at the
Bottom Has Offset Rising US Inequality." In *Proceedings of the National
Academy of Sciences*.

AFL-CIO. 2017. "Labor Commission on Racial and Economic Justice." Labor
Commission on Racial and Economic Justice. January 4, 2017. https://racial
-justice.aflcio.org/.

Agan, Amanda, and Sonja Starr. 2017. "Ban the Box, Criminal Records, and
Racial Discrimination: A Field Experiment." *Quarterly Journal of Economics*
133 (1): 191–235. https://doi.org/10.1093/qje/qjx028.

Agnew, John A. 1984. "Devaluing Place: 'People Prosperity versus Place Prosperity' and Regional Planning." *Environment and Planning D: Society and Space*
2 (1): 35–45.

Ajilore, Olugbenga. 2020. "On the Persistence of the Black-White Unemployment Gap." Center for American Progress. February 24. www.ameri
canprogress.org/article/persistence-black-white-unemployment-gap/.

Alderson, Arthur S., and Francois Nielsen. 2002. "Globalization and the Great
U-Turn: Income Inequality Trends in 16 OECD Countries." *American Journal
of Sociology* 107 (5): 1244–99. https://doi.org/10.1086/341329.

Altig, David, Elias Ilin, Boston University, Alexander Ruder, Federal Reserve
Bank of Atlanta, and Ellyn Terry. 2020. "Benefits Cliffs and the Financial
Incentives for Career Advancement: A Case Study of the Health Care Services
Career Pathway." *Federal Reserve Bank of Atlanta, Community and Economic
Development Discussion Papers*. https://doi.org/10.29338/dp2020-01.

Anderson, Travis. 2022. "'I love you all and I will see you soon,' Jean McGuire
releases first public statement after Franklin Park stabbing." *Boston Globe*.
October 14. www.bostonglobe.com/2022/10/14/metro/i-love-you-all-i-will
-see-you-soon-jean-mcguire-releases-first-public-statement-after-franklin-pa
rk-stabbing/.

American Concrete Institute. 2021. "Concrete Field Testing Technician - Grade I."
www.concrete.org/certification/certificationprograms.aspx?m=details&pgm=
Field%20Concrete%20Testing&cert=Concrete%20Field%20Testing%20Tech
nician%20-%20Grade%20I. Accessed November 4, 2021.

Amos, Brian, Michael P. McDonald, and Russell Watkins. 2017. "When Boundaries Collide: Constructing a National Database of Demographic and Voting

Statistics." *Public Opinion Quarterly* 81 (S1): 385–400. https://doi.org /10.1093/poq/nfx001.

Anderson, Elijah. 2000. *Code of the Street: Decency, Violence, and the Moral Life of the Inner City.* New York: W. W. Norton & Company.

———. 2003. *A Place on the Corner.* Chicago: University of Chicago Press.

———. 2013. *Streetwise: Race, Class, and Change in an Urban Community.* Chicago: University of Chicago Press.

Andersson, Fredrik, Harry J. Holzer, and Julia I. Lane. 2005. *Moving Up or Moving On: Who Gets Ahead in the Low-Wage Labor Market?* New York: Russell Sage Foundation.

Arrow, Kenneth. 1973. "The Theory of Discrimination." In *Discrimination in Labor Markets.* Princeton, NJ: Princeton University Press. www.jstor.org/stab le/j.ctt13x10hs.

Associated Press. 2021. "COVID-19 Creates Dire US Shortage of Teachers, School Staff." *US News & World Report.* September 22, 2021. www.usnews.com/news /business/articles/2021-09-22/covid-19-creates-dire-us-shortage-of-teachers -school-staff.

Atkinson, Daryl V., and Kathleen Lockwood. 2016. "The Benefits of Ban the Box." *Southern Coalition for Social Justice.* www.congress.gov/116/meeting/house /109189/documents/HMKP-116-GO00-20190326-SD013.pdf.

Autor, David H. 2009. "Studies of Labor Market Intermediation: Introduction." In *National Bureau of Economic Research Conference Report*, 1–23. Chicago: University of Chicago Press.

———. 2021. "Good News: There's a Labor Shortage." *New York Times*, September 4. www.nytimes.com/2021/09/04/opinion/labor-shortage-biden-covid.html.

Autor, David, and Arindrajit Dube. 2022. "The Unexpected Compression: Employment and Wage Dynamics before and After the Pandemic." Working paper.

Autor, David H., David Dorn, and Gordon H. Hanson. 2019. "When Work Disappears: Manufacturing Decline and the Falling Marriage Market Value of Young Men." *American Economic Review: Insights* 1 (2): 161–78. https://doi .org/10.1257/aeri.20180010.

Autor, David, Lawrence Katz, and Alan Krueger. 1998. "Computing Inequality: Have Computers Changed the Labor Market?" *Quarterly Journal of Economics* 113 (4): 1169–1213.

Avery, Beth, and Han Lu. 2020. "Ban the Box: U.S. Cities, Counties, and States Adopt Fair Hiring Policies." *National Employment Law Project* (blog). September 30. www.nelp.org/publication/ban-the-box-fair-chance-hiring-sta te-and-local-guide/.

Baert, Stijn, Bart Cockx, Niels Gheyle, and Cora Vandamme. 2015. "Is There Less Discrimination in Occupations Where Recruitment Is Difficult?" *ILR Review* 68 (3): 467–500. https://doi.org/10.1177/0019793915570873.

Bailey, Martha J., and Sheldon Danziger. 2013. *Legacies of the War on Poverty.* New York: Russell Sage Foundation. http://muse.jhu.edu/book/26311.

Baker, Dean. 2007. "Behind the Gap between Productivity and Wage Growth." Center for Economic and Policy Research. February. https://core.ac.uk/downl oad/pdf/71339708.pdf.

Ball, Laurence, and N. Gregory Mankiw. 2002. "The NAIRU in Theory and Practice." *Journal of Economic Perspectives* 16 (4): 115–36.

Ball, Laurence M., Daniel Leigh, and Prakash Loungani. 2013. "Okun's Law: Fit at Fifty?" Working Paper 18668. Working Paper Series. National Bureau of Economic Research. January. https://doi.org/10.3386/w18668.

Banaji, Mahzarin R., and Anthony G. Greenwald. 2013. *Blind Spot: Hidden Biases of Good People.* New York: Delacorte Press.

Banks, Nina. 2019. "Black Women's Labor Market History Reveals Deep-Seated Race and Gender Discrimination." *Economic Policy Institute* (blog). February 19. www.epi.org/blog/black-womens-labor-market-history-reveals-deep-seat ed-race-and-gender-discrimination/.

Barnes, Mitchell, Lauren Bauer, and Wendy Edelberg. 2021. "11 Facts about the Economic Recovery from the COVID-19 Pandemic." The Hamilton Project. Brookings. September. www.brookings.edu/wp-content/uploads/2021/09/CO VID-Facts-v3.pdf.

Barron, John M., Dan A. Black, and Mark A. Loewenstein. 1989. "Job Matching and On-the-Job Training." *Journal of Labor Economics* 7 (1): 1–19.

Bartel, Ann, Maya Rossin-Slater, Christopher Ruhm, Meredith Slopen, and Jane Waldfogel. 2021. *The Impact of Paid Family Leave on Employers: Evidence from New York.* Cambridge, MA: National Bureau of Economic Research. https://doi.org/10.3386/w28672.

Bayer, Patrick, and Kerwin Kofi Charles. 2017. "Divergent Paths: Structural Change, Economic Rank, and the Evolution of Black-White Earnings Differences, 1940-2014." NBER Working Paper 22797. September. National Bureau of Economic Research, Cambridge, MA. www.nber.org/papers/w22797.

BBC. 2020. "US Election 2020: Trump's Impact on Immigration—in Seven Charts." *BBC News*, October 21. www.bbc.com/news/election-us-2020-5463 8643.

Becker, Gary S. 1957. *The Economics of Discrimination.* Chicago: University of Chicago Press.

———. 1962. "Investment in Human Capital: A Theoretical Analysis." *Journal of Political Economy* 70 (5, Part 2): 9–49.

———. 1973. "A Theory of Marriage: Part I." *Journal of Political Economy* 81 (4): 813–46.

Belmonte, Adriana. 2018. "Construction Industry 'Is Still Dealing with the Ramifications' of the Financial Crisis." *Yahoo Finance* (blog). September 15.

https://finance.yahoo.com/news/construction-industry-still-dealing-ramificat
ions-financial-crisis-120542471.html.

———. 2019. "The U.S. Construction Industry Is Facing 'a Uniquely Post-Great
Recession Experience.'" *Yahoo Entertainment* (blog). September 10. www.yah
oo.com/entertainment/construction-industry-after-recession-140430175.html.

Benner, Chris, Laura Leete, and Manuel Pastor. 2007. *Staircases or Treadmills?
Labor Market Intermediaries and Economic Opportunity in a Changing
Economy*. Illustrated edition. New York: Russell Sage Foundation.

Bennett, Neil G., David E. Bloom, and Patricia H. Craig. 1989. "The Divergence
of Black and White Marriage Patterns." *American Journal of Sociology* 95 (3):
692–722.

Berger-Gross, Andrew. 2018. "Out of Prison, into the Workforce: Ex-Offenders
and North Carolina's Tight Labor Markets." North Carolina Department of
Commerce. July 30. www.nccommerce.com/blog/2018/07/30/out-prison-wor
kforce-ex-offenders-and-north-carolina%E2%80%99s-tight-labor-market.

Berger, Suzanne, and Michael J. Piore. 1980. *Dualism and Discontinuity in
Industrial Societies*. Cambridge, UK: Cambridge University Press.

Bernstein, Jared. 2018. *The Importance of Strong Labor Demand*. Hamilton
Project. Washington, DC: Brookings Institution.

Bernstein, Jared, and Dean Baker. 2003. *The Benefits of Full Employment*.
Washington, DC: Economic Policy Institute. www.epi.org/publication/boo
ks_full_employment/.

Bertrand, Marianne, and Sendhil Mullainathan. 2004. "Are Emily and Greg More
Employable Than Lakisha and Jamal? A Field Experiment on Labor Market
Discrimination." *American Economic Review* 94 (4): 991–1013.

Binder, Ariel J., and John Bound. 2019. "The Declining Labor Market Prospects
of Less-Educated Men." *Journal of Economic Perspectives* 33 (2): 163–90.

Birkelund, Gunn Elisabeth, Lars E. F. Johannessen, Erik Børve Rasmussen, and
Jon Rogstad. 2020. "Experience, Stereotypes and Discrimination. Employers'
Reflections on Their Hiring Behavior." *European Societies* 22 (4): 503–24.
https://doi.org/10.1080/14616696.2020.1775273.

Bitler, Marianne, and Hilary W. Hoynes. 2010. "The State of the Safety Net in the
Post-Welfare Reform Era." Working Paper 16504. October. National Bureau of
Economic Research. https://doi.org/10.3386/w16504.

———. 2015. "Heterogeneity in the Impact of Economic Cycles and the Great
Recession: Effects within and across the Income Distribution." *American
Economic Review* 105 (5): 154–60. https://doi.org/10.1257/aer.p20151055.

Bivens, Josh. 2021. "The Promise and Limits of High-Pressure Labor Markets for
Narrowing Racial Gaps." *Economic Policy Institute* (blog). August 24. www
.epi.org/publication/high-pressure-labor-markets-narrowing-racial-gaps/.

Bivens, Josh, and Ben Zipperer. 2018. "The Importance of Locking in Full
Employment for the Long Haul." *Economic Policy Institute* (blog). August 21.

www.epi.org/publication/the-importance-of-locking-in-full-employment-for
-the-long-haul/.

Black, Sandra E., Diane Whitmore Schanzenbach, and Audrey Breitwieser. 2017. "The Recent Decline in Women's Labor Force Participation." *The Hamilton Project* 51: 5–17.

Blanchard, Olivier, and Lawrence F. Katz. 1999. "Wage Dynamics: Reconciling Theory and Evidence." *American Economic Review* 89 (2): 69–74.

Bloome, Deirdre, Derek Burk, and Leslie McCall. 2019. "Economic Self-Reliance and Gender Inequality between U.S. Men and Women, 1970–2010." *American Journal of Sociology* 124 (5): 1413–67. https://doi.org/10.1086/702278.

Board of Governors of the Federal Reserve System. 2020. "What Economic Goals Does the Federal Reserve Seek to Achieve through Its Monetary Policy?" Federal Reserve. August 27. www.federalreserve.gov/faqs/what-economic-goa ls-does-federal-reserve-seek-to-achieve-through-monetary-policy.htm.

Bolton, Roger. 1992. "'Place Prosperity vs People Prosperity' Revisited: An Old Issue with a New Angle." *Urban Studies* 29 (2): 185–203.

Bonacich, Edna. 1972. "A Theory of Ethnic Antagonism: The Split Labor Market." *American Sociological Review* 37 (5): 547–59.

Borjas, George J. 2014. *Immigration Economics*. Cambridge, MA: Harvard University Press.

Boshier, Roger, and Derek Johnson. 1974. "Does Conviction Affect Employment Opportunities." *Britain Journal of Criminology* 14: 264.

Boston Housing Authority. N.d. www.bostonhousing.org/en/Departments/Plan ning-and-Real-Estate-Development/Mixed-Finance-Development/Orchard -Gardens.aspx. Accessed October 6, 2022.

Boston Planning and Development Agency Research Division. 2019. "Boston in Context: Neighborhoods." January. www.bostonplans.org/getattachment/834 9ada7-6cc4-4d0a-a5d8-d2fb966ea4fe.

Boushey, Heather. 2019. *Unbound: How Inequality Constricts Our Economy and What We Can Do about It*. Cambridge, MA: Harvard University Press.

Boushey, Heather, and Elisabeth Jacobs. 2018. "Addressing 21st-Century Economic Risk in the United States." Washington, DC: AEI-Brookings.

Boustan, Leah Platt, and William J. Collins. 2014. "The Origin and Persistence of Black-White Divergences in Women's Labor Force Participation." In *Human Capital in History*. Chicago: University of Chicago Press.

Bradbury, Katharine L. 2016. "Levels and Trends in the Income Mobility of U.S. Families, 1977–2012." Working Papers 16-8. Federal Reserve Bank of Boston.

Breza, Emily, Supreet Kaur, and Yogita Shamdasani. 2017. "The Morale Effects of Pay Inequality." *Quarterly Journal of Economics* 133 (2): 611–63. https://doi .org/10.1093/qje/qjx041.

Bronte-Tinkew, Jacinta, Allison Horowitz, and Jennifer Carrano. 2010. "Aggravation and Stress in Parenting: Associations with Coparenting and Father

Engagement among Resident Fathers." *Journal of Family Issues* 31 (4): 525–55.

Brunello, Giorgio, and Francesca Gambarotto. 2007. "Do Spatial Agglomeration and Local Labor Market Competition Affect Employer-Provided Training? Evidence from the UK." *Regional Science and Urban Economics* 37 (1): 1–21. https://doi.org/10.1016/j.regsciurbeco.2006.06.006.

Brunello, Giorgio, and Patricia Wruuck. 2020. "Employer Provided Training in Europe : Determinants and Obstacles." EIB Working Papers. European Investment Bank. https://library.oapen.org/handle/20.500.12657/43407.

Bucknor, Cherrie, and Alan Barber. 2016. "The Price We Pay: Economic Costs of Barriers to Employment for Former Prisoners and People Convicted of Felonies." Center for Economic and Policy Research. June. https://cepr.net/im ages/stories/reports/employment-prisoners-felonies-2016-06.pdf.

Bui, Ofronama, Christopher Famighetti, Darrick Hamilton. 2021. "Examining the Differential Impact of Recessions and Recovery across Race and Gender for Working- versus Professional Class Workers." *Annals of the Academy of Political and Social Science* 695 (1): 158–72. https://doi.org/10.1177/00027162 211027926.

Bunker, Nick. 2016. "Americans Who Have Been Unemployed for a Long Time Find It Harder to Get a Job. Why?" *World Economic Forum*. October 12. www .weforum.org/agenda/2016/10/americans-who-have-been-unemployed-for-a-l ong-time-find-it-harder-to-get-a-job-why/.

Burchfield, Keri B., and Eric Silver. 2013. "Collective Efficacy and Crime in Los Angeles Neighborhoods: Implications for the Latino Paradox." *Sociological Inquiry* 83 (1): 154–76. https://doi.org/10.1111/j.1475-682X.2012.00429.x.

Bureau of Labor Statistics. 2020a. "The Employment Situation." www.bls.gov/ne ws.release/archives/empsit_05082020.pdf.

——. 2020b. "Job Market Remains Tight in 2019, as the Unemployment Rate Falls to Its Lowest Level since 1969." *Monthly Labor Review*.

——. 2021a. "Quits Levels and Rates by Industry and Region, Seasonally Adjusted." July 7. www.bls.gov/news.release/jolts.to4.htm.

——. 2021b. "Real Weekly Earnings up 3.9 Percent for Year Ending March 2021." *The Economics Daily*. April 16. www.bls.gov/opub/ted/2021/real-week ly-earnings-up-3-9-percent-for-year-ending-march-2021.htm.

——. 2021c. "Table 3. Median Usual Weekly Earnings of Full-Time Wage and Salary Workers by Age, Race, Hispanic or Latino Ethnicity, and Sex, Second Quarter 2021 Averages, Not Seasonally Adjusted." July 16. www.bls.gov/news .release/wkyeng.to3.htm.

——. 2021d. "Unemployed 27 Weeks or Longer as a Percent of Total Unemployed." October 8. www.bls.gov/charts/employment-situation/unemplo yed-27-weeks-or-longer-as-a-percent-of-total-unemployed.htm.

——. 2021e. Average Hourly Earnings of All Employees, Leisure and Hospitality [CES7000000003]. Retrieved from FRED (Federal Reserve Bank of St. Louis). https://fred.stlouisfed.org/series/CES7000000003.Accessed November 22.

Burning Glass Technologies. 2020. "COVID-19 Impact: U.S. Job Postings Fall 43% in March." Burning Glass Technologies. April 7. www.burning-glass.com /covid-19-us-job-postings-impact/.

Burstein, Nancy R. 2007. "Economic Influences on Marriage and Divorce." *Journal of Policy Analysis and Management* 26 (2): 387–429.

Butterfield, Fox. 1988. "What You See Is What You Get." *New York Times*, May 1. www.nytimes.com/1988/05/01/books/what-you-see-is-what-you-get.html.

Cairo, Isabel. 2013. "The Slowdown in Business Employment Dynamics: The Role of Changing Skill Demands." Job Market Paper. Universitat Pompeu Fabra. November 12. www.bde.es/f/webpi/SES/seminars/2014/files/sie1411 .pdf.

Callaci, Brian, and Sandeep Vaheesan. 2022. "Inflation Is No Excuse for Squeezing Workers." *Dissent*. www.dissentmagazine.org/online_articles/infla tion-is-no-excuse-for-squeezing-workers#:~:text=Higher%20unemployment %20reduces%20workers'%20ability,the%20current%20surge%20in%20infla tion. Accessed October 14, 2022.

Cambon, Josh Mitchell, Lauren Weber, and Sarah Chaney. 2021. "4.3 Million Workers Are Missing. Where Did They Go?" *Wall Street Journal*. October 14. www.wsj.com/articles/labor-shortage-missing-workers-jobs-pay-raises-econo my-11634224519.

Campion, Emily D., Brianna B. Caza, and Sherry E. Moss. 2020. "Multiple Jobholding: An Integrative Systematic Review and Future Research Agenda." *Journal of Management* 46 (1): 165–91. https://doi.org/10.1177/014920631988 2756.

Cappelli, Peter. 1999. *The New Deal at Work: Managing the Market-Driven Workforce*. First edition. Boston: Harvard Business Review Press.

———. 2014. "Skill Gaps, Skill Shortages and Skill Mismatches: Evidence for the US." Working Paper 20382. August. National Bureau of Economic Research. https://doi.org/10.3386/w20382.

Card, David. 2001. "The Effects of Unions on Wage Inequality in the United States." *ILR Review* 54: 296–315.

———. 2005. "Is the New Immigration Really So Bad?" *Economic Journal* 115 (507): F300–23.

Card, David, and Alan B. Krueger. 1993. "Minimum Wages and Employment: A Case Study of the Fast Food Industry in New Jersey and Pennsylvania." Working Paper 4509. October. National Bureau of Economic Research. https:// doi.org/10.3386/w4509.

———. 1995. "Time-Series Minimum-Wage Studies: A Meta-Analysis." *American Economic Review* 85 (2): 238–43.

_____. 1997. *Myth and Measurement: The New Economics of the Minimum Wage*. Princeton, NJ: Princeton University Press.

Card, David, Alexandre Mas, Enrico Moretti, and Emmanuel Saez. 2012. "Inequality at Work: The Effect of Peer Salaries on Job Satisfaction." *American Economic Review* 102 (6): 2981–3003. https://doi.org/10.1257/aer.102.6.2981.

Carlson, Marcia J., Sara S. McLanahan, and Jeanne Brooks-Gunn. 2008. "Coparenting and Nonresident Fathers' Involvement with Young Children after a Nonmarital Birth." *Demography* 45 (2): 461–88.

Carmon, Naomi. 1999. "Three Generations of Urban Renewal Policies: Analysis and Policy Implications." *Geoforum* 30 (2): 145–58. https://doi.org/10.1016/S0016-7185(99)00012-3.

Case, Anne, I.-Fen Lin, and Sara McLanahan. 2003. "Explaining Trends in Child Support: Economic, Demographic, and Policy Effects." *Demography* 40 (1): 171–89.

Casselman, Ben. 2019. "Why Wages Are Finally Rising, 10 Years after the Recession." *New York Times*, May 2, 2019.

———. 2021. "Pandemic Wave of Automation May Be Bad News for Workers." *New York Times*, July 3. www.nytimes.com/2021/07/03/business/economy/automation-workers-robots-pandemic.html.

Cengiz, Doruk, Arindrajit Dube, Attila Lindner, and Ben Zipperer. 2019. "The Effect of Minimum Wages on Low-Wage Jobs." *Quarterly Journal of Economics* 134 (3): 1405–54. https://doi.org/10.1093/qje/qjz014.

Cherlin, Andrew J. 2010. *The Marriage-Go-Round: The State of Marriage and the Family in America Today*. New York: Knopf Doubleday.

———. 2014. *Labor's Love Lost: The Rise and Fall of the Working-Class Family in America*. New York: Russell Sage Foundation.

———. 2020. "Degrees of Change: An Assessment of the Deinstitutionalization of Marriage Thesis." *Journal of Marriage and Family* 82 (1): 62–80.

Chetty, Raj, and Nathaniel Hendren. 2018. "The Impacts of Neighborhoods on Intergenerational Mobility I: Childhood Exposure Effects." *Quarterly Journal of Economics* 133 (3): 1107–62.

Chetty, Raj, David Grusky, Maximilian Hell, Nathaniel Hendren, Robert Manduca, and Jimmy Narang. 2017. "The Fading American Dream: Trends in Absolute Income Mobility since 1940." *Science* 356 (6336): 398–406. https://doi.org/10.1126/science.aal4617.

Chetty, Raj, John N. Friedman, Nathaniel Hendren, Maggie R. Jones, and Sonya R. Porter. 2018. "The Opportunity Atlas: Mapping the Childhood Roots of Social Mobility." Working Paper 25147. October. National Bureau of Economic Research. https://opportunityinsights.org/paper/the-opportunity-atlas/.

Chetty, Raj, Nathaniel Hendren, Maggie R. Jones, and Sonya R. Porter. 2020.

"Race and Economic Opportunity in the United States: An Intergenerational Perspective." *Quarterly Journal of Economics* 135 (2): 711–83.

Chetty, Raj, Nathaniel Hendren, Patrick Kline, and Emmanuel Saez. 2014. "Where Is the Land of Opportunity? The Geography of Intergenerational Mobility in the United States." *Quarterly Journal of Economics* 129 (4): 1553–623.

Chung, Hess, Bruce Fallick, Christopher J. Nekarda, and David Ratner. 2014. "Assessing the Change in Labor Market Conditions." *FEDS Notes* (0019), May 22. https://doi.org/10.17016/2380-7172.0019.

Clawson, Dan, and Naomi Gerstel. 2014. *Unequal Time: Gender, Class, and Family in Employment Schedules*. New York: Russell Sage Foundation.

Coleman, James S. 1988. "Social Capital in the Creation of Human Capital." *American Journal of Sociology* 94: S95–120. https://doi.org/10.1086/228943.

Collins, Randall. 2019. *The Credential Society: An Historical Sociology of Education and Stratification*. New York: Columbia University Press.

Colquitt, Jason A., Donald E. Conlon, Michael J. Wesson, Christopher OLH Porter, and K. Yee Ng. 2001. "Justice at the Millennium: A Meta-Analytic Review of 25 Years of Organizational Justice Research." *Journal of Applied Psychology* 86 (3): 425–45.

Congressional Budget Office (CBO). 2021. "How Increasing the Federal Minimum Wage Could Affect Employment and Family Income." www.cbo.gov /publication/55681. Accessed November 15, 2021.

Cooke, Thomas J. 2011. "It Is Not Just the Economy: Declining Migration and the Rise of Secular Rootedness." *Population, Space and Place* 17 (3): 193–203. https://doi.org/10.1002/psp.670.

Coombs, Kyle, Arindrajit Dube, Suresh Naidu, Calvin Jahnke, Raymond Kluender, and Michael Stepner. 2021. "Early Withdrawal of Pandemic Unemployment Insurance: Effects on Earnings, Employment and Consumption." Harvard Business School Working Paper 22-046. www.hbs .edu/ris/Publication%20Files/22-046_ce11d30f-72bc-4dd6-8367-e1dce9e751 54.pdf.

Cooper, David. 2018. "Workers of Color Are Far More Likely To Be Paid Poverty-Level Wages Than White Workers." Economic Policy Institute, Washington, DC.

Correll, Shelley J., Cecilia L. Ridgeway, Ezra W. Zuckerman, Sharon Jank, Sara Jordan-Bloch, and Sandra Nakagawa. 2017. "It's the Conventional Thought That Counts: How Third-Order Inference Produces Status Advantage." *American Sociological Review* 82 (2): 297–327. https://doi.org/10.1177/00031 22417691503.

Costa, Dora L. 2000. "From Mill Town to Board Room: The Rise of Women's Paid Labor." *Journal of Economic Perspectives* 14 (4): 101–22.

Couloute, Lucius, and Daniel Kopf. 2018. "Out of Prison and Out of Work:

Unemployment among Formerly Incarcerated People." Prison Policy Initiative. July. www.prisonpolicy.org/reports/outofwork.html.

Council of Economic Advisers. 2015. "Economic Report of the President and the Annual Report of the Council of Economic Advisers." February. Washington, DC. https://obamawhitehouse.archives.gov/sites/default/files/docs/cea_20 15_erp_complete.pdf.

Craig, Ryan. 2016. "Tuition Assistance Programs: The Secret Employee Benefit." *Forbes*. November 3. www.forbes.com/sites/ryancraig/2016/11/03/tuition-assi stance-programs-the-secret-employee-benefit/.

Crane, Randall, and Michael Manville. 2008. "People or Place? Revisiting the Who versus the Where of Urban Development." *Land Lines* 20 (3): 2–7.

Cunningham, Jamein P., and Jose Joaquin Lopez. 2021. "Civil Rights Enforcement and the Racial Wage Gap." *AEA Papers and Proceedings* 111 (May): 196–200. https://doi.org/10.1257/pandp.20211111.

Curiel, John A. 2021. "ArealOverlapR." September 13. https://github.com/jcuriel -unc/arealOverlapR. Accessed September 15, 2021.

Curiel, John A., and Tyler Steelman. 2018. "Redistricting out Representation: Democratic Harms in Splitting Zip Codes." *Election Law Journal: Rules, Politics, and Policy* 17 (4): 328–53.

Darity, William A., Jr., and Patrick L. Mason. 1998. "Evidence on Discrimination in Employment: Codes of Color, Codes of Gender." *Journal of Economic Perspectives* 12 (2): 63–90.

Deloitte and the Manufacturing Institute. 2018. "2018 Deloitte and The Manufacturing Institute Skills Gap and Future of Work Study." The Manufacturing Institute. www.themanufacturinginstitute.org/research/2018-deloitte-and-the-manufacturing-institute-skills-gap-and-future-of-work-study/.

Demaria, Kyle, Kyle Fee, and Keith Wardrip. 2000. "Exploring a Skills-Based Approach to Occupational Mobility." June. Philadelphia: Federal Reserve Bank of Philadelphia; Cleveland: Federal Reserve Bank of Cleveland. www.ph iladelphiafed.org/-/media/frbp/assets/community-development/reports/skills -based-mobility.pdf?la=en.

Deming, David. 2020. "The Robots Are Coming. Prepare for Trouble." *New York Times*, January 30. www.nytimes.com/2020/01/30/business/artificial-intellige nce-robots-retail.html.

DeParle, Jason. 2021. "Pandemic Aid Programs Spur a Record Drop in Poverty." *New York Times*, July 28. www.nytimes.com/2021/07/28/us/politics/covid-po verty-aid-programs.html.

DePillis, Lydia, and Jason DeParle. 2022. "Pandemic Aid Cut U.S. Poverty to New Low in 2021, Census Bureau Reports." *New York Times*, September 13. www.nytimes.com/2022/09/13/business/economy/income-poverty-census-bu reau.html.

Derenoncourt, Ellora, and Claire Montialoux. 2021. "Minimum Wages and Racial

Inequality." *Quarterly Journal of Economics* 136 (1): 169–228. https://doi.org/10.1093/qje/qjaa031.

DeWitt, Larry. 2010. "The Decision to Exclude Agricultural and Domestic Workers from the 1935 Social Security Act." *Social Security Administration Research, Statistics, and Policy Analysis* 70 (4). www.ssa.gov/policy/docs/ssb/v70n4/v70n4p49.html.

Dey, Matthew, and Mark A. Loewenstein. 2020. "How Many Workers Are Employed in Sectors Directly Affected by COVID-19 Shutdowns, Where Do They Work, and How Much Do They Earn?" *Monthly Labor Review* (April). www.bls.gov/opub/mlr/2020/article/covid-19-shutdowns.htm.

Dey, Matthew, Harley Frazis, Mark A. Loewenstein, and Hugette Sun. 2020. "Ability to Work from Home: Evidence from Two Surveys and Implications for the Labor Market in the COVID-19 Pandemic." *Monthly Labor Review* (June). www.bls.gov/opub/mlr/2020/article/ability-to-work-from-home.htm.

Diamond, Rebecca, and Enrico Moretti. 2021. "Where Is Standard of Living the Highest? Local Prices and the Geography of Consumption." National Bureau of Economic Research Working Paper 29533.

Dobbie, Will, and Roland G. Fryer Jr. 2011. "Are High-Quality Schools Enough to Increase Achievement among the Poor? Evidence from the Harlem Children's Zone." *American Economic Journal: Applied Economics* 3 (3): 158–87. https://doi.org/10.1257/app.3.3.158.

Dobbin, Frank, John R. Sutton, John W. Meyer, and Richard Scott. 1993. "Equal Opportunity Law and the Construction of Internal Labor Markets." *American Journal of Sociology* 99 (2): 396–427.

Doeringer, Peter B., and Michael J. Piore. 1971. *Internal Labor Markets and Manpower Analysis.* D.C. Heath and Company.

———. 1975. "Unemployment and the Dual Labor Market." *The Public Interest* (Winter).

Du Bois, W. E. B. 2013 [1935]. *Black Reconstruction in America: Toward a History of the Part Which Black Folk Played in the Attempt to Reconstruct Democracy in America, 1860–1880.* New Brunswick: Transaction Publishers.

Dube, Arindrajit. 2021. "Aggregate Employment Effects of Unemployment Benefits during Deep Downturns: Evidence from the Expiration of the Federal Pandemic Unemployment Compensation." National Bureau of Economic Research. https://doi.org/10.3386/w28470.

Dube, Arindrajit, Suresh Naidu, and Michael Reich. 2007. "The Economic Effects of a Citywide Minimum Wage." *ILR Review* 60 (4): 522–43.

Ebbert, Stephanie. 2021. "How Did Boston Miss Its Moment to Elect a Black Leader?" *Boston Globe*, September 15. www.bostonglobe.com/2021/09/15/metro/how-did-black-boston-miss-this-moment-lead/.

"Economic Report of the President 1964." 1964. *Economic Report of the President.* https://fraser.stlouisfed.org/title/economic-report-president-45/1964-8135.

Edin, Kathryn, and Laura Lein. 1997. *Making Ends Meet: How Single Mothers Survive Welfare and Low-Wage Work*. New York: Russell Sage Foundation.

Edin, Kathryn, and Maria Kefalas. 2005. *Promises I Can Keep: Why Poor Women Put Motherhood before Marriage*. Berkeley: University of California Press.

Edin, Kathryn, and Timothy J. Nelson. 2013. *Doing the Best I Can: Fatherhood in the Inner City*. Berkeley: University of California Press.

"Effective Practices in Sectoral Employment Programs." 2016. Commonwealth Corporation. https://commcorp.org/wp-content/uploads/2016/07/resources _2016-effective-practices-in-sectoral-employment-programs.pdf. Accessed November 12, 2021.

Eissa, Nada, and Hilary W. Hoynes. 2006. "Behavioral Responses to Taxes: Lessons from the EITC and Labor Supply." *Tax Policy and the Economy* 20 (January): 73–110. https://doi.org/10.1086/tpe.20.20061905.

Elder, Glen H. 1998. *Children of the Great Depression, 25th Anniversary Edition*. Updated edition. New York: Routledge.

Ember, Sydney. 2021. "How Do They Say Economic Recovery? 'I Quit.'" *New York Times*, June 20. www.nytimes.com/2021/06/20/business/economy/workers -quit-jobs.html.

Escobari, Marcela, Ian Seyal, and Carlos Daboin Contreras. 2021. *Moving Up: Promoting Workers' Economic Mobility Using Network Analysis*. Workforce of the Future Initiative. Washington, DC: Brookings Institution. www.brookings .edu/wp-content/uploads/2021/06/Moving-Up.pdf.

Evans, Lorraine. 2011. "Job Queues, Certification Status, and the Education Labor Market." *Educational Policy* 25 (2): 267–98.

Eyster, Lauren, and Semhar Gebrekristos. 2018. *Fulfilling the Promise of Career Pathways*. Washington, DC: Urban Institute.

Faberman, R. Jason, Andreas I. Mueller, Ayşegül Şahin, and Giorgio Topa. 2020. "The Shadow Margins of Labor Market Slack." *Journal of Money, Credit and Banking* 52 (S2): 355–91.

Faberman, R. Jason, Andreas I. Mueller, Rachel Schuh, and Giorgio Topa. 2017. "How Do People Find Jobs?" *Liberty Street Economics* (blog). April 5. https:// libertystreeteconomics.newyorkfed.org/2017/04/how-do-people-find-jobs/.

Fairless, Tom, and Paul Hannon. 2020. "Europe's Economic Recipe for the Pandemic: Keep Workers in Their Jobs." *Wall Street Journal*, March 24. www .wsj.com/articles/europes-economic-recipe-for-the-pandemic-keep-workers -in-their-jobs-11585083397.

Fall, Jaime S. 2019. "Investing in Education, Training, and Development for Workers." *The Aspen Institute* (blog). July 11. www.aspeninstitute.org/blog-po sts/investing-in-education-training-and-development-for-workers/.

Federal Bonding Program. 2021. "About the FBP." *Federal Bonding Program* (blog). https://bonds4jobs.com/about-us. Accessed November 4, 2021.

Federal Reserve Bank of Atlanta. 2021. "Career Ladder Identifier and Financial

Forecaster (CLIFF)." www.atlantafed.org/economic-mobility-and-resilience /advancing-careers-for-low-income-families/cliff-tool.

Fernandez, Roberto M. 2010. "Creating Connections for the Disadvantaged: Networks and Labor Market Intermediaries at the Hiring Interface." March. SSRN Scholarly Paper ID 1576608. Social Science Research Network. https:// doi.org/10.2139/ssrn.1576608.

Fersterer, Josef, Jörn-Steffen Pischke, and Rudolf Winter-Ebmer. 2008. "Returns to Apprenticeship Training in Austria: Evidence from Failed Firms Josef Fersterer." *Scandinavian Journal of Economics* 110 (December): 733–53. https:// doi.org/10.1111/j.1467-9442.2008.00559.x.

Fitzpayne, Alastair, and Ethan Pollack. 2018. "Lifelong Learning and Training Accounts." The Aspen Institute. www.aspeninstitute.org/publications/lifelong -learning-and-training-accounts-2018/

Flouri, Eirini, and Ann Buchanan. 2003. "The Role of Father Involvement in Children's Later Mental Health." *Journal of Adolescence* 26 (1): 63–78.

FOMC. 2012. "Federal Reserve Issues FOMC Statement of Longer-Run Goals and Policy Strategy." Board of Governors of the Federal Reserve System. www.federalreserve.gov/newsevents/pressreleases/monetary20120125c.htm. Accessed September 25, 2021.

———. 2021. "What Economic Goals Does the Federal Reserve Seek to Achieve through Its Monetary Policy?" Board of Governors of the Federal Reserve System. www.federalreserve.gov/faqs/what-economic-goals-does-federal-res erve-seek-to-achieve-through-monetary-policy.htm. Accessed September 25, 2021.

Foote, Christopher L., and Richard W. Ryan. 2015. "Labor Market Polarization over the Business Cycle." Working Paper 21030. March. National Bureau of Economic Research. https://doi.org/10.3386/w21030.

Fortin, Nicole M., Thomas Lemieux, and Neil Lloyd. 2021. "Labor Market Institutions and the Distribution of Wages: The Role of Spillover Effects." *Journal of Labor Economics* 39 (S2): S369–412.

Freeman, Richard B. 1990. "Employment and Earnings of Disadvantaged Young Men in a Labor Shortage Economy." Working Paper 3444. September. National Bureau of Economic Research. www.nber.org/papers/w3444.

———. 2001. "The Rising Tide Lifts . . . ?" Working Paper 8155. March. National Bureau of Economic Research. www.nber.org/papers/w8155.

Frey, Carl Benedikt. 2019. "Learning from Automation Anxiety of the Past." *MIT Sloan Management Review.* November 12. https://sloanreview.mit.edu/article /learning-from-automation-anxiety-of-the-past/.

Fuentes, J. Rodrigo, and Edward E. Leamer. 2019. "Effort: The Unrecognized Contributor to US Income Inequality." Working Paper 26421. November. National Bureau of Economic Research. https://doi.org/10.3386/w26421.

Furman, Jason. 2021. "Most of the Economic Problems We're Facing (Inflation,

Supply Chains, Etc.) Are High Class Problems. We Wouldn't Have Had Them If the Unemployment Rate Was Still 10 Percent. We Would Instead Have Had a Much Worse Problem." Tweet. @*jasonfurman* (blog), October 14. https://tw itter.com/jasonfurman/status/1448442874828410881.

Furman, Jason, and Wilson Powell III. 2021. "US Workers Are Quitting Jobs at Historic Rates, and Many Unemployed Are Not Coming Back despite Record Job Openings." *Peterson Institute for International Economics* (blog). June 28. www.piie.com/blogs/realtime-economic-issues-watch/us-workers-are-quitti ng-jobs-historic-rates-and-many-unemployed.

Galster, George C. 2008. "Quantifying the Effect of Neighbourhood on Individuals: Challenges, Alternative Approaches, and Promising Directions." *Schmollers Jahrbuch* 128 (1): 7–48.

Gans, Herbert J. 2011. "The Moynihan Report and Its Aftermaths: A Critical Analysis." *Du Bois Review: Social Science Research on Race* 8 (2): 315–27. https://doi.org/10.1017/S1742058X11000385.

Gans, Herbert J. 1982. *Urban Villagers: Group and Class in the Life of Italian-Americans*. New York: Free Press.

Gardner, Jennifer M. 1994. "The 1990–91 Recession: How Bad Was the Labor Market?" *Monthly Labor Review* 117 (6): 3–11.

GBD 2019 Police Violence US Subnational Collaborators. 2021. "Fatal Police Violence by Race and State in the USA, 1980–2019: A Network Meta-Regression." *The Lancet* 398 (10307): 1239–55. https://doi.org/10.1016/S0140 -6736(21)01609-3.

Gilchrist, Troy, and Bart Hobijn. 2021. "The Divergent Signals about Labor Market Slack." *FRBSF Economic Letter* (15): 6.

Glaeser, Edward L., Matthew E. Kahn, and Jordan Rappaport. 2008. "Why Do the Poor Live in Cities? The Role of Public Transportation." *Journal of Urban Economics* 63 (1): 1–24.

Golden, Lonnie, and Jaeseung Kim. 2020a. "The Involuntary Part-Time Work and Underemployment Problem in the US." Center for Law and Social Policy. August 6, 2020. www.clasp.org/wp-content/uploads/2022/01/GWC2029_Ce nter-For-Law.pdf

———. 2020b. "Underemployment Just Isn't Working for U.S. Part-Time Workers." Center for Law and Social Policy. May 20, 2020. www.clasp.org/pu blications/report/brief/underemployment-just-isnt-working-us-part-time-wo rkers/.

Goldin, Claudia. 1977. "Female Labor Force Participation: The Origin of Black and White Differences, 1870 and 1880." *Journal of Economic History* 37 (1): 87–108.

———. 2021. *Career and Family: Women's Century-Long Journey toward Equity*. Princeton, NJ: Princeton University Press.

Goldstein, Dana. 2022. "Why You Can't Find Childcare: 100,000 Workers Are

Missing." *New York Times*, October 13, 2022. www.nytimes.com/2022/10/13
/us/child-care-worker-shortage.html. Accessed October 13, 2022.

Goodman, Peter S. 2017. "The Robots Are Coming, and Sweden Is Fine." *New York Times*, December 27. www.nytimes.com/2017/12/27/business/the-robots-are-coming-and-sweden-is-fine.html.

Goplerud, Max. 2015. "Crossing the Boundaries: An Implementation of Two Methods for Projecting Data across Boundary Changes." *Political Analysis* 24: 121–29.

Gotway-Crawford, Carol A., and Linda J. Young. 2004. "A Spatial View of the Ecological Inference Problem." In *Ecological Inference: New Methodological Strategies*. Edited Gary King, Ori Rosen, and Martin A. Tanner, 233–44. Cambridge, UK: Cambridge University Press.

Gould, Elise. 2020. "State of Working America Wages 2019: A Story of Slow, Uneven, and Unequal Wage Growth over the Last 40 Years." *Economic Policy Institute* (blog). February 20. www.epi.org/publication/swa-wages-2019/.

Gould, Elise, and Heidi Shierholz. 2020. "Not Everybody Can Work from Home: Black and Hispanic Workers Are Much Less Likely to Be Able to Telework." *Economic Policy Institute* (blog). March 19. www.epi.org/blog/black-and-hispanic-workers-are-much-less-likely-to-be-able-to-work-from-home/.

Gould, Elise, and Jori Kandra. 2021. "Only One in Five Workers Are Working from Home Due to COVID." Economic Policy Institute. June 2. www.epi.org/blog/only-one-in-five-workers-are-working-from-home-due-to-covid-black-and-hispanic-workers-are-less-likely-to-be-able-to-telework/.

Granovetter, Mark. 1973. "The Strength of Weak Ties." *American Journal of Sociology* 78 (6): 1360–80.

———. 1974. *Getting a Job: A Study of Contacts and Careers*. Cambridge, MA: Harvard University Press.

Grusky, David, Bruce Western, and Christopher Wimer. 2011. *The Great Recession*. New York: Russell Sage Foundation.

Gürtzgen, Nicole, Benjamin Lochner, Laura Pohlan, and Gerard J. van den Berg. 2021. "Does Online Search Improve the Match Quality of New Hires?" *Labour Economics* 70 (101981): 1–16.

Hackman, Michele. 2022. "Add Declining Immigration to Problems Weighing on the Labor Market." *Wall Street Journal*, April 5.

Hamilton, Gayle, and Judith M. Gueron. 2002. "The Role of Education and Training in Welfare Reform." *Brookings* (blog). November 30. www.brookings.edu/research/the-role-of-education-and-training-in-welfare-reform/.

Haney, Lynne. 2018. "Incarcerated Fatherhood: The Entanglements of Child Support Debt and Mass Imprisonment." *American Journal of Sociology* 124 (1): 1–48.

Hannerz, Ulf. 1969. *Soulside: Inquiries into Ghetto Culture and Community*. New York: Columbia University Press. http://eric.ed.gov/?id=ED036587.

Harding, David J. 2003. "Jean Valjean's Dilemma: The Management of Ex-Convict Identity in the Search for Employment." *Deviant Behavior* 24 (6): 571–95. https://doi.org/10.1080/713840275.

———. 2010. *Living the Drama: Community, Conflict, and Culture among Inner-City Boys*. Chicago: University of Chicago Press.

———. 2019. *On the Outside: Prisoner Reentry and Reintegration*. Chicago: University of Chicago Press.

Harding, David J., Lisa Gennetian, Christopher Winship, Lisa Sanbonmatsu, and Jeffrey R. Kling. 2010. "Unpacking Neighborhood Influences on Education Outcomes: Setting the Stage for Future Research." June. National Bureau of Economic Research. www.nber.org/papers/w16055.

Harknett, Kristen, Daniel Schneider, and Véronique Irwin. 2021. "Improving Health and Economic Security by Reducing Work Schedule Uncertainty." *Proceedings of the National Academy of Sciences* 118 (42). https://doi.org/10.10 73/pnas.2107828118.

Harrison, B., and J. Kluver. 1989. "Reassessing the 'Massachusetts Miracle': Reindustrialization and Balanced Growth, or Convergence to 'Manhattanization'?" *Environment and Planning A: Economy and Space* 21 (6): 771–801. https:// doi.org/10.1068/a210771.

Harvey, David. 2001. *Spaces of Capital*. New York: Routledge.

Haugen, Michael. 2017. "Ten Years of Criminal Justice Reform in Texas." *Right on Crime*, August 1. https://rightoncrime.com/2017/08/ten-years-of-criminal-jus tice-reform-in-texas/.

Henly, Julia R., and Susan J. Lambert. 2014. "Unpredictable Work Timing in Retail Jobs: Implications for Employee Work–Life Conflict." *ILR Review* 67 (3): 986–1016. https://doi.org/10.1177/0019793914537458.

Henninger, Daniel. 2019. "Story of the Year." *Wall Street Journal*, March 7. www .wsj.com/articles/story-of-the-year-11551916962.

Hershbein, Brad, and Lisa B. Kahn. 2018. "Do Recessions Accelerate Routine-Biased Technological Change? Evidence from Vacancy Postings." *American Economic Review* 108 (7): 1737–72.

Hickes Lundquist, Jennifer, and Herbert L. Smith. 2005. "Family Formation among Women in the US Military: Evidence from the NLSY." *Journal of Marriage and Family* 67 (1): 1–13.

Hobijn, Bart, and Ayşegül Şahin. 2021. "Maximum Employment and the Participation Cycle." September. National Bureau of Economic Research. www .nber.org/papers/w29222.

Hock, Jennifer. 2013. "Bulldozers, Busing, and Boycotts: Urban Renewal and the Integrationist Project." *Journal of Urban History* 39 (3): 433–53. https://doi .org/10.1177/0096144212467310.

Hofferth, Sandra L., Stephen Stanhope, and Kathleen Mullan Harris. 2002.

"Exiting Welfare in the 1990s: Did Public Policy Influence Recipients' Behavior?" *Population Research and Policy Review* 21 (5): 433–72.

Hollenbeck, Kevin. 2008. "Is There a Role for Public Support of Incumbent Worker On-the-Job Training?" Upjohn Institute Working Papers. January. https://doi.org/10.17848/wp08-138.

Holmes, Aaron. 2019. "The 2010s Were the Decade Amazon Took over the World. Here's How the Company Grew Its Business Tenfold in the Past 10 Years." *Business Insider*. December 16. www.businessinsider.com/amazon-decade-review-2010s-growth-2019-12.

Holzer, Harry. 2013. "Workforce Development Programs." *Legacies of the War on Poverty*. Edited by Martha J. Bailey and Sheldon Danziger. New York: Russell Sage Foundation. http://muse.jhu.edu/book/26311.

Holzer, Harry J., Steven Raphael, and Michael A. Stoll. 2003. "Employment Barriers Facing Ex-Offenders." March 19. Urban Institute. www.urban.org/sites/default/files/publication/59416/410855-Employment-Barriers-Facing-Ex-Offenders.PDF.

Horn, Wade. 2005. *Welfare Reform: Reauthorization of Work And Child Care.* Hearing before the Subcommittee on 21st Century Competitiveness of the Committee on Education and the Workforce, U.S. House of Representatives 109th Congress First Session. March 15. https://files.eric.ed.gov/fulltext/ED496063.pdf.

Horsley, Scott. 2021. "Fed Chair Powell Says Recent Spike in Prices in Temporary." *NPR* (blog). July 14. www.npr.org/2021/07/14/1016093402/fed-chair-powell-says-recent-spike-in-prices-is-temporary.

Hotchkiss, Julie L., and Robert Elijah Moore. 2018. "Some Like It Hot: Assessing Longer-Term Labor Market Benefits from a High-Pressure Economy." SSRN Scholarly Paper ID 3140774. March 15. Social Science Research Network. https://doi.org/10.2139/ssrn.3140774.

Howell, David R., and Arne L. Kalleberg. 2019. "Declining Job Quality in the United States: Explanations and Evidence." *RSF: The Russell Sage Foundation Journal of the Social Sciences* 5 (4): 1–53. https://doi.org/10.7758/RSF.2019.5.4.01.

Hoynes, Hilary W., and Ankur J. Patel. 2018. "Effective Policy for Reducing Poverty and Inequality? The Earned Income Tax Credit and the Distribution of Income." *Journal of Human Resources* 53 (4): 859–90. https://doi.org/10.3368/jhr.53.4.1115.7494R1.

Hoynes, Hilary, Douglas L. Miller, and Jessamyn Schaller. 2012. "Who Suffers during Recessions?" *Journal of Economic Perspectives* 26 (3): 27–48. www.aeaweb.org/articles?id=10.1257/jep.26.3.27.

Internal Revenue Service. 2021. "Work Opportunity Tax Credit." September 24. www.irs.gov/businesses/small-businesses-self-employed/work-opportunity-tax-credit.

———. 2022. "Gig Economy Tax Center | Internal Revenue Service." 2022. www
.irs.gov/businesses/gig-economy-tax-center.

International Association of Administrative Professionals. 2019. "State of the
Administrative Profession." https://cdn.ymaws.com/www.iaap-hq.org/resour
ce/resmgr/files/state_of_the_profession_benc.pdf. Accessed July 19, 2021.

"Investing in America's Workforce." 2019. National Skills Coalition, Washington,
DC. www.nationalskillscoalition.org/wp-content/uploads/2020/12/CIAW-Inv
est-in-AW-1.pdf.

Jacobs, Elisabeth. 2018. "Paid Family and Medical Leave in the United States:
A Research Agenda." Washington Center for Equitable Growth. October 22.
https://equitablegrowth.org/research-paper/paid-family-and-medical-leave
-in-the-united-states/?longform=true.

Jacobs, Elisabeth, and Liz Hipple. 2018. "Are Today's Inequalities Limiting
Tomorrow's Opportunities? A Review of the Social Sciences Literature on
Economic Inequality and Intergenerational Mobility." Washington Center for
Equitable Growth. October 3. https://equitablegrowth.org/research-paper/are
-todays-inequalities-limiting-tomorrows-opportunities/?longform=true.

Jargowsky, Paul A. 1997. *Poverty and Place: Ghettos, Barrios, and the American
City*. New York: Russell Sage Foundation.

Jencks, Christopher, and Susan E. Mayer. 1990. "The Social Consequences of
Growing up in a Poor Neighborhood." *Inner-City Poverty in the United States*
111: 186.

Jones, Janelle. 2020. "Black Women Best." *Data For Progress* (blog), July 15. www
.dataforprogress.org/blog/2020/7/15/black-women-best.

Jovanovic, Boyan. 1979. "Job Matching and the Theory of Turnover." *Journal of
Political Economy* 87 (5, Part 1): 972–90.

Jones, Jeffrey M. 2022. "LGBT Identification in U.S. Ticks Up to 7.1%" Gallup.
October 14. https://news.gallup.com/poll/389792/lgbt-identification-ticks-up
.aspx.

Kain, John F. 1992. "The Spatial Mismatch Hypothesis: Three Decades Later."
Housing Policy Debate 3 (2): 371–460. https://doi.org/10.1080/10511482.1992
.9521100.

Kallas, Johnnie, Leonardo Grageda, and Eli Friedman. 2022. "Labor Action
Tracker: Annual Report 2021." Cornell ILR: The Worker Institute. February
21. www.ilr.cornell.edu/worker-institute/blog/reports-and-publications/labor
-action-tracker-annual-report-2021.

Kane, Jennifer B., Timothy J. Nelson, and Kathryn Edin. 2015. "How Much
In-Kind Support Do Low-Income Nonresident Fathers Provide? A Mixed-
Method Analysis." *Journal of Marriage and Family* 77 (3): 591–611.

Kanno-Youngs, Zolan. 2018. "'I Thought I Was Done For': Tight Job Market
Opens Doors for Ex-Convicts." *Wall Street Journal*, December 19. www.wsj

.com/articles/i-thought-i-was-done-for-tight-job-market-opens-doors-for-ex
-convicts-11545215400.

Kaplan, Greg, and Sam Schulhofer-Wohl. 2017. "Understanding the Long-Run Decline in Interstate Migration." *International Economic Review* 58 (1): 57–94. https://doi.org/10.1111/iere.12209.

Karney, Benjamin R. 2021. "Socioeconomic Status and Intimate Relationships." *Annual Review of Psychology* 72: 391–414.

Kazis, Richard, and Frieda Molina. 2016. "Implementing the WorkAdvance Model." Policy Brief. October. MDRC. www.mdrc.org/publication/implementi ng-workadvance-model.

Kearney, Melissa S., and Phillip B. Levine. 2021. "Will Births in the US Rebound? Probably Not." *Brookings* (blog). May 24. www.brookings.edu/blog /up-front/2021/05/24/will-births-in-the-us-rebound-probably-not/.

Kearney, Melissa S., and Riley Wilson. 2017. "Male Earnings, Marriageable Men, and Nonmarital Fertility: Evidence from the Fracking Boom." NBER Working Paper 23408. May. National Bureau of Economic Research. https://doi.org/10 .3386/w23408.

Kearney, Melissa S., Benjamin H. Harris, Elisa Jácome, and Lucie Parker. 2014. "Ten Economic Facts about Crime and Incarceration in the United States." May. Brookings. www.brookings.edu/wp-content/uploads/2016/06/v8_thp _10crimefacts.pdf.

Kelly, Erin L., Samantha K. Ammons, Kelly Chermack, and Phyllis Moen. 2010. "Gendered Challenge, Gendered Response: Confronting the Ideal Worker Norm in a White-Collar Organization." *Gender & Society* 24 (3): 281–303.

Kesavan, Saravanan, Susan J. Lambert, Joan C. Williams, and Pradeep K. Pendem. 2022. "Doing Well By Doing Good: Improving Retail Store Performance with Responsible Scheduling Practices at the Gap, Inc." *Management Science*. March 2. https://doi.org/10.1287/mnsc.2021.4291.

Kirchner, Stefan, and Elke Schüßler. 2020. "Regulating the Sharing Economy: A Field Perspective." In *Theorizing the Sharing Economy: Variety and Trajectories of New Forms of Organizing*. Bingley: Emerald Publishing Limited.

Kirschenman, Joleen, and Kathryn M. Neckerman. 1991. "'We'd Love to Hire Them, But...': The Meaning of Race for Employers." In *The Urban Underclass*. Edited by Christopher Jencks and Paul E. Peterson, 203–34. Washington, DC: Brookings Institution.

Knight, Louise W. 2010. *Jane Addams: Spirit in Action*. New York: W. W. Norton & Company.

Kochhar, Rakesh. 2020. "Unemployment Rose Higher in Three Months of COVID-19 Than It Did in Two Years of the Great Recession." *Pew Research Center* (blog). June 11. www.pewresearch.org/fact-tank/2020/06/11/unemplo yment-rose-higher-in-three-months-of-covid-19-than-it-did-in-two-years-of -the-great-recession/.

Koerin, Beverly. 2003. "The Settlement House Tradition: Current Trends and Future Concerns." *Journal of Sociology and Social Welfare* 30 (2): 53–68.

Konczal, Mike and Niko Lusiani. 2022. "Price, Profits, and Power: An Analysis of 2021 Firm-Level Markups." Roosevelt Institute. https://rooseveltinstitute.org /wp-content/uploads/2022/06/RI_PricesProfitsPower_202206.pdf. Accessed October 14, 2022.

Kopczuk, Wojciech, Emmanuel Saez, and Jac Song. 2010. "Earnings Inequality and Mobility in the United States: Evidence from Social Security Data since 1937." *Quarterly Journal of Economics* 125 (1): 91–128.

Kroft, Kory, Fabian Lange, and Matthew J. Notowidigdo. 2013. "Duration Dependence and Labor Market Conditions: Evidence from a Field Experiment." *Quarterly Journal of Economics* 128 (3): 1123–67. https://doi.org /10.1093/qje/qjt015.

Krueger, Alan. 1993. "How Computers Have Changed the Wage Structure: Evidence from Microdata, 1984–1989." *Quarterly Journal of Economics* 108 (1): 33–60.

Lambert, Susan J., Peter J. Fugiel, and Julia R. Henly. 2014. "Precarious Work Schedules among Early-Career Employees in the US: A National Snapshot." https://crownschool.uchicago.edu/sites/default/files/uploads/lambert.fugiel .henly_.executive_summary.b_0.pdf, p. 24.

Lambert, Susan J., and Anna Haley. 2021. "Implementing Work Scheduling Regulation: Compliance and Enforcement Challenges at the Local Level." *ILR Review* 74 (5): 1231–57. https://doi.org/10.1177/00197939211031227.

Lampe, David R., ed. 1988. *The Massachusetts Miracle: High Technology and Economic Revitalization.* Cambridge, MA: MIT Press.

Langdon, David S., Terence M. McMenamin, and Thomas J. Krolik. 2002. "U.S. Labor Market in 2001: Economy Enters a Recession." *Monthly Labor Review* (February).

Lee, Woong. 2009. "Private Deception and the Rise of Public Employment Offices in the United States, 1890–1930." In *Studies of Labor Market Intermediation,* 155–81. Chicago: University of Chicago Press.

Lee-Johnson, Margie. 2020. "Give Job Applicants with Criminal Records a Fair Chance." *Harvard Business Review,* September 21. https://hbr.org/2020/09 /give-job-applicants-with-criminal-records-a-fair-chance.

Lerman, Robert Irving, Pamela J. Loprest, and Daniel Kuehn. 2020. "Training for Jobs of the Future: Improving Access, Certifying Skills, and Expanding Apprenticeship." IZA Policy Paper. October. IZA Institute of Labor Politics. www.iza.org/publications/pp/166/training-for-jobs-of-the-future-improving -access-certifying-skills-and-expanding-apprenticeship.

Levitt, Hannah. 2022. "'Soft Landing' Is Unlikely for US Economy, JP Morgan's Dimon Says." *Bloomberg.* www.bloomberg.com/news/articles/2022-10-13/jp

morgan-s-dimon-says-soft-landing-is-unlikely-for-us-economy. Accessed
October 14, 2022.

Levy, Brian L., et. al. 2017. "Why Did People Move during the Great Recession?
The Role of Economics in Migration Decisions." *RSF: The Russell Sage
Foundation Journal of the Social Sciences* 3 (3): 100–25.

Lewis, Oscar. 1959. *Five Families: Mexican Case Studies in the Culture of
Poverty.* New York: Basic Books.

Livingston, Gretchen. 2018. "Facts on Unmarried Parents in the U.S." *Pew
Research Center's Social & Demographic Trends Project* (blog). April 25. www
.pewresearch.org/social-trends/2018/04/25/the-changing-profile-of-unmarri
ed-parents/.

Livingston, Gretchen, and Deja Thomas. 2019. "Why Is the U.S. Teen Birth Rate
Falling?" *Pew Research Center* (blog). August 2. www.pewresearch.org/fact-ta
nk/2019/08/02/why-is-the-teen-birth-rate-falling/.

Logan, John Allen. 1996. "Opportunity and Choice in Socially Structured Labor
Markets." *American Journal of Sociology* 102 (1): 114–60.

Lohr, Steve. 2021. "Workers, in Demand, Have a New Demand of Their Own: A
Career Path." *New York Times*, August 18. www.nytimes.com/2021/08/18/bu
siness/workers-in-demand-have-a-new-demand-of-their-own-a-career-path
.html.

Long, Heather, and Andrew Van Dam. 2021. "'The Struggle Is Real': Why These
Americans Are Still Getting Left behind in the Recovery." *Washington Post*,
October 7.

Lukas, J. Anthony. 2012 [1985]. *Common Ground: A Turbulent Decade in the
Lives of Three American Families.* New York: Knopf Doubleday Publishing
Group.

Lundberg, Shelly, and Robert A. Pollak. 2007. "The American Family and Family
Economics." *Journal of Economic Perspectives* 21 (2): 3–26.

Lundquist, Jennifer Hickes. 2004. "When Race Makes No Difference: Marriage
and the Military." *Social Forces* 83 (2): 731–57. https://doi.org/10.1353/sof.20
05.0017.

———. 2006. "The Black–White Gap in Marital Dissolution among Young Adults:
What Can a Counterfactual Scenario Tell Us?" *Social Problems* 53 (3): 421–41.
https://doi.org/10.1525/sp.2006.53.3.421.

Manning, Alan. 2011. "Imperfect Competition in the Labor Market." In *Hand-
book of Labor Economics*, 973–1041. Amsterdam: Elsevier.

Manning, Wendy D., Pamela J. Smock, and Marshal Neal Fettro. 2019. "Cohabitation and Marital Expectations among Single Millennials in the U.S." *Population Research and Policy Review* 38 (3): 327–46.

Manning, Wendy D., Susan L. Brown, and Krista K. Payne. 2014. "Two Decades
of Stability and Change in Age at First Union Formation." *Journal of Marriage
and Family* 76 (2): 247–60.

Marschall, Daniell. 2021. "Workforce Intermediary Partnerships: Key to Success in High-Performing Labor Markets." AFL-CIO Working for America Institute. September. www.workingforamerica.org/wfi.

Mason, J. W. 2021. "Inflation for Whom?" *Slackwire* (blog), August 23. https://jwmason.org/slackwire/inflation-for-whom/.

Mauer, Marc. 2011. "Addressing Racial Disparities in Incarceration." *The Prison Journal* 91 (3): 87S–88S.

Mazumder, Bhashkar. 2015. "Estimating the Intergenerational Elasticity and Rank Association in the US: Overcoming the Current Limitations of Tax Data." Working paper. Federal Reserve Bank of Chicago.

McLanahan, Sara. 1985. "Family Structure and the Reproduction of Poverty." *American Journal of Sociology* 90 (4): 873–901.

McLanahan, Sara, Laura Tach, and Daniel Schneider. 2013. "The Causal Effects of Father Absence." *Annual Review of Sociology* 39: 399–427.

McLean, Caitlin, Lea J. E. Austin, Marcy Whitebook, and Krista L. Olsen. 2021. "Early Childhood Workforce Index 2020." Center for the Study of Childcare Employment. https://cscce.berkeley.edu/workforce-index-2020/wp-content/uploads/sites/3/2021/02/Early-Childhood-Workforce-Index-2020.pdf. Accessed April 2022.

McNutt, Timothy. 2020. "9 Myths about Hiring People with Criminal Records." The ILR School, January 26. www.ilr.cornell.edu/work-and-coronavirus/employer-best-practices/9-myths-about-hiring-people-criminal-records.

Miller, Kaitlin. 2021. "How Much the US Minimum Wage Was Actually Worth the Year You Were Born." *Chicago Tribune.* April 5. www.chicagotribune.com/featured/sns-minimum-wage-worth-value-living-wage-year-you-were-born-20210405-avg3tjkmynfdldepxvwg6dtniq-photogallery.html. Accessed November 15, 2021.

Miller, Rich. 2021. "Powell Risks Rerun of 1960s Inflation from Confusing Jobs Market." Bloomberg.com, October 31. www.bloomberg.com/news/articles/2021-10-31/powell-risks-rerun-of-1960s-inflation-from-confusing-jobs-market.

Miller, Robert A. 1984. "Job Matching and Occupational Choice." *Journal of Political Economy* 92 (6): 1086–120.

Minor, Dylan, Nicola Persico, and Deborah Weiss. 2017. "Should You Hire Someone with a Criminal Record?" *Kellogg Insight* (blog). February 3. https://insight.kellogg.northwestern.edu/article/should-you-hire-someone-with-a-criminal-record.

Mishel, Lawrence, and Jori Kandra. 2020. "Wage for the Top 1% Skyrocketed 160% since 1970 While the Share of Wages for the Bottom 90% Shrunk." *Working Economics Blog* (blog). December 1. www.epi.org/blog/wages-for-the-top-1-skyrocketed-160-since-1979-while-the-share-of-wages-for-the-bottom-90-shrunk-time-to-remake-wage-pattern-with-economic-policies-that-generate-robust-wage-growth-for-vast-majority/.

Mishel, Lawrence, and Josh Bivens. 2021. "Identifying the Policy Levers Generating Wage Suppression and Wage Inequality." Economic Policy Institute, Washington, DC. www.epi.org/unequalpower/publications/wage-suppression-inequality/. Accessed August 2022.

Mitchell, Josh. 2013. "Who Are the Long-Term Unemployed?" Urban Institute. July. www.urban.org/sites/default/files/publication/23911/412885-Who-Are -the-Long-Term-Unemployed-.PDF.

Modestino, Alicia Sasser, Daniel Shoag, and Joshua Ballance. 2016. "Downskilling: Changes in Employer Skill Requirements over the Business Cycle." *Labour Economics* 41 (August): 333–47. https://doi.org/10.1016/j.labe co.2016.05.010.

———. 2019. "Upskilling: Do Employers Demand Greater Skill When Workers Are Plentiful?" *Review of Economics and Statistics* (June): 1–46. https://doi .org/10.1162/rest_a_00835.

Molloy, Raven, Christopher L. Smith, and Abigail Wozniak. 2017. "Job Changing and the Decline in Long-Distance Migration in the United States." *Demography* 54 (2): 631–53. https://doi.org/10.1007/s13524-017-0551-9.

Moran, Gwen. 2019. "More Employers Are Considering Hiring People with Criminal Records." *Fast Company*, August 15. www.fastcompany.com/903895 58/more-employers-are-considering-hiring-people-with-criminal-records

Morath, Eric, and Greg Ip. 2021. "Tight Labor Market Returns the Upper Hand to American Workers." *Wall Street Journal*, June 20. www.wsj.com/articles/tig ht-labor-market-returns-the-upper-hand-to-american-workers-11624210501.

Mosley, Jane, and Elizabeth Thomson. 1995. "Fathering Behavior and Child Outcomes: The Role of Race and Poverty." In *Fatherhood: Contemporary Theory, Research, and Social Policy*. Edited by W. Marsiglio, 148–65. Thousand Oaks, CA: Sage Books.

Moss, Philip, and Chris Tilly. 2003. *Stories Employers Tell: Race, Skill, and Hiring in America*. New York: Russell Sage Foundation.

Mouw, Ted, and Arne L. Kalleberg. 2010. "Occupations and the Structure of Wage Inequality in the United States, 1980s to 2000s." *American Sociological Review* 75 (3): 402–31. https://doi.org/10.1177/0003122410363564.

Moynihan, Daniel Patrick. 1965. *The Negro Family: The Case for National Action.* 3. Washington, DC: US Government Printing Office.

Mueller-Smith, Michael. 2015. "The Criminal and Labor Market Impacts of Incarceration." University of Michigan Department of Economics. Unpublished paper. https://sites.lsa.umich.edu/mgms/wp-content/uploads/si tes/283/2015/09/incar.pdf. Accessed October 2022.

Mullaney, Tim. 2018. "Why Companies Are Turning to Ex-Cons to Fill Slots for Workers." *CNBC* (blog). September 18. www.cnbc.com/2018/09/18/why-comp anies-are-turning-to-ex-cons-to-fill-slots-for-workers.html.

Muro, Mark, and Yang You. 2022. "Coastal Cities Have Dominated Tech Work.

A New Analysis of Pandemic Trends Suggests New Possibilities." *Brookings* (blog). March 8. www.brookings.edu/blog/the-avenue/2022/03/07/coastal-ci ties-have-dominated-tech-work-a-new-analysis-shows-the-pandemic-may-be -changing-that/.

Murray, Charles. 2012. *Coming Apart: The State of White America, 1960–2010*. New York: Crown Forum.

National Center for Education Statistics. 2019. "Status in and Trends in the Education of Racial and Ethnic Groups: Indicator 27, Educational Attainment." https://nces.ed.gov/programs/raceindicators/indicator_rfa.asp. Last updated February 2019.

National Research Council. 2014. *The Growth of Incarceration in the United States: Exploring Causes and Consequences*. Edited by Jeremy Travis, Bruce Western, and Steve Redburn. Washington, DC: National Academies Press.

Nepomnyaschy, Lenna, Allison Dwyer Emory, Kasey J. Eickmeyer, Maureen R. Waller, and Daniel P. Miller. 2021. "Parental Debt and Child Well-Being: What Type of Debt Matters for Child Outcomes?" *RSF: The Russell Sage Foundation Journal of the Social Sciences* 7 (3): 122–51.

Neumark, David, and Peter Shirley. 2021. "Myth or Measurement: What Does the New Minimum Wage Research Say about Minimum Wages and Job Loss in the United States?" NBER Working Paper 28388. January. National Bureau of Economic Research. https://doi.org/10.3386/w28388.

Newman, Katherine S. 1995. "To Prevent Teen-Age Pregnancy, Think Jobs." *New York Times*, August 16. www.nytimes.com/1995/08/16/opinion/l-to-prevent-te en-age-pregnancy-think-jobs-257295.html.

———. 1999. *Falling from Grace: Downward Mobility in the Age of Affluence*. Berkeley: University of California Press.

———. 2000. *No Shame in My Game: The Working Poor in the Inner City*. Third edition. New York: Vintage.

———. 2003. *A Different Shade of Gray: Mid-Life and beyond in the Inner City*. First edition. New York: The New Press.

———. 2008. *Chutes and Ladders: Navigating the Low-Wage Labor Market*. Cambridge, MA: Harvard University Press.

———. 2012. *The Accordion Family: Boomerang Kids, Anxious Parents, and the Private Toll of Global Competition*. Boston, MA: Beacon Press.

Newman, Katherine S., and Hella Winston. 2016. *Reskilling America: Learning to Labor in the Twenty-First Century*. New York: Metropolitan Books.

Newman, Katherine S., and Victor Tan Chen. 2008. *The Missing Class: Portraits of the Near Poor in America*. Second edition. Boston: Beacon Press.

Ngo, Madeleine. 2021. "Skilled Workers Are Scarce, Posing a Challenge for Biden's Infrastructure Plan." *New York Times*, September 9. www.nytimes.com /2021/09/09/us/politics/biden-infrastructure-plan.html.

NobelPrize.org. 2021. "David Card-Facts-2021." www.nobelprize.org/prizes/econo
mic-sciences/2021/card/lecture/. Accessed October 14, 2022.

Nunn, Ryan, Jana Parsons, and Jay Shambaugh. 2019. "How Difficult Is It to
Find a Job?" *Brookings* (blog). May 2. www.brookings.edu/blog/up-front/20
19/05/02/how-difficult-is-it-to-find-a-job/.

O'Connor, Thomas H. 1995. *Building a New Boston: Politics and Urban Renewal,
1950–1970*. Boston: Northeastern University Press.

Office of Population Affairs. 2021. "Trends in Teen Pregnancy and Childbearing
| HHS Office of Population Affairs." https://opa.hhs.gov/adolescent-health/re
productive-health-and-teen-pregnancy/trends-teen-pregnancy-and-childbea
ring.

Okun, Arthur M. 1973. "Upward Mobility in a High-Pressure Economy." *Brookings Papers on Economic Activity* 1. www.brookings.edu/wp-content/up
loads/1973/01/1973a_bpea_okun_fellner_greenspan.pdf.

Oppenheimer, Valerie Kincade. 1988. "A Theory of Marriage Timing." *American
Journal of Sociology* 94 (3): 563–91.

Oppenheimer, Valerie Kincade, Matthijs Kalmijn, and Nelson Lim. 1997. "Men's
Career Development and Marriage Timing during a Period of Rising Inequality." *Demography* 34 (3): 311–30.

Orrell, Brent. 2021. "Benefits Cliffs: Highlights from My Conversation with Alex
Ruder." AEI. November 10. www.aei.org/poverty-studies/benefits-cliffs-highli
ghts-from-my-conversation-with-alex-ruder/.

Osterman, Paul. 2001. "Gains from Growth? The Impact of Full Employment on
Poverty in Boston." In *The Urban Underclass*. Edited by Christopher Jencks
and Paul E. Peterson, 122–34. Washington, DC: Brookings Institution Press.

———. 2014. *Securing Prosperity: The American Labor Market: How It Has
Changed and What to Do about It*. Princeton, NJ: Princeton University Press.

Osterman, Paul, and Beth Shulman. 2011. *Good Jobs America*. New York: Russell
Sage Foundation.

Pager, Devah. 2003. "The Mark of a Criminal Record." *American Journal of
Sociology* 108 (5): 937–75. https://doi.org/10.1086/374403.

———. 2009. *Marked: Race, Crime, and Finding Work in an Era of Mass Incarceration*. Illustrated edition. Chicago: University of Chicago Press.

Pager, Devah, and Diana Karafin. 2009. "Bayesian Bigot? Statistical Discrimination, Stereotypes, and Employer Decision Making." *Annals of the
American Academy of Political and Social Science* 621 (1): 70–93. https://doi
.org/10.1177/0002716208324628.

Pager, Devah, Bruce Western, and Bart Bonikowski. 2009. "Discrimination in a
Low-Wage Labor Market: A Field Experiment." *American Sociological Review*
74 (5): 777–99.

Panos, Georgios A., Konstantinos Pouliakas, and Alexandros Zangelidis. 2014.
"Multiple Job Holding, Skill Diversification, and Mobility." *Industrial*

Relations: A Journal of Economy and Society 53 (2): 223–72. https://doi.org/10.1111/irel.12055.

Pattillo, Mary. 2013. *Black Picket Fences: Privilege and Peril among the Black Middle Class*. Second edition. Chicago: University of Chicago Press.

Patrick Hilton, Timothy, and Susan J. Lambert. 2015. "Understanding Employers' Use of Labor Market Intermediaries in Filling Low-Level Jobs: Attracting Retainable Employees or Replenishing High-Turnover Jobs?" *Journal of Poverty* 19 (2): 153–76.

PayScale. 2021. "Racial and Gender Pay Gap Statistics for 2021." *PayScale* (blog). www.payscale.com/data/gender-pay-gap.

Pennell, Michael. 2007. "'If Knowledge Is Power, You're about to Become Very Powerful': Literacy and Labor Market Intermediaries in Postindustrial America." *College Composition and Communication* 58 (3): 345–84.

Peri, Giovanni. 2014. "Do Immigrant Workers Depress the Wages of Native Workers?" *IZA World of Labor*. May. https://wol.iza.org/uploads/articles/42/pdfs/do-immigrant-workers-depress-the-wages-of-native-workers.pdf.

Peril, Lynn. 2011. *Swimming in the Steno Pool: A Retro Guide to Making It in the Office*. New York: W. W. Norton & Company.

Petrosky-Nadeau, Nicolas, and Robert G. Valletta. 2021. "UI Generosity and Job Acceptance: Effects of the 2020 CARES Act." Federal Reserve Bank of San Francisco, Working Paper Series. May, 1.000-34.000. https://doi.org/10.24148/wp2021-13.

Pew Research Center. 2015. "Job Seekers Find Internet Essential for Employment Search." *Pew Research Center: Internet, Science & Tech* (blog). November 19. www.pewresearch.org/internet/2015/11/19/1-the-internet-and-job-seeking/.

———. 2019. "Views on Marriage and Cohabitation in the U.S." *Pew Research Center's Social & Demographic Trends Project* (blog). November 6. www.pewresearch.org/social-trends/2019/11/06/marriage-and-cohabitation-in-the-u-s/.

Piketty, Thomas, and Emmanuel Saez. 2003. "Income Inequality in the United States, 1913-1998." *Quarterly Journal of Economics* 118 (1): 1–39. https://doi.org/10.2307/25053897.

Pilkauskas, Natasha V., and Rachel E. Dunifon. 2016. "Understanding Grand-families: Characteristics of Grandparents, Nonresident Parents, and Children." *Journal of Marriage and Family* 78 (3): 623–33. https://doi.org/10.1111/jomf.12291.

Pilkauskas, Natasha V., Irwin Garfinkel, and Sara S. McLanahan. 2014. "The Prevalence and Economic Value of Doubling Up." *Demography* 51 (5): 1667–76. https://doi.org/10.1007/s13524-014-0327-4.

Pleck, Joseph H., and Brian P. Masciadrelli. 2004. "Paternal Involvement by U.S. Residential Fathers: Levels, Sources, and Consequences." In *The Role of the Father in Child Development,* fourth edition, 222–71. Hoboken, NJ: John Wiley & Sons Inc.

Pollmann-Schult, Matthias. 2005. "Crowding-out of Unskilled Workers in the Business Cycle: Evidence from West Germany." *European Sociological Review* 21 (5): 467–80. https://doi.org/10.1093/esr/jci033.

Porter, Eduardo. 2021. "Black Workers Stopped Making Progress on Pay. Is It Racism?" *New York Times*, June 28. www.nytimes.com/2021/06/28/business /economy/black-workers-racial-pay-gap.html.

Powell, Jerome. 2022. "Preliminary Transcript of Chair Powell's Press Conference, September 21, 2022." Accessed October 14, 2022. www.federalres erve.gov/mediacenter/files/FOMCpresconf20220921.pdf.

Press, Eyal. 2021. *Dirty Work: Essential Jobs and the Hidden Toll of Inequality in America*. New York: Farrar, Straus, and Giroux.

Quillian, Lincoln. 2006. "New Approaches to Understanding Racial Prejudice and Discrimination." *Annual Review of Sociology* 32 (January): 299–328.

Quillian, Lincoln, and Devah Pager. 2001. "Black Neighbors, Higher Crime? The Role of Racial Stereotypes in Evaluations of Neighborhood Crime." *American Journal of Sociology* 107 (3): 717–67. https://doi.org/10.1086/338938.

Quillian, Lincoln, Devah Pager, Ole Hexel, and Arnfinn H. Midtbøen. 2017. "Meta-Analysis of Field Experiments Shows No Change in Racial Discrimination in Hiring over Time." *Proceedings of the National Academy of Sciences* 114 (41): 10870–75. https://doi.org/10.1073/pnas.1706255114.

Rabben, Linda. 2013. "Credential Recognition in the United States for Foreign Professionals." Migration Policy Institute. May. www.migrationpolicy.org/rese arch/credential-recognition-united-states-foreign-professionals.

Rampell, Catherine. 2014. "The College Degree Has Become the New High School Degree." *Washington Post*, September 9. www.washingtonpost.com/op inions/catherine-rampell-the-college-degree-has-become-the-new-high-scho ol-degree/2014/09/08/e935b68c-378a-11e4-8601-97ba88884ffd_story.html.

Rao, J. N. K. 2003. *Small Area Estimation*. Hoboken: John Wiley and Sons Inc.

Recht, Hannah. 2020. "censusapi" v 0.7.1, R package on CRAN. https://github .com/hrecht/censusapi. Accessed October 7, 2022.

Reed, Debbie, Albert Yun-Hsu Liu, Rebecca Kleinman, Annalisa Mastri, Devlin Reed, Samina Sattar, and Jessica Ziegler. 2012. *Effectiveness Assessment and Cost-Benefit Analysis of Registered Apprenticeship in 10 States*. U.S. Department of Labor Employment and Training Administration. Washington, DC: Mathematica Policy Research. https://wdr.doleta.gov/resear ch/FullText_Documents/ETAOP_2012_10.pdf.

Reeves, Richard V., and Christopher Pulliam. 2020. "Middle Class Marriage Is Declining, and Likely Deepening Inequality." Brookings. March 11. www.broo kings.edu/research/middle-class-marriage-is-declining-and-likely-deepening -inequality/.

Romanoff, Kent, Ken Boehm, and Edward Benson. 1986. "Pay Equity: Internal and External Considerations." *Compensation & Benefits Review* 18 (6): 17–25.

Romich, Jennifer L., Scott W. Allard, Emmi E. Obara, Anne K. Althauser, and James H. Buszkiewicz. 2020. "Employer Responses to a City-Level Minimum Wage Mandate: Early Evidence from Seattle." *Urban Affairs Review* 56 (2): 451–79. https://doi.org/10.1177/1078087418787667.

Rose, D. 1984. "Rethinking Gentrification: Beyond the Uneven Development of Marxist Urban Theory." *Environment and Planning D: Society and Space* 2 (1): 47–74. https://doi.org/10.1068/d020047.

Rosen, Andy. 2020. "Encore Plans to Replace Some Behind-the-Scenes Bartenders with Machines." *Boston Globe*, January 9. www.bostonglobe.com /business/2020/01/09/encore-replace-some-its-bartenders-with-machines/gj faFWePWrvC5On3lfmEHP/story.html.

Rosenberg, Eli, Taylor Telford, and Aaron Gregg. 2021. "Weekly Jobless Claims Plunge to 199,000, the Lowest Level in More Than 50 Years." *Washington Post*, November 24. www.washingtonpost.com/business/2021/11/24/jobless-cl aims-pandemic/.

Rosenberg, Eli. 2021a. "A Record 4.4 Million Americans Quit Their Jobs in September as Labor Market Tumult Continued." *Washington Post*, November 12. www.washingtonpost.com/business/2021/11/12/job-quit-september-open ings/.

———. 2021b. "These Businesses Found a Way around the Worker Shortage: Raising Wages to $15 an Hour or More." *Washington Post*, June 10. www.washi ngtonpost.com/business/2021/06/10/worker-shortage-raising-wages/.

Rosenfeld, Jake. 2014. *What Unions No Longer Do*. Cambridge, MA: Harvard University Press.

———. 2021. *You're Paid What You're Worth and Other Myths of the Modern Economy*. Cambridge, MA: Harvard University Press.

Ross, Martha, and Nicole Bateman. 2019. "Meet the Low-Wage Workforce." Report. Brookings Institute. November. https://vtechworks.lib.vt.edu/handle /10919/97785.

Russell, Stuart. 2019. *Human Compatible: Artificial Intelligence and the Problem of Control*. New York: Penguin.

Sampson, Robert J. 1999. "What Community Supplies." In *Urban Problems and Community Development*. Edited by R. Ferguson and W. T. Dickens, 241–92. Washington, DC: Brookings Institution.

Sampson, Robert J., Jeffrey D. Morenoff, and Felton Earls. 1999. "Beyond Social Capital: Spatial Dynamics of Collective Efficacy for Children." *American Sociological Review* 64 (5): 633–60. https://doi.org/10.2307/2657367.

Sampson, Robert J., Stephen W. Raudenbush, and Felton Earls. 1997. "Neighborhoods and Violent Crime: A Multilevel Study of Collective Efficacy." *Science* 277 (5328): 918–24.

Sarkadi, Anna, Robert Kristiansson, Frank Oberklaid, and Sven Bremberg. 2008.

"Fathers' Involvement and Children's Developmental Outcomes: A Systematic Review of Longitudinal Studies." *Acta Paediatrica* 97 (2): 153–58.

Sawhill, Isabel V., and Ron Haskins. 2002. "Welfare Reform and the Work Support System." Brookings Institution. March 2. www.brookings.edu/resear ch/welfare-reform-and-the-work-support-system/.

Schneider, Daniel, and Adam Reich. 2014. "Marrying Ain't Hard When You Got a Union Card? Labor Union Membership and First Marriage." *Social Problems* 61 (4): 625–43.

Schneider, Daniel, and Kristen Harknett. 2019. "Consequences of Routine Work-Schedule Instability for Worker Health and Well-Being." *American Sociological Review* 84 (1): 82–114. https://doi.org/10.1177/0003122418823184.

———. 2021. "Hard Times: Routine Schedule Unpredictability and Material Hardship among Service Sector Workers." *Social Forces* 99 (4): 1682–1709. https://doi.org/10.1093/sf/soaa079.

Schneider, Daniel, Kristen Harknett, and Matthew Stimpson. 2018. "What Explains the Decline in First Marriage in the United States? Evidence from the Panel Study of Income Dynamics, 1969 to 2013." *Journal of Marriage and Family* 80 (4): 791–811.

———. 2019. "Job Quality and the Educational Gradient in Entry into Marriage and Cohabitation." *Demography* 56 (2): 451–76. https://doi.org/10.1007/s135 24-018-0749-5.

Schoppe-Sullivan, Sarah J., Sarah C. Mangelsdorf, Cynthia A. Frosch, and Jean L. McHale. 2004. "Associations between Coparenting and Marital Behavior from Infancy to the Preschool Years." *Journal of Family Psychology* 18 (1): 194.

Sharkey, Patrick, and Jacob W. Faber. 2014. "Where, When, Why, and for Whom Do Residential Contexts Matter? Moving Away from the Dichotomous Understanding of Neighborhood Effects." *Annual Review of Sociology* 40: 559–79.

Sharone, Ofer. 2021. "A Crisis of Long-Term Unemployment Is Looming in the U.S." *Harvard Business Review*, March 18. https://hbr.org/2021/03/a-crisis-of -long-term-unemployment-is-looming-in-the-u-s.

Shimer, Robert. 2005. "The Cyclical Behavior of Equilibrium Unemployment and Vacancies." *American Economic Review* 95 (1): 25–49. https://doi.org/10 .1257/0002828053828572.

Siegel, Rachel. 2022. "Fed Official: Inflation Falls Hardest on Poor Families." *Washington Post*, April 5.

Simon, Ruth. 2019. "'I Don't Want to See Him Fail': A Firm Takes a Chance on Ex-Inmates." *Wall Street Journal*, May 14. www.wsj.com/articles/i-dont-want -to-see-him-fail-a-firm-takes-a-chance-on-ex-inmates-11557845943.

———. 2020. "The Company of Second Chances." *Wall Street Journal*, January 25. www.wsj.com/articles/the-company-of-second-chances-11579928401.

Small, Mario L. 2004. *Villa Victoria the Transformation of Social Capital in a Boston Barrio*. Chicago: University of Chicago Press.

———. 2009. *Unanticipated Gains: Origins of Network Inequality in Everyday Life*. New York: Oxford University Press.

Small, Mario L., and Katherine Newman. 2001. "Urban Poverty after The Truly Disadvantaged: The Rediscovery of the Family, Neighborhood, and Culture." *Annual Review of Sociology* 27: 23–45.

Small, Mario Luis, and Jessica Feldman. 2012. "Ethnographic Evidence, Heterogeneity, and Neighbourhood Effects after Moving to Opportunity." In *Neighbourhood Effects Research: New Perspectives*, 57–77. Frankfurt: Springer.

Small, Mario Luis, David J. Harding, and Michèle Lamont. 2010. *Reconsidering Culture and Poverty*. Los Angeles: Sage Publications.

Small, Mario Luis, Robert A. Manduca, and William R. Johnston. 2018. "Ethnography, Neighborhood Effects, and the Rising Heterogeneity of Poor Neighborhoods across Cities." *City & Community* 17 (3): 565–89.

Smialek, Jenna. 2022. "September Inflation Report: Prices Rise Faster Than Expected." *New York Times,* October 13. www.nytimes.com/live/2022/10/13/business/inflation-cpi-report.

Smith, Neil. 1982. "Gentrification and Uneven Development." *Economic Geography* 58 (2): 139–55.

Smith, Sandra Susan. 2007. *Lone Pursuit: Distrust and Defensive Individualism among the Black Poor*. New York: Russell Sage Foundation.

Smith, Sandra Susan, and Kara Alexis Young. 2017. "Want, Need, Fit: The Cultural Logics of Job-Matching Assistance." *Work and Occupations*, November. http://journals.sagepub.com/doi/10.1177/0730888416676513.

Society for Human Resources Management. 2018. "Workers with Criminal Records." May 17. www.shrm.org/hr-today/trends-and-forecasting/research-and-surveys/documents/shrm-cki%20workers%20with%20criminal%20records%20issue%20brief%202018-05-17.pdf.

Somers, Meredith. 2019. "The 'High-Road' Approach to Worker Compensation." MIT Sloan. https://mitsloan.mit.edu/ideas-made-to-matter/high-road-approach-to-worker-compensation. Accessed December 1, 2021.

Spielman, Seth E., Cynthia A. Golembeski, Mary E. Northridge, Roger D. Vaughan, Rachel Swaner, Betina Jean-Louis, Katherine Shoemaker, et al. 2006. "Interdisciplinary Planning for Healthier Communities: Findings from the Harlem Children's Zone Asthma Initiative." *Journal of the American Planning Association* 72 (1): 100–8. https://doi.org/10.1080/01944360608976727.

Stack, Carol B. 1975. *All Our Kin: Strategies for Survival in a Black Community*. New York: Basic Books.

Steelman, Aaron. 2013. "Full Employment and Balanced Growth Act of 1978 (Humphrey-Hawkins)." November 22. www.federalreservehistory.org/essays/humphrey-hawkins-act.

Steelman, Tyler, and John A. Curiel. 2022. "The Accuracy of Identifying Constituencies with Geographic Assignment Within State Legislative Districts." *State Politics and Policy Quarterly*.

Stevens, Ann Huff, and Ariel Marek Pihl. 2016. "Labor Markets and Poverty in the US: Basic Facts, Policy and Research Needs." UC Davis Center for Poverty Research. https://poverty.ucdavis.edu/research-paper/labor-markets-and-poverty-us-basic-facts-policy-and-research-needs.

Stevenson, Betsey, and Justin Wolfers. 2007. "Marriage and Divorce: Changes and Their Driving Forces." *Journal of Economic Perspectives* 21 (2): 27–52.

Stobierski, Tim. 2020. "Average Salary by Education Level: Value of a College Degree." *Northeastern University* (blog). June 2. www.northeastern.edu/bachelors-completion/news/average-salary-by-education-level/.

Strain, Michael. 2021. "Republican Plan to Raise the Minimum Wage Is Self-Defeating." *American Enterprise Institute - AEI* (blog). February 23. www.aei.org/op-eds/republican-plan-to-raise-the-minimum-wage-is-self-defeating/.

Swidler, Ann. 1986. "Culture in Action: Symbols and Strategies." *American Sociological Review* 51 (2): 273–86. https://doi.org/10.2307/2095521.

Taube, Stephanie, and Rachel Lipson. 2021. "Covid-19 and the Changing Massachusetts Healthcare Workforce." The Project on Workforce. www.pw.hks.harvard.edu/post/ma-healthcare-workforce.

Thompson, Owen. 2021. "Human Capital and Black-White Earnings Gaps, 1966–2017." NBER Working Paper 28586. National Bureau of Economic Research. March. www.nber.org/papers/w28586.

Thornton, Daniel L. 2011. "What Does the Change in the FOMC's Statement of Objectives Mean?" *Economic Synopses*, no. 1. https://doi.org/10.20955/es.2011.1.

Tilcsik, András. 2021. "Statistical Discrimination and the Rationalization of Stereotypes." *American Sociological Review* 86 (1): 93–122.

Trading Economics. 2021. "United States Long Term Unemployment Rate." https://tradingeconomics.com/united-states/long-term-unemployment-rate.

United Way. 2020. "On Uneven Ground: ALICE and Financial Hardship in the U.S." December. https://perma.cc/5XNA-E72M.

University of Michigan Surveys of Consumers. 2021. "Preliminary Results for November 2021." November 15. www.sca.isr.umich.edu/.

US Congress House Committee on Education and the Workforce Subcommittee on 21st Century Competitiveness. 2005. *Welfare Reform: Reauthorization of Work and Child Care: Hearing Before the Subcommittee on 21st Century Competitiveness of the Committee on Education and the Workforce, U.S. House of Representatives, One Hundred Ninth Congress, First Session, March 15, 2005*. Washington, DC: US Government Printing Office.

US Department of the Treasury. 2021a. "Child Tax Credit." Accessed November 14, 2021. https://home.treasury.gov/policy-issues/coronavirus/assistance-for-american-families-and-workers/child-tax-credit.

———. 2021b. "Economic Impact Payments." Accessed November 14, 2021. https://home.treasury.gov/policy-issues/coronavirus/assistance-for-american -families-and-workers/economic-impact-payments.

Valletta, Robert, and Catherine van der List. 2015. "Involuntary Part-Time Work: Here to Stay?" FRBSF Economic Letter. June 8. Federal Reserve Bank of San Francisco. www.frbsf.org/economic-research/publications/economic-letter/20 15/june/involuntary-part-time-work-labor-market-slack-post-recession-une mployment/.

Volling, Brenda L., and Jay Belsky. 1992. "The Contribution of Mother-Child and Father-Child Relationships to the Quality of Sibling Interaction: A Longitudinal Study." *Child Development* 63 (5): 1209–22.

von Hoffman, Alexander. 2008. "The Lost History of Urban Renewal." *Journal of Urbanism: International Research on Placemaking and Urban Sustainability* 1 (3): 281–301.

Waddoups, C. Jeffrey. 2016. "Did Employers in the United States Back Away from Skills Training during the Early 2000s?" *ILR Review* 69 (2): 405–34. https:// doi.org/10.1177/0019793915619904.

Waldfogel, Jane, Terry-Ann Craigie, and Jeanne Brooks-Gunn. 2010. "Fragile Families and Child Wellbeing." *The Future of Children/Center for the Future of Children, the David and Lucile Packard Foundation* 20 (2): 87.

Walsh, Carl E. 1993. "What Caused the 1990–1991 Recession?" *Economic Review*, Federal Reserve Bank of San Francisco, no. 2. www.frbsf.org/economic-resear ch/wp-content/uploads/sites/4/93-2_34-48.pdf.

Warner, Mark R. 2021. "Warner Introduces Bicameral, Bipartisan Legislation to Boost Workforce Training as Part of COVID-19 Economic Recovery Efforts." www.warner.senate.gov/public/index.cfm/2021/4/warner-introduces-bicamer al-bipartisan-legislation-to-boost-workforce-training-as-part-of-covid-19-eco nomic-recovery-efforts. Accessed November 12, 2021.

Watts, William. 2022. "'Soft landing' unlikely as Fed tries to get grip on inflation, says former Treasury Secretary Robert Rubin" *Market Watch*. www.marketwa tch.com/story/soft-landing-unlikely-as-fed-tries-to-get-grip-on-inflation-says -former-treasury-secretary-robert-rubin-11665690271. Accessed October 14, 2022.

Weber, Lauren. 2021. "Forget Going Back to the Office—People Are Just Quitting Instead." *Wall Street Journal*, June 13. www.wsj.com/articles/forget-going-ba ck-to-the-officepeople-are-just-quitting-instead-11623576602.

Weil, David. 2014. *The Fissured Workplace: Why Work Became So Bad for So Many and What Can Be Done to Improve It*. Cambridge, MA: Harvard University Press.

Weise, Karen. 2021. "Amazon's Profit Soars 220 Percent as Pandemic Drives Shopping Online." *New York Times*, April 29. www.nytimes.com/2021/04/29 /technology/amazons-profits-triple.html.

Weissman, Jordan. 2022. "Why Larry Summers Thinks We Need Massive Interest Rate Hikes to Beat Inflation." *Slate*. https://slate.com/business/2022/07/larry-summers-massive-unemployment-fed-inflation.html.

West, Darrell. 2018. *The Future of Work: Robots, AI, and Automation*. Washington, DC: Brookings Institution Press.

West, Stacia, Amy Castro Baker, Sukhi Samra, and Erin Coltrera. 2021. "SEED: Stockton Economic Empowerment Demonstration." https://static1.squaresp ace.com/static/6039d612b17d055cac14070f/t/6050294a1212aa40fdaf773a/16 15866187890/SEED_Preliminary+Analysis-SEEDs+First+Year_Final+Repo rt_Individual+Pages+.pdf.

Western, Bruce. 2006. *Punishment and Inequality in America*. New York: Russell Sage Foundation.

———. 2018. *Homeward: Life in the Year after Prison*. New York: Russell Sage Foundation.

Western, Bruce, and Becky Pettit. 2005. "Black-White Wage Inequality, Employment Rates, and Incarceration." *American Journal of Sociology* 111 (2): 553–78.

Western, Bruce, and Christopher Wildeman. 2009. "The Black Family and Mass Incarceration." *The ANNALS of the American Academy of Political and Social Science* 621 (1): 221–42.

Western, Bruce, and Jake Rosenfeld. 2011. "Unions, Norms, and the Rise in U.S. Wage Inequality." *American Sociological Review*, no. 76: 513–37.

Western, Bruce, Jeffrey R. Kling, and David F. Weiman. 2001. "The Labor Market Consequences of Incarceration." *Crime & Delinquency* 47 (3): 410–27. https://doi.org/10.1177/0011128701047003007.

Weszkalnys, Gisa. 2007. "Book Review: Ulf Hannerz, *Soulside: Inquiries into Ghetto Culture and Community* (with a New Afterword). Chicago: University of Chicago Press, 2004. ISBN 0-226-31576-2 (Pbk)." *Critique of Anthropology* 27 (3): 342–43. https://doi.org/10.1177/0308275X070270030602.

Whitehurst, Grover J., and Michelle Croft. 2010. *The Harlem Children's Zone, Promise Neighborhoods, and the Broader, Bolder Approach to Education*. Brown Center on Education Policy. Washington, DC: Brookings Institution.

Whyte, William Foote. 1943. *Street Corner Society: The Social Structure of an Italian Slum*. Chicago: University of Chicago Press.

Wiemers, Emily E. 2014. "The Effect of Unemployment on Household Composition and Doubling Up." *Demography* 51 (6): 2155–78. https://doi.org/10.1007/s13524-014-0347-0.

Wilcox, W. Bradford, and Wendy Wang. 2017. "The Marriage Divide: How and Why Working-Class Families Are More Fragile Today." Institute for Family Studies. September 25. https://ifstudies.org/blog/the-marriage-divide-how-and-why-working-class-families-are-more-fragile-today.

Wilkerson, Isabel. 2020. *Caste: The Origins of Our Discontents*. New York: Penguin Random House.

Wilmers, Nathan. 2018. "Wage Stagnation and Buyer Power: How Buyer-Supplier Relations Affect U.S. Workers' Wages, 1978 to 2014." *American Sociological Review* 83 (2): 213–42. https://doi.org/10.1177/0003122418762441.

Wilson, Valerie, and William M. Rodgers. 2016. "Black-White Wage Gaps Expand with Rising Wage Inequality." *Economic Policy Institute* (blog). September 20. www.epi.org/publication/black-white-wage-gaps-expand-with-rising-wage-inequality/.

Wilson, William Julius, and Kathryn M. Neckerman. 1987. "Poverty and Family Structure: The Widening Gap between Evidence and Public Policy Issues." In *Fighting Poverty: What Works and What Doesn't*, 232–59. Cambridge, MA: Harvard University Press.

Wilson, William Julius. 1987. *The Truly Disadvantaged: The Inner City, the Underclass, and Public Policy*. Chicago: University of Chicago Press.

———. 1990. *The Truly Disadvantaged: The Inner City, the Underclass, and Public Policy*. Reprint edition. Chicago: University of Chicago Press.

———. 1997. *When Work Disappears: The World of the New Urban Poor*. New York: Vintage.

Wingfield, Adia Harvey. 2008. *Doing Business with Beauty: Black Women, Hair Salons, and the Racial Enclave Economy*. Rowman & Littlefield.

Wodtke, Geoffrey T., David J. Harding, and Felix Elwert. 2011. "Neighborhood Effects in Temporal Perspective: The Impact of Long-Term Exposure to Concentrated Disadvantage on High School Graduation." *American Sociological Review* 76 (5): 713–36.

Wozniak, Abigail. 2010. "Are College Graduates More Responsive to Distant Labor Market Opportunities?" *Journal of Human Resources* 45 (4): 944–70.

Wrigley-Field, Elizabeth, and Nathan Selzer. 2020. "Unequally Insecure: Rising Black/White Disparities in Job Displacement, 1981–2017." Working Paper. Washington Center for Equitable Growth, Washington, DC.

Wursten, Jesse, and Michael Reich. 2021. "Racial Inequality and Minimum Wages in Frictional Labor Markets." February. https://irle.berkeley.edu/files/2021/02/Racial-Inequality-and-Minimum-Wages.pdf.

Xie, Yu, James M. Raymo, Kimberly Goyette, and Arland Thornton. 2003. "Economic Potential and Entry into Marriage and Cohabitation." *Demography* 40 (2): 351–67.

Yagan, Danny. 2019. "Employment Hysteresis from the Great Recession." *Journal of Political Economy* 127 (5): 2505–58.

Yeung, W. Jean, Greg J. Duncan, and Martha S. Hill. 2000. "Putting Fathers Back in the Picture: Parental Activities and Children's Adult Outcomes." *Marriage & Family Review* 29 (2–3): 97–113.

Yu, Weihsin, and Shengwei Sun. 2019. "Race-Ethnicity, Class, and Unemployment Dynamics: Do Macroeconomic Shifts Alter Existing Disadvantages?" *Research in Social Stratification and Mobility* 63 (October) 100422: 1–15.

Yuen, Victoria. 2020. "The $78 Billion Community College Funding Shortfall." Center for American Progress. October 7. www.americanprogress.org/article /78-billion-community-college-funding-shortfall/.

Zuk, Miriam, Ariel H. Bierbaum, Karen Chapple, Karolina Gorska, and Anastasia Loukaitou-Sideris. 2018. "Gentrification, Displacement, and the Role of Public Investment." *Journal of Planning Literature* 33 (1): 31–44.

Zundl, Elaine, Daniel Schneider, Kristen Harknett, and Evelyn Bellew. 2022. "Still Unstable: The Persistence of Schedule Uncertainty During the Pandemic." Shift Project Research Brief. January. https://shift.hks.harvard .edu/still-unstable/.

Index

Note: page numbers followed by *f* and *t* refer to figures and tables respectively. Those followed by n refer to notes, with chapter and note number.

Founded in 1893,
UNIVERSITY OF CALIFORNIA PRESS
publishes bold, progressive books and journals
on topics in the arts, humanities, social sciences,
and natural sciences—with a focus on social
justice issues—that inspire thought and action
among readers worldwide.

The UC PRESS FOUNDATION
raises funds to uphold the press's vital role
as an independent, nonprofit publisher, and
receives philanthropic support from a wide
range of individuals and institutions—and from
committed readers like you. To learn more, visit
ucpress.edu/supportus.